Technology in Schools

Exploring the Curriculum

This book is one of a series designed to assist teachers to review practice in schools and classrooms. The series has been prepared by members of the Open University team for the course: *Applied Studies in Curriculum and Teaching*. Each volume follows a common sequence of issues relating to the nature of an area of specialization, its place in contemporary society, its treatment in schools, particular features of its teaching and learning, and consequences for organization and evaluation.

The titles in the series are:

J. Brown, A. Cooper, T. Horton, F. Toates and D. Zeldin (Eds.): *Science in Schools*
A. Cross and R. McCormick (Eds.): *Technology in Schools*
V. J. Lee (Ed.): *English Literature in Schools*

Technology in Schools

A Reader edited by
Anita Cross and Robert McCormick
at the Open University

Open University Press
Milton Keynes • Philadelphia

Open University Press
Open University Educational Enterprises Limited
12 Cofferidge Close
Stony Stratford
Milton Keynes MK11 1BY, England

and
242 Cherry Street
Philadelphia, PA 19106, USA

First Published 1986

British Library Cataloguing in Publication Data
Technology in schools. — (Exploring the curriculum)
 1. Technology — Study and teaching (Secondary — Great Britain
 I. Cross, Anita II. McCormick, Robert III. Series
 607'.1241   T107

 ISBN 0-335-15237-6
 ISBN 0-335-15236-8 Pbk

Library of Congress Cataloguing in Publication Data
Main entry under title:
Technology in schools.
 1. Technical education. I. Cross, Anita. II. McCormick, Robert.
 T65.T38 1986   607'.11   86-12607

 ISBN 0-335-15237-6
 ISBN 0-335-15236-8 Pbk

Text design by Carlton Hill
Typeset by Burns & Smith
Printed in Great Britain
by Butler & Tanner Ltd, Frome and London.

Contents

Acknowledgements

All possible care has been taken to trace ownership of the material included in this volume, and Open University Press would like to make grafeful acknowledgement for permission to reproduce it here.

1. Reprinted from Naughton, J., Introduction to *Living with Technology* (T101) 2nd Edition, 1981, by permission of the Open University.
2. Reprinted from the *Journal of the Royal Society of Arts*, vol. 129, September 1981, pp. 653–66 by permission of the RSA and the author.
3. Reprinted from Jacques, R. and Powell, J.A. (eds.), *Design : Science : Method* pp. 18–29 by permission of Butterworth and Co. (Publishers) Ltd. and the authors of the article.
4. Reprinted from *Higher Education Review*, vol 11, no. 2, pp. 43–56, 1979 by permission Tyrell Burgess Associates Ltd.
5. Reprinted from *Design Studies* vol. 1, no. 1, July 1979, pp. 17–20 by permission of Butterworth and Co. (Publishers) Ltd. and the author.
6. Reprinted from Weiner, M.J., *English Culture and the Decline of the Industrial Spirit 1850–1980*, Cambridge University Press, 1981 pp. 157–66, 205–7 by permission of author and publisher.
7. Reprinted from Cross, N., Elliot, D. and Roy, R. (eds.) *Man-made Futures*, Hutchinson, 1974, pp 31–8, 333–9 by permission of the copyright holder, the Open University.
8. Reprinted from RSA *Newsletter*, Spring 1984 and from Education for Capability: 1985 Recognition Scheme (aims), RSA, 1985 by permission of the RSA.
9. Reprinted from *The Times Educational Supplement*, 1982 by permission of the TES.
10. Reprinted from McCulloch, G., Jenkins, E. and Layton, D., *Technological Revolution*, 1984, pp. 207–15 by permission of Falmer Press.
11. Reprinted from *Design Studies*, vol. 5, no. 1, pp. 31–9, 1984 by permission of Butterworth and Co. (Publishers) Ltd. and the author.
12. Reprinted from *Studies in Design Education, Craft and Technology*, vol. 16, no. 3, Spring 1984, pp. 68–74 by permission of Trentham Books.
13. Reprinted from *In Place of Confusion: Technology and Science in the School Curriculum* by permission of the Nuffield-Chelsea Curriculum Trust and the National Centre for School Technology, Trent Polytechnic.
14. Reprinted from Dodd, T. *Design and Technology in the School Curriculum*, 1978, pp. 63–5 by permission of Hodder and Stoughton.
15. Reprinted from *Studies in Design Education, Craft and Technology*, vol. 17, no. 1, Winter 1984, pp. 33–40 by permission of Trentham Books.
16. Reprinted from *Studies in Design Education, Craft and Technology*, vol. 14, no. 2, pp. 90–6, 1982 by permission of Trentham Books.
17. Reprinted from *School Science Review*, no. 196, pp. 443–8, 1975 by permission of the Association for Science Education and the author.
18. Reprinted from Studies in *Design Education, Craft and Technology*, vol. 18, no. 1, Winter 1985, pp. 24–5 by permission of Trentham Books.
19. Reprinted from *Design Studies*, vol. 6, no. 3, July 1985, pp. 150–6 by permission of Butterworth and Co. (Publishers) Ltd. and the author.
20. Reproduced with the permission of SCDC Publications from *Ways and Means: The Craft, Design and Technology Education of Girls*, Longman: York, 1985.
21. Reprinted from *Studies in Design Education, Craft and Technology*, vol. 15, no. 1, pp. 19–23, 1982 by permission of Trentham Books.

22. Reprinted from *Studies in Design Education, Craft and Technology*, vol. 17, no. 1, Winter 1984, pp. 10–17 by permission of Trentham Books.
23. Reprinted from Jamieson, I., *Industry in Education*, 1985, pp. 1–22 by permission of SCDC publications and Longmans.
24. Reprinted from *Studies in Design Education, Craft and Technology*, vol. 16, no. 1, Winter 1983, pp. 38–43 by permission of Trentham Books.
25. Reprinted from *The Times Educational Supplement*, October, pp. 36–7 by permission of the TES.
26. Reprinted from *Educational Studies*, vol. II, no. 2, pp. 151–8, 1985 by permission of Carfax Publishing Company and the author.
27. Reprinted from *Teacher's Master Manual*, SCDC Publications, 1981, p. 59 and from *Problem-Solving*, National Centre for School Technology/Oliver and Boyd, 1982, pp. 66–73, both by permission of Longmans.
28. Reprinted from *Design and Technology (Advanced) Instructions and Guidance for teachers on the assessment of the Design Project* by permission of the Joint Metriculation Board.
29. Reprinted from *School Technology*, issue 72, vol. 18:2, December 1984, pp. 10–12 by permission of the National Centre for School Technology.
30. Reprinted from *Craft, Design and Technology in Schools : Some Successful Examples*, pp. 16–17, 24–5, 28–9, 1980 by permission of the Controller of Her Majesty's Stationery Office.
31. Reprinted from *Craft, Design and Technology* : Accommodation in Secondary Schools, pp. 39, pp. 40–3, 1985 by permission of the Controller of Her Majesty's Stationery Office.
32. Reprinted from *Studies in Design Education, Craft and Technology*, vol. 18, no. 1, Winter 1985, pp. 26–37 by permission of Trentham Books.
33. Reprinted from *School Technology Forum*, pp. 11–12, 1979 by permission of the National Centre for School Technology.
34. Reprinted from *Technology in Schools : Developments in CDT Departments*, pp. 5–12, 1982 by permission of the Controller of Her Majesty's Stationery Office.
35. Reprinted from *School Technology*, issue 30, vol. 7:4, June 1974, pp. 19–23 by permission of the National Centre for School Technology.
36. Reprinted from Studies in *Design Education, Craft and Technology*, vol. 15, no. 1, pp. 6–9, 1982 by permission of Trentham Books.

Introduction

In this collection of readings we are concerned with what is increasingly being called *technological education*. One of the most significant changes in this aspect of education has been the introduction of the concept of 'technology' itself. Twenty years ago, the word would probably not have appeared in any school curriculum. Now, we are becoming used to seeing subjects and topics such as 'craft, design and technology', 'design and technology', as well as 'technology and society', and perhaps to hearing discussions of the relationships (and demarcations) between science and technology, art and design, and other such combinations. This variety of appearances of technology in the curriculum points to what we see as a wide audience for this Reader. We have prepared it for teachers who are concerned with technological education, whatever their particular subject or curriculum area.

There have been several significant inputs to developments in technology in the school, notably the work of 'Project Technology' and the initiatives of some pioneering local authorities. Some developments have been stimulated by changes such as the reorganization of schools along new departmental or faculty lines. And last, but by no means least, there has been the introduction of new examinations.

As with most educational changes, the forces for change have been both internal and external. From inside schools themselves, there has undoubtably been a 'grass-roots' movement and desire for change, particularly in the development of design as a co-ordinating focus for many of the newer aspects of technology and for some of the more well established areas of the curriculum such as craft, art, home economics and sciences.

In the early 1980s, this internal focus on design has happened to correspond very closely with an external force for change – the virtually unprecedented acknowledgement, encouragement and support for design from the government. It is argued that Britain is faltering as an industrial nation because the design standards of its manufactured goods are lower than those of its competitors. Yet it is also widely acknowledged that the British educational system produces some of the world's best designers! So the remedy is not simply to improve our design education, but perhaps to ensure that the development of design awareness spreads much more rapidly through our educational system and includes an awareness of commercial and industrial values. This recent, high-level acknowledgement of the importance of design has done much to boost the already gathering confidence of the new design groupings within schools. It has also helped to ensure, through central initiatives from, for example, the DES, that design is treated on a par with other subjects: the GCSE national criteria for CDT is an example of this.

Another external force for change in this area has been in the recent emphasis on vocational education – an obvious partner in the desire to promote industry and the preparation for working in it. The funds from TVEI and its sister TRIST will give a substantial boost to technology in schools. Teachers in these areas face massive problems, of course, in trying to prepare their students for 'the world of work' when that world is changing so rapidly – and in many cases actually disappearing. In fact, the rapidity of technological change is a recurring problem for teachers in all the technology-related areas of the school curriculum.

Many teachers, therefore, are now faced with new challenges, new opportunities and new problems, focused on technology in schools. These teachers may be relatively new entrants to the profession who have already decided that 'technology' is their teaching specialism. Many others will be teachers who originally saw themselves as specialists in science, in crafts or arts, but who also now need and want to move into this area of the curriculum. Teachers will therefore enter the debate about technology from a variety of stances and personal backgrounds and it is for all of them that we have prepared this Reader.

With so many developments, changes, movements and pressures in and around the teaching of technology in schools, we cannot pretend to cover everything, or to offer hard-and-fast guidelines for what should be taught and how it should be taught. We have tried to cover those aspects which we think are likely to be significant and long-lasting in their implications, and which we feel are fundamental to an educational perspective on technology.

Our concern is not just to show the various approaches and interests in technology, but also to cover the range of concerns of a school, and a teacher, trying to teach it. Thus we start with trying to define technology. Many of the confusions and disagreements in the debate, about the place of technology in the school curriculum, stem from differences in understanding of the *nature of technology*. We go on to see how, as a form of human activity, it represents aspects of our values and culture. In particular how it can, or perhaps should, encapsulate a unique set of *human values*.

By its very nature, technology is about changing society – deliberately or otherwise. Not only are the effects of *technology on society* the potential subject matter of your teaching of technology, but your attitudes towards the effects will constitute your (more or less) hidden curriculum.

These first three sections (nature of technology, technology and human values, and technology and society) provide the backcloth for the inputs to the debate about *technology and education*. Here we consider three aspects of technology (in the sense we are using it):

(a) its role in education;
(b) the kind of technological education;
(c) what form it should take in the curriculum.

At this stage the readings we have chosen talk only in generalities. But they are crucial generalities, for any amount of technological activity in schools is to no avail unless it is based on a sound idea of why it is being done. Nor should it be assumed that such activity is the preserve of particular groupings of teachers – though the readings present a range of views on this!

The progression through the Reader is towards what goes on in classrooms and workshops, etc., but before we get there we consider three central *issues*: gender, special needs, and industry. All of these need to be taken into account in planning the curriculum and in designing learning activities.

Teaching and learning technology is, as we have already implied, the focus of concern for a teacher. Here we have chosen to highlight some characteristic aspects including 'problem-solving' and project work. These two represent the key to teaching and learning in technological education.

As befits a Reader concerned with curriculum and teaching, we end with *planning the technology curriculum*. Here we offer a number of plans, drawn from the work carried out in schools. These examples, along with the earlier readings, should provide you with a start to thinking about the curriculum which will promote technology in the school.

A number of people have helped us come to grips with this growing field of work, particularly Professor Geoffrey Harrison and his colleagues at the National Centre for School Technology, Trent Polytechnic and the Open University E803 Course Team, in particular Dr Nigel Cross of the Design Discipline. To them we offer grateful thanks. However, we must take full responsibility for the selection and editing.

Anita Cross and Robert McCormick

I WHAT IS TECHNOLOGY?

It is no mere academic exercise to try and define what we mean by technology. It is important to say what it is so that we can see its place in education, but it is also important to say what it is not. Foremost amongst the confusions of meanings of technology is to equate it with science. All of the articles we have selected for this section reject a simple equation. They examine different legitimate definitions and uses of the word in different contexts. These range from equating 'technology' with machinery to dealing with forms of social organization. This wide-ranging use of the concept of technology indicates social and intellectual dimensions to what is usually regarded as a practical aspect of human endeavour.

The authors represented here do not all speak with one voice, nor do they clear up all the conceptual confusions. We are left, for example, wondering about the place of 'engineering' and 'design' and the 'systems approach'. Cross, Naughton and Walker, in Chapter 3, would not see 'engineering' as being wide enough a concept to embrace their definition (derived from Naughton's discussion in Chapter 1). Although they argue for design as a technological activity, they also refer to design *and* technology. Lewin, in the second chapter, clearly sees design as the engineer's equivalent of scientific method. But he also equates it with a 'systems approach', whereas it is more usual to see this as an alternative methodology within technology. Our concern is not to propose a definitive definition of technology, although we lean towards John Naughton's view (Chapter 1), but to enable you to see the consequences of different definitions and to alert you to uses later in the Reader. Even if the definition of technology is unclear, its importance as an aspect of human activity is not – so much so that it is seen by many as a definite aspect of our culture. This we explore in the next section.

1   *What is 'technology' anyway?*

● J. Naughton

EDITORS' INTRODUCTION

This is taken from the 'Introduction' of the OU course Living with Technology, *written by John Naughton. It sets the scene for that course by discussing the kind of definitions which exist within the course material.*

TECHNOLOGY AS 'THINGS'

Equating technology with machinery (sometimes spoken of as hardware) is very common nowadays. I have before me as I write an advertisement for an expensive Danish hi-fi system. Over a photograph of this magnificent piece of equipment is the caption: 'Isn't Technology Beautiful?' This definition of technology as machinery clearly has its uses, and not just in advertisements. For example, in Block 1 of *Living with Technology*, 'Home' (OU 1981), the authors talk about the 'technology of the home', or refer to a house as a piece of technology, 'a machine for living in', as a famous architect (Le Corbusier) once put it.

    The equation of technology with machinery is clearly valid in the sense that it represents common usage, but it also has severe limitations. Consider, for example, the American moon programme of the 1960s (the Apollo Project, as it was named). The success of the programme was hailed as a 'major technological achievement'. This claim makes little sense if technology is defined in terms of machinery only. For although the programme made use of amazingly sophisticated machines, the machinery by itself was not sufficient to account for the achievement of putting men on the moon and returning them safely to earth. Clearly, something more than machinery was involved.

    What were the extra ingredients? Well, first of all there was a *practical task*. This was set by President Kennedy as the task of getting a man onto the moon by the end of the 1960s. Secondly there were *people*, namely scientists, engineers, technicians and computer experts, who were often very specialized and highly skilled. This implies that a third ingredient was *knowledge* of certain kinds.

As individuals, however, all these people (and there were more than 40 000 of them at the height of the project) could not have achieved the task, no matter how numerous or individually skilled they were. So the fourth ingredient was some form of *social organization* to manage and direct the combined effort of all the people involved; in this case it was the managerial structure of the National Aeronautics and Space Administration (NASA).

How might we combine these ingredients to form a definition of technology that is wider than just machinery?

TECHNOLOGY AS SOCIAL PROCESS

Here is a first shot at a definition that meets the above requirements:

'Technology is the application of *scientific knowledge* to *practical tasks* by organizations that involve *people* and *machines*.'

In fact this is almost good enough, but not quite. A brief critical examination will show why.

First, you will notice a little sleight of hand on my part, because instead of the knowledge that I identified as one of the 'extra ingredients' needed, I have specified a special kind of knowledge, namely the kind called 'scientific'. This may be a reasonable way of tightening up the definition, but you should not take it on trust. So let me ask the question, 'Is technology necessarily the application of only one type of knowledge, the scientific kind?'

Now, if you're smart, you'll refuse to answer the question until I've been forced to explain what I mean by the term 'scientific knowledge'. What kind of knowledge is it, and how does it differ from other kinds?

Imagine you're listening to a conversation between two ten-year-old children. One of them is trying to pump up his bicycle tyre – with some difficulty, it would seem. (There's probably something wrong with the valve.) 'Ouch,' he says, 'this pump's getting hot'.

'Pumps always do,' replies his companion, 'I've noticed that.'

'But why do they get hot?' asks the first child.

'Dunno,' says his friend, 'they just do.'

The second child clearly possesses knowledge of some kind about the behaviour of bicycle pumps under pressure. But is it scientific? The answer is no, and the clue to why I say that is contained in the child's answer to the question: why?

Now imagine that an older brother arrives on the scene and is asked why the pump gets hot. Fresh from his O-level chemistry class, he has the answer pat. 'Because when you pump you're really compressing the air in the pump, and Boyle's Law says that the temperature of a gas is related to its volume and pressure.'

This answer might not have enlightened the ten-year-olds, but from our point of view it is sufficient to indicate that the older boy possesses scientific knowledge about this particular matter. The clue which indicates this is the fact that he explains a particular phenomenon (the heating of a bicycle pump) in terms of a general, theoretical 'law' – called Boyle's Law after its discoverer. This states that for any gas, its volume multiplied by the pressure under which it is kept is a quantity which is proportional to its temperature. Mathematically this is written as

$$pV = kT$$

where *p* stands for pressure, *V* for volume, *T* for temperature, and *k* is a constant number. [*Editors note*: This is a statement combining Boyle's and Charles' laws.]

This law was discovered centuries ago and, having been tested over the years, has been found to be reasonably accurate for low pressures. It is a *scientific* law because (a) it can be tested (e.g. by experiments), and (b) because it explains a wide variety of different phenomena in one general, abstract statement. It is not, in other words, just a law of bicycle pumps; it applies to motor-driven compressors, and similar machinery, as well.

I described Boyle's Law as being 'theoretical'. By that I mean that it is expressed in terms of abstract *concepts* (pressure, volume, temperature) rather than in terms of concrete things. And if you were to ask *why* Boyle's Law holds, a scientist would explain it in terms of another, more fundamental set of theoretical statements called the molecular theory of gases. And this theory, in its turn, can be explained by a still more fundamental one, the atomic theory of matter.

I mention all this not to try and impress you, but simply to highlight two important features of scientific knowledge. The first is its tendency to explain everyday events, problems or phenomena in abstract, theoretical terms. The second is the tendency, described above, for scientific theories to be conceptually linked to other theories at deeper levels of abstraction.

Having gone through all this, let's return to our original question: is technology just the application of scientific knowledge?

Having posed the question, I immediately have to concede that the answer is *no*, because there are many examples of activities that I regard as technology despite the fact that they involve the application of types of knowledge other than the scientific kind. For example, I regard the construction of Durham Cathedral in the eleventh and twelfth centuries as a technological achievement. The men who built it had to solve a very difficult practical problem, namely that of constructing a high, wide church with a stone ceiling or 'vault'. The problem arose in the first place because the physical properties of stone mean that it cannot be used over wide spans. The builders of the time had learnt about this deficiency by bitter experience (the collapse of earlier attempts at wide spans), but they did not know *why* stone had this property. They lacked, in other words, the scientific knowledge about the internal structure of materials that is provided by the modern specialism known as materials science.

Not only did the builders of Durham Cathedral lack a scientific explanation of their problem, but they were also able to solve it without recourse to science. What they did was to divide the vault into small areas of 'shell' by means of stone ribs, that is, arches which crossed the church both transversely and diagonally, as shown in Figure 1.1. By doing this they simultaneously made the roof stronger and lighter.

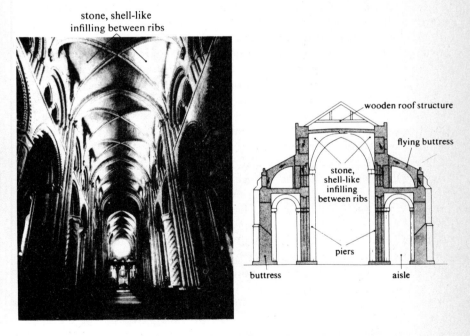

Figure 1.1 *The structure of Durham Cathedral. Arrows show how thrusts (forces) from the ribs are carried partly by the flying buttresses.*

However, this brilliant technical solution in turn gave rise to another serious structural problem, because the forces resulting from the weight of the vault could not simply be supported by the piers and walls of the building. This was because these forces exerted an outward rather than a downward thrust, thereby threatening to push the walls apart. Nowadays this problem could be routinely analysed using standard techniques of the science of engineering mechanics. The Durham builders knew nothing of this; nevertheless, they solved the problem by supporting the piers of the building using what are called 'flying buttresses' (see Figure 1.1 again).

This is a simple example, but it illustrates very well the point that technology need not necessarily involve the application of *scientific* knowledge. The cathedral builders in fact applied another kind of knowledge, namely the 'craft' knowledge they picked up from experience and passed on through successive generations of master masons.

Talking about medieval cathedrals may seem to you to be going too far back into the past, so let's consider a more modern example. Take a typical technological problem – the design of a motor car. Clearly there is a good deal of scientific knowledge involved: the theory of thermodynamics helps engineers to design the combustion chambers in which the fuel is burned; the scientific theories of mechanics and fluid dynamics guide the design of suspension elements like shock absorbers; the science of chemistry guides the selection of particular rubber compounds for the tyres. And so on.

But even though a lot of scientific knowledge goes into the design of a car, the task cannot be accomplished without other kinds of knowledge too. For example, one of the most important and distinctive features of a car is how it 'feels' to the driver: is it responsive, lively, stable? Or sluggish and heavy? Does it look elegant, or ugly, or functional? There is no scientific theory which a designer can draw on to help him here: he has to draw on other sources of knowledge like experience and craft and on his own feelings for particular configurations. Science, in other words, though vital to the technologist, is not enough.

Nor is knowledge-about-things like craft knowledge the only thing the technologist needs to supplement science. He also needs knowledge about how to make things happen in industrial or governmental organizations. Consider, for example, the Apollo Project. Here again the same point holds. For although much of the knowledge applied to the design of the machinery necessary to land on the moon *was* scientific, the managerial skills and knowledge necessary to manage the whole gigantic enterprise effectively were definitely not scientific. For there is no 'management science' in the sense that there is, say, a 'science' of physics. So you have to concede that, once again, forms of knowledge other than scientific were also involved in this particular technology.

This leads me to amend further my definition in the following way:

'Technology is the application of scientific *and other organized knowledge* to practical tasks by organizations that involve people and machines.'

However, this definition, although an improvement on what went before, is still too vague in one crucial respect: it does not specify what kinds of organizations are used to manage the application of the various types of knowledge involved.

Let's use the Apollo Project again as a vehicle for analysing this problem. The form of organization used by NASA in managing the project was of a specific and important kind, the kind called *hierarchical*. The word *hierarchy* was originally a theological term used to describe the three divisions of angels, graded in order of their supposed importance and influence. Those at the top of the hierarchy, the seraphim, cherubim and thrones, were reckoned to be closest to God. Nowadays 'hierarchy' is still used in this sense, but without the divine overtones: it nowadays describes a certain type of command structure in which people at one level control a greater number of people on the level below them.

You may ask why I think hierarchy is so important to technology. After all, perhaps NASA could just as easily have used some other, non-hierarchical structure? Is it necessarily the case that modern technology *requires* hierarchical forms of social organization to run it?

Some writers argue that the answer to this question is *yes* if the practical task involved is one requiring the co-ordinated effort of many specialists and if the machinery involved is complex. This is how one of these writers, the economist John Kenneth Galbraith (1974: 31), put it:

> there is no way that organized knowledge can be brought to bear on the production of an automobile as a whole or even on the manufacture of a body or chassis. It can only be applied if the task is so subdivided that it begins to be coterminous with some established area of scientific or engineering knowledge. Though metallurgical knowledge cannot be applied to the manufacture of the whole vehicle, it can be used in the design of the cooling system or the engine block. While knowledge of mechanical engineering cannot be brought to bear on the manufacture of the vehicle, it can be applied to the machining of the crankshaft. While chemistry cannot be applied to the composition of the car as a whole, it can be used to decide on the composition of the finish or trim.
>
> Nor do matters stop here. Metallurgical knowledge is brought to bear not on steel but on the characteristics of special steels for particular functions, and chemistry not on paints or plastics but on particular molecular structures and their rearrangement as required.
>
> Nearly all of the consequences of technology, and much of the shape of modern industry, derive from this need to divide and subdivide tasks and from the further need to bring knowledge to bear on these fractions and from the final need to combine the finished elements of the task into the finished product as a whole.

The crucial problem, from our point of view, is how the combining of 'the finished elements of the task into the finished product as a whole' is to be accomplished. The solution that has evolved in the kind of technology discussed by Galbraith is to use a hierarchical structure to organize the combining. The reasoning behind this is fairly straightforward, and goes roughly as follows. Left to themselves, the various specialists working on the various sub-tasks will try to find the best solutions to the particular problems they've been set. Often this will be at the expense of some other specialists' solution to *their* problem. The best overall solution to the main task will not be the sum of best solutions to all the sub-tasks. So it is essential that the overall management of the task should be entrusted to people who possess enough power and authority to resolve conflicts over resources, designs, linkages, etc. that arise between those who are working on individual bits of the task. These requirements, so it is argued, imply that technology needs hierarchical structures.

Now many people don't like the idea of hierarchies, and certainly they don't take kindly to the notion that hierarchy might be a necessary feature of certain kinds of technology. When I put forward this idea in an earlier draft of this text, some of my colleagues on the Course Team looked very unhappy. Their reaction, I think, was typical of people trying to cope with a conflict between different sets of values. On the one hand their values lead them to dislike hierarchies and on the other hand they strongly approve of technology; the suggestion that they cannot have technology without hierarchies therefore distresses them very much.

Anyway, I suggest that hierarchical forms of social organization may, whether one likes it or not, be a *defining characteristic* of technology in my second sense. This leads to the final version of my definition of technology as a social process:

'Technology is the application of scientific and other organized knowledge to practical tasks by hierarchically ordered systems that involve people and machines.'

IMPLICATIONS

We have two very different definitions of 'technology'. Which of them is the 'correct' one? The answer is that they are both correct, in the sense that both have legitimate uses. But neither is appropriate for all cases, and they are not necessarily interchangeable. In Block 1 of *Living with Technology*, 'Home' (OU 1981), for example, it is appropriate to use the 'technology as things' definition, but it might be inappropriate to use this definition when discussing the technology of electricity generation in the United Kingdom. There you will be considering the question of whether certain power stations might be designed to provide heat as well as power. The answer to this question depends partly on technical factors, in which case the 'technology as machinery' definition is adequate, but it is also partly a question of how the organization that controls and manages the machinery, in this case the Central Electricity Generating Board, views the matter.

In fact, if you examine the interpretations of the word 'technology' that are most common in everyday use, you will find that my two definitions lie at two extremes. On the one hand, the 'technology as things' definition seems the simplest one possible. On the other hand, my 'technology as social process' definition seems very complex. Everyday use of the word 'technology' generally lies between these two extremes, as, for example, when we talk about the technology of crafts like pottery, implying the application of human skill and knowledge and simple machinery to practical tasks, but without any form of social organization. You will find different interpretations used in different places, but you will also find that they all lie within my two extreme definitions. All you have to do is to ensure that you understand which interpretation is being used at any given point.

Before leaving the topic of definitions, one further point needs to be made. The second of my definitions has one very important implication, which arises out of the phrase 'scientific *and other organized knowledge'*. Scientific knowledge (by which I mean knowledge gained by the study of subjects like physics and chemistry) is very different from other forms of knowledge in that it is the product of a continual and sustained effort to reduce the extent to which values and value-judgements creep into it. I am not suggesting for a moment that the scientific community has been completely successful in these efforts, only that scientists try harder than most professionals to keep value-judgements out of their work. If technology were just the application of scientific knowledge to practical tasks, then perhaps we shouldn't have to worry quite so much about values and their effect on technological decisions. But technology also includes 'other organized knowledge', for example management techniques or craft knowledge, where it is inevitable that values have intruded to a greater or lesser extent.

REFERENCES

Open University (1981) Block 1 'Home' *Living with Technology: a foundation course* OU Press.

Galbraith, J. K. (1974) *The New Industrial State*. Penguin edition.

2 *Engineering philosophy – the third culture?*

● D. Lewin

EDITORS' INTRODUCTION

Worried about the lack of social and intellectual respectability afforded to engineering, Professor Lewin attributes this lack to the confusion between engineering and science. He proposes a distinct engineering philosophy centred upon systems theory. In the original lecture he also dealt with a variety of views on scientific method; we have left these for Cross, Naughton and Walker in the next chapter.

Engineering: the finest career for a young man. An engineer knows all the sciences. (Gustave Flaubert, *Dictionary of Received Ideas*)

[...] Why is it that engineering is seen to lack both social and intellectual respectability? In this paper the author postulates that this is due to a lack of understanding of what constitutes engineering, the confusion between engineering and science but more specifically the lack of an *identifiable engineering philosophy*. Whilst engineering is seen simply as a confluence of science and industrial practices, a view still strongly held in schools and universities, engineers will always be considered as second-rate scientists.

The main objective of this paper is to show that there is a distinct engineering philosophy, centred on systems theory, which could also provide the basis for a general education to equip our children to live and work in the technology-based society of the future.

EXPOSING THE JARGON

Perhaps the four most misused, misunderstood and important words in our language today are science, technology, engineering and design. To the Luddites in our society of course they all mean the same thing – doom! As a first step in unravelling this confusion let us consider in more detail what is understood by these terms. Science is concerned with endeavouring to understand and determine the laws of natural phenomena and in so doing to contribute to the growth of knowledge. Engineering on the other hand is concerned with the artificial world (in the sense of man-made) and the design and manufacture of artifacts. Thus inherent in all engineering endeavour is the process of synthesis, in its highest form creative design, which brings about changes in the total environment. Thus it will be seen that design is an integral part of the engineering process and indeed, as we shall see later, is its central philosophy. Or to put it another way, quoting from Simon,[1] 'Engineering is the science of the artificial'.

If that is the case what then is applied science, a term which has become synonymous with engineering? Moreover it is the use of this term, with its implied assumption that applied must in some way be inferior to pure science, that has helped to denigrate engineering. But can there be any difference between so called pure and applied science? Applied science is usually taken to mean those branches of science which have practical utility, and in the case of engineering schools generally represents a selection of topics which are deemed to be useful in engineering practice. In both cases we are talking about knowledge; applied science, if it means anything, simply represents a certain subset of all scientific knowledge. Moreover, who is to say which branches of science will be useful? In fact it is easy to show that many aspects of so called pure science can readily and usefully be applied to solve practical problems. To sum up, applied science has exactly the same objective and methodology as pure science – science is science is science! Thus the use of adjectives like applied science or engineering science to describe engineering courses conceals but does not change the fact that these courses are predominantly based on a study of mathematics and physics.

Another ambivalent word is technology, the dictionary definitions of which are the practical application of knowledge, or the science and art of industrial manufacture. Defined in this latter way technology is, to all intents and purposes, equivalent to *Technik* – the principles of and the methods used for, the design and manufacture of artifacts. Again technology can be considered as the science of industrial arts, which is the continental usage of the word, i.e. *technologie, teknologi,* etc. Another common use of the word is to describe a set of craft techniques – the art of the industrial arts. That the term is confused is apparent, particularly so in the media where we have both physicists and engineers being called technologists (applied scientists?). It has been suggested by Fores and Rey[2] that the confusion could be resolved by restricting the use of the word to mean 'the scientific study and teaching of techniques'. However, the word is too deeply embedded in our language to expect any major changes in its use; in the words of de Bono[3] 'technology is an impression rather than a definition . . . the closer you get to it the more it is not there'.

Last, but certainly not least, on our list of abused terminology is design. Since the end product of a design exercise is generally expressed as a drawing, sketch or plan (the design) anyone who produces such work is thought of as a designer, as for example the design draughtsman. Moreover, because in many cases the designer actually makes the original prototype of the artifact, be it a pair of jeans or a chair, we also have the concept of the designer craftsman. Again it is also held that design is primarily concerned with the functional appearance of an artifact, that is the aesthetic view of design. It is perhaps because of these differing points of view that the common but mistaken belief that design is in some way different from engineering and requires a lower level of intellect is held by many educationists. But as we have seen, engineering is wholly concerned with the design and manufacture of artifacts, be they hardware or software.

Many and varied accounts of the engineering design process have been expounded and it is essential that these confused ideas be resolved and that engineering and design be established as a unified discipline in its own right with a coherent and well defined philosophy.

SCIENCE AND ITS PHILOSOPHIES

[...] The basic tenet of Popper's argument is that though it is logically impossible, by inductive methods, to verify the proof of a statement it is possible to produce proof of its falsification. Thus Popper substitutes refutation, in place of justification, as the central tool of theory evaluation. Consequently, it is argued that empirical generalizations though not verifiable are certainly falsifiable and theories can be tested by setting up experiments designed to refute them. [...] Popper's philosophy of scientific method goes much further than a simple rejection of inductive principles inasmuch as it emphasizes a *problem-solving approach* with the starting point being the postulation of a hypothesis (the solution to the problem) followed by experimental tests to refute the original hypothesis. Thus Popper turns the traditional Baconian method of scientific investigation on its head and in the process of course again eliminates the need for an inductive approach.

Popper's methodology may be stated as follows:

(a) *Formulation of problem*, for example the need to explain some new phenomenon or extend an existing theory.

(b) *Proposed solution*, i.e. the new theory or hypothesis.
(c) *Deduction of testable propositions* involves setting up a model.
(d) *Experimental tests*, based on refuting the propositions.
(e) *Evaluation of Theory*.

Note that the real starting point is the problem itself, which will in the main presuppose some *a priori* knowledge, and that the method highlights the need to precisely formulate the problem before attempting a solution. Note also the iterative nature of the process, with step (e) above leading naturally back to step (a).

Popper views this problem-solving process as one of continuous development parallel to Darwinian evolution, in which the response to a problem is generated as a hypothesis and then subjected to environmental pressures which lead either to its rejection, acceptance or modification. Thus the process may be depicted as:

$$P_1 \longrightarrow TS \longrightarrow EE \longrightarrow P_2 \longrightarrow TS \ldots$$

where P_1 is the initial problem, TS the proposed trial solution, EE the experimental evaluation (falsification) and P_2 the resulting solution (or new problem). In general a definitive solution will never appear, only one which with due regard to the constraints imposed by the environment (or model) provides a currently plausible explanation.

This view also emphasizes the pure creative nature of the problem-solving process since it is modelled on Darwinian rather than Lamarkian evolution theory. Thus solutions are seen to arise from the imagination of the problem-solver and not from prior experience (this point of course constitutes a controversial issue!) [...]

Two further ideas have played a dominant role in establishing scientific thought and methodology; these are *reductionism* and *mechanism*.

Reductionism is the belief that all things can be reduced or decomposed into simple parts which, once understood, can then be reassembled and used to give an explanation of the whole thing. Thus reductionism gives rise to an analytical way of thinking where problems are broken down on the assumption that the solution to the whole is given by the sum of the solutions to the *independent* parts. Mechanism has, as its central theme, the argument that all phenomena may be explained on a cause-effect basis. Thus since a cause was taken to be sufficient for its effect, the surrounding environment was excluded from immediate consideration thus leading to the concept of a *closed system* and a *deterministic* viewpoint of the world. Consequently the experimental scientist isolates a small part of the real world, systematically investigates a few variables under carefully controlled laboratory conditions and then attempts to extrapolate this research to the world in general.

Many of these traditional ideas of science are being vigorously re-examined, particularly in those fields which deal with complex systems such as the life and social sciences.[4, 5] These principles, however, are still being inculcated in students at schools and universities and since they differ markedly from the engineering approach could be educationally very bad for the engineer.

SYSTEMS APPROACH TO ENGINEERING

The need for a more formal approach to the design of engineering artifacts became apparent during the Second World War when it was essential to undertake the development of complex weapons systems. This approach called *systems engineering*[6] was a major change from the then accepted practice of engineering and laid the foundations for a philosophy of engineering.

What is meant by 'systems' in this context? The word systems has become very fashionable in our language and is used loosely by all and sundry, especially the mass-media, to describe anything from social organizations to bathroom showers! In a sense, that of General Systems Theory, there is nothing wrong with this view. Weinberg[7] makes the point 'a system is a way of looking at the world . . . a point of view'. However in this paper we shall adopt a more formal definition, albeit still a general one – a system is a set of interrelated elements forming a collective entity, where related implies that information and or energy are exchanged or shared between the elements. Note that contrary to the principle of reductionism the whole can be more than the sum of its parts and that the characteristics of the system could well change with time. Though the initiative for systems engineering arose out of the need to synthesize and analyse complex structures (note that complex does not necessarily imply large) the methodology is quite general in its application.

The systems engineering approach is fundamentally one of problem-solving, where the problem presented is the artifact (or system) to be designed and implemented. The basic steps in evolving a solution to an engineering problem are as follows:

(a)   *Problem specification.* Before any problem can be solved it is first necessary to define it as fully as possible, including the basic objectives to be achieved and the constraints imposed on its solution. Since in engineering the point of concern is an artifact, problem specification is in essence a product specification. In most cases design problems are ill-defined and the information necessary to specify the problem (or product) is not immediately available and in some way must be determined or estimated.

(b) *Synthesis stage.* This is the creative stage of the engineering process and requires that a solution be postulated to a design problem. The initial attempt at a solution normally results in an approximate design which is used to establish the economic and technical feasibility of the project; successive solutions are based on the results of the analysis stage which are used to refine the proposed design and or the product specification. Note there is no *unique* solution to any engineering problem, only a best or compromise solution with regard to the constraints imposed by technical, economic, human and environmental factors. Thus engineering can be considered as essentially a decision-making process.

(c) *Analysis stage.* In order to evaluate the proposed design for an artifact and to determine its functional characteristics it is necessary to represent the system in terms of a *model*. In the early stages of the design process it is often not economically viable, or even desirable (in some cases it is technically impossible) to produce a prototype of the artifact. The model can take various forms, a physical analogue or scale model, a formal mathematical description, a computer simulation or simply a thought experiment or intellectual argument. Having established a suitable system model it is then analysed, using logic or mathematical methods, or exercised in the case of a physical model or simulation, to determine its general behaviour and in particular if it satisfies the original specifications.

(d) *Implementation stage.* Once the design has been established it is necessary to examine the detailed means of implementation in terms of available resources, including components and materials, manpower, need for re-tooling and retraining, management methods, etc.

There are a number of important points to be borne in mind when considering the design process outlined above:

(a) The design process is iterative, and feedback can take place between any of the individual stages as well as over the whole process.

(b) Man–machine involvement must be considered throughout the entire design process. The consideration of the total interface between man and machine – that is the function and place of the user, operator, maintenance staff, etc. – is an essential component of design. Coupled with this is the need to consider the effect of the system on the existing environment since every system is itself only an element of a larger system.

(c) The systems approach leads naturally to a 'top-down' design, where initially the system objectives are derived independently from the means of achieving them. The alternative approach is called 'bottom-up' design and starts by considering actual components and available resources building up to a system specification. Both methods are used by practising designers but it is essential that the 'top-down' approach should predominate [...]

TOWARDS AN ENGINEERING PHILOSOPHY

It will now be apparent that the engineering method is very different from that of classical sciences. There is, however, a very close similarity between the systems engineering approach and the logic of scientific discovery as propounded by Karl Popper. The following points of resemblance exist between the two approaches:

(a) Both methods are essentially concerned with problem-solving in the broadest sense, with the initial starting point being the specification of the problem to be solved followed by the postulation of a solution.

(b) Again, both methods proceed by subjecting the postulated solution to analysis and test in the light of experience and existing theory. In the engineering sense this corresponds to the evaluation of a proposed design with respect to its specification. Though the principle of falsification is not always strictly observed, the method of deductive testing[8] is used extensively. For example, alternative design solutions are often evaluated by adding or tightening user requirements until only one design remains viable. Again, the principle appears in the breakdown testing of components and sub-systems and the use of random testing methods to discover faults, etc.

(c) Neither method leads to a definitive solution to a problem and both proceed by an iterative feedback process which allows a solution to evolve.

(d) Both methods depend on creative insight and intuition in postulating the solution to a problem and the ability to decide which solutions should be accepted or rejected.

(e) Fundamental to both approaches is the concept that complex systems change in time owing to the inherent feedback processes. This interaction with the environment can be represented in both cases by open-system models.

(f) The two methods are evolutionary in nature, with the engineering approach drawing on past experience, in the same way that Popper relies on 'well corroborated theories', to appraise a solution and determine the next problem.

Though of little practical concern to the engineer, the need to rely on experience or well corroborated theories, both of which depend on inductive assumptions, to appraise and determine a solution is the main point of dissension in Popper's work, which is of course claimed to be independent of inductive argument. It does, however, show the place of experience in the engineering process and should lead to caution in its use in line with the Hebrew proverb 'For example is not proof'.

So far we have established that the methodology of systems engineering is closely akin to Popper's philosphy of science – does that mean that engineering is really science after all? Not quite; a fundamental difference is the engineer's requirement to design complex structures and make decisions in a real-world environment. In order to achieve this it is necessary to resort to the concepts of general systems theory and the use of open-system models. [In contrast to the closed system of experimental science.] Thus engineering philosphy can be seen as a confluence of Popperian and general systems theory applied to the design of complex structures.

The need to model complex structures also occurs in science (in this case natural structures rather than artificial ones) and is particularly so in the life and social sciences where general systems theory has been employed for this purpose.[9, 10] Unfortunately the scientific community have not yet accepted current thinking on complex systems and in many cases considerable doubt has been cast on the validity of general systems models used for this purpose.[11] This has resulted in the new sciences, such as social science, emulating the method of the traditional empirical sciences, often with disastrous results.

Archer[12] has taken a similar view with respect to the need for a third culture in education and calls the new area Design. In this case Design is defined as 'the area of human experience, skill and understanding that reflects man's concern with the appreciation and adaptation of his surroundings in the light of his material and spiritual needs'. Moreover he also states that 'the essential language of design is modelling'.

Engineering philosophy as defined here takes these arguments further in expounding a methodology of problem-solving based on open system models and the use of formal methods of evaluation.

[...]

CONCLUSION

It has been shown in this paper that engineering (the essence of which is design) has a distinct philosophy of its own based on the principles of deductive problem-solving and comprising an amalgam of Popperian logic and general systems theory. Furthermore, engineering philosophy has been shown to be fundamentally different from that of the traditional sciences and arts and can be considered as constituting a Third Culture.

Thus it is proposed that engineering philosophy should form the core element for a liberal education which would result in uniting the arts and sciences and dispelling the view that engineering is an anti-social and academically inferior activity.

[...]

REFERENCES

1. H. A. Simon, *The Sciences of the Artificial*, MIT Press, Cambridge, Mass., 1969.

2. M. Fores and L. Rey, 'Technik: the Relevance of a Missing Concept'. *Higher Education Review*, Spring 1979, pp. 43–57. [See Part II of this Reader.]

3. E. de Bono, *Technology To-day*, Routledge and Kegan Paul, London, 1971.

4. E. Lazio (ed.), *The Relevance of General Systems Theory*, G. Braziller, New York, 1972.

5. J. Beishon and G. Peters (eds), *Systems Behaviour*, Open University Press, Harper and Row, London, 1972.

6. H. A. Affel, 'Systems Engineering,' *Int. J. Science and Technology*, vol. 35, 1964, pp. 18–26.

7. G. M. Weinberg, *An Introduction to General Systems Thinking*, John Wiley, New York, 1975.

8. K. R. Popper, *The Logic of Scientific Discovery*, Hutchinson, London, 1972, pp. 32–3.

9. F. E. Emery (ed.), *Systems Thinking*, Penguin Education, 1969.

10. H. A. Simon, *Models of Man*, John Wiley, 1957.

11. David Berlinski, *On Systems Analysis*, MIT Press, Cambridge, Mass., 1977.

12. Bruce Archer, 'Design as a Discipline', *Design Studies*, vol. 1, 1979, pp. 17–20. [See Part II of this Reader.]

3 *Design method and scientific method*

- N. Cross, J. Naughton and D. Walker

INTRODUCTION

There is a major concern in design research to relate (in some way or other) design method and scientific method. This concern has been noticeable at many of the design research/design methods conferences that have been held over a period of nearly twenty years now. It was perhaps most prevalent at the 1966 Birmingham conference on 'The Design Method' (Gregory 1967). In the preface to the published proceedings of that conference, Gregory noted that a major aim in setting up the conference had been the hope 'to establish a common basis of agreement about the nature of "the design method", using this phrase in the same way as "the scientific method".' Such an aim suggests an implicit desire to emulate scientists who were presumably supposed to have a definite method that they practised and which was instrumental in their successes.

However, it was clear even then that designers could not hope simply to *copy* the scientists' method, since designers and scientists have radically different interests and goals. As Gregory himself noted, a few pages later in the 1966 conference proceedings, 'the scientific method is a pattern of problem-solving behaviour employed in finding out the nature of what exists, whereas the design method is a pattern of behaviour employed in inventing things of value which do not yet exist. Science is analytic; design is constructive.'

So from the early days of design research and design methodology there has been a seemingly paradoxical attitude in those seeking to relate design method and scientific method. On the one hand there has been a desire to interpret design in ways similar to those in which science is interpreted; and on the other hand there have been the simultaneous *caveats* or declarations that, of course, design is *not* like science.

The basic text on which is founded the faith of the would-be 'design scientists' appears to be H. A. Simon's (1969) *'The Sciences of the Artificial'*. In this slim volume the paradoxical 'design science' attitude is again strikingly evident. 'The natural sciences are concerned with how things are,' Simon said, whereas 'design, on the other hand, is concerned with how things ought to be'.

Despite this openly acknowledged fundamental distinction between science and design, Simon went on to outline a series of elements that would embody 'the science of design', which is something that he wants to be 'a body of intellectually tough, analytic, partly formalizable, partly empirical, teachable doctrine about the design process'. The examples of the elements of this emerging doctrine that Simon offered included several that are now regarded as of dubious value in a design context; for example, methods of optimization borrowed from management science (sic), and methods of problem structuring based on the hierarchical decomposition techniques developed by Manheim and Alexander. (One might also wonder just why design *should* be 'intellectually *tough*'? Why shouldn't the pleasure and delight of designing be accessible to everyone, rather than reserved only for intellectual toughs like H. A. Simon?).

If science is *not* the same as design, why has there been this urge to create a 'design science'? There is obviously some strong attraction in science which has been drawing to it many design theorists. We suspect that this attraction lies not so much in the *method* of science, but in the *values* of science. These are the values (apart from 'intellectual toughness') of rationality, neutrality and universalism.

In the early part of this century, the Modern Movement in design aimed to adopt very similar values, and it is these values that still permeate design theory. When, for instance, might the following quotations have been made?

> Our epoch is hostile to every subjective speculation in art, science, technique, etc. The new spirit, which already governs almost all modern life, is opposed to animal spontaneity, to nature's domination, to artistic flummery and cookery. In order to construct a new object we need a method, that is to say, an objective system.

> The use of the house consists of a regular sequence of definite functions. The regular sequence of these functions is a traffic phenomenon. To render that traffic exact, economical and rapid, is the key effort of modern architectural science.

The first quotation, made in 1923, is from Van Doesburg, one of the founders of the influential *De Stijl* movement in design theory. The second, made in 1929, is from Le Corbusier, one of the founders of the supposedly rational, objective, 'International Style' of modern architecture. Yet both quotations might also have been made by any sufficiently outspoken design theorist or methodologist in the past ten to twenty years.

The values of 'design science', then, are rooted in the notions of objectivity, rationality and universalism that were believed to constitute the 'scientific' ways of seeing the world that were prevalent at the beginning of this century. These philosophical roots were realized by Hillier *et al.* (1972), who proposed a significant reorientation of design method to bring it more in line with some of the more recent philosphy of scientific method. The earlier views of design method were based on rationalist and empiricist philosophies of science, they suggested. There had, however, been a 'slow but decisive shift in philosophy and scientific epistemology over the past half-century or so', that had been overlooked by the design methodologists of the 1960s. One of the results of this shift was a recognition that preconceptions, or 'pre-structures', are an unavoidable element in scientific method.

Thus they introduced to design methodology the concept of 'pre-structure'; 'We cannot escape from the fact that designers must, and do, pre-structure their problems in order to solve them, although it appears to have been an article of faith among writers on design method (with a few exceptions) that this was undesirable because unscientific.' What Hillier *et al.* had managed to do was to reclaim the preconception as a perfectly valid, indeed inescapable, element of design method. If scientists themselves 'really operate' on the basis of pre-structures, they argued, 'then why should such a procedure be thought unscientific in design?'

Another important concept brought into design methodology by Hillier *et al.* was that of the 'conjecture'. Again, it was a concept legitimated by its role in science: 'It was once thought that conjecture would have no place in a rigorous scientific method. It was thought to be akin to speculation, and science sought to define itself in contradistinction to such notions. Since Popper we know that science cannot progress without conjecture, in fact that together with rigorous means of testing, conjectures constitute the life blood of science.' (Hillier *et al.* 1972)

They therefore proposed, following Popper's (1963) 'Conjectures and Refutations' model of scientific method, a 'conjecture-test' model of design method, in place of the old 'analysis-synthesis' model. This model of design method now seems to predominate in the bastard field of design science. One reason for its success is that, unlike some other design theories and models, it appears to fit in many different areas of design – for example, in engineering (Lewin 1979) as well as in architecture (Darke 1979). It is another mark of this model's success that what have been categorized as the first two 'generations' of design methods are now, according to Broadbent (1979), 'giving way to a third which takes a Popperian view of designing'.

However, Popper's 'conjectures and refutations' model of scientific method is not without its critics, as we will show later, and neither is its apparently very successful adaptation to design method. March (1976) notes that 'the philosophy of Karl Popper has had some influence' in design theory, but suggests that 'in the main its impact has been pernicious.' March's line of argument is one that, once again, emphasizes the distinctions between design and science. 'To base design theory on inappropriate paradigms of logic and science is to make a bad mistake,' he quite rightly points out. 'Logic has interests in abstract forms. Science investigates extant forms. Design initiates novel forms.'

Some of the basic tenets of the Popperian view of science are actually untenable when applied to design, according to March. For instance, Popper is opposed to the idea of inductive logic operating in scientific method, whereas in design, March says, 'the chief mode of reasoning is inductive in tenor, that is to say, synthetic rather than analytic.' And for Popper a good scientific hypothesis must be stated so as to be falsifiable, but March comments that 'a good design hypothesis is chosen in the expectation that it will succeed, not fail.'

We are left, therefore, with the distinct feeling that there are some important flaws in 'the Popperian view of designing', which is not surprising in view of the differences that exist between science and design. Indeed, it seems to us that there is an inherent aberration in attempts to build models of design that are derived from models of science. We believe that this aberration arises because, as we have noted, the attraction of a 'design science' lies not really in scientific *method* but rather in scientific *values*. We further believe that the particular value-laden view of science apparently held by the design scientists is no longer a tenable view and this we shall attempt to show in the following section.

SCIENTIFIC METHOD AND ITS PROBLEMS

For some decades now, the philosophy of science has been in a ferment, the origins of which reach back to the early years of this century and to the subsequent development of what has come to be known as *logical empiricism*. The basic premise of this movement was the belief that scientific theories and progress are amenable to *logical reconstruction*, and its main product was a formalized representation of the structure of scientific theories in axiomatic form. This concept constitutes the basis of what Suppe (1977) has designated 'the Received View'.

It has been consistently argued, however, that the Received View suffers from serious deficiencies. Some of these may be described as 'internal' – i.e. stemming from logical problems inherent in the Received View. Others may be termed 'external' in the sense that they stem from considerations outside the Received View – for example reflections on how scientists actually use theories in practice.

'Internal' problems include the difficulties of axiomatizing many theories commonly regarded as scientific, the untenability of the Received View's distinction between theoretical and observational terms, and its general treatment of the former. The 'external' problems have been formulated in the writings of various philosophers who objected, in one way or another, to the way the Received View focused exclusively on the finished product of the scientific enterprise – *viz.* theories – and ignored the process of reasoning through which laws, hypotheses and theories come to be proposed. There are various strands to this line of attack – epistemological, psychological, sociological, and historical.

Popper and Kuhn

Distinguishing between the internal and external criticisms of the Received View provides a convenient framework for considering the specific contributions of two particularly influential philosophers – K. R. Popper and T. S. Kuhn. For our purposes, Popper's work may be viewed as an attempt to overcome (or to sidestep) some of the internal deficiencies of the Received View without sacrificing the basic principle of the logical reconstructability of science. Kuhn, on the other hand, came at the Received View from quite another angle, with an historical study which seemed to cast doubt on the whole principle of logical reconstructability – at least in relation to the most significant cases of scientific progress.

From the outset, Popper's work (Popper 1963, 1968) has been removed from the *logical empiricist* movement, though he is often (and incorrectly) subsumed into it. 'Critical rationalism' is a term sometimes used to describe his position, and it is accurate at least insofar as he maintains that science is a 'rational', logical business in its testing of theories and hypotheses. So although he would not agree with proponents of the Received View that the growth of scientific knowledge can be reduced to the study of artificial languages and logical calculi, Popper would maintain that the *justification* of scientific discoveries must be amenable to rational reconstruction.

His philosophy may briefly be summarized thus: theories are genuine conjectures which, though not verifiable, can be subjected to severe critical tests. Such tests consist of attempts to *falsify* the theory in question. Scientific research always starts with a problem, and discoveries are always guided by theory rather than theories being discoveries due to observation. It is not possible to draw a distinction between theoretical and observational terms, and the descriptive language of science is theory-laden. Various competing theories can (indeed must) exist simultaneously and can be compared on the basis of their record in falsifiability tests and their degrees of corroboration. The scientist's obligation is to test his theories ruthlessly by seeking potential falsifiers rather than confirmations. All theories (and therefore all scientific knowledge) are ultimately conjectural.

Popper's account of scientific method has proved astonishingly popular with lay audiences and seems to have been largely accepted as 'the' picture of what science is about. The reasons for this are doubtless complex and beyond the scope of this paper, but two factors are worth noting. The first is the fact that the 'hypothetico-deductive' characterization of science has been ably popularized by distinguished scientists like P. B. Medawar and John Eccles and, through this, has probably acquired some degree of public credibility. The second factor is that there are strong romantic overtones to the Popperian picture, with its portrayal of scientists as dedicated searchers after truth, endlessly seeking falsifiers for their most cherished hypotheses.

However attractive this picture may be, it has to be said that it has some serious drawbacks as an account of scientific method. The chief difficulty is that the falsification by which Popper sets such store is difficult if not impossible to achieve in practice. The problem is twofold. In the first place, falsification can only work if there exists a *neutral observational language* in which to formulate the (falsifying) observation statements. But no such language exists: all observation is theory-laden. The second difficulty arises because, in real scientific practice, the entity that is being tested is rather more complex than a single hypothesis; it will include, for instance, laws and theories governing the behaviour of any instruments being used, plus specifications of initial conditions and of the experimental set-up, and so on. Popper of course recognized this from the outset, and tried to deal with it by introducing an element of professional judgement into decisions about whether to accept (falsifying) observation statements. But this really amounts only to an evasion of the issue, and to the inevitable conclusion that, since observation statements must always be tentative and fallible, the falsificationist position is drastically undermined.

Perception of these basic flaws at the core of Popper's position has led to various rescue attempts, the most notable of which is Lakatos's 'Methodology of Scientific Research Programmes' (Lakatos 1970). But this proposal also founders, largely because it cannot provide criteria for determining whether one research programme is 'better' than another. The inevitable conclusion to this line of development seems therefore to be that the attempts which have been made to date to impose rational reconstructions on scientific progress – whether in terms of the Received View of the logical empiricists, or the sophisticated falsification of Popper and Lakatos – appear to have failed. This apparent failure is one of the considerations which have led philosphers like Feyerabend (1975) to proclaim that the only general methodological rule which could have universal validity in science is 'anything goes'.

Chalmers (1978) has also noted that 'An embarrassing historical fact for falsificationists is that if their methodology had been strictly adhered to by scientists then those theories generally regarded as being among the best examples of scientific theories would never have been developed because they would have been rejected in their infancy.' Study of the history of science, therefore, would seem to offer little consolation to logical reconstructivists. Certainly that seems to have been the general conclusion drawn by many of them from T. S. Kuhn's celebrated historical study (Kuhn 1962). In this he presented a picture of science as a process involving two very distinct phases. The first (and in a temporal sense the dominant phase) is 'normal science', ie. a phase in which a community of scientists who subscribe to a shared 'paradigm' engage in routine puzzle-solving by seeking to apply the agreed-upon theories within the paradigm to anomalies of various sorts which are observed in the physical world.

The second phase of scientific activity Kuhn called 'revolutions'. These are periods of frenetic activity during which the failure of a paradigm to resolve anomalies throws a particular discipline into a state of crisis, from which it is rescued by the overthrow of the old paradigm and its replacement by another which can then serve as the basis for the next phase of 'normal science'. Kuhn's picture of science was profoundly disturbing to logical reconstructivists for a variety of reasons. In the first place they disliked his portrayal of 'normal' scientific practice, carrying as it did the implication that scientists working within such a tradition are unwilling to contemplate the abandonment of their paradigm even in the face of its apparent falsification. Failure to reconcile a paradigm with experimental or observational evidence, Kuhn claimed, will be seen as a failure on the part of the 'normal' scientist rather than as a reason for rejecting the specific theories in question ('only a poor craftsman blames his tools').

Secondly, Kuhn's description of scientific revolutions – the phases during which paradigms are overthrown – was distressing because of the implication that the revolutionary process cannot be 'rational'. This is because rival paradigms are 'incommensurable' – there exists no metalanguage which would enable their merits and demerits to be compared and evaluated – and because a paradigm is never abandoned until another is available to replace it. The process of paradigm-switch is therefore a matter of faith rather than of rational judgement – something akin to a religious conversion perhaps. Some of Kuhn's critics even went so far as to accuse him of characterizing scientific revolutions as outbreaks of 'mob psychology'.

Like Popper's 'logic of scientific discovery', Kuhn's historically inspired picture of science has also achieved widespread popular currency. The terms 'paradigm' and 'scientific revolution' have found their way into methodological discussions in hundreds of disciplines – though often with interpretations that their originator would be unlikely to countenance. They have even found their way into writings on design. And there are good reasons for their popularity. For Kuhn's picture of science has seemed intuitively plausible to many practitioners; many of his ideas, in other words, resonated with scientists' experience. For example, his concept of a paradigm highlighted the importance of shared intellectual values, 'craft' knowledge, apprenticeship, etc. among a community of researchers and teachers. And his concept of a 'revolution' squared with developments in a variety of disciplines – for example, plate tectonics in geophysics and the quantum theory in physics.

Just as Popper's position has been eroded by criticism, so has Kuhn's. His central notion of a 'paradigm', for example, has been challenged so effectively that Kuhn himself seems virtually to have retracted it, retreating to a concept of what he calls 'disciplinary matrices' and shared 'exemplars' (Kuhn 1977). Other critics have argued that the demarcation between normal and revolutionary science is by no means as sharp as he claimed. And, of course, there has been the overriding criticism that his emphasis on the incommensurability of paradigms leads in the nihilistic direction of a portrayal of scientific progress as a non-rational process.

The present position

The picture we have been assembling is one of highly sophisticated epistemological chaos. Various powerful attempts have been made to arrive at generalized descriptions of 'science', but each in turn has collapsed under criticism. None of the alternative views – whether those of Kuhn, Feyerabend, Hanson (1958), Toulmin (1953), Lakatos or others – has managed to attract majority support among philosophers of science. The most recent attempts at deriving some form of workable synthesis has been the work of Sneed (1971) and Stegmuller (1976) who have argued that a set-theoretic representation of theories allows for a bridge between Kuhn and the logical reconstructivists. But it is still too early to say whether this bridge has, in fact, been successfully constructed.

Transferring this discussion back into the realms of design theory, the important lesson to be drawn seems to be as follows. Attempts to equate 'design' with 'science' must logically be predicated upon a concept of science that is epistemologically coherent and historically valid. The history of the twentieth-century debate in the philosophy of science suggests that such a concept does not yet exist. It would therefore seem prudent for writers on design method to back away from this particular line of argument, at least for the time being.

In the meantime it may be worth seeking an alternative model for 'design'. We propose that it will be more fruitful to view design as a *technological* rather than a *scientific* activity.

DESIGN AS A TECHNOLOGICAL ACTIVITY

> This scientific age too readily assumes that whatever knowledge may be incorporated in the artifacts of technology must be derived from science. This assumption is a bit of modern folklore that ignores the many nonscientific decisions, both large and small, made by technologists as they design the world we inhabit. Many objects of daily use have clearly been influenced by science, but their form and function, their dimensions and appearance, were determined by technologists – craftsmen, designers, inventors and engineers – using nonscientific modes of thought. (Ferguson 1977)

There is, as yet, no developed 'philosophy of technology' analogous to the philosophy of science. It is therefore not yet possible to construct a 'technological' model of design in the same sense as 'scientific' (e.g. Popperian) models of design have been constructed. The best we can do is to begin to construct a view of design which draws upon some of the acknowledged features of technological activity. In particular we shall draw upon the acknowledged role of 'non-scientific modes of thought' in technology.

The concept of technology

[...]

We offer the following as a definition which meets these considerations: 'Technology is the application of scientific and other organized knowledge to practical tasks by social systems involving people and machines.'

It would seem that many of the observed features of design-as-practised map neatly onto such a concept of technology. It is strongly directed, for example, towards *practical tasks*, solutions or action. Designers make use of a *variety of kinds of knowledge* – from scientific knowledge of the properties of materials to the ineffable craft knowledge (derived from apprenticeship, experience, trial and error, etc.) which enables a skilled practitioner to say that a given design solution 'feels' right (or wrong). And, finally, design usually takes place within a *commercial or organizational framework*. Indeed organizational constraints are sometimes cited as explanations of why ingenious designs fail to be implemented or effective.

A 'technological' view of design therefore seems to be a reasonable proposition. We also believe that it will bear fruit in terms of furnishing insights into the design activity.

The use of non-scientific knowledge

We find useful the acknowledgement within a 'technological' model that a variety of kinds of knowledge can legitimately be drawn upon. Designing relies heavily on modes of thought and ways of knowing which (so far) are incompletely defined and poorly understood, but which are characterized by being neither 'scientific' nor 'literary'. This argument has been made by Archer (1979) in the context of defining design as a neglected 'third area' of general education. A related argument has also been made by Ferguson (1977) in the context of the history of technological development. Ferguson emphasizes the role of 'non-verbal thought' in technology, especially the role of images, visualizations, and pictorial modes of thought.

Balchin (1972) has used the term 'graphicacy' to summarize the human intellectual and practical abilities concerned with graphic and other non-verbal forms of understanding and communicating. Graphicacy is an equivalent concept to the other three, more generally acknowledged, areas of human ability: articulacy, numeracy, and literacy. It encompasses the ability to perceive and operate on the world by means of models which are neither verbal, nor numerical, nor literary. These 'graphical' modes of thought are central to designing and making. Yet they are consistently ignored or undervalued by those articulate theorists of cognitive processes who are so deeply immersed in the numerate-literate subculture of the scientific-academic world.

The activity of designing also relies heavily on the skilled performance of the designer. This again is something which is openly and legitimately recognized in technology, but tends not to be in science. It also happens to be something which is difficult to analyse in the classic reductionist ways of science. Skilled behaviour, according to Singleton (1978), 'can only be understood in terms of organized patterns and directed series and any attempt to consider a particular stimulus-response combination in isolation is a simplification at the expense of losing the essence of the whole business.'

Like other skilled behaviour, designing is a 'whole business'. A designer attends simultaneously to many levels of detail as he designs. The level of attention encompasses the range of design considerations from overall concept to small particulars such as materials and dimensions, and a skilled designer is adept at recognizing when concept and particulars clash. A naive designer characteristically allows particulars to intrude or to dominate, to the detriment of the overall design quality.

Many of the small particulars of a design actually appear to be dealt with, or 'attended to', by the skilled designer in a subconscious way. They only surface to be dealt with consciously when they become critical. This is typical of all kinds of skilled behaviour; if the small particulars become dominant then the 'organized patterns' of the skill are lost.

The impossibility of 'attending to' all the details of the skill by the skilled performer is recognized by Polanyi (1962) in his concept of 'tacit knowing'. 'There are things that we know but cannot tell', he argues. These things relate to skills and to qualities which can only be learned by ostensive definitions – i.e., learning from example. The knowledge which is conveyed by ostensive definition is *know-how*.

Knowing how and knowing that

In his book *The Concept of Mind*, Ryle (1949) offered a useful distinction between two categories of knowledge: *knowing how* and *knowing that*. The philosophical tradition behind this distinction stretches back a long way. For our purposes it surfaces in English philosophy in Russell's (1910) distinction between 'knowledge by acquaintance and knowledge by description'. We will stick to Ryle's terms of 'knowing how' and 'knowing that', which seem particularly relevant to our present discussion.

Knowing that is the kind of knowledge which can be made explicit, which can be formulated into advice, into procedures or into organized rules of conventional wisdom. For example, an architect *knows that* so many square metres of space are necessary (by convention) to a four-person house. Similarly he *knows that* a minimum-sized bathroom will occupy a floor area of 2m × 2m using standard sanitary ware. He knows that drains should fall at a minimum gradient of 1:40, and so on.

Knowing how can *not* be made explicit. It is that tacit knowledge which 'we know but cannot tell'. The architect's 'know-how' derives from the experience of planning and designing and constructing *many* houses, in discovering subtle tactics within the rules, of finding incidental, spontaneous ways of subverting the rules to greater benefit.

The differences between *knowing that* and *knowing how* may become easier to understand if we think of an example outside design. For instance, *knowing that* is the kind of knowledge possessed by a football spectator or football coach. He *knows that* the way to play football is so and so. He understands the rules of the game, he can cite chapter and verse. He has ideas about strategy in play and methods of scoring and so on. His knowledge *can* be made explicit.

The game clearly cannot proceed without this kind of knowledge; knowledge of the rules, which forms a public currency between the participants and observers of the game. Yet it is not the same as the incommunicable *know-how* of the players. A football player knows how to play football. His know-how is embodied and embedded in the tiny interrelated details of performance. He cannot say how he does it. The knowledge cannot be transferred in talk or on pieces of paper. This is not because the player is inarticulate, but rather that his form of knowledge is intrinsically non-verbal.

The corollary of this is the *knowing that* is to do with explicit descriptions, to do with rules and procedures. *Knowing that* determines competence. If you do not know the off-side rule, then you are likely to make mistakes. If you do not know the minimum size of bathrooms, then the WC pedestal may interfere with the opening of the bathroom door, and so on. You are incompetent. *Knowing that* seeks to avoid mistakes, seeks competence.

But playing football or designing bathrooms is not judged to be successful merely by the avoidance of mistakes. *Knowing how* is to do with standards of performance that go beyond competence. *Knowing how* determines quality.

There are three main points to be made about these epistemological categories.

First, for very many ordinary human activities *knowing that* is unnecessary. We learn how to see, how to talk, walk, eat, drink, etc. *without* explicit instructions. After trials and errors we *know how* to do it. We acquire the knowledge as children and the skills become locked into us. It is conceivable that even sophisticated rule-bound skills, such as playing chess, can be developed without explicit instruction. (See Ryle 1949: 41)

Second, *knowing that* depends upon *knowing how*. Our ability to perceive, assess, and relate to the world of particulars depends on rudimentary know-how. The accumulated content of *knowing that* is composed from records of those individual acts of perception, measurement and so on. The one kind of knowledge is prior to the other. Polanyi (1962) goes further. His use of the term 'tacit knowledge' embraces know-how and what he calls 'knowing by relying on'. 'Tacit knowing can indeed be identified with understanding, if understanding is taken to include the kind of practical comprehension which is achieved in the successful performance of a skill.' This kind of tacit understanding Polanyi calls the 'central act of knowing'.

Third, under many conditions of practice the two types of knowledge are mutually exclusive – they actually *interfere* with one another. In the employment of know-how, in the practice of a skill (such as playing football), the rules of play, the instructions of the coach (*knowing that*), the concentration upon the explicit, *inhibit* the smooth operation of the skills themselves.

When actually performing skilfully it is necessary that the rules, the advice, the instructions, should be internalized and 'forgotten'. The exercise of know-how is unself-conscious – if not without thought. It is inhibiting to concentrate on rules and explicit procedures when engaged in skilled performance. The centipede *knows how* to walk – if he were to think about it too much, the centipede would stumble!

What does all this mean for designers? Well, the three lessons are reiterated in a more specific form.

Firstly, *knowing that* is *not* of necessity part of design. Theory may not be all that helpful. Tacit knowledge embodied in craft seems quite capable of producing objects which are well made, fitting to their context, appropriate to the users, and rich in significance – in short 'good' designs.

Secondly, *knowing how*, i.e. the inexplicit, manipulative non-verbal acts of skill, lies at the core of design. Historically design has arisen from craft, and it contains very many skills and embodiments of know-how. But also, no artifact exists just because of theory. As Pye (1964) notes, 'If there had been no inventions, there would be no theory of mechanics. Invention comes first.'

Thirdly, *knowing that*, i.e. knowledge of the explicit 'rules' of design, can actually inhibit practice. The focus of attention can be in the wrong domain – in the explicit procedures rather than the subtle details of performance.

We can now see that the activity of science is directed by *knowing that* – towards error-free explanation, towards scientific 'truth'. Design and technology, on the other hand, are directed by *knowing how* – towards seeking performances and products of skill and quality.

CONCLUSIONS

We have argued that the commonly adopted 'scientific' models of design are not really tenable in view of the current epistemological chaos surrounding the concept of 'scientific method'. Further, we wholeheartedly agree with the 'design scientists' themselves that design *simply is not like* science. As an alternative, we have proposed that design should be viewed as a technological activity, and that a 'technological' model of design would be more fruitful than continued attempts to construct a 'scientific' model.

However, models (of whatever kind) of the design process have no value in themselves. Their utility derives from the extent to which they enable us to understand and improve teaching and practice. In this connection, a 'technological' model such as we propose does seem to have something to offer. For example, it encourages us to include and develop within design theory concepts of other forms of knowledge than the simply 'scientific' forms, and leads us to recognize the importance of craft knowledge in the acquisition of design skills.

To some people it may seem that we have simply (or perhaps not so simply) stated the obvious, in the sense that many designers have always subscribed to an implicit model of design which resembles the one we propose. If that is indeed the case, our attempts to make the foundations of such a model more explicit may at least serve to reassure these designers that their basic instincts about the teaching and practice of design are sound. And those who disagree, or who wish to continue their advocacy of a 'scientific' model, will at least have an opposing conjecture to refute.

REFERENCES

Archer, L. B. (1979), 'Design as a Discipline: the three Rs', *Design Studies*, vol. 1, pp. 18–20. [See Chapter 5 of this Reader.]

Balchin, W. G. V. (1972), 'Graphicacy', *Geography*, vol. 57, pp. 185–95.

Broadbent, G. (1979), 'The Development of Design Methods', *Design Methods and Theories*, vol. 13, pp. 41–5.

Chalmers, A. F. (1978), *What Is This Thing Called Science?* Open University Press, Milton Keynes.

Darke, J. (1979), 'The Primary Generator and the Design Process', *Design Studies*, vol. 1, pp. 36–44.

Ferguson, E. S. (1977), 'The Mind's Eye: non-verbal thought in technology', *Science*, 26 August, pp. 827–36.

Feyerabend, P. (1975), *Against Method*, New Left Books, London.

Gregory, S. A. (1967), *The Design Method*, Butterworth, London.

Hanson, N. R. (1958), 'The Logic of Discovery', *Journal of Philosophy*, vol. 55, pp. 1073–89.

Hillier, B., Musgrove, J., and O'Sullivan, P. (1972), 'Knowledge and Design', in Mitchell, W. J. (ed.) *Environmental Design: Research and Practice*, University of California, Los Angeles.

Kuhn, T. S. (1962), *The Structure of Scientific Revolutions*, University of Chicago Press, Chicago.

Kuhn, T. S. (1977), 'Second Thoughts on Paradigms', in Suppe, F. (ed.) *The Structure of Scientific Theories*, University of Illinois Press, Urbana; 2nd edition.

Lakatos, I. (1970), 'Falsification and Methodology of Scientific Research Programmes', in Lakatos, I., and Musgrave, A. (eds) *Criticism and the Growth of Knowledge*, Cambridge University Press, Cambridge.

Lewin, D. (1979), 'On the Place of Design in Engineering', *Design Studies*, vol. 1, pp. 113–17. [Chapter 2 of this Reader is an enlarged version of this article.]

March, L. J. (1976), 'The Logic of Design and the Question of Value', in March, L. J. (ed.) *The Architecture of Form*, Cambridge University Press, Cambridge.

Polanyi, M. (1962), 'Tacit Knowing: its bearing on some problems of philosophy', *Review of Modern Physics*, vol. 34, pp. 601–16.

Popper, K. R. (1963), *Conjectures and Refutations*, Routledge and Kegan Paul, London.

Popper, K. R. (1968) *The Logic of Scientific Discovery*, Hutchinson, London.

Pye, D. (1964) *The Nature of Design*, Studio Vista, London.

Russell, B. (1910) *Mysticism and Logic, and Other Essays*, George Allen and Unwin, London.

Ryle, G. (1949), *The Concept of Mind*, Hutchinson, London.

Simon, H. A. (1969), *The Sciences of the Artificial*, MIT Press, Cambridge, Mass.

Singleton, W. T. (1978), *The Analysis of Practical Skills*, MTP Press, Lancaster.

Sneed, J. D. (1971), *The Logical Structure of Mathematical Physics*, Reidel, Dordrecht.

Stegmuller, W. (1976), *The Structure and Dynamics of Theories*, Springer-Verlag.

Suppe, E. (ed.) (1977), *The Structure of Scientific Theories*, University of Illinois Press, Urbana; 2nd edition.

Toulmin, S. (1953), *The Philosophy of Science: an introduction*, Hutchinson, London.

II TECHNOLOGY AND HUMAN VALUES

The readings in this section develop the ideas presented in the previous section. They explore the notion that technology represents an identifiable and definable aspect of culture with differing values, responses and codes operating within it. Lack of appreciation and understanding of this culture is linked to the conceptual impoverishment of the English language (and thus the British people). There is a lack of an adequate vocabulary which relates to this culture, and the German word 'Technik' is offered by Fores and Rey, in the first reading, to illustrate this. (Unlike the writers in the first section they are not content with the word 'technology'). The implications of this for education are only hinted at by Fores and Rey when they note that 'applied science' is not a sufficient representation of this aspect of culture. Archer, in Chapter 5, goes much further, saying that we need, as Lewin suggested, a third area of education concerned with making and doing aspects of human activity. It is argued that, since the British educational system has shaped our national character, there is now an inherent resistance to technological change, with implications for the decline of the economy. Weiner argues that we are instinctively opposed to high technology industry and salesmanship and to change a national frame of mind and value system is a political challenge facing governments. This stance puts the burden on education to reverse the anti-industrial culture. But can education fulfil such a role in society? One response of the education system (being promoted in this decade) is to suit the needs of the economy: vocationalism. Another is concerned not with content (e.g. scientific and technological knowledge) but with the values and attitudes of the industrial culture. While Archer does not start from this point, he shares with this response, a belief in a neglected aspect of a technological society.

4 Technik: *the relevance of a missing concept*

● M. J. Fores and L. Rey

In the English language, a very large number of commentators and their readers have come to think and to express themselves in a verbal system which is defective but still widely used and beloved. In this system, 'science' and 'technology' are considered to be two key features in modern life, and for the development of civilization and the culture. Both are thought to be important, with the former influencing the latter in a direct way. In particular, this relationship underlies virtually all teaching of scientists, engineers and 'technologists'. 'Science' and 'technology' are closely connected in the minds of many, because of this assumed causal influence, and because practitioners of each share part of an education. Indeed, the connection between the two is sometimes taken to be so close that 'science' and technology' are known as an 'indivisible pair'.[1] At other times they are wrapped up together in a single conceptual package and simply known as 'science'. Always discussion is overshadowed, in Britain at least, by the fact that there are establishments with names such as Imperial College of Science and Technology, University of Manchester Institute of Science and Technology, University of Wales Institute of Science and Technology.

Unfortunately for clarity of thought, this conception of science and technology incorporates a number of important errors, which serve to confuse a wide range of people about the role and importance of what was once known, rather more helpfully, as the 'useful arts' of manufacture. And it means too that the education of engineers has often been misconceived. It has also, incidentally, been consistent with the adoption in English of quite a different idea of 'science' from that used in other major languages; English-language 'science' tends to include only knowledge of natural phenomena; whereas the equivalent word in other languages includes all knowledge.[2]

To illustrate the nature of these errors of conception, we will introduce and use a word, that is new to English, to help improve understanding of the activities and policies connected with manufacturing, engineering and an educational process which is suitable for work in both. We aim to show that this new word represents a missing concept in the English language, the adoption and wider use of which could greatly facilitate analysis and treatment of a number of important subjects. It is important to add that the adoption of this idea also serves to underline the dignity of work in manufacturing.

TECHNIK

The word we choose is the German *Technik*. The concepts of *technik* and *teknik* are well established in Germany and Sweden respectively; the words are widely used and the ideas behind them are rarely misunderstood. The meaning of these two words differs subtly but substantially from the English 'technology', the German and Swedish *verbal* correspondence for which are *Technologie* and *teknologi* respectively. The basis for this difference between *Technik* and 'technology,' as will be shown later, is a conceptual one in that area which in English is covered by the ideas of 'science', 'humanities' and the 'arts'. It is a difference in perceptions of, and analysis of, the general culture; so in this way it is important.[3]

Technik has to do with the functioning of natural and man-made things and the methods used in their manufacture. So, it has come to signify a whole subculture, along the lines of 'science' and the 'arts' in English, *Wissenschaft* and *Kunst* in German. *Technik* includes the set of particular principles according to which artifacts (man-made objects) work and the particular principles of the methods used in manufacturing them. It is not the same as what, in English, would be called the 'technique' of doing something. The English idea of technique is normally contrasted with related scientific principles, whereas *Technik* includes those principles.

Due to the predominance of the English language in the general discussion of industrial matters, the English idea 'technology' has crept into both the German and Swedish languages, and probably into most other languages as well. In translation, the words *Technologie* and *teknologi* have been used for the English 'technology', despite the fact that they both mean something rather different. This practice has added to a general conceptual confusion about important terms and important activities. It has led to a situation that can only be rectified by restricting the use of the word 'technology' in the English language to meaning the scientific study and teaching of techniques. If such a restriction were enforced, the word 'technology' would then, as an additional benefit, have a meaning equivalent to philology, sociology and biology, in parallel with other words based on the Greek 'logos'. After all, nobody seriously expects philology to produce a new language, sociology to build a new town, or biology to create a new Frankenstein's monster. Why, then, should technology be expected to build a jet engine or a pipe-line under the sea? By its very use and construction, English-language 'technology' turns the sage miraculously into an inventor.

TECHNIK AND CULTURE

Difficulties arise in the English language, in correct interpretation of the role and importance of the useful arts and methods of manufacture, from basic misconceptions about the role of science. For instance, Bronowski and Mazlish, in the preface to a study entitled *The Western Intellectual Tradition*, have illustrated one way in which that treatment can go off the rails. The authors' stated aim for the study was to see 'all history, certainly all intellectual history, as a unity'. In particular, they aimed to bring the development of 'science and techniques' into the stream of conventional history. Yet, they quoted from Snow:[4]

> What is needed is that in the general history books the development of science should take its place along with political and economic developments. It is only just that this should be done even from the historian's point of view, for the world we live in is as much the product of science as of politics and economics. The steam engine helped to shape the modern world at least as much as Napoleon and Adam Smith, but only rarely do historians admit the fact. There are few living historians who can write history in this way; but this is one way in which history must be written if the worlds of science and the humanities are not to drift still farther apart.

Where Snow, Bronowski and Mazlish go wrong is at the very heart of their analysis. Certainly the steam engine has had an extremely important influence on the modern world. Few serious historians would dispute this view now, even if they would have done in previous times. But, equally certainly, the steam engine cannot sensibly be thought of as being the 'product' of science', as the authors have it to be. The product's first construction and later development was never very significantly influenced by the possession of scientific knowledge by its pioneers. Of the earliest pioneers, Newcomen and Trevithick were craftsmen, admittedly curious about the knowledge of natural science, but scarcely able to find anything to use in their work from that body of knowledge. James Watt, an instrument maker, had worked in Glasgow University and was quite aware of what was happening concurrently in experimental natural science. The separate condenser for the steam engine, for which he is best known, was based on an idea about the latent heat of steam which turned out to be quite incorrect. One of the most distinctive features of the famous Birmingham factory of Boulton and Watt was its improved practice in machining metal.

Probably the most famous pioneer of the steam engine, and so the man most responsible for shaping the modern world by its use, was George Stephenson. As he was virtually illiterate at the time of his breakthrough, it is very unlikely that he followed developments in scientific knowledge in the conventional fashion, by reading. Indeed, all Stephenson's biographers stress his possession of technical, rather than scientific skills. Undoubtedly the steam engine was an important influence in general economic and social change from the time of its first use. But study of its inception and development shows that this process was not much influenced by the development of natural science; even a guide put out by the so-called Science Museum in South Kensington admits this.[5] The steam engine can hardly be an archetypal product of science.

More generally, for the period up until the last years of the nineteenth century, most specialist historians agree that the development of natural science and that of methods of manufacture lay far apart. An attempt, by any commentators, to wrap both of them up within the boundaries of the development of science, or latterly of science and technology, is quite inappropriate. Bronowski and Mazlish's grasp of the 'Western intellectual tradition', or at least their presentation of it, is flawed through lack of the idea *Technik*, as a vital part of cultural development.

Crossing from Britain to continental Europe, in Germany, if there are two cultures or sub-areas of the general culture, they are not 'science' and 'humanities' of the split generally thought to exist in Britain, this being the split which a number of cultural analysts have set themselves up to try to heal. Instead, if there is a two-way split at all, it is between *Wissenschaft*, concerned with all knowledge and all the subjects taught in the classical university, and *Technik* concerned with making things, making them work and studies in the technical universities and faculties. In most discussion and analysis however, there are three German subcultures: *Wissenschaft*, with broadly the same meaning as before; *Kunst*, describing the notion of 'art', in the sense of 'fine arts' and the performing arts of English, including theatre, opera and ballet. Then there is *Technik* again, which is generally thought of as being quite separate from both. Swedish usage follows the German: *vetenskap* for *Wissenschaft*, *konst* for *Kunst*. Significantly, both the *vetenskap* and *Wissenschaft* terms literally mean 'knowledgeship', the art of handling knowledge, akin to the constructions 'gamesmanship' and 'seamanship'.

Rarely therefore, if ever at all, is the German cultural area *Technik* thought to peep out of the pocket of *Wissenschaft*, in the same way that English-language 'technology', to the uninformed layman, peeps out of the pocket of 'science'. In Germany, everyone accepts that *Technik* and *Wissenschaft* are quite separate as cultural areas, generating separate patterns of work and employment for those involved in them. Essentially the first area is concerned with manufacturing industry and making things; the second is concerned with the universities, teaching and research. The German prefix *Wissen* and the Swedish *veten* are derivatives of the corresponding words for knowledge; so this serves to forge more closely the science-knowledge connection. Few people in Germany imagine that changes in *Technik* are determined primarily and directly by changes in *Wissenschaft*. All major continental European languages contain a conception of cultural splits broadly along the German lines, rather than along English lines. All the ideas expressed in this section of the paper could as well have been put forward using Swedish terms as German ones.

THE NATURE OF *TECHNIK*

Bronowski has also written that man is distinctive because his evolution is continuing. Furthermore, evolutionary change has always been determined by the outside circumstances in which the species finds itself, 'and the name of the culture is technology'.[6] In terms appropriate to this article, Bronowski's assertion should read that man's continuing development is mainly determined by *Technik*, and with his aim to make artifacts and to improve the general environment.

While it is not necessary for present purposes fully to accept Bronowski's view, which he rightly points out to be a startling one, the importance to the general culture of *Technik* can be discerned from the assertion that it has always been a prime concern of the species from the time when man came down from the trees. In contrast, science and systematic knowledge came very much later as a major force in cultural development. Man has always lived in an age of *Technik*, in which his style of life has always been constrained by the possibilities of making useful artifacts and using them as an extension of his own abilities. In contrast, most specialist treatments consider that we have only lived in an 'age of science' for about two hundred years at the very most.

Technik started with the fashioning of stones and the collection of sticks by early man. As one commentator, Forbes, puts it: 'civilization began with man's first attempt to convert into artifacts the materials which he found in nature'.[7] Some of the first tools were stones which could be used, and later sharpened, to break protective coverings to reach food and to kill animals for food. Stones could also be used to kill or ward off dangerous animals for purposes of protection. A diet based on meat-eating left more time for doing other things. Sticks could be used too for protection and attack, to build shelter from the weather and crucially to make primitive machines.

Essentially a machine, then as now, is most often a contrivance whereby force can be applied in one place and a desired effect accomplished in another. The first machine was almost certainly the club or the lever, something which could harness human effort to multiply force applied and so further to extend man's abilities. Later came the harnessing of material resources, especially water and wind, for driving machines and for pumping water. Later on, primitive workshops and factories were created, few of which are available to today's archaeologists to examine, because tools and materials have decayed. A few have been preserved however by chance, such as Egyptian carpenters' tools from about 1500 BC, recognizably similar to tools we see today. A dig through archaeology itself shows two things. First, a society prided itself for the sophistication of its artifacts, and is also remembered for them. Second, *Technik* is best understood as being involved with the efforts of the human species to extend its powers and abilities from those simply exercised directly by its own body and limbs. A machine driven by human power performed this purpose at one remove: that driven by other types of power, animal or from mineral resources, did it at two removes. The accent in this treatment on physical force does not preclude the use of brainpower and ideas. Each machine in its development required a conceptual notion of its utility: and human powers of imagination were critical in this. Indeed, the history of *Technik* shows that man has always used all the knowledge and ingenuity at his disposal to create useful artifacts; but, through most of history, formal, written-down knowledge of natural science has not, as a rule, been directly useful in creating and improving these artificial products. Man's unique powers of foresight and imagination have been more directly useful to him through the exercise of *Technik*, rather than indirectly useful through building up a structured body of scientific knowledge.

TECHNIK AND THE CONQUEST OF NATURE

One school of thought considers the history of *Technik* to be that of the 'conquest of nature';[8] but this is a misleading idea for a number of reasons. Problems of *Technik* have never been cast in terms connected with the notion of nature, but rather in terms of a specific job to be done and an artifact to be made. Indeed it is doubtful, too, whether early man had a very clear idea of conquest, where artifacts and artificial uses were concerned. A stick or a stone could just be used to do a particular job, fashioned or otherwise. 'Conquest' is an idea adopted subsequently by those historians who track these exploits, not typically by those who performed them.

As tools and contrivances became more complex, they were always adopted for useful and understood purposes, which strayed farther and farther from the materials from which they were made. A stick, as a lever, was obviously made of wood, fairly directly from the natural world. But a potter's wheel could be made from various materials, probably in combination. A governor to control the speed of a rotating machine is a tool to control a tool, a contrivance to control a contrivance; in a crucial way it does not deal with nature directly. Nature is rather far away from the specification of such an artifact.

Another reason to doubt the utility of the depiction of *Technik* as conquering nature follows the first and concerns the preoccupations of exponents. The exponent of *Tecknik* must necessarily be obsessed with the artificial; whereas the exponent of natural science has always, and properly so, been obsessed with what is natural. These two obsessions have come into contrast more markedly as the years have gone on. As the artificial has become more complex, so it became even more artificial; and so the preoccupation of the exponent of *Technik* has drifted further away from what is found in nature. That Koestler could class the invention of the printing press amongst 'discoveries' of science is patently absurd.[9] Where did Gutenberg discover it? Behind a gooseberry bush? The most essential fact about putting together a new artifact is that it is a new configuration which has not yet existed; so it cannot be 'discovered'.

Of course even the most sophisticated artifact is made from materials originating in nature. But that is no proper reason to describe the action of *Technik* as the conquest of nature. Products of German *Kunst*, Swedish *konst*, and the English-language 'fine arts', are equally well made from natural materials. But few people think of sculpting or pottery as being characterized by 'the conquest of nature'; nor would they think of shirt-making or cooking in these terms. The practice of modern *Technik* – making, running and maintaining complex and useful artifacts – is just as little distinctively the conquest of nature, as is the practice of making decorative artifacts.

Technik produces what is thought to be useful at any one time by a particular group of people in their own particular culture; furthermore, as Bronowski points out, *Technik* has a major determining influence on that culture. If the operations of *Technik* shade into those of either of the other two cultural areas, they shade into *Kunst*, rather than *Wissenschaft*. A dig by archaeologists will turn up pottery, cutlery, tools, ornaments and jewellery. The first two groups of artifacts are most likely to have been useful in purpose of manufacture, but may have been partly ornamental. The last two groups are most likely to have been ornamental in purpose. But even ornaments have their uses: for instance, to impress potential clients. Craft skills will have been shared between the making of the products of fine art and of the useful arts; metal-working skills are an obvious example of that point. So two sets of activities of manufacture, within *Technik* and *Kunst*, shade into each other; they continue to do so in the circumstances of today.

TECHNIK AND SCIENCE

The juxtaposition of these two concepts introduces immediately a significant contrast in treatment of a common topic, the manufacture of useful artifacts. *Technik* is essentially a continental European idea; whereas applied science only makes any sense in the context of English-language classifications. The verbal equivalent *angewandte Wissenschaften* is an alien topic in German culture; the equivalent Swedish phrase *tillämpad vetenskap* makes little sense either, and it is not in use. Even in English, as we shall argue, 'applied science' does not make very much sense. Instead it incorporates a misleading conception of what happens in manufacturing, one which is associated with the 'indivisible pair' depiction referred to earlier.

Technik is, as we have noted and in its extended sense, the cultural area involved with the making, improving, maintaining, using and running of artifacts of the type which were once called 'contrivances', and which are very often machines of a sort. Amongst those with a higher education qualification, the most important group of exponents of *Technik* are engineers. These are people who are sometimes loosely known as 'technologists' in English, but they normally have a qualification in engineering nonetheless. Many other groups are concerned in practising *Technik*, notably a range of those known, in Britain, as 'technicians', and a range of those with craft skills. Amongst the last are fitters, boiler-makers, electricians, tool-makers, machine operators, in the English parlance: either skilled manual workers or semi-skilled. Modern man is far more concerned occupationally with the useful arts than the fine arts, more concerned with outputs which are not in the form of knowledge than those which are.

The principal specific functions of *Technik*, those concerned directly with the making of artifacts, can be read from any list of jobs done by engineers, or jobs which have a high engineering content. Design of products, production, product development, technical sales and maintenance are the most obvious ones within manufacturing industry. These functions together account for at least three-quarters of graduate engineers in Swedish manufacturing.[10] Other jobs and tasks are associated with *Technik* but are less obviously a part of it, although they are essential to the manufacture of goods nontheless. Jobs in finance, general sales and general industrial management are much more closely connected with this subcultural area than they are with *Kunst* or *Wissenschaft*. Some practising natural scientists in manufacturing may feel themselves more closely associated with the latter of these other two areas than with *Technik*; but these people are few and far between, and their jobs and tasks are quite untypical. For Swedish manufacturing again, there are thirty times as many graduate engineers employed in top-level jobs as there are graduate natural scientists, seven times as many in product development.[11]

The English-language 'applied science' concept is essentially a peg on which natural scientists and other members of the academy can hang their views. They use it when they wish to comment on topics outside their specialist experience and competence, and inside the broad area of *Technik*, which normally they do not adequately understand. Only in English, of the major European languages, could 'applied science' possibly exist, since only English has a meaning of 'science' which makes this word include only knowledge of natural phenomena or, alternatively the process by which this knowledge is derived. So, only in English, can a spurious connection be forged in the mind to relate knowledge (science) and manufacture (applied science), through the fact that the products of manufacture are inevitably made from nature (the subject of science).

In practice, tasks and jobs in continental European *Technik* and in English-language 'applied science' turn out to be much the same; they are virtually constrained to be such. But grasp and understanding of their essential nature and purposes varies substantially between the rival conceptions. Those who use the *Technik* conception concentrate on the production of artifacts and what used to be known in English as 'the useful arts' of manufacture; they concentrate on the product, its utility, its specification and the methods used in making it. Those who use the 'applied science' conception concentrate on inputs of knowledge which are allegedly important to manufacturing processes: the output part of the manufacturing process becomes less important. For these reasons alone the *Technik* idea should be preferred to the 'applied science' one, for describing and understanding the process of making artifacts in industry. Those engaged in this process are invariably more concerned with the product than with knowledge inputs.

Another set of reasons renders the 'applied science' concept doubly misleading. The useful existence of the phase 'applied science' implies that some kind of contrast can exist with 'pure science', whatever that might be. Yet, there can never be any body of pure science at all, if the criterion to be used in this classification is lack of utility, or lack of applicability, of knowledge produced. All scientific knowledge is put out freely for verification or falsification; so all can be used freely and with no attribution. Even the most basic ideas of natural science, such as Ohm's law and Newton's laws of motion, turn out to be applicable in practical circumstances. A third law of thermodynamics is potentially very useful and applicable as well. The ridiculous conclusion has therefore to be drawn that the 'purest' of science is more widely useful in practical circumstances than work which is done for particular applications, the so-called 'applied' type of work.

If the 'pure science' idea bites the dust, and with it the idea of 'applied science' as a body of knowledge, what of 'applied science' as a sensible near-alternative to *Technik* along the lines argued previously? The phrase fails as a body of knowledge simply because all knowledge of natural phenomena is applicable. It fails as an alternative to the concept of *Technik*, simply because technical work cannot be characterized as the application of scientific knowledge; such work is more concerned with personal skill instead. One well-known study commissioned by the British Association for the Advancement of Science has the rate of technical progress to be the same as the rate of adoption, or use, of science; we cannot agree with such an assumption.[12]

TECHNIK AND TECHNOLOGY

Unlike the case of the phrase 'applied science' English-language 'technology' has, as we have pointed out, an etymological equivalent in most other European languages. However, meanings have diverged, with the result that an assumed equivalence of sense turns out not to be so, when comparison is made with the most common English usage of the term.

Technologie and *teknologi*, in German and Swedish, invariably mean roughly what one would expect the words to mean from their Greek roots. In contrast the most common English-language meaning of 'technology' differs significantly from its essential derivation. Furthermore, the English-language word is a variable entity itself. This variation reflects the imprecision with which activities concerned with producing useful artifacts have been described for the general reader. It also reflects a connected factor, whereby discussion put forward in terms of 'technology', like that put forward in terms of 'applied science', has served as an excuse for natural scientists, and other outsiders to manufacturing, to discuss elements of manufacturing they do not properly understand and do not have sufficient competence to deal with.

One meaning of the English-language word 'technology' is roughly equivalent to *Technik*; this makes it the science and art of industrial manufacture, and of designing and producing useful artifacts.[13] Another meaning of the word, that which is most common amongst engineers themselves, describes a set of craft techniques; this might be summarized roughly as the art of the industrial arts. A third, but less common, meaning runs roughly along the lines of *Technologie/teknologi* of continental languages; this has it to mean, roughly, the science and the discussion of the industrial arts. A fourth meaning, ironically, includes all of, or at least most of, natural science as well as most of the industrial arts of manufacture. So a physicist turns out to be a 'technologist' as well as an engineer, in the same way that an engineer turned out to be a 'scientist' in the depiction of the first paragraph of this article: certainly an ironic enough result, and a highly confusing one, as well.

Evidence on what is the most common English language meaning of 'technology' comes from the observation that the majority of people imagine technologists to be the same as engineers. British official statistics tend to group all engineers as 'technologists' and to show that most technologists are engineers: so these are the people who were thought to be 'applied scientists' by the criteria of the last section of this paper.

A more important point to make however, is that engineers are not distinctive for a working output of principles of manufacturing techniques, but rather for an output of manufactured products. So, since one would expect people called 'technologists' to produce a main output of 'technology', then the last term must mean much the same as 'applied science' of the last section. Both ideas turn out to describe the same set of activities: those practised, at the higher level by engineers, and normally known as 'engineering' to the exponents themselves. Again the idea of *Technik* is presented here as a means of clearing up confusion. The engineer, and others whose principal working aim is to make and run three-dimensional useful artifacts tend to be different sorts of individuals from those working in the other cultural areas. They have acquired different sorts of responses too. We consider that the use of the concept *Technik* avoids the treacherous wastes of misunderstanding associated with the term 'technology', with its variable meanings, and the close connections it is assumed to have with natural science.
[...]

CONCLUSION

In this article, we have attempted to demonstrate an important point about man, his nature, activities and education. As individuals both of whom were trained within the cultural area of *Technik*, but have worked for some time outside it, we have tried to explain the process and its concept not, we hope, as outsiders from natural science all too often have done, in distinct ignorance of the process of making things; but with some understanding born of personal curiosity and experience, using the insights which go with them.

If man has anything at all which can be thought of as his 'nature', prominent within this must be his constant and untiring aim to increase his powers and skills by artificial means. Constantly he tries to improve on what he was born with, to stretch out in capability. The young child's obsession with cars, boats or planes reveals this interest. His/her parents work or play with other tools and gadgets, which are intended to be useful in their functions. If the child or the man or the woman wants to know how something works, this is not essentially a part of the curiosity of science, but rather with an aim to perform and perfect the use of operations in the general area of *Technik*. *Technik*, an obsession of the species from the early days of sticks and stones, remains a present obsession as we try, for good or ill, to expand our powers even further with each generation, as we try to alter our immediate environment to suit what we imagine our ends to be.

Technik is a separate cultural area with codes of behaviour, responses and a dignity of its own. Those working within it do not have constantly to look over their shoulders at 'science' or 'arts'. 'Science' and 'arts' do not care much for utility, in the way that *Technik* does; furthermore they have a different grasp of the artificial. *Technik* remains a missing concept in English. Its non-existence is the English-speaker's, and the English-speaking student's, loss.

NOTES

Part of the argument of this article was published in summary form in *Nature*, 1 September 1977.
1. Hilary and Steven Rose. *Science in Society*. Penguin, 1969, p.xi.
2. For further discussion of the varying meanings of 'science' see M. Fores, 'Science of Science: A Substantial Fraud'. *Higher Education Review*, Summer 1977.
3. We have used a comparison with Swedish to show that the German method of classification is used elsewhere as well. See also M. Fores, 'Applied Science Is Pure Nonsense in Myopic Britain'. *The Times Higher Education Supplement*, 19 March 1976.
4. J. Bronowski and Bruce Mazlish. *The Western Intellectual Tradition*, London 1969. Penguin edition, pp. 7–8.
5. John van Riemsdijk and Paul Sharp, *In the Science Museum*, 1968, p. 23.

6. J. Bronowski, 'Technology and Culture in Evolution', *Cambridge Review*, vol. 8, May 1970.
7. R. J. Forbes, *The Conquest of Nature*, Penguin, 1968, p. 19.
8. As in the title of Forbes' book, note 7.
9. Arthur Koestler, *The Act of Creation*, 1964.
10. Svenska Arbetsgivareforeningen, *Loner for Tjansteman*, Stockholm, 1973.
11. *Ibid.*
12. C. F. Carter and B. R. Williams, *Industry and Technical Progress*, London, 1957, p. 1.
13. See also: M. Fores, 'Some Terms in the Discussion of Technology and Innovation,' *Technology and Society*, October 1970; L. Rey, *'Innovations politik?'* Swedish Ministry of Industry, unpublished, 1973.

5   **The three Rs**

   ● B. Archer

EDITORS' INTRODUCTION

*Professor Archer argues that not only is 'design' represented as a third
fundamental area in education, but it is distinct from science and humanities
(the two cultures).*

The world of education is full of anomalies. Take that extraordinarily
durable expression 'The Three Rs', for example. It is very widely held
that when all the layers of refinement and complexity are stripped away,
the heart of education is the transmission of the essential skills of
reading, writing and 'rithmetic. This expression is internally
inconsistent, to begin with. Reading and writing are the passive and
active sides, respectively, of the language skill, whilst arithmetic is the
subject matter of that other skill which, at the lower end of the school,
we tend to call 'number'. So the expression 'The Three Rs' only refers to
two ideas: language and number. Moreover, the word 'arithmetic' is
mispronounced as well as misspelled, giving the impression that the
speaker takes the view that the ability and the necessity to do sums is
somehow culturally inferior. If challenged, most who use the expression
would deny they intended any such bias, but aphorisms often betray a
cultural set. Explicit or implied denigration of science and numeracy in
favour of the humanities and literacy was certainly widespread in
English education up to and beyond the period of the second world war,
and was the subject of C. P. Snow's famous campaign against the
separation of 'the two cultures' in 1959. The two cultures may be less
isolated from one another these days, and may speak less slightingly of
one another, but the idea that education is divided into two parts,
science and the humanities, prevails. There are many people, however,
who have always felt that this division leaves out too much. Art and
craft, dance and drama, music, physical education and sport are all valid
school activities but belong to neither camp. There is a substantial body
of opinion, not only amongst teachers but also amongst groups outside

that profession, which holds that modern society is faced with problems – such as the ecological problem, the environmental problem, the quality-of-urban-life problem, and so on – all of which demand of the population of an affluent industrial democracy competence in something else besides literacy and numeracy. Let us call this competence 'a level of awareness of the issues in the material culture' for the time being. Under present circumstances, it is rather rare for a child who is academically bright to take art of craft or home economics or any of the other so-called 'practical' subjects having a bearing on the material culture to a high level in the fourth, fifth or sixth forms. Universities and professional bodies do not usually accept advanced level qualifications in these subjects as admission qualifications for their courses, even where the course, such as architecture, engineering, or even, in some cases, art and design, is itself concerned with the material culture. It is really rather an alarming thought that most of those who make the most far-reaching decisions on matters affecting the material culture, such as businessmen, senior civil servants, local government officers, members of councils and public committees, not to mention members of parliament, had an education in which contact with the most relevant disciplines ceased at the age of thirteen.

A THIRD AREA IN EDUCATION

The idea that there is a third area in education concerned with the making and doing aspects of human activity is not new, of course. It has a distinguished tradition going back through William Morris all the way to Plato. When St Thomas Aquinas defined the objects of education in the thirteenth century he adopted the four cardinal virtues of Plato (prudence, justice, fortitude and temperance) and added the three Christian virtues (faith, hope and charity). These have a quaint ring in modern English, but Plato's virtues, rendered into Latin by St Thomas Aquinas, were taken to mean something quite specific and rather different from their modern English interpretations. To St Thomas Aquinas *prudentia* meant 'being realistic, knowing what is practicable'; *justitia* meant 'being ethical, knowing what is good'; *fortitudo* meant 'being thorough, knowing what is comprehensive'; *temperentia* meant 'being economic, knowing when to leave well enough alone'. It is no coincidence that in our own day Dr E. F. Schumacher, in the epilogue to his book *Small Is Beautiful*, quotes the four cardinal virtues of Plato as the basis for the socially and culturally responsible use of technology in the modern world. Certainly the craft guilds, who bore a major responsibility for the general education of the populace following the Renaissance, took the view that a virtuous education meant learning to know what is practicable, what is good, what is comprehensive, and what is enough, in a very broad sense. It is a curious twist in fortunes that when the craft guilds lost their general educational role somewhere between the fourteenth and eighteenth centuries, it was the rather narrow, specialist, bookish universities, academies and schools which had been set up to train priests to read and translate the scriptures which became the guardians of what we now call general education. No wonder our education system came to be dominated by the humanities.

When Sir Williams Curtis, MP, coined the phrase 'The Three Rs' in or about 1807, he placed an emphasis on literacy which reflected the virtual monopoly that the church then had in the running of schools. I had an old great-aunt who protested fiercely whenever the phrase 'The Three Rs' was mentioned. She swore that Sir William had got it all wrong. The Three Rs were:

(1) Reading and writing.
(2) Reckoning and figuring.
(3) Wroughting and wrighting.

By wroughting she meant knowing how things are brought about, which we might now call technology. By wrighting she meant knowing how to do it, which we would now call craftsmanship. From reading and writing comes the idea of literacy, by which we generally mean more than just the ability to read and write. Being literate means having the ability to understand, appreciate and value those ideas which are expressed through the medium of words. From reckoning and figuring comes the idea of numeracy. Being numerate means being able to understand, appreciate and value those ideas that are expressed in the language of mathematics. It was from literacy that the rich fabric of the humanities was woven. It was from numeracy that the immense structure of science was built. But what of wroughting and wrighting? It is significant that modern English has no word, equivalent to literacy and numeracy, meaning the ability to understand, appreciate and value those ideas which are expressed through the medium of making and doing. We have no word, equivalent to science and the humanities, meaning the collected experience of the material culture. Yet the output of the practical arts fills our museums, and galleries, equips our homes, constructs our cities, constitutes our habitat.

Anthropology and archaeology, in seeking to know and understand other cultures, set at least as much store by the art, buildings and artefacts of those cultures as they do by their literature and science. On the face of it, if the expression of ideas through the medium of doing and making represents a distinctive facet of a culture, then the transmission of the collected experience of the doing and making facet should represent a distinctive area in education.

THE VACANT PLOT

If there *is* a third area in education, what distinguishes it from science and the humanities? What do science and the humanities leave out? It now seems generally agreed amongst philosophers of science, that the distinctive feature of science is not the subject matter to which the scientist turns his attention, but the kind of intellectual procedure that he brings to bear upon it. Science is concerned with the attainment of understanding based upon observation, measurement, the formulation of theory and the testing of theory by further observation or experiment. A scientist may study any phenomenon he chooses; but the kind of understanding he may achieve will be limited by the observations he can make, the measures he can apply, the theory available to him and the testability of his findings. Some sorts of phenomena may therefore be inappropriate for scientific study, for the time being or for ever. Some sorts of knowledge will be inaccessible to science, for the time being or for ever. Moreover, the scientist is concerned with theory, that is, with generalizable knowledge. He is not necessarily competent or interested in the practical application of that knowledge, where social, economic, aesthetic and other considerations for which he does not possess any theory may need to be taken into account. He would regard most of the making and doing activities of the material culture as outside his scope, although he would be prepared to bring a scientific philosophy to bear upon the study of the making and doing activities of other people.

Amongst scholars in the humanities there seems to be less agreement about the nature of their discipline, apart from unanimity in the view that it is quite distinct from science. There is a fair consensus that the humanities are especially concerned with human values and the expression of the spirit of man. This justifies scholars in the humanities in studying the history and philosophy of science, but not in contributing to its content. There also seems to be a measure of agreement, by no means universal, that the humanities exclude the making and doing aspects of the fine, performing and useful arts, although their historical, critical and philosophical aspects would still be fair game for the humanities scholar. It is interesting to note that writers on the science side frequently mention technology and the useful arts as being excluded from their purview, presumably because they are only just outside the boundary. Writers on the humanities side frequently mention the fine and performing arts as being excluded, presumably because they, too, are only just outside. A third area in education could therefore legitimately claim technology and the fine, performing and useful arts, although not their scientific knowledge base (if any) or their history, philosophy and criticism (if any) without treading on anyone else's grass.

THE NAMING OF THE PARTS

Clearly, the ground thus left vacant by the specific claims of science and the humanities extends beyond the bounds of 'the material culture' with whose pressing problems we began. The performing arts are a case in point. There are other areas, such as physical education, which have not been mentioned at all. It would be tempting to claim for the third area in education everything that the other two have left out. However, we should stick to our last, if I may take my metaphor from the doing and making area, and clarify the question of education in the issues of the material culture. Any subject which relates with man's material culture must necessarily be anthropocentric. A discipline which claims, as some kinds of science do, to deal with matters that would remain true whether man existed or not, would be ruled out from our third area. Material culture comprises the ideas which govern the nature of every sort of artefact produced, used and valued by man. Those ideas which take the form of scientific knowledge would belong to science. The historical, philosophical and critical ideas would belong to the humanities. What is left is the artefacts themselves and the experience, sensibility and skill that goes into their production and use. If the human values, hopes and fears on which the expression of the spirit of man are based are shared with the humanities, the striving towards them, and the inventiveness that goes into the production and use of artefacts, is a necessary characteristic of our third area. Any discipline falling into this area must therefore be aspirational in character, and, to take them clearly out of both the science and the humanities fields, it must be operational, that is to say, concerned with doing or making. Under these tests, how do the subjects ordinarily left out by the traditional science/humanities division fare? The fine arts, which in schools can be executed in a variety of materials such as ceramics and textiles as well as through the medium of painting and sculpture, clearly fall into the third area. In the useful arts, woodwork and metalwork would usually qualify. Technical studies are sometimes conducted in such a way that they are not actually concerned with doing and making, and therefore may or may not rank as science, instead. Similarly environmental studies might or might not fall into the third area, according to their manner of treatment.

Home economics presents a problem. Taken as a whole, home economics is clearly anthropocentric, aspirational and operational, and therefore falls centrally into the third area. In practice, however, home economics may be taught in schools through the medium of individual subjects ranging from needlecraft taken as fine art through home-making taken as useful arts to nutrition taken as science. So home economics, too, may fall into science, the humanities or the third area, according to the manner of treatment adopted.

Outside the bounds of the material culture altogether are the other subjects explicitly left out by the first and second areas. Amongst the performing arts, music might qualify as anthropocentric, aspirational and operational. So might drama and perhaps dance. So might gymnastics, the way it is pursued these days, but probably not the other areas of physical education. But this is going too fast. Any number of objections can be raised and counter-arguments offered in respect of many, but perhaps not all, the subjects I have mentioned as belonging or possibly belonging to an alleged third area in education. The point I wanted to make is simply this. The justification for the nomination of a third area in education lies not in the existence of subjects which do not fit readily into the definitions of science and the humanities, but in the existence of an approach to knowledge, and of a manner of knowing, which is distinct from those of science and the humanities. Where science is the collected body of theoretical knowledge based upon observation, measurement, hypothesis and test, and the humanities is the collected body of interpretive knowledge based upon contemplation, criticism, evaluation and discourse, the third area is the collected body of practical knowledge based upon sensibility, invention, validation and implementation.

THE NAMING OF THE WHOLE

This leaves us with the problem of finding the correct title for the third area. The term 'the arts' would be ideal, if the expression had not been appropriated by, and used more or less as a synonym for, the humanities. Plato would not have objected to 'aesthetics', but that has taken on a special and distracting meaning in modern English. 'Technics' has been used, and is in the dictionary, but has not proved very popular in educational or common use. A term which has gained a good deal of currency especially in secondary schools in England and Wales, is 'Design', spelt with a big D and used in a sense which goes far beyond the day-to-day meaning which architects, engineers and other professional designers would assign to it. Thus design, in its most general educational sense, where it is equated with science and the humanities, is defined as the area of human experience, skill and understanding that reflects man's concern with the appreciation and adaptation of his surroundings in the light of his material and spiritual needs. In particular, though not exclusively, it relates with configuration, composition, meaning, value and purpose in man-made phenomena.

We can then go on to adopt, as an equivalent to literacy and numeracy, the term 'design awareness', which thus means 'the ability to understand and handle those ideas which are expressed through the medium of doing and making'. The question of the language in which such ideas may be expressed is an interesting one. The essential language of science is notation, especially mathematical notation. The essential language of the humanities is natural language, especially written language. The essential language of design is modelling. A model is a representation of something. An artist's painting is a representation of an idea he is trying to explore. A gesture in mime is a representation of some idea. Everybody engaged in the handling of ideas in the fine arts, performing arts, useful arts or technology employs models or representations to capture, analyse, explore and transmit those ideas. Just as the vocabulary and syntax of natural language or of scientific notation can be conveyed through spoken sounds, words on paper, semaphore signals, Morse code or electronic digits, to suit convenience, so the vocabulary and syntax of the modelling of ideas in the design area can be conveyed through a variety of media such as drawings, diagrams, physical representations, gestures, algorithms – not to mention natural language and scientific notation. With all these definitions in mind, it is now possible to show the relationships between the three areas of human knowledge according to the diagram in Figure 5.1.

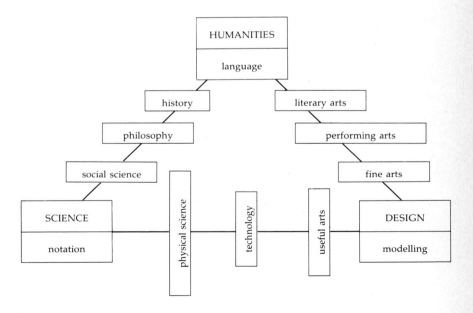

Figure 5.1

The repository of knowledge in science is not only the literature of science but also the analytical skills and the intellectual integrity of which the scientist is the guardian. The repository of knowledge in the humanities is not simply the literature of the humanities but also the discursive skills and the spiritual values of which the scholar is the guardian. In design, the repository of knowledge is not only the material culture and the contents of the museums but also the executive skills of the doer and maker.

6   *English culture and the decline of the industrial spirit, 1850–1980*

● M. J. Weiner

EDITORS' INTRODUCTION

This reading is taken from the final chapter of Weiner's book and gives an overview of an anti-industrial culture which not even the Industrial Revolution was able to counter. Today we are, he argues, still faced with this 'frame of mind' and to change it politicians must engage in a cultural contest.

> It is a very difficult country to move, Mr. Hyndman, a very difficult country indeed, and one in which there is more disappointment to be looked for than success. (Disraeli to H. M. Hyndman, 1881)

> Now we ask ourselves more and more if the so-called progress we see going on about us at breakneck speed is what we really want. This is the age of the international companies – the commercial dinosaurs that stride from continent to continent. It is the age of supertankers, superstores, supersonic flight. The only thing which for many is not super is life itself. (Folkestone Herald, 31 July 1971)

THE CULTURAL DOMESTICATION OF THE INDUSTRIAL REVOLUTION

At the time of the Great Exhibition of 1851, Britain was the home of the industrial revolution, a symbol of material progress to the world. It was also the home of an apparently triumphant bourgeoisie. Observers like Carlyle and Marx agreed in pointing to the industrialist as the new aristocrat, a figure that was ushering in a radically new order and a new culture. Yet they were misled. From the time of their assertions, social and psychological currents in Britain began to flow in a different direction.

By the 1970s, falling levels of capital investment raised the spectre of outright 'de-industrialization' – a decline in industrial production outpacing any corresponding growth in the 'production' of services.[1] Whether or not such a spectre had substance, it is true that this period of recognized economic crisis in Britain was preceded by a century of psychological and intellectual de-industrialization. The emerging culture of industrialism, which in the mid-Victorian years had appeared, for good or ill, to be the wave of the future, irresistibly washing over and sweeping away the features of an older Britain, was itself transformed. The thrust of new values borne along by the revolution in industry was contained in the later nineteenth century; the social and intellectual revolution implicit in industrialism was muted, perhaps even aborted. Instead, a compromise was effected, accommodating new groups, new interests, and new needs within a social and cultural matrix that preserved the forms and even many of the values of tradition. Potentially disruptive forces of change were harnessed and channelled into supporting a new social order, a synthesis of old and new. This containment of the cultural revolution of industrialism lies at the heart of both the achievements and the failures of modern British history.

The new society created by the later Victorians rested on a domestication of the wilder traits of earlier British behaviour; the riotous populace, the aggressive and acquisitive capitalists, and the hedonistic aristocrats of the Georgian world became endangered, if not extinct, species of Englishmen. Their descendants were more restrained, more civilized, and also more conservative, in that they now had an established and secure place in the social order, or, in the case of the aristocracy, had come to terms with social change and recemented their place in the *status quo*. By Victoria's death, British society had weathered the storms of change, but at the cost of surrendering a capacity for innovation and assertion that was perhaps the other face of the unruliness and harshness of that earlier Britain.

In particular, the later nineteenth century saw the consolidation of a national elite that, by virtue of its power and prestige, played a central role both in Britain's modern achievements and its failures. It administered the most extensive empire in human history with reasonable effectivenss and humanity, and it maintained a remarkable degree of political and social stability at home while presiding over a redistribution of power and an expansion of equality and security. It also presided over the steady and continued erosion of the nation's economic position in the world. The standards of value of this new elite of civil servants, professionals, financiers, and landed proprietors, inculcated by a common education in public schools and ancient universities and reflected in the literary culture it patronized, permeated by their prestige much of British society beyond the elite itself. These standards did little to support, and much to discourage, economic dynamism. They threw earlier enthusiasms for technology into disrepute, emphasized the social evils brought by the industrial revolution, directed attention to issues of the 'quality of life' in preference to the quantitative concerns of production and expansion, and disparaged the restlessness and acquisitiveness of industrial capitalism. Hand in hand with this disparagement went the growth of an alternative set of social values, embodied in a new vision of the nation.

The dominant collective self-image in English culture became less and less that of the world's workshop. Instead, this image was challenged by the counter-image of an ancient, little-disturbed 'green and pleasant land.' 'Our England is a garden,' averred the greatest poet of imperialism; another imperialist, a poet laureate, celebrated England at the height of imperial fervour for its 'haunts of ancient peace'; and an anti-imperialist socialist has inspired his readers with the aim of making England once again, as it had been before the Industrial Revolution, the 'fair green garden of Northern Europe.' The past, and the countryside - seen as inseparable - were invested with an almost irresistible aura. These standards and images supported a very attractive way of life, geared to maintenance of a *status quo* rather than innovation, comfort rather than attainment, the civilized enjoyment, rather than the creation, of wealth.

British political opinion bore the imprint of the aristocracy long after the demise of the aristocracy's power. The politicians, civil servants, churchmen, professional men, and publicists who did so much to shape modern British political opinion and policy moved in a climate of opinion uncongenial to the world of industry. Most of them showed a striking fondness for gentry tastes and standards, making such tastes an essential part of the modern British style of government. Political calls for economic growth went against the grain of the values and style of life actually believed in by most politicians and civil servants, as well as by the rest of the elite.

Industrialists themselves were far from immune to this anti-industrial culture; like others, they breathed it in ever more deeply the higher they rose in social position. The new British elite was open to industrialists, if they adapted to its standards. With few exceptions, they were ready to do so, although such adaptation required a degree of disavowal of their own former selves and their very function in society. By modelling themselves - in varying proportions - upon civil servants, professional men, and men of landed leisure, industrialists found acceptance at the upper reaches of British society. Thus, the famed 'establishment' and its consensus was created. Social integration and stability were ensured, but at a price - the waning of the industrial spirit.

POST-INDUSTRIALISM OR DE-INDUSTRIALISM?

The peculiar pattern of British social and cultural history has involved both benefits and costs. Which, however, has predominated? Has this pattern been on balance a fortune or a misfortune for Britain? And what signposts to the future – if any – does this cultural history set out?

Many, within and without Britain, have praised the cultural path thus taken. Even the business historian D. C. Coleman was at pains to point out in his argument for the importance of the gentlemanly ideal that he was not *criticizing* its sway:

> If, by some unlikely magic [Victorian and Edwardian businessmen] had turned themselves into single-minded, constantly profit-maximizing entrepreneurs, what sort of world might have resulted? If it is true that one of the costs of Public Schools producing 'first-class administrators' was some lag in industrial advance, how can we know that the price was not worth paying?[2]

Others, on both left and right, have thought the gain certainly more than worth the price. The *Times* spoke for many of them in 1971 when it reflected on the lack of enthusiasm for 'wealth, as such', and found it good. 'The secret hope of Britain,' it concluded.

> is indeed that the monetary obsession has penetrated our society less deeply than it has others. There are probably still more people in Britain who will give total effort for reasons of idealism than for reasons of gain.[3]

A peculiar English gift for the 'quality' rather than the 'quantity' of life was claimed as early as 1907, by the cosmopolitan novelist Ford Madox Ford. 'The especial province of the English nation,' he reflected, 'is the evolution of a standard of manners . . . The province of the English is to solve the problem of how men may live together.'[4] Around the same time, foreign visitors (particularly Americans) began to note the pleasantness and relaxed quality of English life. Arthur Shadwell, an Edwardian 'efficiency expert', reported: 'An American gentleman said to me one day: "We are a tearing, driving, scheming lot here. The Englishman leads a tranquil, happy life, and I for one envy him." '[5] The direct descendant of this nameless American was the *New York Times*, London correspondent during the later 1960s and early 1970s, Anthony Lewis, who observed in a farewell 'love letter': 'There is a larger reality than the pound and inflation and the GNP. It is life, and the British are good at that'.[6] Some have gone even further in their admiration, and see the British as pioneering new forms of 'postindustrial society'. John Kenneth Galbraith, interviewed on the BBC, told his hosts that

> your real problem is that you were the first of the great industrialized nations, and so things happen here first. You are living out the concern for some more leisurely relationship with industrial life that the other people have been discussing for 50 years or more.[7]

To Bernard Nossiter, London correspondent for the *Washington Post* during the 1970s, 'Britons . . . appear[ed] to be the first citizens of the post-industrial age who are choosing leisure over goods on a large scale,' and he heartily approved of their choice.[8]

However, others have sounded a more sombre note, portraying rustic-gentlemanly values as sliding imperceptibly into decadence. Donald Horne expressed it with the vehemence of an expatriate:

> Kindness, tolerance and love of order become snobbery, woolliness and love of the past. Effortless ease becomes the ease of not making any effort to do anything. Gentlemanly intuitive wisdom becomes the inability to make up one's mind. Doing the decent thing comes to mean that there should be no sharp clash of attitudes, no disagreeable new beliefs, that might disturb someone. The sense of fairness becomes the belief that competition is unfair: it might benefit some new person, but it might also harm some old person.[9]

This point of view was expressed succinctly by Lord Nuffield in 1959, when he called Britain a 'nation in semi-retirement'.[10] Others have shared Nuffield's perception of a failure of national energies, adaptability, or will. One of the most eloquent and earliest was C. P. Snow, who in the same year, 1959, delivered this warning to his fellow members of the British governing class:

> More often than I like, I am saddened by a historical myth. Whether the myth is good history or not, doesn't matter; it is pressing enough for me. I can't help thinking of the Venetian Republic in their last half-century. Like us, they had once been fabulously lucky. They had become rich, as we did, by accident. They had acquired immense political skill, just as we have. A good many of them were tough-minded, realistic, patriotic men. They knew, just as clearly as we know, that the current of history had begun to flow against them. Many of them gave their minds to working out ways to keep going. It would have meant breaking the pattern into which they had crystallised. They were fond of the pattern, just as we are fond of ours. They never found the will to break it.[11]

Nearly two decades later, Snow's Venetian analogy seemed more relevant than ever to the Marxist Tom Nairn. 'The House of Lords,' he complained in 1977.

> is a better gauge of British futures than IBM. Underneath the ceaseless speechifying about new starts, the dominant dream is of a Venetian twilight: a golden-grey steady state where staid arts and moderate politics join to preserve the tenor of things English. The true impulse is not really to 'catch up' with the greater, evolving world outside, but to hold one's own somehow, anyhow, and defend the tribe's customs and weathered monuments.[12]

Sixteenth-century Venice, of course, had nothing equivalent to North Sea oil; but similar windfalls to other nations, when unreinforced by a favourable social environment, have had little lasting effect. The classic historical example is seventeenth-century Spain. The historian J. H. Elliot laid responsibility for that nation's decline at the feet of its ruling class, which

> lacked the breadth of vision and the strength of character to break with a
> past that could no longer serve as a reliable guide to the future . . . At a
> time when the face of Europe was altering more rapidly than ever before,
> the country that had once been its leading power proved to be lacking the
> essential ingredient for survival – the willingness to change.[13]

The vision was given literary form when one of Britain's best contemporary writers, known previously as a novelist of personal relations, was impelled by the crisis of the seventies to explore the condition of the national spirit. Margaret Drabble had become increasingly concerned by what seemed to her to be negative and retreatist social values,[14] and in her novel *The Ice Age* portrayed an English elite in a state of psychic and moral exhaustion. Returning to the moralist tradition of the early Victorians, Drabble sought within her dark canvas for sources of renewal, and was unafraid to court ridicule by calling upon John Milton and his vision of 'a noble and puissant Nation, rousing herself like a strong man after sleep'. *The Ice Age* summed up one view of the 'condition of England'.

It has also been argued that the pleasant vision of English 'post-industrialism' is a mirage; that the quality of life cannot be readily opposed to the quantity or even their constituents easily separated.[15] Recent studies of public opinion, moreover, suggest that, as Rudolf Klein has regretfully put it, 'altruism appears to be largely a function of economic prosperity'.[16] A no-growth society does not seem likely to be a more humane, more tolerant, or even more comfortable society. One recalls Edward Heath's 1973 warning:

> The alternative to expansion is not, as some occasionally seem to suppose,
> an England of quiet market towns linked only by trains puffing slowly and
> peacefully through green meadows. The alternative is slums, dangerous
> roads, old factories, cramped schools, stunted lives.[17]

'MODERNIZATION': UN-ENGLISH?

To mention Edward Heath is to raise the question of whether this national culture can be – or is being – changed. The gentlemanly consensus of 'domesticated progress' began to come under strain in the early 1960s, as the continental economic surge sowed anxiety about national decline in the minds of British observers. These anxieties brought the issue of modernization into the political arena. Beginning in 1964, this new issue played an important role, at least rhetorically, in every general election. The general election of 1979, in particular, was fought around the question of national economic decline. In a historic exchange, whose outlines were first perceptible in 1970, the Labour Party stood for English tradition, the *status quo*, and 'safety first', whereas the Conservatives – their leader especially – gave the calls for sweeping change. 'I am a reformer,' Margaret Thatcher announced, 'and I am offering change.'[18] The Conservative victory gave Britain a leader well known for her resolve to reverse the pattern of the past century. Thatcher indeed seeks, as her opponents charged, to 'turn the clock back' – to restore nineteenth-century economic dynamism by reintroducing the disciplines and incentives of the market [...]

The outcome of Thatcher's crusade may turn on how successful methods like lowering marginal tax rates and restricting the money supply will be in altering cultural attitudes formed over many years.[19] The least tractable obstacle to British economic 'redevelopment' may well be the continuing resistance of cultural values and attitudes. A recent survey of British attitudes toward money and work commissioned by *New Society* revealed a nation 'remarkably unambitious in a material sense':

> Very few sincerely want to be rich. Most people in Britain neither want nor expect a great deal of money. Even if they could get it, the vast majority do not seem prepared to work harder for it: most of our respondents thought we should work only as much as we need to live a pleasant life . . . It seems clear that the British today prefer economic *stability* to rapid economic growth.[20]

Indeed, the 1970s saw in Britain (as elsewhere) a *reaction* against the calls of the 1960s for modernization and growth. Edward Heath, after painfully imposing the gospel of efficiency upon the Conservatives, failed even more painfully to impose it upon the nation. The acute Labour Minister Richard Crossman commented on Heath's difficulties with 'the traditional Right' in the 1960s: 'The policy he is putting across seems to me to be attractive only to young and thrusting businessmen' – no prescription for successful politics.[21] 'Technophobia', as two journalists put it in 1967, persisted in the grass roots of the Tory party:

> What[ever] aspirations the present leadership may have [they warned] . . . the party traditionalists take little account of doctrines of business efficiency, and largely loathe the Americans who invented most of the concepts. How lonely the evangelistic Mr. Marples looks in the Tory Party when he tries to convince the ranks of the devoted that their concern is with technology and business efficiency, and how curious has been his fate! What applause there was for Mr. Angus Maude's 'for Tories simply to talk like technocrats will get them nowhere'![22]

Nonetheless, Heath pushed on, seeking to break the psychological resistance, within and outside the party, to modernization. He described Britain in December 1969 as 'a Luddite's paradise . . . a society dedicated to the prevention of progress and the preservation of the status quo'. He seized the surprise Conservative victory in 1970 as a mandate for the transformation of Britain, announcing to the first party conference after the election that 'we were returned to office to change the course of history of this nation – nothing less.' More and more Heath saw the root problem facing him as psychological: the short-sighted tendency of his countrymen to 'prefer comfort to progress'.[23] Yet it was by no means clear how this tendency could be changed by government. Heath was soon labelled a 'radical' and a 'divisive' figure,[24] and most of his initial programme was abandoned, gutted, or proven ineffective even before his government was swept away in the wake of the 1973–4 confrontation with the miners.

After a taste of Heath's crusade, in February 1974 the public found more appealing the Labour campaign, which, despite the party programme's pledges of nationalization and redistribution, was remarkably conservative in spirit. The party leadership had moved from promising in 1964 to reshape Britain in the 'white heat of a new technological revolution' to pledging a decade later an end to 'divisiveness', a taming of the 'ruthless, pushing society', and 'a quiet life'.[25]

In office, Harold Wilson, and especially his emollient successor, James Callaghan, followed the tone set by the general election, seeking above all to promote social harmony and stability, and cushioning the social fabric and the economic *status quo* from stresses of change. The modernizing rhetoric of the 1960s, evoking Joseph Chamberlain and Lloyd George, was gently laid to rest, and the spirit of Stanley Baldwin hovered over Downing Street. Both Wilson and Callaghan, in contrast to Heath, acquired farms and were often photographed there, appearing in Baldwinesque fashion as men of the country. For both men these farms (neither was a serious agricultural enterprise) maintained a link to what Callaghan's wife called 'the peasant in us'.[26]

Many intellectuals and publicists took the two Conservative electoral defeats in 1974 as a repudiation of 'growthmania'. Christopher Price, a Labour MP, was one of a number who argued that 'Labour is now the natural party to rein back' from such misguided zeal. The 'ancestral virtues' of the party, which had provided a 'moral authority' during the Attlee–Cripps era of austerity, could now again, Price argued, do good service.[27] In the 1960s, he later reflected, whatever party, 'The message was the same: "Out with the old, on with the new." ' New Towns, new tower blocks, new supersonic planes, new motorways. And if a few greenhouse windows were broken to let Concorde fly, if good houses were torn down for roads and redevelopment, too bad, 'You couldn't make omelettes . . .' Now it is all suddenly different.' Novelty had soured, and 'bigness' – which, Price recalled, 'some Socialists had been preaching against for a century' – had become unfashionable. Price set out a 'non-economic' agenda for what he called a socialist political program. Its aim was to protect the existing 'social and environmental fabric of Britain' – its 'pleasant, fraternal, convivial' character, and its countryside. 'All this,' he conceded, 'may sound negative.' Well and good. 'Labour has always been used to start things. I suspect its role in the future will be more concerned with stopping them.'[28]

After 1974, educated opinion seemed more disillusioned than ever with 'progress'. Ramsay Macdonald's biographer, David Marquand, found Macdonald's anti-materialism freshly relevant: 'Ten or fifteen years ago,' he remarked in 1977, 'Macdonald's warning that the quality of life might be sacrificed in the pursuit of material prosperity, and that socialists might lose sight of their non-material objectives in the struggle for votes, could be dismissed as a piece of sentimental obscurantism. It cannot be dismissed so easily today.'[29]

A new cultural phenomenon came of age in the 1970s: explicit and organized opposition to the results of technical and material advance. This was of course part of a development embracing the entire industrialized world, where anti-growth and anti-technology movements had taken root among left-wing university students and had become a force to be reckoned with in public life. In Britain, this general movement took on a more popular and nationalistic form. The ranks of English critics of progress extended far beyond the universities or the left; these critics tended to see their mission as inseparable from English patriotism – to save traditional English life from unwelcome change. The great variety of new or resurgent causes taken up in the late 1960s and early 1970s from environmentalism to historical preservation to the Campaign for Real Ale, constituted a non-partisan 'movement to protect English culture'.[30] As Marquand argued (all the more powerfully for being a well-known critic of the left): 'The issue of the future is small against big, community against *anomie*, peace-of-mind against rate-of-growth, grass roots against tower blocks, William Morris against both Sidney Webb and Henry Ford.'[31]

Perhaps the chief literary embodiment of this spirit of resistance was the immensely popular poet laureate John Betjeman, who was more widely read than any previous laureate. Betjeman extended the pastoral nostalgia of his predecessors, John Masefield and Alfred Austin, to suburbia, now an integral part of Old England. His writing disparaged the new and evoked the security of old, familiar things. The public responded with enthusiasm to his Tory 'longing for the simplicity of irremovable landmarks'.[32] This longing moved the left as well as the right: The *New Statesman* in 1973 hailed Betjeman's denunciation of urban redevelopment. 'At last,' it announced in its front-page leader, a Poet Laureate has expressed the nation's feelings. This week Sir John Betjeman observed that destroying the surroundings in which people live – and which they like, and are accustomed to – amounts to straightforward robbery. It is stealing the people's property, said Sir John; exactly the same as being burgled. In some ways maybe worse. You can buy substitutes for the contents of a house. A familiar narrow street, with its obscure chapel, tree and corner shop, is irreplaceable.[33]

Similarly, the socialist playwright and critic Dennis Potter wrote with approval in the *Sunday Times* (London) that 'Betjeman is the surviving proof that it is all right, after all, to be an Englishman. He stands at the wrought-iron gates, ready to hold back the flood.'[34]

The identification of 'English' with 'holding back the flood' of change had been made familiar by that widely read man of the left, J. B. Priestley, who had by the 1970s become a popular authority on the national character. He revelled in attacking the modernizers, arguing in 1970 that they failed to understand that, as he had implied as early as 1949, the modern world was 'alien to the English temperament'. It was natural and good that the English did not take readily to its characteristic activities. 'We are instinctively opposed,' he announced, 'to high-pressure industry and salesmanship, wanting something better than a huge material rat race.' The nation's future, Priestley urged three years later, hung upon resisting 'change for change's sake.'[35]

At the end of the day, it may be that Margaret Thatcher will find her most fundamental challenge not in holding down the money supply or inhibiting government spending, or even in fighting the shop-stewards, but in changing this frame of mind. English history in the 1980s may turn less on traditional political struggles than on a cultural contest between the two faces of the middle class.
[...]

REFERENCES

1. See Frank Blackaby (ed.), *De-Industrialization* (London, 1978); see also Peter Jenkins, 'A Nation on the Skids', *Manchester Guardian Weekly*, 8 October 1978, and [Paul Barker], 'Europe's Merseyside', *New Society* 46 (14 December 1978), p. 623.

2. 'Gentlemen and Players', *Economic History Review*, series 2, 26 (1973), p. 115.

3. 'What Is the British Disease?', *Times* (London), 29 April 1971.

4. *The Spirit of the People* (London, 1907), p. 151.

5. *Industrial Efficiency* (London, 1906), vol. 2, p. 459.

6. 'Leaving the Village', *International Herald Tribune*, 2 August 1973. See also Lewis's comparison of English and American life, in which England comes out, for all its faults, the home of 'human values' ('Notes on the New York Skyline . . .', *Atlantic*, June 1971, pp. 58–62).

7. Quoted in Krishnan Kumar, 'A Future in the Past?', *New Society* 42 (24 November 1977), pp. 418–9. See the reflections by Christopher Price, MP, provoked by Galbraith: 'A Dunce as Prizewinner', *New Society* 39 (3 March 1977), pp. 452–3.

8. *Britain – A Future That Works* (Boston, Mass., 1978), p. 100.

9. *God Is An Englishman* (Sydney, Australia, 1969), p. 71.

10. Quoted by R. R. James, *Ambitions and Realities: British Politics, 1964–1970* (London, 1972), p. 293.

11. *The Two Cultures and the Scientific Revolution* (New York, 1959), p. 42.

12. 'The Politics of the New Venice', *New Society* 42 (17 November 1977), p. 352.

13. *Imperial Spain, 1469–1716* (London, 1963), p. 378. This was a failure, he stressed elsewhere, of a society, and not a handful of leaders: 'Behind this inert government . . . lay a whole social system and psychological attitude which themselves blocked the way to radical reform' ('The Decline of Spain' [1961], in *The Economic Decline of Empires*, ed. Carlo Cipolla [London, 1970], p. 185). 'Spanish Main Gold,' as Peter Jenkins recently remarked, 'was to Castille what North Sea oil may prove for Britain – the agent of de-industrialization' ('Going Down with Great Britain', *Harper's*, December 1979, p. 28).

14. See the *Guardian*, 26 November 1973.

15. See, for example, Wilfred Beckerman, *In Defense of Economic Growth* (London, 1974).

16. Review of James Alt, *The Politics of Economic Decline* (Cambridge, 1979), in *New Society* 50 (8 November 1979), p. 332.

17. Pre-conference message to Conservative party workers, 28 September 1973, quoted in *Sunday Telegraph*, 30 September 1973.

18. Quoted in *Manchester Guardian Weekly*, 22 April 1979.

19. See, for a similar argument during the election campaign, Peregrine Worsthorne, 'Do British Want to Lose Their Chains?', *Sunday Telegraph*, 8 April 1979, p. 16.

20. Tom Forester, 'Do the British Sincerely Want to Be Rich?', *New Society* 40 (28 April 1977), pp. 158, 161.

21. *The Diaries of a Cabinet Minister* (New York, 1976), vol. 1, p. 351.

22. Glyn Jones and Michael Barnes, *Britain on Borrowed Time* (Harmondsworth, 1967), p. 268. Maude saw himself as keeper of the Tory conscience, and denounced preoccupation with economic growth as no part of the Conservative tradition. Echoing R. H. Tawney, he labelled it (in *The Consuming Society* [London, 1967]) a 'fetish' producing 'a sterile cycle of increasing production for increasing consumption of increasingly trivial things.'

23. Anthony Lewis, 'The Radical of 10 Downing Street', *New York Times Magazine*, 14 March 1971, p. 46.

24. See David Marquand, 'Compromise Under Attack', *New Society* 16 (5 November 1970), p. 829, and Paul Johnson, 'Ted Heath's Britain', *New Statesman* 83 (18 February 1972), p. 196.

25. See David Butler and Dennis Kavanagh, *The British General Election of February 1974* (London, 1974), pp. 125–6, 162–3; David Butler and Michael Pinto-Duschinsky, *The British General Election of 1970* (London, 1971), p. 169; and Robert Rhodes James, *Ambitions and Realities: British Politics, 1964–1970* (London, 1972), pp. 220, 239. See the suggestive analysis of the key words and phrases used by the candidates by Shelley Pinto-Duschinsky, 'A Matter of Words', *New Society* 27 (7 March 1974), pp. 570–1. Wilson continued this winning line in the October election: 'What the people want,' he affirmed, 'what every family needs, is a bit of peace and quiet' (David Butler and Dennis Kavanagh, *The British General Election of October 1974* (London, 1975), p. 134).

26. Quoted in *People* (New York), March, 1977, p. 32.

27. 'The Politics of Austerity', *New Statesman* 87 (3 May 1974), pp. 607–8. The decade of the 1940s was harked back to as a model by a number of left-wing writers. It now seemed an age of elevating austerity and common purpose, before prosperity opened the floodgates of selfishness and the frantic pursuit of artificial wants. Mervyn Jones, novelist and regular contributor to the *New Statesman*, greeted the year 1975 ('A New Year Salute', *New Statesman* 89 [3 January 1975], pp. 3–4) with a reassurance that prolonged zero growth was all for the best: 'I never believed that human happiness can be measured in gross national product per capita.' He and others, he recalled, had spent the 1950s deploring the pursuit of affluence; they were right then, and should hardly be despondent now that 'the affluence show is closed down', at least 'for the time being'. 'There have been,' he went on, 'only two periods in my lifetime that justified a positive pride in being a citizen of this country: the war, and the early post-war years.' In Attlee's Britain, for all the shortages, 'the number of people who felt deprived, who got nothing of value out of life, was surely less than it is now.' (The irony of such nostalgia is inescapable if one looks at a cartoon in the 4 October 1944 issue of *Punch*, in which a scene of a queue of shoppers draws the [humorous] observation from a bystander, 'I suppose in about thirty years' time people will insist on describing this as the good old days.' [Precisely on the nose!]).

28. 'Labour after the Defeats', *New Statesman* 92 (12 November 1976), pp. 659–60.

29. *Ramsay Macdonald* (London, 1977), p. 462.

30. Lincoln Allison, 'The English Cultural Movement', *New Society* 43 (16 February 1978), pp. 358–60. Allison offered a 'culturist manifesto': 'Join the organisations which oppose harmful modernization and development. Do it thoughtfully but with determination. Protect your communities. Learn ancient skills. Renovate old houses. Defend quality, whether of beer or of landscape; the substitutes rarely satisfy. In doing so you will reward not merely yourself, but your society.'

31. 'Farewell to Westminster,' *New Statesman* 93 (7 January 1977), p. 2.

32. Anthony Hartley, *A State of England* (London, 1963), p. 129n.; see also Clive James, 'Supplier of Poetry', *New Statesman* 88 (22 November 1974), p. 745: 'The urge to preserve supplied him with his most important creative impulse.'

33. *New Statesman 85* (23 February 1973), p. 253.
34. Quoted in Allison, 'English Cultural Movement', p. 360.
35. *The Edwardians* (London, 1970), p. 289; *The English* (London, 1973), p. 242.

III TECHNOLOGY AND SOCIETY

In this section Robin Clarke considers the impact which contemporary technology has upon individuals, the environment and social organization. He considers a variety of responses to problems created by technology, favouring not the rejection of it, but the development of 'alternative technology'. Although it is common to focus upon the problems of technology, rather than its benefits, Clarke does not take a negative view of technology; instead he wants it to be seen as a moral activity. This reinforces definitions of technology which raise it above mere technical considerations. The five differing types of responses to technological problems ('technical dilemmas') identified and analysed by him, provide a background to view contemporary technological issues, such as the effect of microelectronics on the world of work.

7 *The pressing need for alternative technology*

● R. Clarke

'Technology – Opium of the Intellectuals' was the title of a famous article in the *New York Review of Books* a few years ago.[1] In it, the author argued that we in the industrialized nations had become enslaved and addicted to technology which, by providing material comforts, covered up the deeper and more important social, psychological and political shortcomings of present forms of society. This view of technology, while by no means a majority one in any part of the world, has recently grown in importance, particularly in the industrialized world and especially among the young. It has led to a view that it might in the future be a good idea to do away with technology altogether and return to forms of society in which human and social issues again become the main concern.

To some extent, I believe this critique of technology to be justified. It seems almost wholly so in those cases where an improved technology is urged on people to cover up more fundamental problems, such as a lack of social justice. Thus the argument that new technology will promote economic growth so that a country's gross national product (GNP) becomes larger and everyone's slice of the economic cake will get bigger is often used as an excuse for not cutting that cake in a more equitable manner. At this level technology can indeed be used as a hard drug which promises nirvana but only at a huge and hidden social cost.

I shall deal mainly with a different but related problem. The view just outlined implicitly assumes that there is only one form of technology, and that that form is the existing type of technology we see today widely used in the developed countries and increasingly applied in the developing ones. This idea creates much confusion, for the shortcomings of contemporary technology then become the evils of all technology – and hence the rise of anti-technological schools of thought in the industrial civilizations.

[...]

THE NATURE OF CONTEMPORARY TECHNOLOGY

In the developed world, contemporary technology is almost universally regarded as polluting. Though this is by no means the most serious of the criticisms which can be levelled at today's technology, we will deal with it first because it is by far the most common. And, of course, it is unquestionably correct. The technology we use is polluting in many different ways: factories discharge effluents, sometimes noxious and always offensive, into rivers, the sea and the atmosphere.

In several parts of the world the eating of shellfish has become dangerous due to the high levels of heavy metal residue found in them. Nuclear devices, both military and peaceful, liberate unwanted and potentially harmful amounts of radiation into both water and air. Particulate matter accumulates in the atmosphere leading to smog. The air is so heavily dirt-infested in industrial areas that household cleaning becomes a twice-a-day routine. Dangerous chemicals accumulate in foodstuffs, giving them peculiar tastes and other undesirable properties. The discharge of waste heat from factories and power plants heats river and lake water to such a degree that eutrophication and subsequent death of aquatic life becomes a familiar problem. Agricultural soil is treated as though it were some kind of chemical blotting paper whose only function is to provide domestic plants with sufficient nitrogen, phosphorus and potassium. The soil structure deteriorates mechanically, and the highly complicated ecology of important soil organisms is irreversibly upset. According to one calculation, the United States has lost, since the time the prairies were first put under the plough, one-quarter of the topsoil available.

Such a list of the polluting effects of contemporary technology could be, and indeed has been many times in the past few years, greatly extended. To this problem there are now a number of standard responses. The first can be described as the 'price response': pollution, this riposte runs, is the price we pay for an advanced technology, and it is well worth the price; true, we have a pollution problem (though it is greatly exaggerated), but it is of 'minor' importance in comparison to the real benefits technology produces. The price response is heard most often in the developed world but it is also found in developing countries in a slightly differing form: bring us your polluting factories and we will learn to live with the pollution that results, for it is a small price to pay for a means of escape from the grinding poverty in which we live.

The second rejoinder, and this is the one most widely found in scientific and technical circles, is the 'fix-it' response. Advocates of this position accept the seriousness of the pollution problem, or of much of it, and claim that serious and concerted action must be taken to restore the environment. This action, however, will involve more technology, not less, and the clever use of sophisticated devices to monitor and then lower pollution levels, if this is found necessary. Into this category of declamation fit advertisements for electricity boards urging users to take to 'clean fuel' and substantial international programmes, such as Unesco's own Man and Biosphere. The 'fix-it' response is primarily scientific and technical, and sometimes technocratic.

The next two possible responses are more radical. The first of them – the away-with-it response – has already been discussed. The argument used here is that the price we pay for advanced technology is far too heavy, and that we have to learn to live either without technology at all or at least with a great deal less than is now the case. This response is almost solely confined to the developed countries, and is remarkable in its absence in the developing countries where there may be a very minimum of technology in practice. Generally, it seems, people who are forced to live without technology quickly become unhappy with their situation when they see others benefitting from it.

THE ALTERNATIVE POSSIBILITY

Fourth, there is the 'alternative response'. In essence, this claims that the form of technology now in use is intrinsically polluting, and no amount of extra technical effort will ever change that situation. This response claims, however, that not *all* technologies are intrinsically polluting and that new forms of technology can and should be devised to remedy a deteriorating situation. Thus instead of burning fossil or nuclear fuels, with their particulate and thermal pollution, we should develop technologies such as the use of solar and wind power which are intrinsically non-polluting. The alternative response [. . .] needs careful distinction from the 'fix-it' answer which sees nothing *fundamentally* wrong with the form of technology in current use. The alternative response sees current technology as fundamentally flawed and advocates radical alternatives. The alternative response is becoming increasingly common in the developed countries but is also found (though less commonly) in the developing countries.

These retorts to the most common criticism of contemporary technology – the pollution it produces – are all based to some extent on technical evaluations. There is, however, a fifth response which is not technical but political, and radical. It suggests that pollution is an invention of capitalist elites to disguise from the people their real political plight and the facts of their exploitation by profiteers. Pollution, it is argued, is not important except in the sense that it is a product and symptom of capitalist society, whether that society be the victim of either private capitalism or what is known as state capitalism.

Each of these five rejoinders has powerful advocates and (as we shall see) the choice between them is made usually on ethical and emotional grounds, rather than on logical ones. Indeed, it may be impossible to characterize any one as more logical than any other, or even as simply 'better'. It is largely a question of taste and philosophy, not subject to scientific analysis, and this makes the situation complex and difficult. I should stress, however, that each position demands serious consideration and the attempt to characterize them all in a pithy way is not meant to imply criticism of any one of them. Such a characterization is useful, for the five responses are used not only to answer the critique of pollution by contemporary technology but the other criticisms which are now widely voiced. It is to those that we now turn.

Probably the most important feature and criticism of contemporary technology is economic. The type of technology we use in developed countries is extremely capital-intensive, so much so that it tends to become the prerogative of those countries which are richest, and of those groups within the countries which are the richest. What this means is vividly illustrated by a single statistic. In a labour-intensive economy, it takes perhaps the equivalent of six months' salary to buy the equipment needed to provide work for one man. In a capital-intensive, advanced-technology economy, the equivalent figure is 350 months' salary. It is thus easy to see why development using Western technology has been such a slow process.

However large figures for international aid from the rich to the poor countries may be, providing jobs in the developing world by using advanced technology is a very, very expensive business. At the same time, that very same technology is not designed to provide jobs as such; instead, very often it is designed to *eliminate* jobs, to replace them by automatic processes. It has been said, and with some justification, that our technologies are designed to eliminate the need for people and to maximize the need for capital. It should be noted that this is not a political criticism as such, for the economic problem is no less painful for non-capitalist countries. It is simply that the type of technology we use places great emphasis on the economy of large-scale operations and is often poorly adapted to decentralized, local situations. In this sense, contemporary technology is as badly suited to accelerating development as any that can be imagined.

RESOURCES ARE UNEVENLY SHARED

I have tried to summarize how this criticism is subject to the five responses discussed above, in Table 7.1. For instance, the radical political response to this situation is that if resources were equally split both between and within countries, current forms of technology would be equally accessible to all. While this is undeniably true, it is a fact that neither social nor natural resources are evenly split in this way now; and that even if the Herculean task of international legislation improves the accessibility to resources, legislation will not offset the distribution of natural resources within national territories.

The third criticism most commonly made of contemporary technology concerns its use of natural resources. Essentially, our technology is in the sense of the industrialized world an exploitive one, wrenching from the earth mineral resources which have taken billions of years to accumulate and using them up within a few centuries. The arguments about how long our resources will last if used in this way are well known, of course, and can continue interminably. But it is obvious that we have a technology that uses resources such as metals and fossil fuel faster than they are created by natural processes. For this reason, there will come a time when scarcity becomes a serious problem.

In this context, as any competent economist will point out, the question of 'limits' to growth or consumption is not of central concern. What happens is that as a resource becomes scarcer, poorer quality reserves have to be used increasingly and their sources become ever more difficult to get at. Long before any resource runs out, then, an economic crisis is precipitated when the cost of obtaining a resource begins to equal the utility of getting it. If we were to continue burning fossil fuel for a few more centuries (at most), we would probably end up spending more energy obtaining the resource than is liberated by burning it. It should be noted that we have long since passed this energy break-even point in the field of agricultural products. In the developed countries far more calories are used in obtaining a food than are liberated by eating it. This has led the ecologist Howard T. Odum to claim that the potatoes we eat are 'made partly from oil', referring to the petroleum products consumed by farm machinery. In a primitive agricultural tribe, by contrast, every calorie of energy used in farming produces the equivalent of about fifteen calories of food.

The fourth criticism made of technology today is that it is capable of widespread misuse. The technology of nuclear power, for example, is difficult to distinguish from the technology of nuclear warfare; the latest medical advances are apt to find themselves applied in centres developing biological weapons before they are in hospitals; and in the capitalist countries the pace and type of technical advance are very closely geared to the profit motive. The existence of this flaw in modern technology gave rise a few years ago to the whole 'social responsibility' movement in science in which it was argued that scientists are themselves responsible for the uses to which their work is put. Again, there is much argument over exactly what constitutes a misuse of science or technology and what is proper use. But clearly, just as modern technology has made contemporary man more secure from the whims and misfortunes of the environment in which he lives, so too has technology added a new and threatening dimension to life by making possible the annihilation of the human race.

Many more criticisms can be made of technology today but, unlike the previous four, these are more social in nature and closely related to each other. Globally, the most important may be the destructive effect of our form of technology on local, developing world cultures. Built into a technology one can always find the values and ideals of the society that invented it. So when we use contemporary technology in development programmes, we export a whole system of values which includes a certain attitude to nature, to society, to work and to efficiency. As yet no developing, local society has been able to withstand the effects of this onslaught, with the result that such a society always changes to meet the incessant demands of the new technology. The end of this process is a global uniformity of cultures, all perfectly adapted to high technology but everywhere the same.

Similarly, modern technology is highly complicated and requires a trained specialist elite to operate it. As a result, ordinary men and women are deprived of the ability they previously had to control their own environment. There exist opinions as to how unfortunate this is, but we should stress here the fact that it is so; and in any systematic account of the flaws and virtues of contemporary technology the fact must be recorded. Equally, the technology used today is based mainly on the virtues of highly centralized services. To be sure, centralization has many advantages but we should not ignore the disadvantages it brings with it. Technical innovation becomes very expensive, people become totally dependent on the existing system: the system itself, through centralization, becomes highly liable to both technical accidents and the activities of saboteurs. The last have only to remove a weak link in the chain to cause chaos over many interlinked systems covering hundreds or thousands of square kilometres. Centralization also precludes the use of diffuse energy sources, such as solar and wind power, which by their nature are extremely difficult to centralize.

I will make two further points in criticism of contemporary technology. The first is that technical knowledge today has become a separate part of all knowledge. By this, I mean that technical knowledge does not develop naturally out of local technologies but forms a distinct body of knowledge on its own, with almost no links with what preceded it. For this reason, the idea of craft activity – which of course involves its own technology – has become pitted against the demands of new technology. The choice that confronts us almost daily is whether a product can still be something made with skill by craftsmen in limited quantity, or whether that product must be mass-produced in the latest way, by someone requiring a quick training programme only, in large quantities. This disadvantage of modern technology must be held responsible for the widespread alienation of workers in industrial society who are thus reduced to cogs in a machine and condemned to the performance of meaningless and repetitive manipulations as a means of earning their living.

To summarize, the principal criticisms of modern technology are thus: high pollution rate; high capital cost; exploitive use of natural resources; capacity for misuse; incompatibility with local cultures; dependence on a technical specialist elite; tendency to centralize; divorce from traditional forms of knowledge; and alienating effect on workers (see Table 7.1).

As the table shows, to all these points there are in essence five different types of response. And as I have already hinted, it seems very doubtful that there is any rational or logical way of characterizing any one of these responses as being 'better' than another. To do so means answering questions such as: 'What kind of world do we want to live in?' 'How highly do we value an equal technical chance for men all over the globe?' And 'Can men ever really get satisfaction from the activity we call work?' Each of us has his or her own answers to these questions and, consciously or unconsciously, personal views dictate the kind of response we choose to make to these technical dilemmas.
[...]

To take the above criticisms seriously is to say that an alternative technology should be non-polluting, cheap and labour-intensive, non-exploitive of natural resources, incapable of being misused, compatible with local cultures, understandable by all, functional in a non-centralist context, richly connected with existing forms of knowledge, and non-alienating. But immediately one is struck by the fact that the technology of, say, a primitive agricultural tribe in New Guinea or a hunter-gatherer society in the Mato Grosso of Brazil would probably fulfil all these boundary constraints. Yet this is not what we mean by an alternative technology. Primitive technology certainly has some links with alternative technology but is generally held to be a long way from it. Indeed, the evolution seen is that at some time in the past primitive technology led to industrialized technology, and that at some time in the future industrialized technology will lead to alternative technology.

The alternative, in other words, does not seek to jettison the scientific knowledge acquired over the past three centuries but instead to put it to use in a novel way. Space heating, in the primitive context, was achieved by an open wood fire. In the alternative context, it might still be achieved by burning timber – provided the overall rate of use was lower than the rate of natural timber growth in the area concerned – but

Table 7.1 Technical dilemmas and some social responses

Technical dilemma	Price response	'Fix-it' response	'Away-with-it' response	Alternative response	Radical political response
1. Pollution	Pollution inevitable and worth the benefit it brings	Solve pollution with pollution technology	Inevitable result of technology; use less technology	Invent non-polluting technologies	Pollution is a symptom of capitalism, not of poor technology
2. Capital dependence	Technology will always cost money	Provide the capital; make technology cheaper	Costs of technology are always greater than its benefits; use less	Invent labour-intensive technologies	Capital is a problem only in capitalist society
3. Exploitation of resources	Nothing lasts for ever	Use resources more cleverly	Use natural not exploitable resources	Invent technologies that use only renewable resources	Wrong problem: exploitation of man by man is the real issue
4. Liability to misuse	Inevitable and worth it	Legislate against misuse	Misuse so common and so dangerous, better not to use technology at all	Invent technologies that cannot be misused	Misuse is a sociopolitical problem, not a technical one
5. Incompatible with local cultures	Material advance is worth more than tradition	Make careful sociological studies before applying technology	Local cultures better off without technology	Design new technologies which are compatible	Local culture will be disrupted by revolutionary change in any case
6. Requires specialist technical elite	Undertake technical-training schemes	Improve scientific technical education at all levels	People should live without what they do not understand	Invent and use technologies that are understandable and controllable by all	Provide equal chance for everyone to become a technical specialist
7. Dependent on centralization	So what?	No problem, given good management	Decentralize by rejecting technology	Concentrate on decentralized technologies	Centralization an advantage in just social systems
8. Divorced from tradition	This is why technology is so powerful	Integrate tradition and technical know-how	Tradition matters more than technical gadgets	Evolve technologies from existing ones	Traditions stand in the way of true progress
9. Alienation	Workers are better fed and paid; what matters alienation?	More automation needed	Avoid alienation by avoiding technology	Decentralize; retain mass production only in exceptional cases	Alienation has social, not technical, causes

in a cheap and well designed stove which optimizes useful heat output against the need for fuel. Or it might be provided by a cheap solar heating system, a small electrical generating windmill, or simply by first-class insulation. This difference between primitive and alternative technology is important, for it has in the past led to charges that the alternative is retrogressive, essentially primitive, and ignores the utility of modern scientific knowledge. This is not the case.

The most compelling case for alternative technology can probably be made in the field of energy. In the developed world there is much controversy over the future of energy supplies. As our remaining fossil fuels are burnt up, a desperate struggle goes on to make nuclear energy both competitive in price and safe. Neither is easy. Even the future of enriched uranium looks far from being a long-term affair. Breeder reactors are generally held to be a neat solution to this problem, although the technical problems they pose are still far from solution.

There is the added danger that as such reactors breed plutonium, if they were to become widespread over the earth's surface, the possibility of plutonium falling into the 'wrong' hands is very real. Plutonium is not only a very toxic substance in its own right but it can, of course, be used in an atomic bomb. Estimates of the number of nuclear weapons that could be made – without the need for uranium enrichment plants – from the plutonium that will accumulate over the next two decades from nuclear fission are truly staggering. Add to this the problems of disposing of radioactive materials which are the by-products of the fission reaction (a problem still not solved, although the nuclear age is more than twenty years old) and those of preventing sabotage and accident in nuclear power stations, and it is then clear that the path we follow is fraught with danger. The prospect that all these problems will be resolved by the development of safe, controlled nuclear fusion reactors is still too distant to be realistic.

THE FLAW OF THERMAL POLLUTION

In any case, all these energy technologies suffer from one fundamental flaw. Because they use up stored energy, they produce large quantities of thermal pollution. There is a real chance that if we continue to use such sources, and our energy demand mounts over the next hundred years as fast as it has in the past hundred years, we will heat up the earth to a point where noticeable and unwanted long-term changes in climate will ensue.

Is there any alternative? The alternative technology recipe for solving world energy problems runs something like this. First, the developed countries must accept that there is a ceiling to the amount of energy they can use, and they must become more concerned with saving energy than with supplying it. Second, an intensive effort to make use of all those energy sources which are supplied to the earth in real time must be made. These include hydroelectric schemes, geothermal energy, tidal power, solar and wind energy, and timber as fuel. The first three of these are limited to particular regions but this is no reason why they should not be used to the fullest extent. Solar and wind energy are found more universally and if coupled to the energy which could be obtained by burning timber, they form an interesting distribution pattern over the earth's surface. In almost any habitable place, energy is or could be available from the use of the sun or the wind or timber. In places where there is little sun, wind and wood are often common. And where timber and wind are rare, there is usually plenty of sun.

In the developed world, these sources have been largely neglected because no single one of them is capable of supplying all energy needs. In northern latitudes, for instance, it is difficult or impossible to heat a house sufficiently well with solar energy. But as experiments have recently shown, houses in northern France can be designed to gain two-thirds of their heat from a very simple and cheap installation known as a solar wall. If the remainder could be provided with a little wind power and timber burning, the problem is essentially solved at the level of the household. There is a very real chance that if we accepted multiple solutions to our energy problems we could solve them by what have been called biotechnic means: using energy sources at roughly the same rate as they are naturally generated on the earth, hence creating no problems of thermal pollution whatsoever.

The disposal of sewage is another area where the need for an alternative is compelling. The problems of the current system are classic: expensive sewage installations are needed, together with large volumes of scarce and purified water, to sweep our sewage into processing units which discharge into rivers and seas a rich effluent causing severe pollution problems. As sewage contains important quantities of organic materials, the land is consequently always in deficit, particularly where animal excreta are not returned to it. (In modern intensive factory farming, this is becoming more and more of a problem.) So sewage disposal causes huge expense, water wastage, agricultural depletion and severe pollution.

A SOLUTION WE HAVE MADE INTO A PROBLEM

In any rational scheme, we would have found ways of returning our sewage to the land where it belongs. To reduce expense, we would do this not with a centralized scheme but at the family or community level.

And we would use our precious supply of purified water for more suitable purposes and tasks. In fact, all this is technically quite easy to achieve. In Scandinavia there is a device on the market which will compost family sewage and turn it over a period of about one year into a small quantity of extremely rich but sterile and odourless fertilizer which can be applied directly to the garden. The device uses no water and can digest kitchen scraps. Why this solution is not more common in the developed world is hard to understand.

It is nothing short of tragic, furthermore, to see developing countries investing huge amounts of hard-earned foreign exchange into expensive sewage disposal schemes when this, altogether much more efficacious, solution is at hand. The irony of the situation is compounded when we realize that in some of the drier developing countries there simply will never be sufficient water available to provide a 'Western-type' sewage disposal scheme for everyone. In today's society sewage has become a problem: it should be, and could again become as indeed it once was, a solution.

How do these examples of alternatives in energy and sewage disposal measure up to the nine boundary constraints listed in Table 7.1? Clearly, they do well in terms of pollution (no. 1), capital cost (2) and use of resources (3). Equally, they are essentially decentralized techniques (7) and their principles would be easily understood and controlled by anyone (6). Further, partly because they are decentralized, they would be difficult to misuse (4); indeed, a general principle for this constraint is that technical systems designed to operate optimally on the small or medium-small scale are usually difficult to misuse wherever that misuse involves a scaling up (as it usually does). Put another way, it is not easy to envisage what a solar bomb or a wind-powered missile would be like.

Certainly wind-power and composting are old and traditional technologies (8), found in many parts of the world. Neither has been much touched by scientific progress; it is not optimistic to assume that if our new knowledge were applied to either, we would find surely that traditional use had already discovered, perhaps intuitively, many of the important functional principles but that significant and perhaps radical improvements could now be made. The gearing and control mechanisms on a windmill, for example, can be much improved over what was possible in Holland three centuries ago. On this ground also, their development would be compatible with local culture in many areas of the world (5).

About alienation (9), little can be said, for alienation is usually produced primarily under conditions of mass production. True, there might be some mitigating effect through the introduction of technical substitutes, but it would not be a strong one. In general, an alternative technology can be designed to meet the nine boundary constraints listed, but in practice a substitute will always meet some conditions better than others. In a real world, this need not surprise us, nor need it be taken as proof of the impracticality of the idea. The important point is that by listing a series of goals for technology to meet, technology is lifted out of the moral vacuum in which it has existed for so long. It can thus, once again, become a moral activity, and like all human activities will probably always fall short of moral perfection in one or another respect.

NOVEL DESIGNS FOR DWELLINGS

There is not sufficient space to detail all the other possible alternatives to modern technology. Today a great deal of interest in construction is leading to some novel and satisfactory designs for dwellings made from cheap local materials, realized to a high degree of insulation, and with almost complete independence from external services. Designs have been made for dwellings which provide their own energy, process their own proper wastes and trap and purify their water supply. These designs usually fulfil all nine boundary conditions, although their weak points still tend to be that they are too complicated and costly to count yet as perfect examples of alternative technology. But real progress has been made.

Similar advances are now being tested in the field of food production. For example, one small-scale system in the United States produces high-quality fish protein at a truly enormous equivalent yield in relation to surface used, without relying on external sources other than the sun and human excrement. The fertile overflow from a domestic septic tank is led to a small pond over which a timber and glass structure has been built to capture the sun's energy. In the pond are grown insect larvae in great quantities, feeding on the rich nutrient in the pond and thriving in the hot, humid conditions. Once a week these larvae are removed and fed to *Tilapia* fish in another small pond contained in a plastic geodesic dome which acts as a hot-house, heating the water in the pond to the 25°–30° C in which *Tilapia* thrive. In a single summer the fish grow to edible size, and the water is then used to fertilize the vegetable garden. This very ingenious, closed cycle system has much to recommend it; there are without doubt many possible variations applicable in many different parts of the world.

Similarly, much work is being done on the difficult question of protection of domestic crops from predators. Alternative technologists have to find a different solution from that of applying polluting, dangerous and expensive sprays. There are several possible approaches. Perhaps the most important lies in fostering highly diverse, ecological food-growing systems rather than the monoculture to which society is now so addicted. There is evidence that diverse-species food production can be more productive than that of single species. Ecologically, production of this kind clearly stimulates a healthy species balance, with less danger of the monumental and truly savage attacks made by predators and disease organisms where and when only one crop is grown.

Alternative techniques such as these will have to be complemented by the biological control of pests and systematic, companion planting programmes in which the beneficial effect some species of plants appear to have on other species is used to the full. Cheap and biologically degradable sprays might also be acceptable: both nicotine and garlic sprays have been shown to be effective against a wide range of pests. Alternative technology will have to find sound biological and ecological means of maintaining the altered states of nature which farming implies in order to replace those blunderbuss spray technologies which our current clumsy approach to things biological has deemed to be the most appropriate means.

THE FUTURE OF ALTERNATIVE TECHNOLOGY

In the past three or four years the idea of alternative technology has blossomed in the developed world, particularly in the United States, United Kingdom, Sweden and France. Earlier, two organizations, the Intermediate Technology Development Group in the United Kingdom and the Brace Research Institute in Canada, had been set up to design and stimulate the growth of an alternative economic technology which would be labour-intensive and use local materials – and hence be more accessible to the developing countries. Since then, many more, less formal institutes and organizations have appeared, proclaiming additional constraints on the technology they wish to develop, in some cases more than the nine listed earlier.

This year some of these institutes are carrying out their first research, and their membership is growing considerably. It must be stressed that not all of these are concerned with rural alternative technology: some are directing their attention to the urban situation, where the demands of an alternative technology may be different in kind but not different in principle. Considerable numbers of people, many of them young, are seeking life-styles which can be supported by this type of alternative technology in preference to the '9 to 5' office or factory routine which conventional society and technology offer.

The change in attitude that has come about, therefore, is that the alternative which was first seen as a means of more rapid development for the Third World has become something of an obsession for the disenchanted in the so-called developed world. Recently, there has been less talk of the implications of alternative technology for development, and much more of the need for viable alternatives in countries which are usually considered to be developed. Whether this change is for the good is not clear, and at first glance it looks like a regression.

Those who urge labour-intensive, alternative technologies on developing countries place themselves in an exposed position. Countries without a real technological base tend to see alternatives as second-class options. After all (they contend), why should they accept forms of technology which the developed countries themselves do not normally use? The intermediate technologists have thus become, in many eyes, the 'new imperialists' trying to tell the developing world what is good for it. The story sounds all too familiar.

Yet the situation is more complicated than that. For one thing, considerable interest is to be found in the developing world for what is normally termed 'village technology' or small-scale technology which can be operated at the village level and used to improve material conditions on the micro-scale. India, in particular, is a stronghold of such thought, but there are indications from other countries too that they find the idea of value.[2] And if one is discussing the people actually facing development problems in the Third World, they may often be more interested in making a simple pump from local materials than in their governments' far-reaching schemes for a nuclear power programme, or a green revolution which will help only the larger and richer farmers. What people in the developing world think about such things might then be imperfectly articulated by their governments.

The important moral is that what must happen is that the new alternatives be developed. If that is not done, the developing countries will have no choice to make about their own future. They can in effect only continue in their present state or adapt themselves to the existing technology of the developed world. That is a poor choice. Those of us who believe that the future could have more to offer than the technocratic nightmare are intent on widening the options available for ourselves and for future generations wherever they may be.

REFERENCES

1. J. McDermott, *New York Review of Books*, 31 July 1969.
2. *See* J. Omo-Fadaka, 'The Tanzanian Way of Effective Development', *Impact of Science on Society*, XXIII, 2 (April–June 1973).

IV TECHNOLOGY IN EDUCATION

Following through the considerations in earlier sections, we now have a background to consider the place of technology in education. The inclusion of technology as an area of teaching and learning within the school curriculum provokes debate about the nature of technological education which should be offered. This section therefore presents arguments which consider the role which technological education at school level could play in individual and social development as well as toward national prosperity. The idea of 'capability', taken up by the Royal Society of Arts (RSA) (Chapters 8 and 9), is one response to the arguments of Weiner, which we presented in Chapter 6. The ability to act is advocated in addition to what the RSA call 'comprehension' and 'cultivation' – the traditional focus of education. It is tempting to be swept along on this apparently new approach without due regard to the past. McCulloch, Jenkins and Layton, in Chapter 10, not only question some of the assumptions of writers like Weiner, but remind us about issues of how the curriculum changes through an historical account of technological education since the second world war.

Views derived from these arguments and justifications inevitably affect decisions about the kind of technological education which should be offered by schools. For example, should we equip children with the necessary specialized skills and knowledge to enable them to gain employment in industry and commerce when they leave school? Should we prepare children in ways which will ensure that they are technologically 'socialized' and able to make informed decisions in their own lives about technological choices? Or should technological education contribute to the general education of all children by focusing upon ways of learning which distinguish this area of the curriculum from others? Anita Cross (Chapter 11) takes up this latter issue by looking at the contribution of design. She does this in part through a consideration of the findings of research on modes of thinking and the workings of the human brain. Bernard Down in Chapter 12 argues for a focus on social issues having rejected one which sees technological education as a preparation for work. But it would be wrong to assume that those who advocate 'capability', view education in narrow utilitarian terms. In spelling out technological capability, Professors Black and Harrison clearly see it as an aspect of a more general human capability. Their examples of pupil activities in schools puts some flesh on the bones of earlier arguments.

The form which technological education actually assumes in the school curriculum however, is influenced by other considerations in addition to educational aims. For example, the provision which is made for it within the school timetable and the allocation of effective resources; the organization of 'knowledge' into subject areas and the consequent fragmentation of technology teaching across the school curriculum; conflicting views about the aims and nature of technological education across the subject areas. All of which lead to different ideas on the location of technology within the curriculum and, the ability of teachers to assume responsibility for an expanding area of the school curriculum.

Tom Dodd (Chapter 14) offers a variety of models for locating technology in contrast to Bernard Down who, in Chapter 15, considers the nature of one subject area, CDT, where technology has an important place. Colin Tipping (Chapter 16) sees no exclusive place for technology and wants technological education to be part of all subjects: technology across the curriculum. Science teachers often see a special place for technology in their teaching, a stance shared by Brian Woolnough in Chapter 17. He is not arguing for science to have the monopoly over technology in the school, but he does oppose the creation of yet another subject area.

We end this section with a cameo of the growth of CDT, the subject area which may seem to be the 'home' of technology in the curriculum. John Eggleston's snapshot shows the multitude of influences on a subject area indicating that it is not just an intellectual and cultural tradition, but a social institution with a national 'life' as well as one within particular schools. The title of the article indicates an uncertain future; developments in GCSE will make this true for technological education wherever it is found in the curriculum. Will the GCSE, for example, stifle all cross curricular initiatives? Time will tell whether or not other teachers will leave technology to the CDT department – we hope not.

8 *Education for Capability*

- Royal Society of Arts

EDITORS' INTRODUCTION

The RSA have taken up the challenge of the manifesto of Education for Capability through a recognition scheme. Here we reproduce the manifesto and the aims of the education for capability defined in the scheme. In Chapter 9 Peter Gorb gives some of the background and details of this new movement for change.

MANIFESTO OF EDUCATION FOR CAPABILITY

Six years ago, a group of friends who shared similar anxieties about the course British education was taking met informally and drafted the manifesto of Education for Capability:

There is a serious imbalance in Britain today in the full process which is described by the two words 'education' and 'training'. The idea of the 'educated person' is that of a scholarly individual who has been neither educated nor trained to exercise useful skills; who is able to understand but not to act. Young people in secondary or higher education increasingly specialize, and do so too often in ways which mean that they are taught to practise only the skills of scholarship and science. They acquire knowledge of particular subjects, but are not equipped to use knowledge in ways which are relevant to the world outside the education system.

This imbalance is harmful to individuals, to industry and to society. A well-balanced education should, of course, embrace analysis and the acquisition of knowledge. But it must also include the exercise of creative skills, the competence to undertake and complete tasks and the ability to cope with everyday life; and also doing all these things in co-operation with others.

There exists in its own right a culture which is concerned with doing, making and organizing and the creative arts. This culture emphasizes the day-to-day management of affairs, the formulation and solution of problems and the design, manufacture and marketing of goods and services.

Educators should spend more time preparing people in this way for a life outside the education system. The country would benefit significantly in economic terms from what is here described as Education for Capability.

EDUCATION FOR CAPABILITY:
1985 RECOGNITION SCHEME

The aim of Education for Capability

It is the aim of Education for Capability to encourage and develop in people four capacities that are currently under-emphasized in our education system.

The great majority of learners – whether pupils at school, students at universities, polytechnics or colleges, or adults still wanting to learn – are destined for a productive life of practical action. They are going to do things, design things, make things, organize things, for the most part in co-operation with other people. They need to improve their *competence*, by the practice of skills and the use of knowledge; to *cope* better with their own lives and the problems that confront them and society; to develop their *creative* abilities; and, above all, to *co-operate* with other people. It is these four capacities that we want to see encouraged and developed through Education for Capability.

The education system at present gives most of its emphasis to two other educational aims – the development of the abilities to acquire and record specialized knowledge and to appreciate the values inherent in our cultural heritage. We call their achievement *comprehension* and *cultivation*, respectively, which by themselves are not enough; even for those destined to pursue a life of scholarship or contemplation, they do not alone afford an adequate preparation for life in the outside world.

9   *Catalyst for capability*

● P. Gorb

Recently, Anna Bindoff, aged eleven, described to a crowded and attentive audience of eminent educationists and industrialists at the Royal Society of Arts a method she had worked out for counting the flints in the wall of her local church. She was talking about the way children learn at Lewknor Primary School, in Oxfordshire. She told us how a group working together identified the problems of this task, and how they set about solving them. Quite apart from practising mathematics in a way which was relevant to their experience and needs, by referring to the teacher only when a need to know was established, the children also improved their ability to cope with problems, and to do so in co-operation with others.

Anna Bindoff was describing one of the eleven award-winning submissions in the 1981 RSA Education for Capability Recognition Scheme. During the two years of its life, the scheme has attracted more than a thousand enquiries and about 140 applications for recognition. This interest comes from all levels, from primary to postgraduate, from people involved in youth opportunity schemes to industrial training programmes.

There has also been a growing interest in Education for Capability among those who make or influence educational policy, or who are concerned to do so. During last year, the Education for Capability Committee at the RSA was asked (either collectively or individually) to address conferences, visit educational programmes, meet with local education authorities and respond to interest in the newspapers, journals and on radio and television. The weight and quality of this response – to what are, after all, not new educational ideas – has, we think, two main causes.

The first is the timeliness of the message. When, about four years ago, an informal group (most of whom are now members of the committee) sat down to write the Education for Capability manifesto [see Chapter 8], they were aware that they were focusing a set of dissatisfactions that were common to many educators, industrialists and parents. That manifesto received wide support from an influential body of signatories, and prompted the group to seek a platform at the RSA for three lectures by Correlli Barnett, Charles Handy and Tyrrell Burgess, which provided a background to the manifesto.

Economic decline, growing unemployment, the social alienation of young people, the cutbacks in education and the problems of its organization and control – all these issues served to reinforce the timeliness of the Education for Capability movement. By the middle of 1979, we were being carried forward on a tide of uneasiness about education and its place in society.

Another reason for this growing interest has been the home of the movement at the RSA. In introducing the second symposium (at which Anna Bindoff spoke), Ian Hunter, the Chairman of the Council of the Society, touched on the eclectic nature of the Society's work, reflected in the audience, which included polytechnic directors and primary school children, managing directors and trade unionists, central and local government officers, teachers and members of both Houses of Parliament. The RSA, as a wholly independent body, is a natural home for a movement which is trying to focus an educational debate spanning at least three departments of government and organizations from well outside the formal system of education.

There are many worthwhile educational and related reform groups who wish to make connections with us, or to squeeze us into their mould. We therefore welcome every opportunity to restate our main concern, which is to correct a serious lack of balance in our education system. We wish to change the emphasis from a concentration on equipping young people for an 'academic life' to one which equips them for an 'active life'.

We have been accused of disparaging the 'academic', the pursuit of knowledge for its own sake, and the development of the cultivated individual, able to appreciate and evaluate and judge. It is not the case that we wish to abandon what Toby Weaver has encapsulated under the headings of *Comprehension* and *cultivation*. But, as he said in introducing the discussion at the RSA symposium, 'by themselves these two are not enough, except for scholars, critics and contemplatives'.

He went on to emphasize that a 'capably' educated person must learn how to exercise creative skills, to develop one or a number of special competencies, the 'know-how' on which modern society depends; and above all learn how to cope with the problems of life and work. Finally, all these things need to be done, not individually and competitively (as our examination systems demand), but by co-operative effort and joint action. We want young people to be prepared for a life of responsible action in a world where employers are concerned with what young people can *do* as well as what they *know*.

We take no sides in the debate about the pecking order of subjects. We believe all subjects should be taught with a strong emphasis on their relevance to the lives of young people. We believe that young people need to learn how to identify and solve problems, and how to undertake and complete tasks using appropriate knowledge and skills. We believe they can learn to do this in nearly every subject area. It is, for example, sad to observe the extent to which technological subjects have all too often become fixed in an academic mould which treats engineering as an applied science.

The work of the engineering department at Middlesex Polytechnic has received recognition from the RSA for its efforts to re-establish its engineering degree work on a problem-solving basis. A creative problem-solving programme is now part of all three years of their BSc Civil Engineering course. Designed to counteract the view that there are always unique solutions to problems, the programme requires the students to undertake problem-based work outside the polytechnic, and to do so in a situation which demands that they work with others.

Education for Capability should not be classified amongst the various 'understanding industry' schemes. We recognize the importance of these schemes in reinforcing the importance of wealth creation to new generations of school-children. We also admire the attempt to place the relevance of work at the heart of the educational process.

But understanding by itself is not enough, even if it succeeds in creating among the young an admiration for the world of industry and commerce, and a desire to work within it. Effective performance in industry (or indeed in any job) requires action as well as appreciation, and 'know-how' even more than knowledge.

Again, in the field of work and employment, Education for Capability has occasionally, and wrongly, been identified with schemes which attempt to prepare school-leavers, and particularly unemployed school-leavers, for jobs. It is, of course, sensitive to the social and economic problems which motivate these schemes, and it has recognized a number of effective and heartwarming programmes associated with them.

One of these is the 'Service Away from Home' scheme, which enables the young unemployed school-leavers to cope with living and working away from home. But as Rachel Stephens, the organizer, says, 'it is a pity that unemployment was the motivation for this important educational experiment'.

Education for Capability is concerned with the employed as well as the unemployed. It is the capability of the employed which will determine whether or not our immediate economic ills can be cured. This leads to a further confusion, which would confine Education for Capability to those who are unable or unwilling to tackle the examination hurdles towards higher education.

But it is often those who are best at passing examinations who are most in need of the kind of education we are advocating. It is they who will ultimately manage or influence our society. We are hardly likely to do well as a nation if our ablest members are not helped to become doers and makers, organizers and problem-solvers.

Furthermore, the present debate on employment has begun to recognize that employment as we understand it is not necessarily a prerequisite for living a full life and making a contribution to the wealth of the community. Education for Capability may well be a prerequisite to making the kinds of economic, social and emotional adjustments to new and perhaps still unknown ways of living and working.

A criticism levelled at the group is that because we 'preach' rather than 'practise', we do not 'practise what we preach'. Certainly it is not the purpose or the place of the RSA to do more than encourage and motivate the activities of others. In the end it is the education system itself which must make the changes. But, by providing an independent focus and forum, the RSA hopes to be catalytic in helping this particular reform movement.

If schemes designed to enhance capability are to find a stronger place in our system, ways of assessing student performance and validating those assessments need not only to be devised and implemented, but also given status and independence. An assessment of capability which complements and perhaps eventually takes precedence over traditional examinations needs to be sought by employers and those responsible for university admissions, as well as by teachers and parents and, of course, by the students themselves.

One of the most effective points at which to insert a lever for educational change is the admissions level to higher education. The shift from the academic to problem-based ways of learning needs to take place at the universities themselves, most of whose students will never become academics. It was encouraging for the RSA to be able to recognize a scheme at Salford University at postgraduate level which deals with work for an MSc in Environmental Resources in a problem-based way.

Acceptance and encouragement from the highest levels of the system will open the way to many more practical schemes now in operation at schools like Lewknor Primary. It is important to recognize and encourage the enormous and valuable resources which can be nurtured at the earliest educational level – and which were so ably demonstrated to us by Anna Bindoff. To do so remains a priority for the Education for Capability movement.

Details of the scheme are available from the RSA, John Adam Street, Adelphi, London WC2N 6EZ.

10 *Technological revolution?*

● G. McCulloch, E. Jenkins and D. Layton

EDITORS' INTRODUCTION

This is the concluding chapter of an historical account of science and technology in the last forty years. The authors see the problem in technological education to be as much about how to conduct curriculum reform as about definitions of technology.

It is apparent, then, that despite major efforts there has been no 'technological revolution' in the schools. Nevertheless, the mixed record of past endeavours offers some useful lessons for current policy-makers and educationists. Also, in a wider context, the politics of school science and technology comprises a significant aspect of the recent history of England and Wales, giving an insight into the nature and limitations of attempts to reform social attitudes over the last century.

In 1959, C. P. Snow argued that the traditional values of literary culture dominated English society at the expense of science and technology. He concluded that unless the balance between the 'two cultures' was redressed, Britain's relative decline as a world power would accelerate:

> I can't help thinking of the Venetian Republic in their last half-century. Like us, they had once been fabulously lucky. They had become rich, as we did, by accident. They had acquired immense political skill, just as we have. A good many of them were tough-minded, realistic, patriotic men. They knew, just as clearly as we know, that the current of history had begun to flow against them. Many of them gave their minds to working out ways to keep going. It would have meant breaking the pattern into which they had crystallised. They were fond of the pattern, just as we are fond of ours. They never found the will to break it.[1]

By the 1970s, as economic, industrial and social problems increased, Snow's general analysis appealed to several historians as an explanation for national decline. The history of scientific and technical education has come to be seen as a symbol and partial explanation of an 'English disease' which has inhibited social development. Such assessments have tended to suggest a general formula by which Britain might have avoided long-term decline and the discontents of the 1980s: the 'practical' approach to education. Correlli Barnett, for example, has attributed Britain's low industrial productivity to the social attitudes reflected in and reproduced by education: 'The general ethos and thrust of British education are, if anything, hostile to industry and careers in industry.'[2] He argues that only an increase in 'practical' education, which he describes as 'education for capability', can arrest the relative decline which he perceives; indeed, 'Education for capability alone can keep Britain an advanced technological society and save her from becoming a Portugal, perhaps even an Egypt, of tomorrow.'[3] Gordon Roderick and Michael Stephens have also followed this line of reasoning, contending that the 'British disease' is 'synonymous with relative economic failure and an inability to match our industrial productivity to that of our competitors'.[4] They trace this failure from the Victorian period, and ask 'Where Did We Go Wrong?'. In answering this question, they stress the continuity of the 'Great Debate' on the 'British malaise', and point out that the social criticisms made by such figures as Baron Playfair and T. H. Huxley in the nineteenth century had strong affinities with those advanced by Lords Snow and Bowden, among others, in the 1950s and 1960s. Martin J. Wiener has provided a particularly impressive and elaborate version of this kind of argument, concluding that

> leaders of commerce and industry over the past century have accommodated themselves to an élite culture blended of preindustrial aristocratic and religious values and more recent professional and bureaucratic values that inhibited their quest for expansion, productivity, and profit.[5]

However, such analyses, although valuable in exploring the development of social attitudes in Britain, do give rise to certain problems. Firstly, they are based on the assumption that there is a clear and precise link between 'practical' education and improved economic productivity. This is, however, a matter of some dispute. In reality, it is most difficult to predict either the general economic and social requirements of the future, or the specific industrial consequences of changes in education and training.[6] Moreover, such analyses appear to overstate the role played by the aristocratic ethos, especially in the period since 1945. The attitudes of the FBI and the engineering institutions towards school science and technology were primarily designed to enhance the professional standing of industry and engineering – a very modern anxiety. To be sure, they sought academic legitimation for this purpose, but the equation between academic values and the aristocratic ethos is less exact than Wiener in particular seems to suppose. Since 1945, the desire for professional status appears to have played a much more important role in downgrading the 'manual' and 'craft' connotations of engineering and industry in this country than any surviving 'preindustrial aristocratic and religious values'.

Also, this historiography of decline tends to exaggerate the coherence of the many educational and social critics of the last century. It assumes that there is a single 'practical' approach, constituting the 'alternative road'. Roderick and Stephens in particular leave the strong impression that there were no significant differences between the various advocates of a more 'practical' approach, and attribute their failure to the dominance of short-sighted and old-fashioned social attitudes. Yet in fact, the resistance of traditional social and cultural values is an insufficient, and in some respects misleading, explanation for the general failure of attempts to encourage greater awareness of technological and industrial applications of science at the school level in this country. It is true that the secondary technical schools suffered from the effects of ingrained social prejudices against technical education, and that such prejudices persisted until the 1980s. Even so, it is unfair to assume that dominant cultural attitudes of this sort left all such endeavours starved of publicity, resources and sympathy. Figures as prestigious and influential as the Duke of Edinburgh and Sir Harold Hartley were strong supporters of applied science and technology in schools and they enjoyed access, often of an informal kind, to agencies such as the Schools Council, the CBI and the CEI which were important sponsors of projects and initiatives in this field. When the Duke of Edinburgh consulted Hartley over the creation of the SSTC, he saw no difficulty about also contacting Alan Bullock, the chairman of the Schools Council 'to put him in the picture', since Bullock was the Master of St Catherine's, the Oxford college of which the Duke was Visitor.[7] It is clear, therefore, that the various initiatives in respect of the alternative road did not fail through any lack of will or resources, or even sympathy. Rather, their impact was blunted by tensions and divisions among the reformers themselves. There was never any single 'practical' approach; the 'alternative road' embraced many differences of emphasis and opinion. Thus, for example, the leaders of the AHSTS failed to agree on the nature and implications of the 'alternative road'. The Action Group and the Schools Council Project in Technology represented rival factions with conflicting notions of applied science and technology in schools. The SSTC failed to resolve these tensions, and proved unable to formulate a clear prospectus for reform. The SCSST continued to be surrounded by differing interpretations of needs and priorities. To understand the failures and disappointments of these initiatives, it is not enough to point to the overt resistance presented by traditional attitudes and certain entrenched interest groups. The difficulties of individuals and groups well disposed towards applied science and technology in schools were compounded by internal political and ideological tensions. In addition, these tensions, severe enough in themselves, were often exacerbated by simple failures of communications, despite the closeness of the links between the various agencies and individuals seeking to reform the school curriculum. As has been pointed out, Sir Harold Hartley remained unaware of the initiative being taken by the Schools Council until the summer of 1967, and there is little doubt that the strains inherent in the relationship between the Schools Council Project in Technology and the Action Group were increased as a result of breakdowns in communication at crucial moments.

At the school level, the various advocates of the alternative road failed to formulate a clear and positive policy about the role of the traditional craftwork and handicraft departments in their plans. The relationship of design activities to science and technology raised comparable and contentious issues of status, rationale and resources. The further vexed question of whether attempts at curriculum reform should be directed towards particular groups of pupils or types of school was circumvented, at least partially, by the development of a comprehensive system of secondary education. However, it is significant that much of the discussion which accompanied the announcement of the Technical and Vocational Education Initiative of the Manpower Services Commission in 1982 was concerned with identifying the group of pupils for whom it was intended. By many the development was seen as threateningly divisive in relation to the comprehensive ideal.

Differences in approach, emphasis and interpretation between the various participants have persisted into the 1980s, the broad policy issue of the relationship between science and technology being of particular importance. Many prominent advocates of increased recognition of applied science and technology have argued that the allegedly close ties between pure science and technological and industrial applications should be maintained or even strengthened. The Duke of Edinburgh continually emphasized the need for a fruitful alliance between science and technology. Sir Frank Mason, the first chairman of the SCSST, insisted at its inaugural meeting that 'science and engineering should not drift apart', since 'The greatest contributions to improving living conditions had been at times when science and engineering were considered as one unified entity.'[8] However, by the 1980s, and especially since the Finniston Report with its explicit assertion that engineering was different from, and in no sense a subordinate branch of, science,[9] a tendency towards distinct, even competing, 'science' and 'technology' camps could be detected. The effect on the school science curriculum of the emergence of autonomous technology, with its Engineering Council, Finniston's 'engine for change', and its own Fellowship of Engineering as an authoritative and independent voice in national affairs intended to complement that of the Royal Society, is yet to be determined.

Beyond internal conflicts, however, the task of curriculum change which confronted advocates of applied science and technology in schools was more daunting than that faced by reformers of school science who aimed to reinforce its academic and experimental character. According to Leon Trotsky, 'In practice a reformist party considers unshakable the foundations of that which it intends to reform.'[10] It is not necessary to be a Trotskyist to agree with this remark. In the field of school science and technology, the 'reformist party' sought to update science curricula without incorporating much in the way of applied science and technology. The activities of the Science Masters' Association (SMA), the Association of Women Science Teachers (AWST) and the Nuffield Foundation stressed the academic, intellectual and cultural value of the separate sciences in modernized school courses. They led to important reforms, but within the framework of existing attitudes and traditions. The problems of outdated and overloaded curricula could be tackled because it was clear that there was no challenge to the established educational function ascribed to science. The leaders of the SMA, the AWST and the Nuffield Foundation's science teaching project were, in Coulson's phrase, 'forward looking educational conservationists'.[11] Their reforms were designed to conserve as much as they changed. By contrast, advocates of applied science and technology in schools were seeking to change basic attitudes as part of their curriculum reform. Their aims were therefore more far-reaching than were those of the SMA, the AWST and the Nuffield Foundation. They needed not only to formulate curriculum proprosals, but also to construct a rationale for applied science and technology in schools which would be convincing to teachers, administrators and the various interest groups in the field. That they failed to agree among themselves as to the nature and implications of such a rationale served to compound their difficulties.

In addition, proponents of the alternative road often found it difficult to explain how the teaching of applied science and technology could be accommodated within already overcrowded school timetables. Individuals and groups with a precise sense of the changed attitudes which they wished to instil often displayed only a rudimentary understanding of the dynamics of curriculum change. Sir Partrick Linstead argued that a 'taste for technology' should be 'introduced' in schools, but offered no clear prescription as to how this could be done.[12]

The FBI and the IMechE called for greater appreciation of applied science and technology in schools, but struggled to devise a means by which this might be achieved, and were forced to rely upon schemes already developed in schools like Ealing and Sevenoaks. They were perhaps naive in assuming that the unusual conditions associated with such schemes could be reproduced in schools all over the country. They had an overtly instrumental approach to education, with the primary aim of enhancing the image of industry and the engineering profession; but they lacked any detailed knowledge of the complexities of curriculum change. None of the principal initiatives in school science and technology before the late 1960s was informed by theoretical analysis of, and research into, the curriculum. As John Maddox had noted, the work of the Nuffield Foundation Science Teaching Project was largely 'pragmatic and not theoretical in character'.[13]

Given this general lack of appreciation of the complex and ambitious nature of the curriculum reform being attempted, it is understandable that there was a failure to ease sufficiently the constraints affecting teachers in the normal course of their professional duties. In the past, many of those leading curriculum innovation in this field have tended to respond to national priorities and issues, rather than act as, or in conjunction with, representatives who could diagnose the nature of classroom constraints and provide some means of alleviation. The exigencies of the teachers' world which influence their day-to-day ordering of priorities and the coping strategies adopted, are familiar in general terms, though 'a systematic analysis of teachers' concerns, relating them to the various levels of the institutional contexts in which teaching is embedded' is still unavailable.[14] Even without this, however, it is not difficult to discern some of the obstacles to the implementation of a more practical and technologically oriented curriculum in secondary schools. The problems of initiating, managing and assessing project work are a case in point. Although the benefits to students of project work have been widely extolled, adoption of this mode of learning is costly in terms of teacher effort and skills, to say nothing of time and material resources, and is not always easily compatible with traditional constraints on classroom life.

In conclusion it is appropriate to ask whether the prospect for a 'technological revolution' in schools is any brighter in the 1980s than it has been in the period . . . [since the war] Clearly both the national and the institutional contexts of the school curriculum have changed and there is a sense in which some of the obstacles to reform [...] have been removed or diminished. Continuing economic difficulties have undoubtedly encouraged movements toward 'the vocationalisation of secondary education'[15] and the provision of courses perceived as more 'practical and relevant'. In this connection, the considerable resources for technical and vocational education in secondary schools made available from 1982 through the agency of the Manpower Services Commission constituted a major new determinant of the curriculum. Ironically, such developments in England and Wales coincided with the publication in the USA of evaluation research which was critical of the effectiveness of vocational education offered in that country.[16] Within the world of science and technology, it was notable that the Royal Society's report on science teaching in 1982 made specific reference to the need to incorporate applications in the teaching of science,[17] a view which contrasted sharply with opinion that informed the first wave of Nuffield Foundation science teaching projects twenty years before. Also in 1982, the first policy statement of the newly founded Engineering Council placed emphasis on the teaching of technology in schools, additional to science and mathematics; it also expressed concern that greater recognition should be given to courses which adopted a project approach to learning.[18] No such enthusiasm for separate technology in schools characterized the Royal Society's report. Whether accommodation and co-operation or competition and conflict will characterize the relations of school science and school technology remains a critical question for the future.

As for the teachers in schools, by the 1980s the ASE had come to take a more positive interest in technological education and consensus on the nature of school technology appeared nearer. Examination boards had developed syllabuses concerned with engineering science, design, control technology and electronics; together with the schools, they had gained valuable experience of the problems of teaching and assessment in these fields. Perhaps, too, developments in technology, most notably in microelectronics and computing, had contributed to a greater and more personal recognition on the part of many teachers of the alliance of knowledge, skill, creativity and design which, arguably, characterized the alternative road. As but one indication of change, traditional handicraft teaching, with its emphasis on the group acquisition of specific craft skills, was being transformed to CDT, with its broader concern for individual problem-solving.[19] Also, the need to formulate precise criteria for the proposed secondary school examination at 16+ and the prospect of national monitoring of the technological attainments of school children by the Department of Education and Science's Assessment of Performance Unit generated detailed, if ambitious, statements of the objectives of school technology which commanded general support. Their appropriateness to the education of all pupils was more widely accepted; the provision for girls, in particular, was enhanced by legislation for equal opportunities and by a growing understanding of the subtle processes associated with the social construction of sex differences. Perhaps, in the long term, of greatest significance were changes in technology itself. Developments in microelectronics and information technology made the objectives of technology in education more credible by being better matched to the resources and constraints of schools than had been possible hitherto.

A final point might be that the 'doing community' of technology as opposed to the 'knowing community' of science seemed at last within sight of articulating a coherent and persuasive rationale for its educational activities. What had been achieved at school level was paralleled at national level. Though some tensions remained, the engineering community drew its ranks together and, for the first time, offered the prospect of a single powerful voice speaking on behalf of its interests.[20]

For those convinced of the need to establish 'an alternative road' in secondary education, an understandable judgement was that the omens, as they appeared in the early 1980s, had rarely seemed more propitious. Nevertheless, it could be argued that even if it finally proved possible to establish an 'alternative road', such a success might soon be rendered worthless or irrelevant by the impact on society and industry of the 'microelectronics revolution'. Even assuming that 'practical' and 'technical' education will still be required in a post-industrial society, it will presumably not be oriented to the needs of industry and work as currently understood. It would be a cruel irony indeed if the strenuous efforts to adapt school science and technology to the needs of the so-called 'technological revolution' were to succeed twenty years too late. As Hegel pungently observed, 'The owl of Minerva spreads its wings only with the falling of the dusk.'

REFERENCES

1. C. P. Snow, *Two Cultures*, p. 40. [This quote was used by Weiner, p. 61]

2. C. Barnett, 'Technology, Education and Industrial and Economic Strength,' *Journal of Royal Society of Arts*, no. 5271 (February 1979), p. 120.

3. *Ibid.*, p. 127.

4. G. Roderick and M. Stephens (eds), *The British Malaise: Industrial Performance, Education and Training in Britain Today*, 1982, p. 3. Also G. Roderick and M. Stephens (eds), *Where Did We Go Wrong? Industrial Performance, Education and the Economy in Victorian Britain*, 1981.

5. M. J. Wiener, *English Culture and the Decline of the Industrial Spirit, 1850–1980*, 1981, p. 127. [See Chapter 6 of this Reader.]

6. See, e.g., S. B. Prais, *Vocation Qualifications of the Labour Force in Britain and Germany*, 1981, and K. G. Gannicott and M. Blaug, 'Manpower Forecasting Since Robbins: A Science Lobby in Action', *Higher Education Review*, (autumn 1969), vol. 2, no. 1, pp. 56–74.

7. Duke of Edinburgh, memorandum to Sir H. Hartley, 17 April 1968 (Hartley papers, Box 328).

8. SCSST, inaugural meeting, 18 January 1971, minute 7 (SCSST papers).

9. *Engineering Our Future*. Report of the Committee of Inquiry into the Engineering Profession, HMSO 1980, Cmnd. 7794, p. 25.

10. L. Trotsky, *History of the Russian Revolution*, 1934 edn, vol. 3, p. 5.

11. E. Coulson, *Confessions of a Forward Looking Educational Conservationist*, 1972.

12. *TES*, 1 January 1965, report, 'Delay the First Choice'.

13. J. Maddox to B. Young, 8 March 1965 (Nuffield Foundation papers, file EDU/52).

14. D. Barnes, 'Curriculum Developers Versus Teachers' Dilemmas', *Studies in Science Education*, vol. 10 (1983), p. 135.

15. See, e.g. *European Journal of Education*, vol. 18, no. 1 (1983), especially pp. 7–20.

16. *Ibid.*, p. 45.

17. *Science Education 11–18 in England and Wales*. Report of a Royal Society Study Group, Royal Society (1982), pp. 31 and 70.

18. The Engineering Council, *Policy Statement*, September 1982, paras 2.2 and 2.4.

19. George Hicks, 'Infant Phenomenon', *TES*, 7 October 1983, pp. 35–6.

20. The Fellowship of Engineering was established in 1976 and the Engineering Council in 1982.

11 *Towards an understanding of the intrinsic values of design education*

● A. Cross

EDITORS' INTRODUCTION

For further progress to be made in design education – particularly in design as a component of general education – it is necessary to articulate its intrinsic values. Two main inter-related areas in which such values might be found are discussed. The first area is the 'language media' of design, and the second is the modes of thought which relate particularly to design abilities. The latter area draws upon research in the neurosciences which is discovering fundamental differences in the thought modes associated with the two hemispheres of the human brain.

FOUNDATION MEDIA OF DESIGN

Design is being introduced into the curriculum of general education but there is no consensus of opinion on its fundamental role or intrinsic value. Central to the task of clarifying the intrinsic value of design in general education is the necessary recognition of a distinction in education between 'underpinning' or foundation, and superstructure. Balchin and Coleman[1] explain:

> underpinnings or foundations are that part of education on which the superstructure must rest. They involve teaching the individual child to communicate and receive communications, they are the media of communication that the child learns. The superstructure is the content that is taught through these media.

Much debate revolves around the superstructure of design education. That is, the ideas, products, the various facets and constraints of art and design culture into which the child is to be introduced. Further debate is held on ways which have been employed traditionally in the teaching of design subjects, to accomplish this introduction. In comparison to other areas in the school curriculum less attention is given to the underpinning or media which the child learns. These media do not have the same respect or teaching time devoted to them as do those other media, literacy and numeracy, which form the basis of education from the earliest years. A recent UK government document illustrates this emphasis:

> primary schools rightly attach priority to English and Mathematics. This is an overriding priority: it is essential that the early skills in reading, writing and calculating should be effectively learned in primary school since deficiencies at this stage cannot easily be remedied later and children will face the world seriously handicapped.[2]

In contrast, design is introduced and taught as a subject at upper levels of schooling and often appears to consist of superstructure without prior foundation. This is not surprising. If we attempt to clarify what designing *is*, what it involves in terms of thought modes, procedures and 'languages' of communication, we find that we can only go so far. Sooner or later we come up against something intrinsic in designing which is difficult to define, which lies outside our combined concepts of art, science, or mathematics and which it is difficult to reach agreement on how to teach.

It is in the exploration of this difficult area intrinsic to designing that we may begin to understand what the underpinning or media of design may be. Identifying the fundamental human abilities that are relevant to, and fostered by, design activities would seem to be an important step towards defining the intrinsic educational value of design activities. At the same time, such an attempt would help to reveal the 'content' of design as an area of knowledge, since ability cannot be defined outside the context of what it demonstrates.

Graphicacy

Within this context Balchin and Coleman[1] raise the question of whether the commonly accepted underpinnings of literacy, numeracy and verbal articulation provide a wholly adequate foundation or set of media for thought and communication. They decide that although emphasis in education is placed upon the acquisition of these particular learning media, they are inadequate. Their decision is based upon the awareness that other, more suitable forms of communication are resorted to in particular situations. For example:

(a) the owner of a house will use a plan to describe its layout;

(b)   the mathematician will use a graph or diagram to describe an abstraction when words or numbers are inadequate;

(c)   the historian may resort to a picture;

(d)   the geographer will use a map or photograph.

Balchin and Coleman therefore argue that skills in the communication of relationships, especially visual and spatial relationships, complement basic skills in literacy and numeracy as foundation media in education. They call this particular ability range 'graphicacy' (since the syllable 'graph' is common to many of the names for visual aids, e.g. graphs, photographs, cartography, graphic arts) and claim that it refers to the educated counterpart of the visual-spatial aspect of human intelligence and behaviour. Moreover it has been observed that graphical talent in young children appears to be more spontaneous than writing or number.

Bloomer[3] observes that children demonstrate a natural tendency to record visual information by graphic means:

> they are strongly motivated to represent the most important characteristics of the object in question. In doing this, children usually draw objects from the viewpoint that gives the most information. A wagon for instance would be drawn from the side in order to show the wheels, hood and shape, whereas a house would be drawn from the front.

Gardner[4] shows how children's drawings demonstrate shifts in perception, mood and skill levels and are therefore capable of communicating rather more non-verbal information than is often appeciated. Advocates of graphicacy however do not appear to encourage this level of perceptual analysis. In their view it is a concept which emphasizes technical competence in graphic skills:

> it can be said that Art is a form of self expression and communication a skill that involves both an expressor and an expressee. Great Art includes both. Graphicacy however includes only the skill aspect. It is the communication of relationships that cannot be successfully communicated by words or mathematical notation alone.[1]

Silver[5] balances this tendency to polarize the argument of subjectivity versus technical skill in education. He focuses upon the often overlooked ability to represent and develop thought through visual forms. He provides many examples of instances demonstrated by children's drawings which show that the medium is instrumental in gaining conceptual understanding. He proposes that graphic symbols can take over some of the functions of verbal language symbols in the thinking of language-impaired children. In one series of paintings a child demonstrated that he had gained an understanding of the concepts of verticality and horizontality without instruction. Experiences which the child could not verbalize, but could think about whilst painting his pictures, offered the opportunity for self-correction and observation which direct technical teaching does not allow.

Clearly 'graphicacy' hints at aspects of human intelligence relevant to our understanding of 'design abilities'. However it is inadequate to suppose that communication skills can be considered or taught independently of the perceptual reading and thinking aspects of the learning process. A holistic concept must be held in which equal emphasis is placed upon thought/perception, understanding, intellectual manipulation, and appropriate representation of non-verbal, non-numerical relationships and ideas.

A CAPACITY OF MIND

Archer [6] has attempted to define such a holistic concept of design education. He writes:

> by design education I mean making all children aware of the ideas and values and problems of the material world around them and helping them to achieve some competence in doing and making, judging and choosing, inventing and implementing. [He sees this process as] a fundamental capacity of mind equal in importance to the language capacity, that is exploited by designers but is part of everyday life.

Archer calls this capacity 'the capacity for imaging' and he describes it thus:

> Designers can conjure up in their mind's eye an image or system, can rotate and transform it, and make shrewd judgements, about its construction, practicability and worth.

It is a capacity which differs from abstract thinking, but this kind of thought can be externalized by means of drawings, diagrams and constructions. Archer terms this externalization 'modelling' and it relates to 'imaging' as language relates to abstract thinking. Archer believes that a deeper understanding of this mode of thought and its related forms of externalization will contribute to a strengthening of design education at all levels.

Much past and current written work helps to clarify and expand an emerging concept of these intrinsic aspects of design. For example Daley[7] asks:

> are the processes by which designers make their decisions susceptible to systematic examination? If so, what sort of examination? Are such processes conscious in all their facets? What precisely is the nature of the knowledge which designers have and use? What is the nature of the metaknowledge of such skills and practices to which design theorists aspire?

In attempting to develop answers to these questions, Daley proposes that an epistemological approach would seem to be the most appropriate one to take. It enables us to ask 'how' we understand what it is that we understand. This aspect of design theory, she maintains, is inseparable from design knowledge and processes. In developing her argument Daley proposes an explanation of 'mind' and 'consciousness' in which design processes lie outside the bounds of verbal description and allow the systematization of experience to occur in a non-verbal mode.

Non-verbal thought and perception

A considerable body of ideas and research exists which forms a generalized field of study of non-verbal thought, perception and communication. This work stems from a wide range of interests drawing in psychology, neurology, art, education and linguistics.

Ferguson[8] has attempted to demonstrate and clarify the nature of non-verbal thought processes by studying the practice of technologists and physical scientists since the Renaissance. He draws attention to the many drawings, pictures and books that have both recorded and stimulated technological developments. He also reviews the many graphic inventions (such as perspective drawing) that have served to systematize, communicate and thereby exchange non-verbal information. For example, Leonardo Da Vinci's sketch books contain whole series of drawings recording sequences of non-verbal thought in pictorial form. This mode of thinking Ferguson calls the 'non-scientific component of design' and he maintains that it has little educational status beyond the kindergarten.

Non-verbal, visual capacities and thought processes underlie developed abilities to read pictorial information: to understand, infer or deduce from visual cues. Support for the view that these capacities are innate aspects of cognition comes from many directions, and blurs the once sharp distinctions drawn between intelligent thought and sensory perceptions.

Bower[9] describes research work conducted in the field of psychology involving observations of new-born infants. The focus of interest in this particular instance relates to the capacities and developing abilities of young babies in the field of perceptual organization and integration. Evidence suggests that the first few months of life are a critical period for development and learning in perceptual abilities. During this time the perceptual system of the child becomes increasingly competent and at the same time is extremely susceptible to damage. For example, lack of environmental stimulation can damage irreparably the perceptual structure which is present at birth. Children born with correctable visual defects, such as cataracts, appear to make no use of the capacity to see after the condition has been corrected. In cases where vision had been established and used, temporary impairment during the first three years of life has been shown to result in a dramatic loss of capacity which is difficult to reverse. Further evidence suggests that a more destructive process may operate in people who have been blind from birth. Areas of the brain normally involved in vision may be taken over for other sensory functions. Once this has become established, these areas cannot be restored for vision, even if it is technically possible for sight to be restored to the individual.

Visual awareness and understanding of the structure of the world through this sensory channel therefore appears to be dependent upon a critical early period of development and learning. The nature of non-verbal thought remains difficult to examine, however, because of the difficulty of isolation from thought which is language-linked.

Cognitive modelling

Traditional views of learning as developed within academic psychology tend to see cognitive development in relation to the acquisition of verbal language symbols and speech. It is commonly held that sensory perception and concrete experience become less important in learning as the child acquires the verbal symbols which signify reality. This, it is believed, enables thought to proceed internally by abstract manipulation. Different theoretical positions claim varying degrees of emphasis for the role of sensory knowledge in this process. But generally it is assumed that verbal language is the primary element in cognitive development.

The development of spatial thinking and the acquisition of spatial 'languages' to progress and develop this mode of thought is an aspect of cognitive development which has received less attention. Blaut and Stea[10] attempt to explain the nature of this internal process in terms of mental representations of geographical space which they suggest can be thought of as 'hologram' models. The mental 'hologram' is constructed from the sensual and visual perception of information. The process of this construction is called 'cognitive mapping'. They write:

> we have reason to believe that they [cognitive maps] are evolutionary, adaptive and therefore pervasive, featuring in the spatial orientation of all humans and highly mobile animals, are learned but largely untaught, that they depend upon more than simple visual-motor co-ordination (since they also appear in the blind) that the capacity to utilise them develops with development of the organism, and they have a neurophysiological basis and that the neurophysiological basis is likely to be more strongly represented in one hemisphere of the brain than the other.

Similarly, Segel[11] proposes that the comprehension of the external world evolves through an active engagement with it. A consequence of this engagement is an internal construction or mental representation. He argues that comprehension of pictures is analogous to reading the printed word and that the principal mechanism underlying each skill is the process of transformation.

Designerly ways of thinking

Attempts to define the intrinsic value of design education relate to these connected processes of:

(a) perception, construction and comprehension of visual/sensory representations;

(b) their transformation into an external manifestation.

Cross[12] argues that this thought process distinguishes the area of design from other areas such as science and the humanities. He maintains that design values are thus derived from its peculiar 'ways of knowing' and thinking and that these ways rest upon the manipulation of non-verbal codes in the material culture:

> these codes translate messages either way between concrete objects and abstract requirements; they facilitate the constructive, solution-focused thinking of the designer in the same way that the other (verbal and numerical) codes facilitate analytic, problem-focused thinking; they are probably the most effective means of tackling the characteristically ill-defined problems of planning, designing and inventing new things.

Connections between inventing, producing/making and thinking and their relationship with non-verbal codes or 'languages', begin to define a mode of thought within a cultural context which deserves greater clarity and educational attention. Design processes clearly are emerging as aspects of human 'mind' concerned with a particular dimension of understanding and possessing related and distinguished media for thought and communication.

TWO SIDES OF THE BRAIN

Our understanding of many of these cognitive capabilities has been enhanced significantly during the past ten or twenty years by experiments and reflection in the fields of the neurosciences. In particular there has been a series of investigations involving 'split-brain' patients who have had the two halves of their brains surgically disconnected [commissurotomy].[13, 14]

These experiments have shown that quite distinct differences exist between the cognitive functions of the two cerebral hemispheres. In particular the right hemisphere functioning abilities have been shown to play an important and specialized role in visual, spatial, non-verbal and constructional tasks such as arranging, building and drawing. The left hemisphere functioning abilities demonstrate a specialization in verbal language functions.

Reviewing the evidence

In a wide review of the extensive studies and investigations involving brain-injured patients, commissurotomy (split-brain) patients and normal subjects, Bradshaw and Nettleton[15] discuss the difficulties involved in considering hemispheric differences simply as a verbal/non-verbal dichotomy. Although all the evidence points to minimal language ability of right hemisphere functioning, it also shows that the right hemisphere is far from uncomprehending or unresponsive to auditory stimuli, including speech. The right hemisphere is seen to have considerable receptive capacities for speech even though it has little command of speech for articulation. Right hemisphere superiority in comprehension of acoustic stimuli is recognized in areas of discrimination and judgement involving:

(a) pitch;
(b) harmony;
(c) intensity;
(d) timbre;
(e) musical chords;
(f) melody;
(g) environmental sounds;
(h) non-verbal vocalizations (eg whistling);
(i) sonar signals;
(j) emotional tones;
(k) intonation patterns.

Likewise, left hemisphere functioning is demonstrably not limited to verbal language functions. Order, sequence and rhythm, reading and transcribing musical notation and other abstract symbolic representation, as well as co-ordinated and integrated motor control, are all aspects of musical performance which implicate left hemisphere functioning abilities. The verbal/non-verbal dichotomy is thus further confused by the recognition that the right hemisphere is not always – or even solely – responsible for musical ability, but rather that both hemispheres participate in musical functions. A 'synthesis' in performance is thus suggested.

Nebes's investigations[16] similarly distinguish left/right differences other than those which the verbal/non-verbal dichotomy can contain. Tests in which the subjects were required to complete designs from partial patterns (e.g. completing an arc of a circle to make a full circle) showed a right hemisphere superiority on gestalt perception. The left hemisphere was shown to be superior in tasks which involve isolating shapes from an irrelevant background, demonstrating an advantage in conceptual discrimination. Other gestalt tests have demonstrated that the right hemisphere has a greater ability to perceive accurately and remember stimuli which cannot be easily labelled, or which are too complex or similar to distinguish between with words. Using commissurotomy patients, Levy, Trevarthen and Sperry[17] tested a variety of perceptual functions involving recognition of photographs of faces, ambiguous solid black figures, line drawings of familiar items and patterns of squares and crosses. Their summary states: 'Stimuli having no verbal labels stored in long term memory and which are resistant to feature analysis were found to be extremely difficult for the left hemisphere to identify.'

Modes of thought

Generally the findings of the experimental work indicated that the two hemispheres were able to process conflicting information simultaneously and independently in two differing styles. Levy, Agresti and Sperry[18] suggest that:

> the mute (right) hemisphere is specialised for gestalt perception, being primarily a synthesist in dealing with information input. The speaking, major hemisphere in contrast seems to operate in a more logical, analytic, computer-like fashion [and] the findings suggest that a possible reason for cerebral lateralisation in man is a basic incompatibility of language functions on the one hand and synthetic perceptual functions on the other.

These findings indicate a deeper conceptual or structural dichotomy underlying the simpler verbal/visuospatial distinctions of hemispheric differences. Dissatisfaction with the verbal/spatial dichotomy, therefore, has led to attempts to distinguish the characteristics of hemispheric differences in more comprehensive terms. Bogen[19] writes: 'the right hemisphere recognises stimuli (including words), apposes or collects data and while receiving the very same stimuli as the other hemisphere, is often arriving at different results.' Citing Teuber,[20] Bogen agrees that this phenomenon can be credited to different *modes* of organization and processing of information within the two hemispheres. In other words, each hemisphere employs a mode of thinking (in the disconnected condition) which differs in nature from the other. Bogen names these the *appositional* and *propositional* modes of thinking and the implication is made that in the normal brain, both these modes are available.

Propositional and appositional modes

The term 'propositional' describes the sequential analytical and predominantly abstract kinds of mental functioning ascribed to left hemisphere capabilities. The term arises from a background of thought based upon empirical evidence (such as split-brain data) which attempts to understand the complex nature of the differing capacities of the cerebral hemispheres. Is there an innate biological mechanism existing only in the left hemisphere which gives it an advantage in processing verbal information? Does this mechanism also exist in the right hemisphere? If so, why is it so unequally developed in the hemispheres? Is development unequal or are there different kinds of development?

Bogen's[19] contribution to the debate is an attempt to interpret the evidence in a way which structures the left/right dichotomy into different ways of thinking. Within this dichotomy an 'appositional' mode of thinking (associated with right hemisphere function) assumes an equal emphasis and importance with the 'propositional' mode of thinking which is traditionally recognized as being a left hemisphere function. In the field of neurology, Bogen summarizes the important

Table 11.1 *Dichotomies with lateralization suggested*

Jackson (1864)	Expression	Perception
Jackson (1874)	Audio-articular	Retino-ocular
Jackson (1876)	Propositioning	Visual imagery
Weisenburg and McBride (1935)	Linguistic	Visual/kinesthetic
Anderson (1951)	Storage	Executive
Humphrey and Zangwill (1951)	Symbolic/ propositional	Visual/imaginative
McFie and Piercy (1952)	Education of relations	Education of correlates
Milner (1958)	Verbal	Perceptual/non-verbal
Semmes, Weinstein, Ghent and Teuber (1960)	Discrete	Diffuse
Zangwill (1961)	Symbolic	Visuospatial
Hecaen, Ajuriaguerra and Angelergues (1963)	Linguistic	Preverbal
Bogen and Gazzaniga (1965)	Verbal	Visuospatial
Levy, Agresti and Sperry (1968)	Logical/analytic	Synthetic/perceptual
Bogen (1969)	Propositional	Appositional

distinctions which have contributed to the debate on the left/right dichotomy. He places 'propositional' and 'appositional' within this dichotomy, but his terms encompass all the previous distinctions which have been made (see Table 11.1). Bogen further supports his hypothesis by drawing attention to the many dichotomies of dual thought processes which have been recognized and defined in fields other than neurology (see Table 11.2).

Table 11.2 *Dichotomies without reference to lateralization*

C.S. Smith	Atomistic	Gross
Price	Analytic/reductionist	Synthetic/concrete
Wilder	Numerical	Geometric
Head	Symbolic/systematic	Perceptual/non-verbal
Goldstein	Abstract	Concrete
Ruesch	Digital/discursive	Analogic/eidetic
Bateson and Jackson	Digital	Analogic
J.Z. Young	Abstract	Map-like
Pribram	Digital	Analogic
W. James	Differential	Existential
Spearman	Education of relations	Education of correlates
Hobbes	Directed	Free/unordered
Freud	Secondary process	Primary process
Pavlov	Second signalling	First signalling
Sechenov (Luria)	Successive	Simultaneous
Levi-Strauss	Positive	Mythic
Bruner	Rational	Metaphoric
Akhilinanda	Buddi	Manas
Radhakrishnan	Rational	Integral

Creativity and problem-solving

This tendency for each hemisphere to specialize in certain functions and thinking styles is thought by Bogen and Bogen[21] to be of adaptive value in evolutionary terms. It is suggested that a more fundamental function than speech or language is served by this duality, and that is the need and ability to solve problems. Viewed in this context, the specialization of the hemispheres in different modes of thought greatly increases flexibility and creativity when both are available.

The Bogens' argument on this aspect of cognitive behaviour echoes many points which have been raised and discussed by many eminent and creative people in other contexts. Henri Poincaré, Albert Einstein, Henry Moore and Stephen Spender, amongst many others, have each described their own creative activities in ways which indicate substantial degrees of interhemispheric communication, although they do not express it in these terms.[22] The Bogens' suggestion implies that creative solving of problems is a natural cognitive function involving hemispheric interaction. They suggest that if this function is not present in normal people there may be some obvious explanations for its absence. For example, there may be a deficiency in technical competence in a suitable medium – in the case of literacy or mathematics this may be the lack of a propositional skill. Conversely, in the cases of people who have developed proficiency in propositional skills (such as technical drawing, writing or music) deficiencies may exist in the demonstrable lack of the innovative and informative values of appositional modes of thought.

These deficiencies may be the result of genetic inadequacies, or inadequate environmental exposure necessary for the development of the possible potential. Sperry,[23] writing on the same topic, explains this lack of function in terms of a lack of structural (neurological) development within the brain:

> many elements deeper in the brain centres must discharge only in very special activities and if these activities are not exercised – especially during maturational stages when the neurons seem to be particularly dependent on use – the neuron types involved may regress leaving profound functional deficiencies in the integrative machinery.

The term 'culturally disadvantaged' has been used to refer to people whose propositional potential has remained undeveloped for lack of proper schooling. Bogen and Bogen[21] suggest, on the basis of neurological data which provides evidence for the existence of an appositional mode of thought, that it is also a term which can be applied to people whose education consists mainly of reading, writing and arithmetic. This is because education which is predominantly and emphatically in this mode results in a lack of appositional development. They maintain that there must be a free exchange and interaction between propositional and appositional modes of thinking. The difficulty as they see it is that there exists an inbuilt antagonism between analysis (left hemisphere function) and intuition (right hemisphere function). They write: 'Certain kinds of left hemisphere activity may directly suppress certain kinds of right hemisphere activity. Or they may prevent access to the left hemisphere of the products of right hemisphere activity.' Clearly formal education has a direct and important role to play in ensuring the achievement of development in both aspects of thought in the individual.

COGNITIVE DEVELOPMENT AND INTEGRATION

Gazzaniga and LeDoux[14] further develop the argument which places emphasis upon the co-operation of the hemispheres in the normal brain.

Central to their argument is a rejection of the 'specialization' theory which they believe has resulted in the popularization of the left/right dichotomy in a misleading and divisive way. In their view, the argument that each hemisphere is 'specialized', i.e. that it is neurologically 'set' at birth to develop a particular style of thinking, cannot be sustained by neurological evidence. This is because implicit in this argument is the assumption that the type of neural organization that underlies the unique functions of one hemisphere is incompatible with that sustaining the cognitive style of the other. Both hemispheres, however, have demonstrated fundamental similarities in cognitive repertoires (e.g. analysis and synthesis, albeit in differing styles). Perhaps more significantly, the idea that each hemisphere is structurally specialized for a particular mode does not explain how only one hemisphere can develop to sustain *both* styles of thinking when damage is incurred early in life.

They suggest that the human brain is organized so that two potentially independent mental systems exist side by side. Each possesses its own capacities for learning, emoting, thinking and acting, and in the normal brain these independent spheres work together. The demonstrable differences which exist in the hemispheres of the adult brain are explained in the context of the nature of the co-operation which occurs between them.

Gazzaniga and LeDoux claim that right hemisphere advantages are associated with *manual* activities in the perception or production of spatial relationships. They call these functions *manipulospatial*, and they argue that these functions are in that part of the right hemisphere whose corresponding part in the left mediates language. Hence the left hemisphere's language functions are developed at the expense of its potential manipulospatial functions. Further, they claim that the right hemisphere's advantage in this function is by default and in consequence of left hemisphere language development.

The manipulospatial function

This notion of a manipulospatial function which has a neurological basis in the right hemisphere and is associated with appositional modes of thinking, would appear to be central to any justification for the inclusion of design activities in the curriculum of general education. Briefly, it is the idea of a neural/cognitive mechanism which transcends the simple notions of perceptions and motor functions, since it is neither of these *per se*. Rather it is the mechanism by which a spatial concept is mapped into the perceptual and motor activities involved in drawing, arranging, constructing and otherwise manipulating items so that the parts are in an appropriate relationship to one another.

Gibson[24] describes in depth an aspect of what Gazzaniga and LeDoux term the 'manipulospatial function'. He refers to it as 'active touch' and what he describes are the active exploratory manipulations involved in the understanding and evaluation of complex spatial/tactile stimuli. Gibson distinguishes clearly between 'touch' as a receptive, passive sense – being touched by/with something – and 'touch' as an exploratory activity in which the fingers produce the stimulus. What happens at the fingertips depends upon the movements which are made and also upon the object being touched. These movements are not the kind which are usually considered as responses as they do not modify the environment but only the stimulus coming from the environment. They enhance some features of the potential stimulation and reduce others. They explore rather than perform. Gibson suggests therefore that these movements of the fingers are like the movements of the eyes. He believes that they are a tactile scanning process analogous to visual scanning. Moreover, active touch cannot be classified as a single sense. It provides a definite channel of perception of information about the external environment and such use of the hands involves the play of input coming from the whole skeletomuscular system. Manipulospatial functions/mechanisms are therefore the means by which active exploration and alteration of the environment occurs by using the hands.

However, as Gazzaniga and LeDoux point out, it is misleading to consider appositional modes of thought as exclusively right-brain processes located structurally within this hemisphere. Unlike the related mechanisms for language, which seem to be concentrated in one half of the brain, perceptual, spatial and semantic abilities seem to imply an involvement of both hemispheres in the functioning mechanism.

Integrated thought

Investigations by De Renzi[25] led him to the conclusion that *elementary* spatial abilities appear to be confined to a focal area of the right hemisphere. Thus the neural substrata underlying the processing of perceptual cues is represented in this section of the brain. However, the left hemisphere becomes involved as soon as the integration of changing perceptual cues is required. Consequently the superiority of the right hemisphere in spatial tasks subsides as the task becomes more complex and demands spatial abilities which go beyond the perceptual level (e.g. in conceptual tasks or memory tasks). De Renzi's evidence leads him to conclude that the capacity to imagine space is dependent upon neural substrata which are asymmetrically represented between the two hemispheres.

The implication of the 'language mode' of thinking in the solution of spatial tasks has been indicated in further studies. Investigations into tasks of visual and tactile memory for position/orientation in space[26] failed to find differences between patients with left hemisphere damage and patients with right hemisphere damage. Harris[27] makes the point that language modes are not usually suitable for tasks requiring spatial analysis. However some spatial problems can be solved in non-spatial ways. Words which act as 'localizers' can aid in the location of objects. So too do systems which provide 'learned strategies' for acting upon. For example many problems contain analytical as well as synthetic elements requiring the mental rotation of images or the synthesizing or integration of information from different spatial locations (such as the co-ordination of perspectives or problems of conservation).

Franco and Sperry[28] provide an interesting attempt to analyse the 'intuitive' processing of geometric relations. Commissurotomy patients, hemispherectomy (removal of one hemisphere) patients and normal subjects were given a series of tests. These were cross-modal, visuotactile tests involving different levels and kinds of geometrical discrimination. The design of the tests distinguished between Euclidean, affine, projective and topological space. Their findings suggest a right hemisphere advantage or superiority and differences in the left hemisphere capacities, correlating with the four different types of geometry. Franco and Sperry refer to the observations of Piaget and Inhelder[29] that children are able to discriminate between geometrical forms at pre-school age while they are still incapable of verbalizing the discriminating features involved. Similarly, in adult processing Franco and Sperry claim that geometrical properties and theorems can be understood intuitively long before a verbal expression is possible.

> An active interaction of the two hemispheres during processing of geometric problems is implied and a similar interhemispheric integration would seem reasonable also for other cerebral activities involving spatial intuitions and their linguistic expression.

Integrated behaviour and the media of thought

Research investigation such as that reviewed above has developed during the past decade and clearly adds a new dimension to the theories of cognitive development upon which much present-day practice in education rests. In attempting to consider the nature of new theories which fully acknowledge appositional modes of thought, Marks[30] suggests that central to any such theory will be the importance of brain functioning in which will feature internal representations and encoding of information in one or more languages of thought. To support this hypothesis, Marks points to evidence provided by split-brain investigations which emphasizes the normality of the everyday behaviour of the patients. Under controlled laboratory conditions, split-brain patients are denied the use of mechanisms which serve to unite conscious states even in normal people. Under normal conditions those mechanisms are available to them through their interaction with the environment. Some patients do exhibit abnormal behaviour in everyday situations, but it is claimed that the integration of their overall behaviour is not affected. Often the abnormality demonstrates *how* the integration is occurring. For example, some patients demonstrate intermanual conflict, i.e. lack of control of the left hand, or correction of the right hand by the left (situations where right hemisphere dominance occurs) or being slapped awake by the left hand. These are failures of behavioural integration outside the experimental situation and often occur to provoke or 'cue' in the correct behavioural response. These 'failures' are themselves mechanisms for the integration of behaviour and thinking. Marks therefore considers *integrated behaviour* to be an important criterion in any concept of consciousness.

Gazzaniga and LeDoux[14] provide a very good basis for this argument, maintaining that the two hemispheres function together as a single unit, and that 'cross-cueing' strategies play an important role in this integration. It is a phenomenon in which each mental system regards the behaviour of the other, and the two systems communicate through behavioural cueing strategies. This is most dramatically demonstrated in split-brain experimental situations but it is suggested that normal behaviour uses the same strategies. For example, the normally dominant language system occupying the attentional mechanism can be engaged in such a way that information perceived in the right-brain mode can bypass its process and become stored without the verbal system noting it. A common experience is being able to find one's way home from a new place, even though the verbal system was engaged in conversation during the initial experience of the new route. If asked to describe the route the verbal system could not do it, but the critical roads are recognized and correct choices are made when the experience is repeated.

CONCLUSION

Design activities within the school curriculum provide learning situations which can be recognized as crucial to cognitive development. Many theories of cognitive development indicate that thought is progressed, externalized and directed by the acquisition of a suitable 'language' medium. Although attention has traditionally been focused upon the role of verbal language in this process, the relationship between thought, language and interaction with the environment is now becoming sufficiently explicit to allow serious questioning as to whether verbal language is the only medium which can be instrumental in the progression of particular thought modes. Research work being conducted particularly in the neurosciences is revealing the characteristic features of an appositional mode of thinking which is clearly implicated in design thought and behaviour. Media appropriate to the progression and development of this style of thought might therefore be looked upon as 'languages' of thought. They are essential means for the encouragement of intellectual development.

REFERENCES

1. Balchin, W. G. V. and Coleman, A., 'Graphicacy Should be the Fourth Ace in the Pack', *Times Educational Supplement* (5 November 1965).

2. Department of Education and Science, *The School Curriculum*, HMSO (March 1981), p. 10.

3. Bloomer, C. M., *Principles of visual perception*, Van Nostrand Reinhold (1976).

4. Gardner, H., *Artful Scribbles: the Significance of Children's Drawings*, Jill Norman, London (1980).

5. Silver, R. A., *Developing Cognitive and Creative Skills through Art*, University Park Press, Baltimore (1978).

6. Archer, L. B., 'The Minds Eye', *The Designer* (January 1980).

7. Daley, J., 'Design Creativity and the Understanding of Objects', *Design Studies*, vol. 3, no. 3 (July 1982), pp. 133-7.

8. Ferguson, E. S., 'The Mind's Eye: nonverbal thought in technology', *Science*, vol. 197 (1977), p. 827.

9. Bower, T., *The Perceptual World of the Child*, Fontana/Open Books (1977).

10. Blaut, J. M. and Stea, D., 'Studies in Geographic Learning', *Annals Assoc. American Geography*, vol. 61 (1971), p. 387.

11. Segel, S. J., *Imagery: Current Cognitive Approaches*, Academic Press, London (1971).

12. Cross, N., 'Designerly Ways of Knowing', *Design Studies*, vol. 3, no. 4 (1982), pp. 221-7.

13. Gazzaniga, M. S., *The Bisected Brain*, Appleton Century Crofts, New York, NY (1970).

14. Gazzaniga, M. S., and LeDoux, J. E., *The Integrated Mind*, Plenum Press, London (1978).

15. Bradshaw, J. L. and Nettleton, W. C. 'The Nature of Hemispheric Specialisation in Man', *The Behavioural and Brain Sciences*, vol. 4 (1981), pp. 51-91.

16. Nebes, R. D., 'Direct Examination of Cognitive Function in the Right and Left Hemispheres', in M. Kingsbourne (ed.), *Asymmetrical Functions of the Brain*, CUP Cambridge (1978), pp. 99–140.

17. Levy, J., Trevarthen, C. and Sperry, R. W., 'Perception of Bilateral Chimeric Figures', *Brain*, vol. 95 (1972), pp. 66–78.

18. Levy, J., Agresti, J. and Sperry, R. W. 'Differential Perceptual Capabilities in Major and Minor Hemispheres', *Proc. Nat. Acad. Sci.*, vol. 61, no. 1151 (1968).

19. Bogen, J. E., 'The Other Side of the Brain; II: an appositional mind', *Bulletin of the Los Angeles Neurological Societies*, vol. 34, no. 3 (1969), pp. 135–62.

20. Teuber, H. C., 'Postscript: Some Needed Revisions of the Classical Views of Agnosia', *Neuropsychologia*, vol. 3 (1965), pp. 317–78.

21. Bogen, J. E. and Bogen G. M., 'The Other Side of the Brain; III: the corpus callosum and creativity', *Bulletin of the Los Angeles Neurological Societies*, vol. 34, no. 4 (1969), pp. 191–217.

22. Ghiselin, B. (ed.), *The Creative Process*, Mentor Books, University of California Press, CA (1952).

23. Sperry, R. W., 'Embryongenesis of Behavioural Nerve Nets', in Denaan, R. I. and Ursprung, H. (eds), *Organogenesis*, Holt Rinehart and Winston, New York, NY (1965).

24. Gibson, J. J., 'Observations on Active Touch', *Psychological Rev.*, vol. 69 (1962), pp. 477–91.

25. De Renzi, E. 'Hemispheric Asymmetry as Evidenced by Spatial Disorders', in Kingsbourne, M. (ed.) *Asymmetrical Functions of the Brain*, CUP, Cambridge (1978), pp. 49–85.

26. De Renzi, E., Faglioni, P. and Scotti, G., 'Impairment of Memory for Position Following Brain Damage', *Cortex*, vol. 5 (1969), pp. 274–84.

27. Harris, L. J., 'Sex Differences in Spatial Ability: possible environmental, genetic and neurological factors', in Kingsbourne, M. (ed.) *Asymmetrical Functions of the Brain*, CUP, Cambridge (1978), pp. 405–527.

28. Franco, L. and Sperry, R. W., 'Hemisphere Lateralisation for Cognitive Processing of Geometry', *Neuropsychologia*, vol. 15 (1977), pp. 107–114.

29. Piaget, J. and Inhelder, B., *The Child's Conception of Space*, Routledge and Kegan Paul, London (1967).

30. Marks, C. E., *Commissurotomy, Consciousness and Unity of Mind*, MIT Press, London (1981).

12 *Educational aims in the technological society*

● B. K. Down

EDITORS' INTRODUCTION

Starting from three categories of aims of education, and a discussion of the nature of technology and of a technological society, Bernard Down argues for the primacy of an understanding and critical awareness of the social issues of technology. (We have omitted the section on the nature of technology which has been dealt with earlier in the Reader.)

INTRODUCTION

In a previous article I concluded by asking what were the aims of CDT.[1] The difficulties to which I drew attention are made worse to a stranger to the CDT scene who hears enthusiastic pleas being made for education for the technological society through computers and the like, without mention being made of the specific role of CDT. Such a stranger may indeed discover that a number of many so-called CDT workshops appear to differ very little from the school craft shops of the past. He recognizes however that the subject has become upgraded in status partly because of its association with technology but he may not be clear exactly what this is. He is therefore concerned with two major questions:

1. What are the aims of education in a technological society?
2. What contribution does CDT make of such aims?

In order to come to grips with these questions I intend to examine the nature of educational aims, the distinguishing marks of technology and the unique features and problems constituent of the technological society.

THE NATURE OF EDUCATIONAL AIMS

Aims denote intentions or policies, with the possibility of either success or failure. There is always a danger that statements of educational aims will be regarded as platitudes or will operate at such a level of generality that everyone will tend to agree with them, though they may be interpreted in various ways. Everyone wants children to be morally good, but everyone does not want the same thing. Similarly an education in or for technology may be widely supported as an aim but not in the same way by every one, therefore it is important that the aims are given enough detailed exemplification and precision so that their unique character is clear.

For such statements to be effective there must also be a general commitment to the aims and a will to implement them. Research on areas such as mixed ability has shown that where individual teachers disagree with the general school policy, their apparent conformity can conceal different attitudes.

The concept of the hidden curriculum makes the same point. It may be the stated school policy to seek to get all pupils to think for themselves – but some teachers by their general attitudes and authoritarian methods may fail to support this policy. Even if the teachers never apparently think about the aims, nevertheless their practice presupposes particular intentions or attitudes, for teaching must logically be an intentional activity. School policies can only work if staff are prepared to modify their own activities in the light of them. However, some educational aims are of such a general character that they can only succeed if the whole of society supports them. Aims denote priorities, the concentration of effort on the achievement of certain values and a long-term concern with improving pupils in some stated direction, therefore, educational success depends upon the general conditions of society. If we genuinely want individuals to think for themselves then we must be prepared to support individuality and to accept the social consequences of nonconformity.

It is important to make these points because if we want children to be equipped for the technological society, then the school must be backed financially in its provision of appropriate materials, and children must be helped generally, through the mass media and in the home, to have the necessary experiences. Similarly within the school, as it has been realized that language is too important a matter to be left solely to the English teacher, so it will have to be realized that the same may be true about technology. Furthermore this cannot just be recognized at the head-teacher level commitment must be general for the aims to be achieved. This may require changes in the core curriculum, changes in school architecture and changes in teaching organization, and commitment by all involved staff.

Historically there have been three main categories of aims: (1) liberal or intrinsic; (2) child-centred or individualist; and (3) social.

1. *Liberal or intrinsic* aims have, since Greek times, stressed the pursuit of knowledge for its own sake and rejected the idea of activities taught for their usefulness or as means to extrinsic ends. This view has tended to create a hierarchy of activities with the arts being regarded highly and craft or technology being ascribed lowly status. Craft was regarded as largely vocational and practical (for the Greeks this meant using the body rather than the mind) and lacking a coherent structure or form of theoretical knowledge. On this view a technological education could not be liberal.

2. *Child-centred or individualist* aims may not be explicitly stated, for they are concerned with the development of the individual and his needs, interests and happiness, as he may see them. Such aims are often closely associated with creativity, problem-solving and project work where openness is the main feature and the end cannot easily be determined. With its use of problem-solving some writers have seen CDT as operating with a process model of the curriculum and a form of child-centredness.[2]

3. *Social* aims stress the importance of schools in shaping society. Some social aims have been *conservative* being primarily concerned with creating obedient citizens – good Christians or communists. In contrast, some teachers have attempted to use their position to create attitudes of *reform* or radical change in society. A more *democratic* view has supported aims concerned with individual autonomy and integrity based on rationality and social and moral responsibility. It is the democratic view of education that has modified the traditional liberal elitism. While the conservative may seek an unquestioning acceptance of the technological society, the modern liberal educator, pointing to the narrowness of a technology that is concerned with the means-to-ends and mere efficiency stresses the need for wholeness and a general education. Liberal education and social democratic aims are concerned to develop an individual who is both able to understand technology and its related disciplines and can evaluate its moral, social and political effects [...]

THE TECHNOLOGICAL SOCIETY

In short the technological society seems qualitatively different from previous societies. It is grounded in modern science and technology and as such is secular, materialist and optimist in character, being concerned with efficiency and the conquest of nature. On the one hand, it holds the promise of alleviating poverty, starvation and human suffering. It opens doors which we can choose to go through and in this way gives us greater power and freedom of choice than we have had before. On the other hand, we cannot leave its various developments to chance or we will find that the machine has come to rule man and that man is no longer free. Each decision we make lessens our future freedom of action, for its effects seem global and almost irreversible.

EDUCATIONAL AIMS AND THE TECHNOLOGICAL SOCIETY

This brings us to the question of what role education has in the preparation of the young for the technological society. Certain things will now have become clear. We cannot isolate children from technological change and its consequences. At the same time it would be foolish to aim at social conformity and the uncritical acceptance of technology. It is difficult to assume that traditional religious and moral values are not being challenged by the technological emphasis on the means-to-ends efficiency. It is also important to establish that if technological innovation and socially important design require public debate, then the school must cater for political education within a participatory democracy. Design and technological awareness must be part of that political education; indeed these are but elements of a general education required for life in society. To take the subject of geography, design and technology must, in some senses, form an important part of that subject. Think only of discussions about urban and motorway planning, industrial change, energy resources and technology in the developing countries and you must realize the importance of geographical knowledge. The same must be said about many other subjects. Preparation for the technological society cannot be left entirely with departments of technological or science subjects.

In this context the traditional liberal criticism of a technological training cannot be ignored. Blanshard argues that a man may be technically proficient but remain uneducated – ignorant, bigoted and provincial. He may even enjoy solving puzzles about how iron or hydrogen behaves when compressed or frozen or heated to a million degrees, or enjoy harnessing the more mulish forms of matter and make them work for us. But even at this level he is essentially pushing physical things about, and not experiencing a liberation of the spirit which liberal education seeks to achieve:

> The ideal technologist is an infinitely subtle brain at work on an infinitely subtle puzzle. He needs curiosity and endurance; but any appreciation of

human goodness or artistic beauty, of what is funny or tragic or sublime, any sense for music or religion or justice would be for him, simply as a technologist, superfluous baggage.[3]

Of course Blanshard is just pointing to the danger of a blinkered technological education, but it need not be like that, I have argued for the need to relate technology to moral and political education and a long time ago A. N. Whitehead[4] pointed out that the antithesis between technical and liberal education can be reconciled. We cannot afford the mutual incomprehension and hostility between the science and art cultures that C. P. Snow found.[5]. We all live in the technological society and we must all be educated for it. The products of technology can be used in music (with music centres and electronic keyboards) or English (with word-processors), and indeed there are few subjects that may not use the computer. It is essential to remove the fears the uninitiated sometimes experience and render the young competent in the tools of the new technology. In this way technology pervades the arts; and the arts – or at least some of the arts – can contribute to our understanding of the technological society. The virtue of the liberal aims is that they draw attention to the needs of man to be truly human in this context. H. S. Broudy[6] looks both to society and education to help the individual find the power, the freedom and the individuality to render himself morally responsible, socially significant and aesthetically aware. For this, education must include a knowledge of the workings of the technological society – industrially, commercially and politically.

One of the key issues that rises here is how to prepare children for work in the technological society – an issue raised by the great debate about education. The problem is complex[7]. It must be acceptable to give children an understanding of the general factors affecting industrial development and the availability of jobs in society. It is also important to have careers advice and careers education in school. But vocational training in terms of training for specific jobs or an education that is limited by choice of career, cannot be acceptable educationally especially in the kind of changing situation I have described. At this moment many jobs are fragmented, repetitive and boring, requiring little education for them. In the future it is suggested that only a minority in the manufacturing industries may require highly developed and analytical technological positions, while the rest might find themselves replaced by robots. Hence a high standard of general education or even of technological training will not be necessary for the majority as work preparation. Somehow we have to be prepared to give up the Protestant work ethic and find a substitute for work as a central force in determining our social identity. We have to prepare children for a world without work.[8] Our educational aims must therefore be directed beyond work.

EDUCATIONAL AIMS AND CDT

The foregoing arguments have suggested that the first preparation for a technological society is moral, political and social education, conceived as an open approach to the question of what kind of society do we want. I have argued that technological awareness, which is a condition for such preparation, requires social knowledge rather than practical skills. This is how the DES booklet *Technology in Schools* [HMSO, 1982] interprets the phrase 'technological awareness' (p. 15) and similar considerations are offered in the APU booklet *Understanding Design and Technology* [APU, 1981] (pp. 6–7).

For many writers training children in technology means simply training children in the use of computers or giving them an understanding of and practice in electronics. In neither of these areas does CDT have the monopoly. Clearly an education for technology must involve technology across the curriculum.

What then should be the position of CDT? It must be noted that the subject I am focusing on is craft, design and technology and not technology. Both craft and design have something to offer for the technological society. M. W. Thring in considering a future in which robots are developed to do all the routine repetitive subhuman work, argues that our education system must be adaptable to cater for the self-fulfilment of individuals. 'An entirely new system of education will have to be offered, so that a range of creative arts and crafts are taught which people can enjoy doing for their own sake.'[9] Craft, then, has a part to play in our homes at the creative as well as the do-it-yourself level. In this respect craft may be compared to music, painting or literature as a source of enjoyment for many children and adults.

The phrase 'design awareness', as we have seen, is sometimes used to describe a general social attitude towards issues of social planning. Such a notion implies that beyond every individual act of pupil design work, there must be an attempt to develop aesthetic sensibility and a general understanding of design criteria. Getting children to design products is partly an attempt to get them to think about the making of material objects and to consider the various technical and aesthetic factors that are involved, and it is partly an attempt to encourage them to be creatively involved in some craft or technological planning. For this they require some prior knowledge of the material being used as well as the appropriate skills to be employed in the making of the object. One principle of such teaching is that since there is insufficient time for a logical and sequential course in all the necessary skills and knowledge, children must learn how to find things out for themselves. This principle, encapsulated in the phrase 'learning how to think rather than what to think' – is sometimes supported as a necessary procedure to be adopted in a world of great change. As a preliminary to making, involving some research and creative planning, designing has its place, and it may, as *Technology in Schools* indicates, involve some technological work.

This brings us to the element of technology in CDT. We have noted throughout that one may manipulate technological hardware and even innovate in technology, without supportive scientific explanation of why something is happening, though more recent technology involves a closer relationship to science and maths. Sometimes it is said that there are four areas of technology that need to be taught in CDT – control, materials, energy and communications. What is learned within these areas can vary from concrete specifics to the abstract general. Energy may be exemplified in the various forms of propulsion or power that may be employed in specific products. It may also be quantified, measured and used in relation to theoretical problems. It is to be noted that the DES acknowledges a deep concern of CDT teachers that technology should involve practical activities in manipulating mechanical, electrical and related physical aspects of technology. There might be a place for a more theoretical course in technological analysis, involving studies in applied science and in the solving of theoretical problems related to, say, engineering, but such courses which would compete with subjects like physics at 'A' level, might only have minority interest.

The aims, then, of a technological education must be primarily that of preparing children, morally and politically, for understanding and being critically aware of the social issues of technology. Secondly it must involve learning how to employ technological devices, wherever appropriate. Thirdly, in relation to CDT, it must include some involvement in and understanding of the areas of technology that can be related to designing and making.

Such technological awareness would need to be taught through a concerted effort within school and an openness to public debate generally in society. But it could only be adequately catered for, by understanding and learning to operate technological tools and products. This can be done in several subjects.

In so far as CDT is a holistic subject weaving craft, design and technology into one piece, then it can never be regarded as solely technology. Technological concepts are taught operationally whenever an appropriate issue arises in design. Similarly the craft skills of wood and metal are taught whenever the occasion arises in the realization of the appropriate design product. On this view, technology is taught through the act of designing and making, in so far as tests of material efficiency are employed, considerations of specific types of energy are involved, control devices and methods, e.g. electronic devices, are used or computer graphics are utilized. But the emphasis is practical rather than theoretical: it involves the attempt to create a product and any research or theoretical analysis must be related to that end. With this emphasis, however, both design and technology may provide pivotal points whereby the student can be taken beyond some immediate process or product to an act of analysis and research in order to improve the design. Within an integrated curriculum involving team-teaching, such analyses and operational understanding can be developed further through teaching of a more scientific nature.

REFERENCES

1. 'Problem-Solving, CDT and Child-Centredness', *Studies in Design Education, Craft and Technology*, vol. 16, no. 1 pp. 38–43. [See Chapter 24.]
2. A. V. Kelly, 'CDT and the Curriculum', *Studies in Design Education, Craft and Technology*, vol. 13, no. 1 pp. 22–28.
3. B. Blanshard, *The Uses of a Liberal Education*, Alcove Press, 1974, p. 101.
4. A. N. Whitehead, *The Aims of Education*, Ernest Benn, 1962, pp. 66–92.
5. C. P. Snow, *The Two Cultures and a Second Look*, Cambridge University Press, 1963.
6. H. S. Broudy, 'Technology and Educational Values', in K. A. Strike and K. Egan, *Ethics and Educational Policy*, Routledge and Kegan Paul, 1978.
7. V. C. A. Wringe, 'Education, Schooling and the World of Work', *British Journal of Educational Studies*, vol. 29, no. 2, June 1981, pp. 123–37.
8. V. A. G. Watts, *Education, Unemployment and the Future of Work*, Open University Press, 1984.
9. M. W. Thring, 'Machines for a Creative Age', in N. Cross, D. Elliott and R. Roy, *Man-Made Futures*, Hutchinson Educational in association with the Open University Press., p. 305.

13 *Technological capability*

● P. Black and G. Harrison

EDITORS' INTRODUCTION

Professors Black and Harrison, in this extract from their pamphlet, translate general ideas on capability into specific activities in the classroom aimed at developing technological capability.

INTRODUCTION

If we want to know how we should educate children in and through technology, we must first answer two questions:

1. What is technology?
2. For what purposes should it play a part in children's education?

This chapter attempts to answer these questions. The argument is developed as follows:

(a) Section 1 attempts to define the essence of technology.
(b) Section 2 looks at human capability in more general terms.
(c) Section 3 sums up the argument with the concept of Task-Action-Capability.
(d) Section 4 gives examples of situations in which such capability can develop.

THE ESSENCE OF TECHNOLOGY

Technology is the practical method which has enabled us to raise ourselves above the animals and to create not only our habitats, our food supply, our comfort and our means of health, travel and communication, but also our arts – painting, sculpture, music and literature. These are the results of human capability for action. They do not come about by mere academic study, wishful thinking or speculation. Technology has always been called upon when practical solutions to problems have been called for. Technology is thus an essential part of human culture because it is concerned with the achievement of a wide range of human purposes.

In the mid 1960s, those wanting technology to play an important part in education asked 'What is technology?' The question was answered in the following way. 'Technology is a disciplined process using resources of materials, energy and natural phenomena to achieve human purposes.' This definition led to three complementary sets of educational aims:

1. To give children an *awareness* of technology and its implications as a resource for the achievement of human purpose, and of its dependence on human involvement in judgemental issues.
2. To develop in children, through personal experience, the *practical capability* to engage in technological activities.
3. To help children acquire the *resources* of knowledge and intellectual and physical skills which need to be called upon when carrying out technological activities.

However, the above definition and aims have not been totally accepted or understood. Some teachers have concentrated their effort on practical capability, to the neglect of other aspects. Others have emphasized the resources and given little attention to their use. Emphasis on its many harmful effects has called in question the value-free promotion of technology – thus exposing problems about aim 1. Such difficulties suggest that the definition and the aims need to be re-examined.

So, what are the questions which *should* be asked?

How do we describe, and educate our children for, those human activities which bring about change, enhance the environment, create wealth, produce food and entertainment, and generally get things done? What is the nature of capability in these activities, how can it be fostered and what kind of back-up knowledge and experience is needed? How can future citizens be better equipped to foresee consequences and make choices?

HUMAN CAPABILITY

First, let us consider a range of such activities which, although diverse, do perhaps have a common pattern. Then let us examine the implications for education and its opportunities and responsibilities for fostering such capability in young people.

Human capability lies at the heart of such diverse activities as:

   (a) creating a self-propelled flying machine;
   (b) composing a symphony;
   (c) writing and directing a television show;
   (d) organizing an office business system;
   (e) managing a mixed arable and livestock farm;
   (f) creating a three-dimensional mural for a public building.

The activities need not be on a grand scale. Capability is also called for in:

   (a) designing and building a garden shed;
   (b) writing and producing a sketch in a school revue;
   (c) setting up a system of domestic accounts;
   (d) maintaining a car or bicycle;
   (e) putting up shelves;
   (f) carving a piece of sculpture;
   (g) hanging wallpaper.

Large or small, these activities call for a variety of competencies which the capable person knits together in order to achieve success. Maintaining a motor car requires competence in mechanical and electrical fault-finding, in correct and skilful use of tools, in treatment and preservation of materials susceptible to corrosion, in manipulating heavy equipment with safety.

Similarly, setting lyrics to music calls for imagination and intuitive flair. It also calls for perception of meaning in words and in music and an ability to match one to the other. In addition to these imaginative and creative processes, the composer needs to have at his or her fingertips an understanding of harmony, melody, rhythm and structure.

A similar analysis could be made for all of the examples. They have a common pattern. Each requires:

   (a) application of personal driving qualities such as determination, enterprise, resourcefulness;
   (b) personal innovative powers of imagination, intuition and invention;
   (c) powers of observation and perception;
   (d) willingness to make decisions based both on logic and on intuition;
   (e) sensitivity to the needs being served, to the possible consequences, benign or harmful, of alternative solutions, to the values being pursued.

However, overlapping all these is the common necessity to possess a sound base of knowledge and both intellectual and physical skill appropriate to the job in hand. The shed builder must know about the treatment and processing of timber, about how to make effective connections between structural members and about principles of strength and weakness, rigidity and stability, weatherproofing and foundations. The composer needs to know the principles of harmony and rhythm and have the skill to perform on musical instruments. The office manager needs to know the principles of accounts and the techniques for management relevant to his or her business. The farmer needs to know about fertilizers, pesticides, basic medical treatment and the technical requirements of machinery, plant, equipment and building.

Thus the common pattern shows that full capability for personal action calls simultaneously for both action-based qualities and the resources of knowledge, skill and experience.

The first without the second may lead to frustrated, hyperactive, but ineffective individuals. The second without the first leads to individuals who are highly knowledgeable and skilled but who may be incapable of producing new solutions to problems.

This interaction between the *processes* of innovative activity and the *resources* being called upon is itself one of the key elements of successful human capability. It is a continuous engagement and negotiation between ideas and facts, guesswork and logic, judgements and concepts, determination and skill.

TASK-ACTION-CAPABILITY

If the nature of these personal human attributes which bring about a capability to engage in active tasks is becoming clearer, the second question remains to be answered. How do we educate our children with a view to maximizing their individual potential for what might be called 'Task-Action-Capability' (TAC)?

There are three dimensions to TAC which are amenable to educational development. Each might be considered central from particular and different points of view, but, nevertheless, each represents a personal attribute of direct practical value in the real world:

(a) *Resources* of knowledge, skill and experience which can be drawn upon, consciously or subconsciously, when involved in active tasks.
(b) *Capability* to perform, to originate, to get things done, to make and stand by decisions.
(c) *Awareness*, perception and understanding needed for making balanced and effective value judgments.

These three clearly interact. To develop capability and awareness, experience of tackling tasks is essential. Through such tasks we learn how to use and apply resources of knowledge and skill, for the mere possession of such resources does not imply or confer the ability to apply them. The relationship is mutual, for the needs of real tasks can provide a motive for acquiring new knowledge and skills or for consolidating those already learnt.

This mutual interaction between resources, and tasks chosen to develop capability and awareness is represented in Figure 13.1.

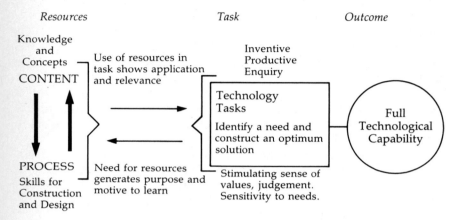

Figure 13.1   *A model of technology education*

TASKS FOR LEARNING

In the particular areas of engineering and design, where the concepts of science and technology play essential roles, the three dimensions of TAC become very obvious. Nevertheless, in order to be able to construct learning systems which will be effective in the overall development of TAC all three dimensions will need to be planned, interwoven and modulated to meet the needs which change with age, ability, interest and motivation. Three brief examples may help to illustrate this point.

Task 1   Moving loads up a long ramp

Thirteen-year-old children were given this task to help develop learning about technological concepts of energy (a *resource*).

They were given assorted motors, electricity supplies, gears, pulleys, wire and other raw material. By giving different briefs to different groups, recognizing diverse abilities, the children were faced with appropriately challenging opportunities to engage in inventive problem-solving (and so develop their process skills as another *resource*).

Between them they were expected to identify, use and compare three choices in transport technologies: the use of a locomotive with a self-contained power unit: electrical power delivered to a vehicle along wires; and power delivered to a vehicle mechanically by string.

The need to compare these led to the idea of power/weight ratios which in turn led to structural design concepts for the vehicles themselves. At this age the concepts could not be quantified except in general comparative terms. It was the beginning, however, of the development of all three dimensions of TAC within the one project.

Children learned to develop *resources* – problem-solving, skills of observation, experiment, evaluation, designing and decision-making, and concepts of power and energy.

Children learned to develop *practical capability* in using these resources. The varied approach led to varied solutions bringing with them the understanding that there is no single correct solution; one had to be evaluated against another, for which criteria needed to be defined. Children learnt that, from the smallest detail (say, wheel bearings) to the overall concept, decisions have to be taken in order to achieve success.

This exercise also promoted wider discussion of examples from all over the world: the two common forms of electric train in this country; the diesel-electric locomotive, diesel multiple units; the cable cars of San Francisco; trams and trolley buses in continental cities. So children developed an *awareness* that the real world has no single optimum solution. The factors which influenced decisions were seen to be environmental; economic costs, energy resource implications, and relations between these and technological optimization could all be touched on in order to awaken a concern for *value judgements*, including moral and aesthetic, in technological developments.

Task 2   The hybrid car

This task involved a class of fifteen-year-olds in an inner city school which, as a group, designed the complete system for a car propelled by a hybrid of petrol and electrical propulsion. The design process involved children in acquiring new *intellectual resources*, including detailed knowledge about high current electronic control circuitry, and about the mechanical, structural and dynamic principles essential in a road vehicle which has to conform to the Road Traffic Acts and win awards in the BP Buildacar competition.

The main purpose of this project was to motivate a group of children to become fully involved in a real task which would not only develop their inventive and design skills and their manufacturing capability but do two further things. It helped those children to become *aware* of the importance of learning some science in order to achieve something useful; it also brought about a vivid realization of the *value judgements* involved when conservation of energy resources and the potential impact of the internal combustion engine on the environment had to be considered.

Task 3   Building the motorway

Both of the previous examples involved children in designing and making as a process. The tasks that might be set for such processes can be modulated to take account of the maturing minds and skills. They can be appropriately modelled for the youngest ages in the primary schools. However, studies may also be more investigative than design based and these too can be adapted to all ages.

For instance, a group of primary school children were engaged in a topic that focused on the construction of a nearby motorway. They had to engage in various *processes* of enquiry: they visited the site and talked to construction workers, nearby residents, and a farmer whose land was being used; the discussion of the advantages and disadvantages of the change raised the problems of choice and conflicting *values*. They went on to study methods of road construction and examined different soil samples, so acquiring new *resources* of knowledge. They also built models of soil-moving machinery using electric motors, simple levers and gears. The theme also involved them in map reading, in studying transport past and present, in drawing and in writing poetry.

The list of possible examples is endless, but they should not be seen as isolated examples. Any successful example illustrates kinds of capability appropriate to particular stages in the development of the individuals involved. An essential condition for success is that the tasks be structured progressively, comprehensively and in close co-ordination between those areas of the curriculum which can contribute to resources of knowledge and skill and those which can help in making the judgements which the exercise of modern technology forces on society.

Indeed, it is only when the three dimensions of TAC have been properly developed that young people become able to take part in decisions, whether these be the complex decisions of any democratic society – such as those concerned with transport, land use and services – or the decisions which face individuals seeking to make a go of running their own homes and gardens.

14   *Technology – a school subject*

●   T. Dodd

Many countries have realized that too early specialization tends to reduce mobility and there has been a consequent swing away from it to avoid 'closed doors'. This is an important factor for curriculum planners, because numbers of parents and pupils wish to keep as many options open for as long as possible. It is thought, for example, that the swing away from technical/vocational courses in Sweden is largely due to parents trying not to commit their children to too early specialization and inevitable vocations.

There are many pupils, and not only those of modest ability, who might benefit from what Crowther calls 'a practical education making progressively exacting intellectual demands'.[1] Age, ability and aptitude need to be taken into account if the idea of individualized learning is to mean anything. Developmental psychologists, particularly Piaget, have established that progress towards abstract thinking is through 'concrete' stages, and thus to omit a vital part of the experience necessary for all children would seem indefensible. The Department of Education and Science Circular 8/71 refers to courses having 'a substantial practical element',[2] often with an emphasis on real tasks, and an emerging view sees technology as having four main purposes: the first two connected with human and social considerations and the latter inspired by psychological and educational reasoning.

1. *Technology and social education.* In this form the guiding principle concerns school and community co-operation. Links need forging between the world of work, further and higher education, and the community generally. Thus the child may be prepared for a place in a particular social system by ensuring that he understands it as a result of having explored it in some practical way.
2. *Technology and people.* The purpose of group-work is to include the pupil in a group of people rather than in society at large. This

involves motivating and organizing a group, first through designing and then through practical work, and the individual requires to find his place in such a group according to his ability, ambitions, personality and knowledge.

3.   *Technology and interdisciplinarity.* The project method used in much technical work stems from psychological and educational considerations and this form shows how a technical problem, or centre of interest, can be used. Disciplines, expertise, skills and techniques are brought together for the purpose of solving practical problems in which the general direction is toward synthesis and practicality.

4.   *Technology and subject disciplines.* Technology may be used as the basis of study of one or more basic subjects which retain their traditional independence. Thus abstract concepts may be studied from their application by using the analytical tools of the disciplines.

Deforge subscribes particularly to the two latter in approaching a new educational situation, in which pupils should become increasingly involved with technology, by the same methods and within the framework of the traditional disciplines such as physical science and history. He makes the point that the tendency to merge one subject with another, justified though it may be in some ways, leads to a certain amount of confusion. This can be supported by the English experience with Project Technology, in which the technological design process seems justified in every way because of the 'everyday' nature of the problems. However, without the deeper analysis and research method of the disciplines, many of the tools required for such work are lost.

There is much to be learned because of the increase of knowledge in the scientific and technological fields. There is a tendency for courses to be longer and more demanding than they were, and there has been an increase in the number of new courses which have been introduced into new situations. As a result there needs to be much questioning of content to remove irrelevant material. The aims of scientific and technological project work allow for selection and choice in content while ensuring that important methodological benefits are gained by all (depending, of course, on individual ability and aptitude). A delicate balance is necessary, and the teacher has an important part to play in helping, guiding and reorientating pupils towards their maximum potential. In this rapidly changing field of science and technology much of the knowledge, being transitory, does not warrant too high a priority, except as it is relevant to the scientific and technological development of the pupil. The notion that education is what is left after the facts have been forgotten is particularly apt in this context.

What is included and what is left out may be a philosophical question, but in practical terms the emphasis and direction of many courses will depend on the training and experience of teachers, the varying facilities of schools and the traditional status of certain kinds of activity. In technology the breadth of content may be determined by the nature of the problem, and different combinations of subjects, different contributions from staff and different constraints must point towards more individualized learning. Most countries seem to find difficulty in recruiting and training sufficient teachers of the right kind for such work, and schemes are being devised whereby teachers with technical knowledge and expertise coupled with pedagogical understanding may be supplied. There are particular difficulties in certain kinds of integrated courses as specialist teachers are asked to submerge their identities in broad fields and undertake work for which they are ill-suited. In Sweden, time is set aside for 'concentration days' when specialist teachers are asked to co-operate with each other in the solution of cross-disciplinary problems – for example, engineers, metallurgists and chemists working together on the problem of corrosion.

The nature of technology, the complexity of its administration in schools and the importance of the specialist contribution require us to pay particular attention to the pedagogical implications of such work. It is possible to identify four teaching patterns which are being increasingly used and which hint at the educational importance and flexibility of such work. In order of decreasing interdisciplinarity they are:

1. Technology as a *guiding theme* in which, to be successful, the teacher needs to develop numerous facets of such work. The necessity for widely different areas of knowledge, skill and technique means that such methods are probably best reserved for the junior groups, for if taken to its extreme form there is no longer any need to timetable separate subjects.
2. Technology as an *end* in itself; in this approach technology stands above a group of subjects taught by specialists working as a team. Technology may thus be regarded as a field in which previously acquired knowledge may be applied.
3. Technology may be regarded as a *subject* in its own right, but it needs to be developed without any formal links with other subjects and it presupposes that a proper definition of the subject area can be made. Development in this form requires specialized teachers, a teaching method, agreed aims and objectives, and the establishment of new curricula.
4. Technology may also be used as a form of *motivation* and each subject specialist may be asked to subscribe to technology from his own teaching. Interdisciplinarity is incidental, and in many circumstances may be non-existent.

A consideration of the main purposes of technology, and the pedagogical evidence from these patterns, both point towards a need for radical restructuring of curricula. That many of these courses have grown out of craft courses and pure science courses underlines the difficulties that many teachers and schools will have in adapting to the new requirements of such a wide-ranging curriculum programme.

REFERENCES

1. Ministry of Education, *15–18* (Crowther Report), 1959.
2. Department of Education and Science, Circular 8/71, 1971.

Should CDT be part of a national common core curriculum?

● B. K. Down

EDITORS' INTRODUCTION

In this extract from Bernard Down's article (in which he analysed recent national reports on the curriculum) he uses the educational ideologies underlying the categories of aims presented in Chapter 12 to examine the place of CDT in the core curriculum. Design, he argues, must occupy a central role in CDT.

CRITICISMS AND JUSTIFICATIONS OF SCHOOL CRAFT

[...] In considering what justifications can be offered for CDT within a national common core curriculum, it soon becomes clear that the issue is one of comparing the educational value of CDT and other subjects in the competition for time and space, within the curriculum. Whether or not there is ever a compulsory national common core curriculum, this competition for status is being fought in every school. In many schools where staff and CDT are respected the subject is already part of the common core curriculum. In others it may seem to lack university credibility, intellectual and academic standing and a staff that is in tune with the demands of a modern curriculum.

CDT has emerged from the craft areas of woodwork and metalwork. It is craft that has been the subject of often spurious justifications or has been attacked as intellectually inadequate. It has been defended on vocational grounds despite the small number who become professionals. It has also been advocated because of certain supposed outcomes. Thus S. Glenister wrote of craft serving to train the memory or to develop logical thinking.[1] S. Nisbet argued that craft helps to create a sympathetic understanding for manual workers 'an essential adjustment for the non-manual worker to make if he is to play a useful part in political life'.[2] (Perhaps a study of politics or experiences of community work might be better!) R. Stewart in an examination of such justifications comments that the diversity of craft might prevent its acceptance as a serious academic subject. He then goes on to say 'It must be shown to demand a sufficient level of intellectual and creative involvement on the part of the pupil and provide an introduction to important human or natural phenomena pertinent to the society in which he lives'.[3]

John White rejects the idea of handicraft as a common compulsory activity on the grounds that it can be understood and its concepts can be made intelligible to the onlooker who does not participate in the activity – its skills are not mysteries into which one requires initiation like looking at paintings.[4] White thus fails to recognize the complex nature of craft know-how. Broudy, Smith and Burnett,[5] writing from an American context, argue that while perhaps it is no longer possible to pick up tool manipulation informally as once one may have been able to, nevertheless such skills can be and are picked up at the level of amateur use by trial and error or by following instructions. At the same time, the understanding of such technological devices or processions such as those involved in electronics can be acquired through the study of science.

Robin Barrow, an English philosopher, argues that, in comparison with history, woodwork is more physical but less intellectually demanding. History can be practical by being studied for the solution of certain problems, it can be pursued for leisure purposes, and it casts more light on the human condition than woodwork.[6] It is noticeable that such writers as these stress academic understanding and undervalue skills and attitudes in their discussion of craft areas.

Patrick Walsh, in a refreshing defence of practical subjects, argues that any set of criteria that is broad enough to apply to the wide range of academic subjects will apply also to the practical subjects. The practical areas have their own values which are equally as important as those of the sciences or humanities.

> To truth, consistency and clarity as intellectual virtues do there not correspond effectiveness, economy and good workmanship as virtues of practical activities and are not these, too, peculiarly 'mental' virtues?[7]

The craftsman's feeling of respect for his material has as much ethical significance as the liberal pursuit of truth. Latin can be pursued mindlessly no less than woodwork. The leisure-time or vocational activities of the many have at least as much right to consideration as the liberal pursuits of the few. The essential question to be asked is whether or not the subject can help the development of the individual.

Walsh is right in maintaining that craft no less than history has intrinsic values, but the critics are asking whether or not the learning of its skills cannot occur elsewhere, and whether systematic long-term instruction is required, with some element of compulsion in order to bring long-term benefits. How is its social and educational value to be measured when placed alongside and competing with other subjects? Is it a subject only for the Newsom-type pupils?

SHOULD CDT BE INCLUDED IN A NATIONAL CORE CURRICULUM?

The creation of CDT should go some way to meeting these objections to craft. It involves three elements woven together by the act of problem-solving and has a different character from that of craft. It should not, therefore, be subject to the same criticisms. Craft involves a product approach to education, with the artefact as the object of assessment; of more concern in design is the process, the thinking, the problem-solving.[8] Of the three paradigms we noted – the social reconstructionist approach stresses social relevance, the child-centred model advocates creativity and personal development, and the liberal model emphasizes certain intellectual values and breadth of outlook.

1. *Social reconstructionist criteria.* Both the design and technological aspects are often regarded as socially relevant. Lawton has pointed out that we are short of high technologists in society and our industrial management lacks engineering qualifications. School technology is grossly neglected because of the time allowed for it, the status and quality of its teachers and its failure to achieve a place in the compulsory curriculum.[9] Schools are said by some to engender a lack of interest or even a positive hostile attitude towards industry. These are all arguments beloved of industrialists and government, because they direct the blame for industrial and economic failure, elsewhere, on teachers.

But there is a danger of identifying high technology with industry, and believing that the major social concern is industrial production. I have argued elsewhere that the aims of a technological education must be primarily that of preparing children, morally and politically, for understanding and being critically aware of the social issues of technology.[10] Incidentally, these are the aspects of technology which girls seem to want to study.[11] There should also be some 'hands on' experience of technological devices, and the understanding of areas of technology, especially those related to designing and making. However, Bernard Aylward is surely right in warning us of the danger of overstressing the theoretical aspects of technology to 'facilitate CDT becoming a training ground for future university students. This falls into the same trap as have academic studies in the traditional curriculum. It is divisive and would tend to elevate the academic study of technology, above the use of technology in serving mankind'.[12] In emphasizing the economic relevance of technology it is easy to create an educational imbalance by stressing present industrial needs to the detriment of future social understandings.

2. *Child-centred criteria.* The problem-solving basis of CDT has its origins in child-centredness. It is not therefore surprising for writers to justify design education in particular by talk of its opportunities for developing students' abilities in tackling 'real-world ill-defined problems',[13] or its advantages in encouraging 'the development of creativity and of problem-solving, decision-taking and evaluation which are valuable in all walks of life'.[14]

The claims about developing problem-solving abilities are no doubt sometimes exaggerated for there is no general problem-solving ability.[15] Also, as Douglas Lewin reminds us, 'it is impossible to teach creativity. All one can do is to encourage and allow the students to experience design situations for themselves, the basic principle being to draw out rather than cram in'.[16] Nevertheless the virtue of getting pupils to design is that they are actively learning and being asked to think about the various issues rather than to follow the teacher's instructions. That cannot be bad.

3. *Liberal criteria.* Hirst argues that a liberal education involves an initiation into the unique forms of propositional knowledge. There are strong arguments for maintaining that there is a unique element to design, for its language is modelling, with designs being expressed through drawings, diagrams, physical representations and other forms of non-verbal as well as verbal representation. Bruce Archer has argued that such graphic thinking involves important skills which have parallels with the skills of literacy.[17] The term 'graphicacy' has been coined to cover such non-verbal communication.[18] While it could not be maintained that modelling or graphicacy is unique to design (it constitutes an essential part of geography) or even that there is an automatic transfer between different forms of graphicacy (such as between map-reading and reading architects' plans), there is no doubt of the value and distinctiveness of this form of representation. We ought to educate children to be graphically literate. Through modelling one is able to conceptualize in design things which do not yet exist. On these grounds, M. J. French sees the prime justification of design education as lying 'in strengthening and uniting the entire non-verbal education of the child'.[19]

Historically craft was regarded as illiberal because of its supposed cognitive narrowness, as well as its practical and vocational element. But CDT is a diverse area of activity, and in the design and making process one may draw on a multitude of disciplines. In a sense far from being illiberal CDT may form the core of liberal studies. The elements of design and technology can be taught across the curriculum. They can be studied within a historical and social context, in which moral and political questions are raised. Technically appropriate mathematical competence and relevant scientific concepts are necessary for the solution of several types of design problems. At the same time design involves aesthetic elements. Because of these factors there are those who see design as integrating the sciences and humanities,[20] or as defined by its ability to synthesize discrete areas of knowledge.[21] Lewin assuming that design is the core of engineering criticizes CDT as paying undue attention to making – the craft aspect of an artefact. Nevertheless he maintains that in schools engineering through problem-solving provides the basis of a liberal education.[22]

In various ways such as these, writers have tried to show the educational value of some model of CDT – particularly one emphasizing design or technology. However these arguments do not take us far in the issue of the core curriculum, for they make it clear that the degree to which such a variety of knowledge will be experienced will depend upon the actual situation in school. All design or technological problem-solving does not provide the basis of a liberal education. Furthermore, one must recognize the obvious point that time is limited and even if it were desirable CDT at best would have to assume other knowledge rather than teach it.

CONCLUSION

This leads us then, finally, to ask what model of CDT, what core skills, knowledge and concepts, and what kind of general conditions operating in schools, are necessary to justify a key position for CDT in a national common core curriculum. Scanning the literature on craft, particularly on woodwork, one cannot help but see a virtual consensus of doubts about its intellectual value, because of its product rather than process model of education, its failure to fully stretch the mind, and because it is thought to be economically less relevant than design or technology. The virtues implied by 'craftsmanship' are often forgotten.

There are those who would want CDT to be more theoretical either by concentrating on design modelling or by offering technological packets of information. However, surely making constitutes part of the uniqueness of this area. Also children learn something about the practicality of their design by making and evaluating the artefact.

Design, nevertheless, must occupy the key role in CDT, because it can help to develop an awareness in the pupil of the way that human needs, social concerns, aesthetic factors as well as technical data and skills affect the final product. It also employs non-verbal models of graphicacy and helps to develop aspects of non-verbal thought. There needs to be some agreement about the ideological emphasis, the aims and appropriate model of CDT necessary for common core teaching. If the child-centred ideology is stressed it would be difficult to prescribe in detail what skills, concepts and knowledge should be taught to all pupils, since a total commitment to problem-solving assumes that what is taught is primarily the general features of problem-solving and the specific craft skills and items of knowledge necessary for solving the particular problem. However, some acceptable minimum of craft skills, technological know-how and graphic skills to be attainable by most pupils by the age of sixteen, may need to be recognized if CDT can become part of a genuine national common core curriculum.

All cannot be put right merely by prescribing an acceptable programme of studies. In the end, as the *School Curriculum*[23] recognizes, everything depends upon the teacher and the facilities he/she has. A high percentage of teachers within this area are skilled craft teachers. They have not all had the opportunity to acquire the relevant technology or design skills. All are not necessarily sympathetic to the changes they see being advocated. Consensus cannot be forced. In the meantime individual departments are gradually winning their right to a place for CDT in the school compulsory curriculum.

REFERENCES

1. S. Glenister, *The Technique of Handicraft Teaching* (3rd edn), Harrap, 1968.

2. S. Nisbet, *Purpose in the Curriculum*, London University Press, 1957, p. 70.

3. R. Stewart, 'Justifying Craft', *Studies in Design Education and Craft*, vol. 6, no. 1, Winter 1973, p. 74.

4. John White, 'Learn as You Will', *New Society*, 4 Dec. 1969.

5. H. S. Broudy, B. O. Smith and J. B. Burnett, *Democracy and Excellence in American Secondary Education*, Rand McNally, 1964, pp. 181–2.

6. R. Barrow, *The Philosophy of Schooling*, Wheatshea, 1981, pp. 112–3.

7. Patrick D. Walsh, 'The Upgrading of Practical Subjects', *The Journal of Further and Higher Education*, vol. 2, no. 3, Autumn 1978, p. 61.

8. Philip Roberts, 'What Is Design?', *Journal of Art and Design Education*, vol. 1, no. 2, 1982, pp. 269–78.

9. D. Lawton, *The Stanley Lecture: 17 October 1979, Curriculum Planning and Technological Change*, Stanley, 1979.

10. B. K. Down, Educational Aims in the Technological Society. [See Chapter 12].

11. Girls and Technology Education Project at Chelsea College, London.

12. B. Aylward, 'Beware of Seduction by High Technology', *Education*, 24 June 1983, p. 483.

13. N. Cross, 'Designerly Ways of Knowing', *Design Studies*, vol. 2, no. 4, 1984, p. 226.

14. Design Council, *Design Education at Secondary Level*, June 1979, para. 3.6.

15. B. K. Down, 'Problem-Solving, CDT and Child-Centredness', *Studies in Design Education, Craft and Technology*, vol. 16, no. 1, pp. 38–43. [See Chapter 24 of this Reader.]

16. D. Lewin, 'On the Place of Design in Engineering', *Design Studies*, vol. 1, no. 2, October 1979, p. 117.

17. B. Archer, 'The Three R's', *Design Studies*, vol. 1, no. 1, p. 19. [See Chapter 5 of this Reader.]

18. Anita Cross, 'Towards an Understanding of the Intrinsic Values of Design Education', *Design Studies*, vol. 5, no. 1, Jan. 1984, pp. 31–9. [See Chapter 11 of this Reader.]

19. M. J. French, 'A Justification for Design Teaching in Schools', *Engineering: Design Education Supplement*, May 1979, p. 25.

20. Stuart Pugh, 'Design – the Integrative – Enveloping Culture – not a Third Culture', *Design Studies*, vol. 3, no. 2, April 1982, pp. 93–8.

21. Clive Dilnot, 'Design as a Socially Significant Activity: An Introduction', *Design Studies*, vol. 3, no. 3, July 1982, pp. 139–46.

22. D. Lewin, 'Engineering Philosophy', *Journal of the Royal Society of Arts*, vol. 129, no. 5302, Sept. 1981, pp. 653–66. [See chapter 2 of this Reader.]

23. DES, *The School Curriculum*, HMSO, 1981.

16 *Technology across the curriculum*

● C. C. Tipping

EDITORS' INTRODUCTION

In the original article, Colin Tipping argued that secondary education tends to develop the left hemisphere of the brain (see Chapter 11) and that design education can nourish both sides. While education based on design activities (as argued by Bruce Archer in Chapter 5) is now accepted, it would be wrong to only associate design (as general problem-solving) with crafts. Below we take up the argument where he explains design's closer relationship with technology and his proposals for technology across the curriculum.

[...]

If design does not belong exclusively with technical studies, or with art or science for that matter, neither does it have an exclusive place anywhere in the curriculum as specific content or knowledge. Rather it is a way of approaching all types of knowledge and applying it in all sorts of ways. It facilitates at the secondary level the kind of learner-centred education which IDE and Guided Discovery methods facilitated at the primary level.

The Design Council recently circularized a consultative document, 'Design Education at Secondary Level' (1979). The response to that document by the National Association of Head Teachers is interesting in this context.

> We believe that the concept of Design Education . . . should feature in our core curriculum, both because of its importance to our economic prosperity as an industrial nation and also because of the need for education for later life and non-work activities required by this coming generation of young people. We welcome the document in as much as it crosses departmental boundaries which we believe is much needed in Secondary Schools today. Having said this however, we do have reservations about the advisability of looking at Design Education as one single independent aspect of the curriculum, and would rather see it fully developed as an element of other subjects.

Design eduation, then, would become an agent of curricular change *in method* if it were implanted into the subject disciplines. It would enable the learner to become cognitively and affectively more personally involved in the subject through a more problem or project-orientated approach. The extent to which this would allow or encourage workshop-based activities to grow out of subject-centred, but learner-directed, project work is a further question.

The fact that the word 'design' can mean either a plan for an intended artifact, the artifact itself, or the process by which it comes into being, accounts for much of the misunderstanding about its meaning. While design education will certainly be concerning itself with plans and products, its main educational claim lies in its value as a process and an activity rather than as content.

Technology on the other hand is 'content' rather than process and it can enter most academic subjects as an element of content. Its exclusivity to craft education, with a sideways glance at science, is an even greater absurdity than was the attachment of design to craft, and will serve to ensure that it remains out of the mainstream of education if it stays this way. It has little or nothing to do with craft other than in very specific ways relating to the material and the techniques associated with it.

The relationship between design and technology on the other hand is extremely close and mutually dependent. One is process: the other content. There is a strong interactive relationship between society and its prevailing technology. Designing is the decision-making process at the interface between society and technology. In this sense both design and technology are absolutely central to human affairs.

While technology draws a great deal of its reference from science, much of science has come about as a result of technological development. Neither one necessarily leads to the other, but clearly there is a relationship between them.

In developing teaching material around the concept of technology we have unfortunately gone the route of packaging instances of 'applied science' as modules of technology. This helps us to teach things like electronics, mechanisms, structures, and hydraulics, etc., which is fine if we consider that to be desirable; it does little to develop the kind of mind which might one day generate new forms of technology.

The applied science approach to technology is, by its nature, knowledge-centred and restricted to the scientific viewpoint. This bounds the concept far too much and tends to remove it from the context of creative design. It does little to promote creativity and the designerly way of thinking which is implicit in the objectives of design education.

The kind of technological creativity promoted by my colleague John

Cave and illustrated in a series of articles in [*Studies in Design Education Craft and Technology*], retains its link with creative design. Though simple and 'low tech', it exemplifies all the concepts and principles that more expensive and 'high tech' equipment and theoretical material would demonstrate. Its very simplicity, cheapness and versatility makes it very flexible and adaptable. It enables it to be applied to work of a highly individual creative kind. The results are still able to be unpredictable, surprising and innovative in non-scientific terms. Instead of becoming ossified as a fixed body of knowledge, technology taught in this way remains fresh, innovative, dynamic and free from any one form of knowledge.

It counters the idea suggested by the modular approach that technology is something that is separable from design context and human affairs, and that it is an extension of science.

Indeed in as much as design and technology are inextricably linked, technology belongs every bit as firmly within the humanities as with science and the arts. While *'Language Across the Curriculum'* was a cry to free verbal communications from the context of English lessons alone, so *'Technology Across the Curriculum'* could suggest valid content for English, environmental studies, history, science, social science, art and maths.

Bronowski showed us through his television series and book, *The Ascent of Man*, how man's cultural development is punctuated, accented and indeed only facilitated by significant technological achievements, crucial to the next stage or phase in the evolution of civilization and mankind. History, and archaeology particularly, makes constant reference to forms of technology as indicative of a way of living and an inferred set of cultural values, just as the social sciences of today infer prevailing norms, ideologies, values and habits from the technology of today. Consider any contemporary scrap heap for example. But technology, and the design procedures that give rise to it, also illustrate prevailing concerns, even by their very non-existence at times. Technology often represents conflicting interests, compromises and moral dilemmas. It is almost always controversial and problematic and provides both the opportunity and the context in which pupils can deal with real controversial issues in a dynamic, evaluative, open-ended and designerly way.

A curriculum development movement suggested by the idea of 'Technology Across the Curriculum' is timely. We are now educating for an age which will be dominated by technology to the extent that it will alter social relationships and the way of life that we know. The human dimension to technology is every bit as important, if not more so, than the scientific facts that underlie it. A curriculum which made more effort to raise students' perceptions of technology and its effect would be very valuable in this respect.

If the concepts of design and technology are released from their narrow association with craft and with science, they become agents for general change in curriculum content and organization. They can provide a focus for study in all the disciplines which would help to relate the subjects more to the real world and current concerns, and would create the situation in which a more problem-based, learner-centred education could operate.

Though this does not imply specialist teachers in CDT to teach in each discipline, since we all should be aware of developments in our subject and general interest area brought about by technological change, teachers with good backgrounds in design and technology might be key figures in this movement. They might be needed to act as 'consultants' across a wide range of subjects. The role of workshops and studios would also be crucial. They would have to provide 'hands-on' practical experimentation, modelling and design realization opportunities – whenever the situation demanded it.

If this strategy were adopted, and if it began to work in this way, the real value of practical education would become more apparent to everyone.

A study of fourteen-year-olds' attitudes to technology and industry, made for the Standing Conference on Science and Technology by Dr Roy Page and Ms Melanie Nash, shows that a curriculum which emphasizes technology, project-based science contact with industry, etc., has direct as well as indirect pay-offs. As reported in the *Guardian* (23 October 1980), it showed, for instance, that from schools with the most positive attitudes towards this kind of emphasis:

(a) All pupils either went on to higher education or obtained employment, in spite of being in areas of high unemployment (employers apparently saw the value).

(b) Pupils were fascinated and excited by modern electronic and mechanical technology and became particularly disposed towards a career in these areas.

(c) Discipline in all the schools was good and pupils were stretched to their limits academically, with exam results well above the norm for 'ability intake'.

Curriculum innovation is however most resisted when it concerns change in attitude, or focus, in the fourth and fifth-year examination work; and this is understandable. Many people would cite the examinations as the reason for not doing anything at all in this direction.

The situation, even in this respect, becomes dramatically altered once the pupils move into the sixth form. In a great many schools sixth-form pupils are obliged to do some general studies as an antidote to A-level specialization.

John Fairhall, *Guardian* (20 January 1981), showed that general studies, in a number of forms, accounts for a very significant part of the curriculum.

It has a great deal of general support from the teaching profession, and the mere fact that it is sixth-form work makes it high-status. It has no rigid academic structure to be defended by subject 'priests'; no bureaucratic organization barriers and systems of evaluation which might prevent it being open-ended, flexible and learner-centred. There is no HMI with responsibility for it; no LEA advisors, and no courses in it at teacher training establishments. There is however a General Studies Association, run by enthusiasts, which acts as a focus of enquiry for teachers who may have been landed the job of organizing general studies in their school; usually either a very junior, or very senior member of the staff. But as things stand, it is a form of curriculum development which is happening fairly organically within schools, and organized by the teachers themselves.

The point is however that it offers the teacher who believes in a designerly approach to education the ideal opportunity to take the lead in this area of sixth-form work. Through general studies, these teachers might have a significant effect, of a kind already shown to be possible with fourteen-year-olds, on the very people who will one day be the leaders in all walks of life.

Such teachers might generate returns of a much greater order than if they had reserved all their effort for the single subject of CDT.

Most of these general studies 'courses' are taught by teams of teachers drawn from the disciplines, the 'creative subjects' and subjects which already have an integrated approach, such as environmental studies, rural studies, social studies. Usually the timetable is unable to release the scientists and the mathematicians, but as I have already pointed out, design and technology draws heavily upon the humanities as well as science and maths, though these could not be excluded, obviously. A teacher with a good background in design and technology, who was able to apply his/her designerly approach to wider issues, could give a strong lead to a general studies team, and ought to be in a position to know when a mathematical contribution or a scientific interpretation was necessary, and to ask for it to be made available.

As argued before, this would make workshops and studios available as learning resources, thereby bringing back some high-level sixth-form work into this area, and even in some cases, preventing their actual closure, which some schools are considering because of staff shortage. Workshops would be essential to this work, to provide the environment in which to make real the connections between practical problem-solving (as opposed to craft) and the rest of the curriculum.

Some very fine people enter the profession to become teachers of CDT. Many have been designers or members of industrial project teams, or have similar valuable experience to offer. They embrace the philosophy of design education, as it is presented to them in the books and through their courses at college, because they can so easily appreciate how well it relates to the world of work and real life that they have just left to become teachers.

But they become frustrated and disillusioned by the reality of the situations they find themselves faced with in the schools. Daunted by the enormity of the problems associated with bringing about significant change, especially in attitudes, they leave the profession, or simply acquiesce.

An alternative strategy for them, and for many of the very fine teachers who are retraining in CDT, might actually be to apply for a post of Head of Sixth-Form Studies, or to suggest to the headmaster that he creates a post like this for them. They might just find that this gives them far greater opportunity to teach design and technology in the most meaningful way than ever would have been possible from within the CDT department alone.

It might even work out that the influence such a teacher might exert at sixth-form level would begin to percolate down to other levels in the curriculum, eventually perhaps giving some semblance of reality to the notion of 'Technology Across the Curriculum'.

POSTSCRIPT

By way of a postscript to this article which tried to set out the relationship of design and technology to the development of a more holistic and humanistic curriculum, I feel that it is necessary to say something more about craft in education. The run of the argument did not leave room enough to take care of some of the implications for craft which arose, nor to explore the nature of some of the choices which might become available to teachers of CDT.

I tried to indicate that in broad general terms neither design nor technology is compatible with craft in the specific sense. I have also argued that design as an educational activity should not only pervade curriculum subjects as a form of holistic method, but also occur as a specific kind of practical activity in workshops and studios.

I also put forward the view in my article in vol. 12, no. 2 of [*Studies in Design Education Craft and Technology*] that it makes very little sense to try and teach the rigour and discipline of craft when children are young. Even in early adolescence they lack the necessary strength and control to achieve any level of skilful performance in crafts like woodwork and metalwork. Yet at the age of eleven or twelve they are in their prime as far as their imaginative and creative abilities are concerned.

All this may have left the impression that I would support the idea that crafts like woodwork and metalwork should be left out of the school curriculum. I definitely would not. Indeed I would argue for a strengthening of craft education and for a separate identity for it. I am not however suggesting that we return to the status quo that existed before the shotgun marriage between craft, design and technology was arranged. Mine is not a reactionary position and anyone looking for a justification of the old 'handicraft' will be disappointed. (I believe that the desire to find a reason to return to the 'old days' is known to be so strong that people in a position to influence the subject have been reticent about criticizing recent developments for fear of being quoted as advocating this. Bandwagons are more difficult to get off than to mount.)

What I am suggesting is while creative design activities should begin as early as possible in a child's education and should be seen as a proper extension of primary methods into the secondary curriculum, craft might be reserved for the senior years of schooling; offered as a special non-examination option in the fifth and sixth years.

In this context it would be offered as something special, challenging and intrinsically worthwhile. It could help to provide a balance in a student's work programme which might otherwise be exclusively academic. A commitment to a high standard in both design and workmanship ought to be demanded of anyone who opted to do it.

Teachers do, it seems, then have a number of choices open to them in terms of the way in which they wish to develop their subject and their personal contribution to it.

Some of those choices I have suggested in the above article; integrated design teams, sixth-form general studies, etc. But whatever happens in the wider school curriculum there are choices open to the teachers within a department to make changes in their own schemes in the light of this kind of analysis. Little need change except attitude.

The apparently radical move to take craft to the top end of the school and to establish its identity as distinct from design and technology requires only that the teachers redefine the nature of the design-based practical activities that would replace it. This would enable design and technology to develop properly from the first year upwards, and provide a consistent and logical route to the design and technology exams. Then we might begin to see a dramatic improvement in the numbers of entrants for them, but not at the expense of craft education.

17 *The place of technology in schools*

● B. E. Woolnough

EDITORS' INTRODUCTION

Although this article was written more than a decade ago, Brian Woolnough's idea that technology should not be a separate subject is still valid today. He argues that science courses are an important place for technology. Indeed, technological science teaching is essential to prevent science from being 'concerned with abstract niceties'.

The need for technology in the schools, as part of the education of tomorrow's citizen, has now become a truism. However (like creativity, equality and love), whilst all agree that it is a 'good thing', there is little agreement as to the precise meaning of the term or of how to implement it in practice. I hope in this article to clarify, in my own mind at least, some of the issues relating to the place of technology in schools and to suggest a practical, pragmatic approach for its implementation.

The juxtaposition of three recent meetings has triggered off my putting pen to paper, as each has illuminated at least one of the significant issues. Firstly, a highly profitable and illuminating visit to study a part of the French educational system in Le Havre, under the auspices of ADEPT. In the French educational system, every pupil in every school in the 12 to 15-year-old range has two periods of technology per week, but no teaching in physics or chemistry until he arrives at the lycee, at sixteen years of age. I would suggest that there is no corresponding slot for technology in the English educational system, nor should there be. Secondly, the educational group of the Institute of Physics had its annual conference on the theme of Project Work in Schools and Higher Education. It was clear from those attending that many saw project work as a key, integral part of a school physics course, and also as fulfilling many of the aims of technology. And thirdly, a meeting organized by the Schools Forum for the Training of Teachers for Technology, where it appeared that many people were using the term technology in quite distinct and different senses, without realizing the widely differing implications.

Taking this third issue first, and facing it head on, it will be seen that the many and conflicting definitions of technology are either too technically restrictive or too all-embracing to have any prescribing influence.

If I may quote just one recent publication[1] – 'Technology is the means by which man adapts the environment and by which he became and remains human' (the first part of that, at least, is specific enough). But it then goes on to be so all-embracing that it means – to me – everything and nothing. 'It is an attitude of mind which has now evolved into an intellectual discipline, confining itself to no specific area and using all other disciplines to achieve its ends.' How do you teach that!

I do not think that any pithy definition of technology would be of much value, indeed I would be happy to bury the word entirely, but I do believe that school technology should contain three elements. The three elements, if I may use the preacher's alliteration, of Applying, Application and Appreciation: applying the principles of science to real problems, and giving the pupils problem-solving activities, projects in which they are able to use their basic scientific skills and knowledge in an individually creative way; application of the facts and principles of science to uses in everyday life and in industry; and an appreciation of the significance, the power and the limitation of science in its wider social and moral context. Now many would say that these three elements are an integral part of the way they teach their subject, especially if it is physics, chemistry or biology, and that, I believe, is the way ahead. Technology ought not to be a separate subject, apart from

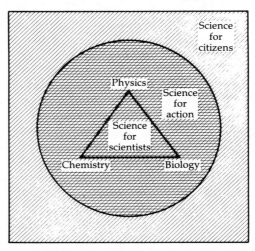

Figure 17.1

the main line teaching, but should be an integral part of all our science teaching. I think it was John Lewis who spoke of our science teaching moving from merely being a pure 'science for scientists', to embrace more applications in 'science for action', and also more significance as 'science for citizens' (Figure 17.1). If our science teaching can widen in this way we will have no need for 'technology' as such.

Indeed, I believe it is positively harmful to urge that 'technology' should be introduced as a separate subject in the timetable. There is no room in the overcrowded curriculum of the English schools to introduce another subject across the board. The only way it could go in would be as an option – and as an option it would only be studied by a few. (And these few would not normally include the ablest pupils.) I believe that all should be exposed to the importance of technology, and not just a random few. The only way for all, or the majority, of the pupils to be influenced is as it is introduced through the main line science periods. One real danger that the introduction of 'technology' could bring would be the polarization of teaching attitudes in science and technology. The science teaching would become even more pure because 'the applications are done in technology'. If we look at the figures for the number of pupils taking the relevant external examinations at A, O or CSE levels we will see that, nine years after the introduction of Project Technology, the engineering sciences or technology courses have been unable to make significant headway. I include in the table below the corresponding figures for physics for comparison.

I would see technology having a real place in the schools through three spheres: through craft and design workshops, through hobbies and technology centres and, most importantly, through normal science periods. And it is to how technology can best be incorporated into the context of science teaching that I would like to look now. Fundamentally, I believe that it is an attitude and approach which can spread through, and enhance, all science teaching. It is more a state of mind than a specific, distinctive course. We do not need to radically

Table 17.1 *GCE and CSE entries for physics and technology, 1974*

	A-level	O-level	CSE	
Number of candidates taking physics in England in 1974	40 597	114 793	88 611	75 242 (Mode 1) 13 369 (Mode 3)
Number of candidates taking any type of engineering science or technology in England in 1974	467	1 140	approx. 5000	≈ 2500 (Mode 1) ≈ 2581 (Mode 3)

Total population of 16-year-olds in England and Wales in 1972 ≈ 700 000.

change the content of current science courses, but to teach the existing material in a technological way – applying, showing applications and teaching appreciation. Much practical work could be directed more as a project, problem-solving activity, and less of a verification of well-established principles. At the pre-O-level stage I do not believe that we can realistically hope for each student to do a significant project for himself; limitations on time, space, facilities, and syllabus pressures add to the pupils' limited scientific background. But smaller, less grandiose exercises could be introduced periodically to specifically encourage problem-solving skills.

Most readers will be familiar with the Berkshire bridges[2] ('Construct a bridge to span a 50 cm gap, weighing not more than 30 g. A prize for the strongest bridge'), and the problems posed in the SC 5–13 project,[3] and this type of exercise encourages constructive creative development. In the long term however, we should aim at reducing the syllabus content for the 16-plus examinations, allowing more time for individual project activity, which could be teacher assessed and included in any 16-plus assessment. At the sixth-form level we can realistically aim for much more in the problem-solving skills, applying their scientific knowledge and the understanding to real open-ended problems, and this can be done best by doing projects or investigations. The inclusion of project work in A-level Nuffield physics,[4] biology and physical science[5] is especially to be welcomed, but project work is no less valuable if it is not externally assessed. Many of us, who have been involved in sixth-form project work, are convinced that this is one of the most significant developments in school science teaching over the past few years. By giving opportunity for developing individual creative problem-solving activities a pupil achieves far more in acquiring the type of cognitive and affective skills that so many science teachers are aiming for.

Applications of the principles of science throughout the course can be introduced to give the syllabus content greater relevance and significance. More textbooks are being published now which include good applications, but the main source of examples will always be the teacher himself. It is instructive to take an O-level science syllabus and work through it systematically, noting down as many applications of each point as possible. If this is done as a workshop activity with a group of local teachers, a composite list can be produced with an impressive selection of applications for reference. Such a list of pooled examples makes a very handy reference sheet. (I think that it would be a mistake, though, to write specific applications into the GCE and CSE syllabuses as they could easily become fossilized, like Davy's miners' lamp.)

Science teachers can also help the students to appreciate the social and moral implications of the science they teach by discussing them as they arise, either from the content of the lesson or from the current news. I am not advocating a wholesale switch to a pseudo-sociological type of science course. But I do believe that we should spend a few minutes as the opportunities arise to discuss how science affects the way we live. There are many who are only too ready to point out the harmful effects of science and technology; are not the science teachers the best people to present a more balanced assessment?

School science teachers have been made increasingly aware of the importance of pupils understanding the underlying concepts of science. And this clearly is a vital aspect of science, dear to the hearts of most science teachers. But perhaps in over-emphasizing these formal, abstract aspects of science, we have been in danger of losing the more concrete, operational emphasis which can be more readily appreciated by many, less intellectual pupils. In over-emphasizing the fundamental principles we have under-emphasized the need for seeing science as a human activity, showing its applications and significance to the world of today. In over-emphasizing the development of a rather convergent 'scientific method' we have under-emphasized the more divergent, lateral approach so important for real problem-solving activities. Some of the more recent courses, such as Nuffield Secondary Science and SCISP, have seen these dangers and sought to redress the balance.

It will be seen that I am not advocating anything radical or revolutionary.[6] Indeed many will say that this is how they are teaching their science now, and in so doing I believe they are training and preparing tomorrow's citizens appropriately. I believe that this is the way that 'technology' can realistically be introduced into the curriculum for all pupils, through the Trojan horse approach rather than the frontal attack.

One vital question remains: do science teachers at the moment wish to teach their science in this way, and if not, could they be persuaded to? Most O-level and CSE examinations certainly do not encourage time being spent on 'technological' skills and applications, with the notable exceptions of SCISP and some of the Mode 3 CSEs. Some interesting work has been done to discover the importance that physics teachers give to various aims. Holley[7] for instance stated fourteen possible aims for physics teaching and asked fifty senior physicists in northern schools to rate them according to their importance. By averaging the scores a crude measure is obtained of a concensus judgement of the importance of the various aims (Table 17.2). Clearly on such a small atypical sample, sweeping generalizations are not in order. It is, however, interesting to speculate on the significance of their results in the light of teaching technology in school science. It appears that physics teachers are still concerned primarily with understanding principles, with knowledge of basic facts, with obtaining good examination results and enjoying

Table 17.2   *Aims of physics teaching rated by sixth-form teachers (after Holley)*

Aim no.	Averaged score
1. Competence and skill in experimental work	2.4
2. Original thinking in physics	2.4
3. Knowledge of basic facts	2.4
4. Appreciation of science as man's achievement	3.2
5. Understanding of principles	1.5
6. Enjoyment of physics	2.2
7. A-level grades	2.3
8. Further and higher education	2.3
9. Preparation for employment	2.7
10. Physics as a creative activity	3.0
11. Application of mathematical methods	2.8
12. Awareness of achievements of modern physics	2.7
13. Finding sources of information on own initiative	2.3
14. Sixth-formers conduct own research	3.4

Rating   1.   Supremely important
2.   Very important
3.   Important
4.   Of relatively minor importance
5.   Unimportant

physics. In teaching technology through science one would expect the aims of 'physics as a creative activity', 'sixth-formers conduct own research', and 'appreciation of science as man's achievement' to rate fairly highly. There is regrettably little evidence for believing this to be the case from these figures. Hopefully teachers are becoming more aware of the need for a more relevant, technological science teaching, showing science as an important human activity and not just a remote academic study. Hopefully, also, the in-service training possible through the new Open University course Technology for Teachers, will encourage many teachers to modify their teaching appropriately. At the initial training stage, I believe all science tutors have a responsibility to try to widen the horizons of their graduate scientists – most of whom have been taught for their previous ten years in a style of science which was almost entirely convergent and academic. At the Oxford Department of Educational Studies we encourage both engineering and science graduates to train to become science teachers, having physics, chemistry or biology as their main field of method work, but we have a supporting Applied Science and Technology option to which we again encourage both engineers and scientists to attend.

Science teaching in the schools is still relatively young, and it has evolved, gradually, over the last 100 years. I believe that our science teaching must change now, becoming less concerned with the abstract academic niceties and more creative and relevant to our technological age. I believe we owe it to our pupils. If we persist in teaching a purely academic science we are in danger of teaching a subject as relevant to the modern, and future, world as the classics were – and science will be in danger of suffering the same fate; with science becoming a minority school subject to be studied for its intellectual stimulation by an erudite minority. However, if we can modify our science teaching so that we give pupils the opportunity of applying their skills to project activities, of seeing the applications of their knowledge and of giving an appreciation of the significance of science in its human context, I believe we as teachers and all the pupils will gain far more satisfaction and enjoyment.

REFERENCES

1. School Technology Forum, Report No. 5, *Discussion Paper on General Studies*, June 1974.
2. Luscombe, N., 'When Berkshire Bridges Came Tumbling Down', in A. R. Marshall (ed.), *School Technology in Action*, English Universities Press, 1974.
3. Schools Council 5–13, *With Objectives in Mind*, Macdonald, 1972.
4. Nuffield Advanced Physics, *Teachers' Handbook*, Chapter 7: 'Individual Investigations', Penguin, 1971.
5. Nuffield Advanced Physical Science, *Introduction and Guide*, Chapter 4: 'The Project', Penguin, 1973.
6. 'An Association View on School Science and Technology', *Education in Science*, November 1973, no. 55.
7. Holley, B. J., Schools Council Research Studies, *A-level Syllabus Studies: History and Physics*, Macmillan, 1974.

18 *Craft, design and technology – the uncertain future*

● J. Eggleston

EDITORS' INTRODUCTION

This lecture, given on 31 October 1985 to commemorate the anniversary of woodwork and metalwork teaching at Bethoven Street School, provides an interesting snapshot in the growth of a subject area, showing some of the influences and problems.

One hundred years ago, the teaching of craft, design and technology (then manual training) began in the playground shed of a Paddington school. The instructor was the school caretaker, John Chenoweth, who happened to be a carpenter. The case for including practical subjects in the school curriculum had already been supported by a Royal Commission, but even so the government refused grants and the City and Guilds of London Institute provided initial funding. Now in its anniversary year CDT seems to have everything going for it. After its years in the outer reaches of the curriculum – and often the school buildings – it has painfully fought its way out of the cold. CDT teachers, advisers, inspectors and teacher trainers have devoted decades of committed work to the struggle. With the assistance of the national projects of the 1960s and 1970s (which probably had more effect on CDT than on any other subject) they have achieved a new identity – from woodwork and metalwork to design and technology.

The subject now enjoys enhanced status enthusiastically accorded by the Department of Education and Science and HM Inspectorate with the accolade of warm approval from Sir Keith Joseph himself. The Manpower Services Commission through its TVEI and related in-service (TRIST) schemes is pumping large sums of money into CDT facilities and those who use them in schools in most local education authorities.

In many, CDT leads the TVEI programme with courses in electronics and control technology and other technical and vocational activities. British School Technology buses are now a familiar sight on the roads of Britain. A wide range of examination courses are attracting able students to the subject and the attention of the universities and polytechnics is slowly but surely being captured. The new grade-related criteria of the GCSE CDT syllabuses are already speeding further developments. The new DESTECH group for CDT has been established. Specialist journals, notably *Studies in Design Education Craft and Technology,* enjoy rising circulations.

Girls are participating in the subject in growing numbers helped by the thrust of the GIST and the GATE projects. Most Local Education Authorities have women CDT teachers; women now comprise 8 per cent of London CDT teachers. In some schools, CDT is also playing a major role in increasing the opportunities for black young people.

New national contests for CDT-related activities produce outstanding entries – for example the prize days of the Design Council awards, the Young Electronic Designer of the Year and the Granada Power Game provide impressive evidence of the dynamism/initiative of CDT departments throughout the land. CDT now has its own television programmes. Even in the primary schools – once the no-go area for CDT – the subject is achieving a major breakthrough.

Is the rise of CDT unstoppable? Beyond the euphoria there are major hazards ahead. One is the risk that the pursuit of technology will distract and even eliminate much of the equally important emphasis on practical design. Design, associated with its concerns for the human environment, expression, identity and aesthetic considerations is an essential part of the liberal education of all children. It is, alas, not a necessary part of technology, as twentieth-century history has demonstrated frequently. CDT in recent years has done much to revive and reinterpret this aspect of education in the lives of all children. Young people know this – for them technology is unacceptable without design – in motor cycles, hi-fi, dress, and much more. Design must be enhanced, not diminished, and the content-loaded courses that are frequently (but not necessarily) a feature of TVEI courses do not help. Paradoxically, design is an aspect of CDT teaching which is far better supported by the professional background of many if not most CDT teachers, hence the urgency of in-service training schemes such as TRIST.

Yet another problem is the unresolved distance and conflict between CDT and applied science. This remains unbridged and even unexplored in most schools. CDT teachers have been moving briskly into teaching electronics, control technology, computer-assisted design and other aspects of technology and applied science. Despite crushing staff shortages, but with immense enthusiasm and in-service training, many have offered outstanding programmes in these areas. But science teachers are also teaching in these same areas under the leadership of the Association for Science Education. Yet, as HMI have recently reported, in many schools there is little or no dialogue between science and CDT – in some there is a marked lack of awareness or recognition of the other's capability and contribution. This leaves a crucial fault into which school technology – and CDT with it – could fall disastrously.

Finally, there is a real risk that CDT and its teachers may fail to realize the magnitude of the task that they have accepted and may be unable to satisfy the often inflated expectations of employers, parents and politicians. CDT alone cannot solve the problems of British industry, make all young people employable, or provide activities to occupy unemployed people fully. Yet implicit global expectations of these kinds surround CDT as its teachers try to respond to too many things at once.

How may these perils be averted?

One solution for CDT is through improved management. The management skills required to run a CDT department are of the same level as a complex small business, yet there is virtually no provision for management training. Such training, if provided, would enable heads of CDT departments to use their limited staffing and resources more effectively and in a more focused way. It could also help them to communicate better with parents, pupils, employers and admissions tutors. It would above all enable them to evaluate the work of the department regularly and efficiently. In the latter the new initiative of the Department of Education and Science Assessment of Performance Unit in Design and Technology (based at Goldsmiths' College, London) is likely to be of long-term significance.

If the management of CDT could be put on a sound and coherent footing with the aid of a new kind of in-service training then the present instability and apparent confusion of much of what is currently happening could be resolved and the subject placed on a far firmer foundation to face the challenges and opportunities of the twenty-first century. Such a management initiative could, in part, be funded by sensitive use of TRIST monies. But it would need the combined effort of MSC and DES to ensure that both its direction and its strength were appropriate. Sensitivity and vision have always been major objectives of CDT teaching; they have never been more urgently needed by the subject itself.

V ISSUES

The three issues we deal with in this section, namely gender, special needs, and industry, are important considerations in planning the technological curriculum and in designing teaching and learning activities. Unlike in previous eras, technological education for all is a major concern and gender is the foremost barrier in this respect. It remains a scandal that so few girls have any kind of technological education and that they do not find their way into occupations associated with technology. Their absence from industry is not only a matter of the failure of equal opportunities, but a loss of their perspective in product development. The first chapter in this section, by Margaret Bruce, addresses this loss within the design process. As a symptom of society's sex stereotyping, the absence of women in industry cannot be rectified only by schools. Indeed teachers often lament the choices of subjects which girls make as a result of earlier stereotyping which they have accepted. However, schools have much to do. It is still possible to find 'needlework' put as an option against CDT, with girls tending to do the former and the boys the latter. John Catton, in the second reading (Chapter 20), considers what steps can be taken within the curriculum to encourage girls to take technology. But that is only one level. Technology is often not taught in a way which attracts girls, and in Chapter 21, Mal Evans shows how project work can overcome this. In a later section, (Chapter 36) we take up the problem of attracting girls to technology through a particular approach to planning a course.

A more difficult aspect of 'technology for all' is to cater for special needs. Most schools have a long way to go in this issue in all areas of the curriculum, with the full impact of legislation yet to be felt; the technological education of children with special needs is no different. We cannot do justice to such a complex topic and David Lund's article (Chapter 22) is only one aspect. It is true, however, to say that there has been very little published on the problems of providing a technological education to children with special needs.

By way of contrast, the amount of work on the relationships between schools and industry is large and in this section we give an extract of the publication of the Schools Council project in this area (Schools into Industry Project – SCIP). This is not just about vocational education, as Ian Jamison makes clear in his overview. Many see school–industry links as two-way, with industry having as much to learn and contribute as schools. In a Reader like this it is not possible to detail examples of work going on in schools and industries, but Jamison's chapter does, nevertheless, provide a good introduction – the book from which we have extracted, is well worth a closer look.

19   *A missing link: women and industrial design*

- M. Bruce

EDITORS' INTRODUCTION

The industrial design process is notable for its absence of practising women designers. It is likely that there will be little change in the future. Currently, there are no initiatives to encourage women to be more involved in the design process as either professionals or as informed consumers.

Consequently, the 'tacit knowledge' of women is not applied in the design process and artefacts are often inappropriate for the needs and concerns of women users. The 'tacit knowledge' of designers entails assumptions about women's needs and roles in society and reinforces and reproduces these.

Proposals for developing the skills and 'tacit knowledge' of women and making these central to the design process include, in the shorter term, post-experience design courses for women, awareness campaigns aimed at employers to recruit women designers, design competitions for girls, awards for female designers and supporting networks of women designers. However, to be successful in the longer term, a change in the design process and male and female roles has to be addressed.

Women are 'invisible' in the profession of industrial design. The consequences of this are twofold. First, women's 'tacit knowledge' is not drawn upon during the design process and second, designs and markets which meet women's needs and concerns are underdeveloped.

This paper considers the position of women practising industrial design and discusses some of the barriers which inhibit women from being involved as design professionals and informed consumers. It is argued that the 'tacit knowledge'[1] of male industrial designers makes assumptions about women's priorities, needs and roles in society. Designs are created which are dissonant with the concerns of many women consumers and users and also reinforce and reproduce certain images of women in society.

In the shorter term, there will not be a substantial increase in the number of women entering the industrial design profession or key positions in the product cycle, as these are currently constituted. Further, the present emphasis in design education is aimed at primary and secondary school level and at higher education to encourage closer collaboration between business schools and industrial design schools. Within this, there is no specific intention to alter the position of girls and women as designers. There is no attempt to build women's confidence in their ability to design and to perceive themselves as designers and inventors or as critical users and consumers.

Interventions can be made to open up the design process to women, as designers, users and buyers, so that women's needs and values are incorporated into the design process. However, such developments do not represent the solution unless, in the longer term, they become part of a wider political and industrial initiative which provides a more radical challenge to the ideology of the sexual division of labour, that is, which roles are appropriate for men and women.

THE SEXUAL DIVISION OF LABOUR

The term 'sexual division of labour' means that system whereby certain types of work are classified as being more appropriately done by one sex rather than another. In its grossest form, all domestic and caring work within the 'private' sphere of the family is classified as women's work, while all economically productive, waged work in the 'public' sphere as belonging to men. In present-day Western Europe few cultures or individual families would subscribe to such a rigid division. However, a sexual division of labour exists in the workplace, with certain types of jobs seen as male and others as female and the environment within which the work is done is also seen as sex specific.

Figure 19.1 demonstrates the areas of employment women are typically involved in.[2] The figures have not changed significantly during 1975–81, despite the implementation of the Equal Opportunities Act in 1975 and the technological and social changes of this period. Women are not found in professional, scientific and technical areas.

Figures are not available for the category of 'design'. However, the Design Innovation Group (DIG) of The Open University has conducted a survey of over 100 firms, during 1980 and 1984, in various areas of manufacturing industry, including domestic heating appliances, office furniture and electronic office equipment. The manufacturers are British, employing a workforce of between 25 and 2000 people, that is,

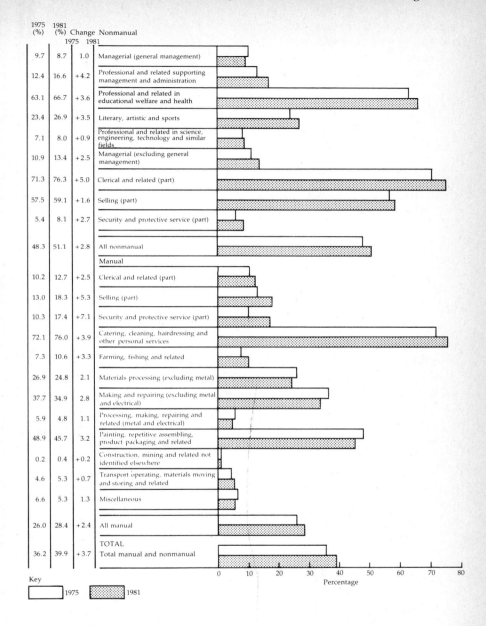

Figure 19.1 *Women as a percentage of occupational labour force, Great Britain 1975 and 1981*

Table 19.1 Comparison of male and female industrial design graduates for 1984

Educational institution	Course	Number of male graduates 1984	Number of female graduates 1984
Royal College of Art	Industrial design	25	3
	Industrial design and engineering course	16	1
	Automotive design	17	0
Kingston Polytechnic	Industrial design	21	2
Newcastle Polytechnic	Three-dimensional design	21	2
Manchester Polytechnic	Industrial design	9	2
	Interior design	5	9
	Wood, ceramics and metals	11	18
Central School of Art	Industrial design	16	3

medium-sized companies. From this, it is clear that less than 1 per cent of industrial designers employed in companies are female. Industrial design is a masculine activity. In the office furniture sector, for example, 72 per cent of firms in the sample employed in-house industrial designers but only *one* company employed a female industrial designer. Yet the main end-users for office furniture and electronic office equipment are women. Indeed, 70 per cent of users of office automation products are female.

DIG has also conducted a small number of international comparisons. European companies have a similar record to British firms. For example, one global electronics company employs ninety male industrial designers but no females. On the other hand, 20 per cent of the industrial design staff employed by two Japanese firms making electronic equipment, which were visited by the Group, are female.

Is this situation likely to change in the near future? A survey of some of the major institutions offering degree courses in industrial design shows the number of females graduating in 1984 in the UK. The figures are presented in Table 19.1. It is clear, from the table, that courses have two or three female graduates for every 19 to 23 male graduates. The automotive design course at the Royal College of Art had 17 male graduates in 1984 and no female graduates.

THE ABSENCE OF WOMEN

Women are absent from the world of product design and planning. Why?

The senior management staff interviewed by the DIG – marketing managers, industrial design managers, managing directors, etc. – attributed the 'invisibility' of female industrial designers to education, to women – 'who are their own worst enemies' – and to the nature of the job which was regarded and presented as 'masculine'.

Most of the male participants of the survey claimed to have 'open minds' about employing women as industrial designers but women 'just don't put themselves forward' or 'if they are offered a job, they turn it down'. There were rumours of there being more women industrial designers 'in other countries, notably America' or in other areas, such as fashion. In contrast, the one female industrial designer in the sample stated that women are not encouraged by industry or by the profession.

However, the statements do not acknowledge that, characteristically, the industrial designer's job is represented as 'masculine'. The interviewees in the survey reiterated the views that industrial design requires the ability to work with production engineers 'who would not take orders from or listen to a woman' or is 'industrial', 'dirty' or 'technical', meaning 'not for women'.

The participants of the DIG's survey, when asked about the skills of female industrial designers, were emphatic that women 'do not' (if they knew or thought they knew of a female industrial designer) or 'should not' (if they did not know of any) have different skills to male designers. Sometimes, women were perceived as having different and better skills in 'styling', 'colour', 'co-ordination' and appreciation of the end-user, especially in the areas of office furniture and office equipment. One man suggested that female industrial designers should be employed in kitchen design, since 'women have practical knowledge of kitchens and could enhance design in this area'.

These attitudes and perceptions of which roles are suitable for men and women are deeply rooted, culturally and historically, and act as a barrier inhibiting women from choosing technical and design careers, even when women have the appropriate knowledge, when they want to do such work and when employers are not discriminating against them. The attitudes reinforce the ideas that women do not typically perceive themselves as being 'technical' and suitable for 'industrial design'. Design education in schools, with the stereotype of male woodwork teachers and female needlework and craft teachers, does not encourage departure from these images.

Employers are not willing to give practical support to women with family commitments. This is one reason why women are in design education and research; the working hours are more flexible. Whilst training schemes in technology and science, notably the Women Into Science and Engineering (WISE) initiative organized by the Equal Opportunities Commission and the Engineering Council,[3] exist for women, Cockburn[4] points out that there are no schemes to train men in 'female' skills, for example, those required for domestic responsibilities, caring, secretarial and other support jobs that women usually do.

TACIT KNOWLEDGE

Cross, Naughton and Walker[1] argue that designers draw upon 'tacit knowledge' in the 'problem-solving' activity of design. This is described as 'knowing how', as 'knowledge we know but cannot tell'. It is 'intrinsically non-verbal', derived 'from experience' and associated with 'quality'. 'Tacit knowledge' is regarded by the authors as an *essential* component of the skills and quality of designers but the 'tacit knowledge' of women is rarely, if ever, applied to the industrial design process. Thus the profession does not reflect the composition of social needs and so is limited in its design endeavours.

More significantly, many technological objects are inappropriate for the needs and preferences of most female consumers and users. Male designers and ergonomists take account of women through anthropometric studies and market research but do not necessarily translate this knowledge into products commensurate with women's requirements and needs.

The ergonomists Pheasant and Scriven[5] tested the hypothesis that 'tools which have evolved for the male user are less satisfactory for women ('who in general have smaller hands and less muscular strength'). They considered handtools, tools, screwdrivers and automatic wheelbraces. Pheasant and Scriven concluded that 'men have sufficient strength to overcome deficiencies in tool design which pose insuperable problems for women'.

In effect, handtools are designed for 'people', but 'people' defined as 'stronger men'. More appropriate tool designs are required which allow 'non-macho' women and men to perform 'physically demanding tasks'. Indeed, it is the designers' 'tacit knowledge', containing assumptions about women's needs and their appropriate roles in society, which is problematical. The assumptions are evaluative in reinforcing and reproducing certain images of women, such as, inactive, physically weak, not logical, poor at manipulating machines and dependent on male colleagues and partners. The following examples are based on these value assumptions about women's attributes and social roles.

The action and 'macho' BMX bike for boys. Where is the equivalent for girls? Think of the 'action' mountain bike for men. Where is the equivalent for women? Think of microcomputers – machines for 'people' but which are generally marketed to boys and men. The parallel uses for 'non-logical' girls and women are not developed. One of the clearest examples of a public computer system designed primarily for middle-class men is British Telecom's videotex system, Prestel. The product was tested in the domestic area by mainly male users. The information provided by Prestel is for the businessman and his 'dependent wife'; the wife being a subset of the man. Why not provide information for different kinds of female users – mothers, single parents, career women, girls, etc.?

WOMEN'S EVALUATION AND DESIGN

Women are the prime consumers and users of many products and artefacts in both public and private spheres. In the shorter term, women can build up confidence to participate in the design process by working collectively to critically assess product and system design.

One successful technique for product evaluation is an approach to technology assessment developed for the Open University's women's studies course.[6] Most of the women taking the course had non-design and non-technical backgrounds. They participated in a technology assessment activity to assess contraceptive and transport technologies. The activity used a brainstorm technique to generate ideas and an 'effects wheel' to present the results of the women's evaluation. The women developed categories of 'women's needs' to assess different technologies. In some cases, these categories formed the basis for developing new designs appropriate to women's needs. Some of the results of the women's evaluation of transport technology are presented in Table 19.2 and Figure 19.2.

These show that women have particular experiences and concerns with regard to the products and artefacts of industrial design. This 'tacit knowledge' could be applied to develop new forms, radical designs and to assign priorities to the development and improvement of designs and artefacts.

What would happen if women's 'tacit knowledge' was utilized in the industrial design process? This is an almost impossible hypothesis to test, not least because there are so few women industrial designers working together to create such artefacts. There is one very stark illustration of potentially different designs. The designs are shown in Figure 19.3. They are irons created by male and female industrial design students who graduated from Kingston Polytechnic in 1983. The

Table 19.2   *Women's criteria and changes in car design*

Women's criteria	Changes in car design
Women and children – health and safety	Rear seat belts Child-proof locks Lead-free petrol Entertainment for children Privacy for breastfeeding Space for buggys, trolleys, etc. Ramp to lift/wheel buggys, trolleys, etc. into car directly – no lifting required
Ergonomic	Adjustable seat height Padded seat belts Awareness of people's different shapes and sizes 'Softer' brake pedals
Women's needs	Low speed cars Functional cars – not for 'status symbols' Durable Knowledge of cost of travel Easy to clean Easy to maintain Labelling of car parts to help repair and maintenance Access to wider variety of vehicles Greater choice over size, performance and fuel Mode of cars to suit different transport needs

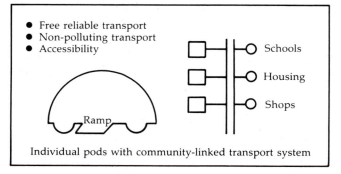

- Free reliable transport
- Non-polluting transport
- Accessibility

Ramp

Schools

Housing

Shops

Individual pods with community-linked transport system

Figure 19.2 *Features of public car transport system designed by women*

Example of a radical change: *public care community transport system*
The community transport system combines high-technology computers with low-energy, renewable and non-polluting fuels. Individual needs for convenience are met by many 'pod-like' vehicles located in community spaces, such as schools, housing estates, health centres, etc. The vehicle is shown in Figure 19.2.

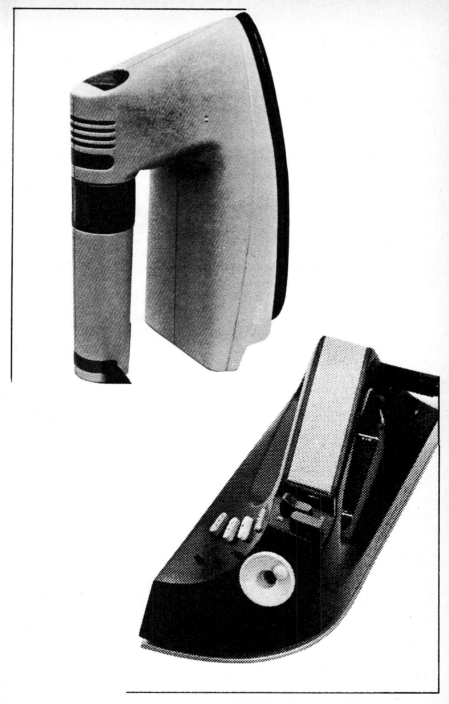

Figure 19.3 *Irons designed by (a) male and (b) female industrial design students*

designers were given the same brief: to redesign the hand grip of the iron. The students spent the same amount of time and worked together on the task analysis. Yet their solutions to the problem were quite different. The male designer was much more concerned with 'style', the female with 'user need', namely, the problem of ironing sleeves and making a compact iron. This is an example of 'tacit knowledge' in operation and an insight into possibilities for new designs.

PROPOSALS FOR ACTION AND CHANGE

There are points of intervention in the design process where the ideology supporting the sexual division of labour can be challenged. In the shorter term, various initiatives could be taken.

One of these is to increase the number of female technologists, designers, planners, etc. through extending training and education and employment opportunities to women. The government should combine post-experience design skills with an employer awareness campaign in order to increase the number of female industrial designers from less than 1 per cent to 5 per cent within the next three to five years, in the first instance. The courses could impart skills and knowledge so that the women have the skills to work as designers. However, such training schemes have to be handled carefully. This is clear from an evaluation of post-experience courses conducted during the WISE initiative in 1984.[7] A major criticism of WISE is that it elicited an individualistic response to encouraging women into science and technology in that it was women's responsibility to demonstrate that they could enter jobs, when in reality doors were closed to them, for reasons which had nothing to do with their level of personal competence. Also, these kind of initiatives have to be treated carefully to avoid tokenism or simple acceptance of the idea that more female designers alone automatically leads to changes in values and the quality of designs produced.

Another solution is to find ways of developing the confidence and skills of female users so they have a stronger effect on the product market.

This demands a much more critical consumer market than we have at present. Again, this has implications for education, as well as trade unions, consumer action groups, local authorities, etc. These organizations could play a part in democratizing the design process for women; for example, via supporting networks of women designers and users, organizing positive action campaigns and assessing products in terms of their ability to meet women's needs.

Critical evaluation activities, such as technology assessment, could be extended for women both with design and technical knowledge and without such knowledge. The activities should be built into formal educational settings and outside this context. This would help to build critical awareness of the design process and to prioritize women's needs in the design process. The Design Council could use the exhibition space in its shops to reveal how good or bad different products are at meeting the physical, visual, emotional and practical needs of women. Feminist criteria could be one of the Design Council's categories of selecting products for the Design Selection.

Support could be given to schemes which encourage girls and women to design and work collectively to develop their 'tacit knowledge' and to build confidence. For example, design competitions for girls (how many girls currently enter schools competitions?), awards specifically for female designers, the development of networks of women industrial designers, supported by the Design Council, SIAD and the Ergonomics Society, etc. and more support given to existing networks which bring women designers together, such as the Feminist Art Network and Matrix.[8]

For the longer term, design education should be directed at girls at primary and secondary school levels. This should impart skills and knowledge and encourage girls to perceive themselves as designers and inventors.

Also, awareness campaigns should be directed to employers to recruit female industrial designers and women in key positions of design and product planning. Employers should have working arrangements for women and men with family responsibilities.

Some critical scholarship in design has begun to address some of these issues. It is interesting that women scholars and designers who are involved in analysing the problem of design and women's lives often see it systemically, in terms of changing social structures, and are concerned to redesign large-scale environments such as cities[8] and 'self-cleaning' houses.[9]

There are also instances where women are working together collaboratively, and separately from men, to challenge the social relations underpinning the design process. The Women's Peace Movement in Britain through the establishment of 'peace camps', has challenged the development of military technology, created public awareness about the likely effects of nuclear war and wakened many people to the possibilities of using these resources to design alternative products. Many of the women regard weapons as a symbol of gendered designs which have rejected the values of non-violence, supportiveness and caring; values which they have been expected to embody as 'female'.

ACKNOWLEDGEMENTS

Thanks to Gill Kirkup for helping to develop some of the ideas in the paper and to Georgy Leslie, Robin Roy, John Towriss and Viv Walsh, members of the Design Innovative Group. Sally Boyle, Design Discipline, The Open University, prepared the artwork for Figure 19.2. The Joint ESRC-SERC Committee and The Open University have funded DIG's study.

REFERENCES

1. Cross, N., Naughton, J. and Walker, D., 'Design Method and Scientific Method', *Design Studies*, October 1981, [See Chapter 3 of this Reader.]
2. Equal Opportunities Commission, *Seventh Annual Report*, HMSO, 1983.
3. Equal Opportunities Commission and The Engineering Council, *What Is WISE Year All About?*, 1984.
4. Cockburn, C., 'Women and Technology', BSA Conference paper, April 1984.
5. Pheasant, S. and Scriven, J., 'Sex Differences in Strength? Some Implications for The Design of Handtools', *Procs. Ergonomics Society Conf.*, 1983.
6. Bruce, M., Kirkup, G. and Thomas, C., *Teaching Technology Assessment to Women*, Design Discipline, The Open University, 1984.
7. Bruce, M., and Kirkup, G., 'Post-Experience Course in Technology for Women: Aims and Processes', *Adult Education*, July 1985.
8. Matrix, *Making Space — Women and the Man-Made Environment*, Pluto, 1983.
9. Gabe, F., 'The Self-cleaning House', in J. Zimmerman (ed.) *Technological Woman*, Praeger, 1983.

20 *Girls and the CDT curriculum*

● J. Catton

The welcome development in the CDT curriculum over recent years is involving girls and boys alike in the subject area. The change in emphasis from a strong craft tradition to designing is reported by Dodd and Clay (1982). They say that 'pupils are now encouraged to become more involved in the planning aspects of their work. Teachers tend to favour a problem solving approach and there is general agreement that emphasis should not be on the product alone, but on the educational process leading to it.' I consider this philosophy and approach an essential prerequisite for girls' full involvement in the subject, for two reasons:

(a) a fresh start in the subject provides an opportunity for girls to break into a traditionally male subject;
(b) it enables the individual pupil, girl or boy, to decide on the specific direction of the subject content in order that a particular aspect or interest may be pursued.

Furthermore, the value of the traditional craft curriculum is very limited in the 1980s.

If girls are to take a full and active part in this important area of the curriculum, this change in emphasis in the work must be made, though that change alone will be unlikely to result in the mass take-up of CDT by girls in their fourth and fifth years. The CDT department within the design faculty in one of the eight GIST action schools has long been recognized as an example of good practice in curriculum development, but this has not led to the involvement of more girls, at fourth-year level, than in other mixed comprehensive schools.

GIRLS' AND BOYS' INTERESTS

When considering the type of project work to be set, it is well to bear in mind the current interests of pupils, though these have changed over the years and will of course continue to change. The GIST team found striking differences between girls' and boys' preferences for essay titles at the age of eleven years. Details of these findings are reported by Barbara Smail (1985) and in Table 20.1.

Table 20.1   *Girls' and boys' essay title preferences* (from Science Knowledge test)

Girls	%	Boys	%
Human body	25.7	Rockets	19.9
Birds	21.8	How cars work	18.1
Seeds	21.2	Human body	15.2
Pond life	14.0	Birds	11.7
Rocks/fossils	10.3	Pond life	11.2
How cars work	3.5	Seeds	10.3
Chemistry set	2.9	Rocks/fossils	9.1
Rockets	0.6	Chemistry set	4.5

Reproduced from Kelly *et al.* (1981), with permission from the Girls in Science and Technology Project.

The boys' top two titles – rockets and space travel, and how cars work – were largely unpopular with the girls. The same team, through their Scientific Curiosity questionnaire, also found that girls were uninterested in physical science and boys uninterested in nature study. Given the similarity between work in physical science and work in CDT, the implications for girls' enjoyment of CDT could be alarming.

Some interests overlap, however, and these provide clues to the type of material which may form useful starting points. One of the conclusions of the GIST research is that, 'if we were to devise a syllabus based on what is interesting to boys *and* girls at 11 years of age a large part of it would be linked to the human body and how it works, with another large section exploiting the spectacular aspects of science (as in scientific programmes on television)'. A topic of interest can be a very useful lead-in to other areas of work so that 'although girls are not interested in how machines work, they would like to find out more about how our muscles work and this could lead to learning about moments and forces' (Kelly *et al.* (1981).

John Pratt *et al.* (1984) found stark differences between the hobbies of girls and boys. The ten most popular hobbies for each sex, listed in order below, are taken from his fuller information:

Girls	Boys
1. Swimming	1. Football
2. Cooking	2. Sports
3. Music	3. Music
4. Dancing	4. Youth club
5. Knitting/sewing	5. Swimming
6. Youth club	6. Cycling
7. Reading	7. Fishing
8. Art/drawing	8. Cars
9. Horses	9. Motorbikes
10. Ice skating	10. Model making

Adapted from a chart in *Option Choice* published by NFER/Nelson.

Despite the obvious differences, there *are* similarities. For example, music is third in popularity in both lists, and youth club and swimming occur in both. This suggests that 'design and make' activities which focus on specific needs in those three areas may appeal to both sexes. By looking at the lower end of the full lists of hobbies, we can identify activities with no strong association for either girls or boys. Such neutral topics have the advantage of not making the majority of pupils of one sex feel that the topic is the prerogative of members of the opposite sex. Included in this category are: cinema, birdwatching, skating, rock climbing, walking, collecting, first aid, interior design, archery, television and photography. In other words, we can cater for a wide range of interests without reinforcing stereotypes.

It is important that such information is used positively to expand girls' and boys' mutual interests, not to emphasize the differences between pupils. I recently visited a second-year mixed CDT lesson in a multi-material workshop in which all of the girls were working in wood and the boys in metal. The teacher had divided the group. To provide totally different experiences, particularly when girls are asked to work in a less resistant material which is regarded as a soft option, is wholly inappropriate. Such a mistake is often made on the assumption, for instance, that jewellery work is appropriate for girls, whereas boys are free (able) to tackle other engineering-based types of work – the real meat of the subject!

Grant (1982) analysed pupil entries for the Schools Design Prize competition. He found that whereas boys' projects invariably focused on some *technical principle*, girls' projects almost always focused on a *social problem* or need. From this, Grant proposes an approach to teaching CDT which is likely to interest girls and help to change the male image of the subject. He refers to this approach as 'design and technology from issues and situations'.

This view is supported by girls who have studied CDT at some depth. A sixth-form girl taking A-level design recently wrote that CDT 'links economic, social and historical events and dilemmas, and enables one to appreciate and criticise society carefully'. Another girl on the same course wrote, 'I find this [analysis] a particularly interesting and enjoyable step in the design procedure, it required talking to many and varied people.'

EXAMPLES OF CDT WORK TO APPEAL TO GIRLS AS WELL AS BOYS

One of the GIST action schools found that girls have been attracted to the CDT department through their involvement with the School

Concern scheme. The scheme aims to improve the quality of life of disabled people in the area. Involvement is voluntary, and a group of five girls and six boys met regularly at lunchtime and after school for eighteen months. In that time they produced an activity centre for a blind boy, a shower bed for a physically handicapped girl, and a writing aid for someone who suffers from severe arthritis. Much time is spent by pupils at various homes and hospitals in the area and their commitment to the work appears to stem from the knowledge that they are being of direct help to other people. This type of project, with its focus on human needs and the quality of life, is worth serious consideration for inclusion in CDT lessons.

Another area with considerable scope for interesting both girls and boys in CDT might be described as having natural fascination. Many of the resulting projects are children's toys or 'executive toys'. At the heart of this work is the CDT Curriculum Research Unit at Middlesex Polytechnic, where John Cave and colleagues have developed ideas for alternative technology in schools. Possibly the most versatile idea to emerge from the unit is the simple pneumatic system in which a balloon is connected to a discarded washing-up liquid bottle with a piece of PVC tubing. When the bottle is squeezed the balloon expands. The scope of this delightfully simple and low-cost system is limited only by the imagination. Various toys using the simple, closed system pneumatics, from a jumping frog to a working model of a fork lift truck, have come from Middlesex. As John Cave (1980) says, this type of work 'holds out the promise of being instructive, interesting and – unashamedly – just good fun'.

These activities benefit from the fascination of controlled movement at a distance and provide ample scope for using and learning a wide range of practical skills – all at minimal cost.

THE WOODPECKER PROJECT

The Woodpecker project, undertaken by girls in their extra-curricular CDT club at Green Park, also has natural fascination. The idea was taken from the old toy which was operated by cotton reels at the end of strings. Since the girls were twelve to thirteen years old and had next to no experience in CDT at the time, the early stages of the project were tightly structured. The girls were presented with a partially completed woodpecker toy. The profiled woodpecker was pivoted on the legs using dowel rod; the legs were fixed to a base. The problem set to the group was how the bird could be made to 'peck' constantly, as in real life.

In the group discussion that followed, all kinds of possible methods were suggested, one or two clues being interjected by me from time to time. Some of the suggestions included elastic bands, strings and weights, springs, cams (although the girls didn't know the name at that stage), magnets, pendulums, and electric magnets. After this, the girls worked on detailed sketches and notes of 'their own' designs. The early stages of the practical work was, quite unashamedly, little more than woodwork-by-numbers. I wanted each girl to reach the stage of pivoting the bird on the baseboard as quickly and easily as possible. Hence my template was used to mark out the woodpecker profile and to mark positions of holes. There was ample opportunity for each girl to make her own contribution to the work when it came to arranging for the bird to 'peck' constantly.

The Woodpecker project was carefully chosen. I was mindful of the GIST research which suggested that many girls were interested in nature study. This, combined with the fascination of the pecking movement, and the desire to provide the girls with new experience in basic practical mechanics/electrics, lead to the final selection.

Towards the end of the project, when I asked if they had enjoyed the work, all but one of the girls said yes. Four or five of them were most enthusiastic about their interest, pleasure and satisfaction in the work. But I regard the fact that most of the girls voluntarily attended the sessions over a long period as the more reliable yardstick.

There are many other possibilities for similar projects. Some of the Victorian working toys are useful sources of ideas as are the various books on working toys and models. A word of caution, however. In this type of work, pupils can end up doing little more than copying and making up an existing idea. This, of course, is far from the spirit of current thinking in CDT and is of very limited value. Projects should always allow pupils a substantial piece of honest design activity. Even in the early stages, it can be combined with appropriate structure to the work, as in the case of the Woodpecker project. It is insulting to leave pupils with only minor decisions – where to round off the edges, or shapes of end-pieces, or colour of paint, for example.

The GIST research indicates that girls and boys alike are interested in the spectacular and fantastic aspects of science as depicted in television programmes such as *Tomorrow's World*. This kind of programme, and dramatized scientific/technical documentaries – like books – contain a wealth of material for discussion work, written material and even practical CDT projects. Though such material will all too often illustrate the domination of men (who had the opportunities) in the past – something we must be aware of as teachers – they are valuable and interesting for pupils. They demonstrate dramatically how technologies were conquered, and breathtaking moments of human intellect and craft were realized. Such material shows the very real way CDT is concerned with the quality of life; it can also produce ambition and goals for girls as well as boys.

The design activity we involve our pupils in should relate to the outside world – in all its magnitude – whenever possible. Woodpeckers, projects on toys and simple everyday artefacts, are valuable to a degree, but to convey an accurate impression of CDT (and hence its purpose and value) we must engage girls and boys in design beyond the school and domestic context. The difficulties in this are by no means insurmountable. The cost of materials for larger-scale work is an increasing problem, as is the physical movement of pupils. Some argue these pupils should learn on small and harmless work which is specifically set for that purpose, until they have mastered certain skills, although I would disagree.

There are solutions: special funds are still forthcoming from various sources and not every project has to be realized fully. It may be enough for pupils to complete some or all of the design stages and perhaps finish with a scale model. In other situations, discussion of a problem with the people concerned will be worth many hours of school-based work, in pupils' appreciation of a concept. For example, first-hand experience of visiting some local industry with a problem in its work, and a discussion with perhaps a member of their design staff and one of the site team, can be of immense value. Most of us CDT teachers do not organize enough of this liaison outside of our schools, perhaps because routine is easier. Yet it is as difficult to justify that routine as it is for pupils to appreciate the full meaning of our subject without such experiences.

The kind of work selected for pupils in CDT is all-important. We know the work must be appropriate for pupils in the progression of experiences and difficulties within the framework of their whole course. Often overlooked, or given little serious consideration, is that the subject matter must appeal to the majority of pupils – girls as well as boys. It is also vital to ensure that the nature of the work does not reinforce the 'maleness' of the subject area in the eyes of the girls. Failure to achieve this is likely to result in many of the girls taking no serious part in the work.

THE PRESENTATION OF CURRICULUM TOPICS

Even more crucial than the *type* of topic or project presented to girls and boys in CDT, is the *way* it is introduced. In the north-west, the Granada Power Game is an annual competition, designed to interest school pupils of all ages in technical design activities. Very few girls have entered the competition in the three years it has operated. The problem for 1982 was as follows:

GRANADA POWER GAME – 1982 PROJECT DEFINITION

The aim of the competition is to design and construct a device which, from a standing start, will travel along a straight track in the shortest possible time. En route the device will be required to cross two barriers positioned one metre and three metres from the start. (The timed track will be 4 metres long).

Each barrier will consist of blocks, a minimum of 60 mm high and 100 mm wide (this represents the same approximate section as a standard metric housebrick). The barriers will extend the full width of the track. The device must make contact with the track after crossing each barrier.

The height of the obstacles can be raised or lowered at the discretion of the competitors by adding or substracting blocks of the same cross-section and any increased scale of difficulty will be reflected in the score.

Scores will be decided on the basis of two runs. The score for each run will be obtained by dividing the time by a factor related to the height of the obstacles.

  (i) with both barriers 60 mm high (representing one brick) the time will be divided by 1.
 (ii) with both barriers 120 mm high (representing 2 bricks) the time will be divided by 4.
(iii) with both barriers 180 mm high (representing 3 bricks) the time will be divided by 10.

(Note: Both barriers must be at the same height and no barrier can be more than 180 mm high.)

The sum of the first two valid runs out of a maximum of four attempts will be used to determine the winner of the competition (in this case the smallest total will win).

The only power source will be a standard 150 mm length of rubber contained within the device (catapults will not be allowed). The rubber will be FAI Flight quality $\frac{1}{4}$ inch width, available from model shops. At both the Local Authority finals and Grand Final the organisers will provide these lengths of rubber so as to ensure a standard power source. The track for the Grand Final will be 4 metres long and 1.2 metres wide, laid out on the reverse side (the textured side) of standard sheets of hardboard. The track will extend beyond the start and finish lines but no flying starts will be allowed.

On the basis of the theories of Ormerod (1981) and Grant (1982), we should not be too surprised that boys dominate the Power Game. Whereas boys may happily grapple with the technological problems of the design brief, girls may well first wonder why such a device is required, where it will be used and who will use it. This is not at all unreasonable; after all, who needs a device which will travel along the ground, passing over house bricks spaced two metres apart?

The abstract quality of the problem does little to attract interest. It is related to nothing and appears to exist purely for the sake of the competition exercise. How does this contribute to a CDT concern with the quality of human life? The problem could well have been made more attractive to girls (and boys) by placing it in context, perhaps in the form of a game for a summer fair, or as a vehicle for travel across rough country. There are many other barriers to girls' full involvement in competitions of this type, but careful consideration of the presentation of the problem is likely to help.

It is interesting that, in the 1983 Power Game, a team of two girls from a Sefton school reached the final. Although their teachers spoke of the girls' tremendous persistence and determination, it may be significant that the girls had the active support of their families; most of the practical work was undertaken in the workshop bedroom of one of the girls whose father worked in engineering.

Dodd and Clay (1982) in 'A Plea for Balance' suggest 'time' as a topic which provides scope for the integration of a technological approach with some of the more traditional constructional work in CDT. This is useful, and has the additional advantage of being a neutral area of study. It may be tempting to begin such a piece of work with a technical investigation of timing devices, from electronic circuits to complex mechanical devices. However, the topic may have wider appeal if introduced through a discussion of the nature of time, patterns of waking and sleeping amongst different people, the need for measurement of time and degree of accuracy required for different situations. Pupils might then (as Schools Council/Nuffield Foundation Science 5–13 project (1972) suggests) move into making their own timing devices using throwaway materials. The possibilities of working across the subject area in schools are considerable with such a topic.

The CDT staff in one project school became conscious of the assumption they were making about pupils' interest in the work. They decided to make a positive attempt to present a technical project in a way which would capture the interest of girls as well as boys. At the same time, staff felt they should begin to move their emphasis away from the traditional craft skills in favour of a pupil-centred, problem-solving approach.

In the past pupils had made a small wheeled toy from drawings supplied by the teacher. The work had begun by showing pupils a completed model and then demonstrating the first stages of manufacture. They decided to give pupils much more freedom to decide on the nature of the wheeled toy and also to introduce the project from a wider and more general aspect, including the need for, the variety of, and the different uses of wheels in our everyday lives. A mixed ability group of second-year pupils were to undertake the project. A pupil workbook entitled 'Wheels' was produced to assist in the introduction of the work and also to provide structure in the design process pupils were to follow. The attempt to interest girls focused on the inclusion of illustrations and notes based on everyday examples, where possible. It was also considered important to depict girls actively involved with 'Wheels'.

The project was attempted with two groups of pupils who were to work in wood for six weeks as part of their second-year craft 'circus'. It is extremely difficult to be certain about the success of its appeal to girls. The teachers reported that more girls took part in class discussion than was often the case, and that both girls and boys appeared interested in the pupil booklet. One teacher observed that it was 'hard work' compared with the way he had taught for the past twelve years. It was also felt that in future the project need not be based upon the chassis since it often hindered the development of sound design ideas.

Materials of this type can be produced by teachers or adapted from what is already in use. The 'masculine' image of CDT will slowly be changed by efforts like this, particularly if the production of non-sexist teaching materials is co-ordinated in a department. Commercial publishers have yet to respond to the need for CDT textbooks and other printed materials to focus on *people*: *girls* as well as boys, *women* as well as men. Subject teachers have the opportunity to take the initiative and put their own house in order before publishers eventually act on this matter.

Craft, design and technology is about improving our environment and thus the quality of our lives. For a subject with this objective, the preoccupation with materials, tools and processes is rather ironic. In our attempts to improve the lot of human beings, we frequently omit them from our discussions and deliberations! The social aspects have been shown to be an important motivator for girls in the subject and it is therefore vital that we focus on the broader relationship between any one project and the wider society. We have seen that even when curriculum content and presentation cater well for the interests of both girls and boys, it does not necessarily follow that significant numbers of girls will opt in when given a choice. However, it is one necessary factor amongst many which should be planned for the needs and interests of all pupils.

SUMMARY

The development of the former 'technical crafts' into craft, design and technology, with all the implications for the new forms, nature and approach to the subject, is likely to be helpful in encouraging more girls to continue their study of the subject. The new approach should help to change the image of the subject which has dissuaded girls in the past. Furthermore, CDT is more pupil-centred, allowing individual pupils much greater involvement and influence in the nature and direction of their work. This is also likely to appeal to girls (and boys alike).

Curriculum topics

When selecting topics for pupils, it is important to remember that girls and boys have many different interests. We must cater for these interests without reinforcing stereotypes. For example, it is not uncommon for girls (but not boys) to be invited to make jewellery; it is unwisely assumed that jewellery will interest them, simply because of their sex.

Despite the range of pupils' interests, there appear to be overlapping areas and these should be exploited. For example, in the GIST research, both girls and boys declared an interest in the human body. Here is a starting point in the study of structures and other mechanical principles.

Other topics might be described as neutral areas (e.g. time, photography, rock climbing), having little or no association with either male or female. Such areas are likely to provide useful starting points in CDT.

Table 20.2 Summary of CDT projects for mixed groups

Type of project	*Examples*
1. Projects based on *shared interests* such as human body, music, swimming, youth club	Human structures, cassette holders, trophies for sporting achievement
2. Projects arising from a *social issue*	Aids for disabled members of the community, safety in various situations
3. Projects in *neutral areas*	Photography, bird watching, collecting, cinema, skating
4. Projects with their own 'natural fascinations'	'Executive' and children's toys based upon *movement* of some form, closed system pneumatics, control at a distance
5. Projects with a strong *cross-curricular* aspect	Puppets, wheels, shelter, information-handling, saving energy, travel

The presentation of curriculum topics

Topics are likely to appeal more to girls if they are presented as a *need* of individuals or society. Whenever possible, the full context of the need should be made clear and projects linked to society, such as local public building schemes or some particular industry. More abstract ideas, in common with techniques/tools/equipment, as starting points are much less likely to appeal to girls. It is important, however, that these areas are covered by girls, after their interest has been captured.

Work sheets and source materials should reflect your expectation of girls' full involvement, rather than reinforce society's stereotyping; show girls as well as boys, and women as well as men, involved with tools, machines, electronics and other technical areas.

REFERENCES

Cave, J. (1980), 'Technology in School: some alternative approaches', *Studies in Design Education, Craft and Technology*, 13, Winter.

Dodd, T. and Clay, B.E. (1982), 'A Plea for Balance', discussion paper for teachers based on a small research project in Craft, Design and Technology, Department of Design and Technology, Brunel University, September.

Grant, M. (1982), 'Starting Points', *Studies in Design Education, Craft and Technology*, 15, Winter [Chapter 36 of Reader].

Kelly, A., Smail, B. and Whyte, J. (1981), *The Initial GIST Survey: Results and Implications*, GIST.

Omerod, M.B. (1981), 'Factors Differentially Affecting the Science Option Preferences, Choices and Attitudes of Boys and Girls', in Kelly, A. (ed.), *The Missing Half*, Manchester University Press.

Pratt, J., Bloomfield, J. and Seale, C. (1984) *Option Choice: a Question of Equal Opportunity*, NFER/NELSON.

Schools Council/Nuffield Foundation Science 5–13 Project (1972–4), *Time*, Macdonald Education.

Smail, B. (1985), *Girl Friendly Science: Avoiding Sex Bias in the Curriculum*, Schools Council Programme Pamphlet, Longman for the School Curriculum Development Committee.

21 *Project 'JAM' (Jar Air Mechanism)*

● M. Evans

EDITORS' INTRODUCTION

Mal Evans describes a project involving boys and girls. The work and views of the girls are given here, illustrating how technological projects appeal to them.

This project was initiated as a standard item of course-work related to the Oxford Board's O-level in CDT. The problem posed, that of removing tight lids from screw-top jars, was taken directly from a past Oxford paper.

The new fourth form group to which this problem was presented, consisted of twenty-one boys and seven girls. The group was to be taught primarily by myself, but with occasional assistance from other departmental staff who were sometimes available.

The project topic when announced, got a mixed reception (not a pun!), the boys feeling initially that there *was* no problem here, as *they* had never encountered any difficulty in removing lids from jars!

As discussion proceeded however, it transpired that some of them had! and, of course, as the discussion proceeded further to consider those weaker than the norm, they became aware of those who did not have the male physical strength advantages. What about elderly people with arthritic hands? or for some reason having insufficient strength in their hands and fingers – what about girls?! The girls of course readily accepted the problem, they had encountered this difficulty many times, and there were situations in the kitchen when you needed to tighten jar lids securely as well as remove them afterwards! And what about elderly people and those generally who might be handicapped in some way? This really concerned them!

So, off we all went, in search of a simple effective answer to the problem – quite a tall order for 14/15-year-olds particularly, one would have thought, the girls, who had only one year's experience of designing and making things anyway. It so happened that during the latter half of the year, a letter arrived concerning the 'Young Inventors' Awards' which were in turn related to the 'Homeware and Hardware Exhibition' at Olympia. I felt that here was an opportunity to add further realism and incentive to the project, and, as it happened, what we were doing particularly suited the requirements.

I decided to ask initially if any of them would be interested in competing, and most were. As it was virtually impossible to bring the work of all twenty-eight to a stage which satisfied the entry requirements in the time available, each pupil's project was assessed in terms of suitability and progress. The work of six of the girls and five of the boys would meet the deadline (an interesting comparison?).

To be honest, some of the devices that the boys produced (as I said to them at the time) would look better in a garage jacking up a car than in a kitchen taking lids off screw-top jars! Most accepted this criticism with good humour and in the spirit in which it was levelled. From my point of view, the main educational aims had been achieved; they had each followed a detailed design process in considering the problem and their devices would indeed take off tight lids from screw-top jars – even if they were also capable of jacking up cars! Some of the proposed solutions were very cleverly and painstakingly arrived at – a sequential mechanism which unfortunately relied on the elastic strength of a loop, which if formed from a material strong enough for the task in hand, would need a Herculean operator! There were sliding jaws which moved in curved inclined planes, pivoting hooks, wedge devices, spring-loaded moving platforms, cone sections which moved in converging arcs, the Kitchen 'Toucan', a device based on arcs tangential to two circles of differing diameters – and so on.

Each pupil's work consisted of two A2 'design sheets', a working drawing plus models/prototypes and a written (or typed) report.

Of particular interest in this project was the work of the girls, and their philosophies and career aspirations in choosing to take design, given in answer to a questionnaire. Their answers are both interesting as well as sometimes amusing!

LILIAN CHONG

Although art is my favourite subject, I find design the most interesting as it covers most aspects of life. It helps us to understand people's needs and once you've successfully achieved something, you will feel satisfied. I enjoy the practical side of design more, although the thinking side helps to improve our imagination and the theory lessons help us to acknowledge the materials available and their individual uses, as well as the different methods and machines we can use.

Design and technology sounded exciting and because it was more useful than cookery or needlework, both of which could be learnt in the spare time. But now I find it useful in other subjects like geography, where we had to find out how steel was produced.

When I leave school, I would like to go to art college and if possible get an A-level in art and graphics. After college, I would like to take up a job as a graphics designer.

KIRSTEN CLAYTON

I chose design and technology for four reasons:

1. Design and technology was a mixture of academic and practical, and to be able to do something practical is a restful change (sometimes!).
2. My better subjects tend towards the arts, e.g. English, history. I don't do so well at maths and science and as really I couldn't make a career in either of the former I took a subject which took other skills apart from artistic ones.
3. I tend to be a very forgetful, scatty person and in design and technology it is necessary to be very precise and definite and to formulate your ideas clearly.
4. Design and Technology gives experience in practical skills such as working on the machines, turning wood, etc. I find that by taking design and technology I approach problems differently and even solve them differently. I thought that design and technology was quite boring when I did it in the third year, but now that I've really become involved in this problem I find the subject fascinating.

I'm still not really sure what I'd like to do when I leave school. Most of all I should like to become an actress, but acting is not the most secure of professions and I will probably do something to do with medicine, either a doctor or a medical researcher, or perhaps a barrister, thus combining acting and English!

SARA DEVITT

I chose design because I liked it best out of the four subjects I had available. I was told by Mr Evans that I was quite good at design so I thought it would be worthwhile taking it up. And lastly I find design quite interesting as well as practical.

NINA PAWAR

There were no 'ifs' or 'maybes' about choosing design and technology because since the first year of Orange Hill I have wanted to take design O-level. Why?

1. My dad is a hospital consultant architect, and I do admire the work he has done so I'd like to see what design is like.
2. From the choice of doing needlework, cookery and design, design is the better option, because the other two options can be learnt at home and design involves a lot of thinking.
3. I think the idea of being confronted with a design problem is a challenge, and after one has solved a problem, however trivial it is, one has achieved something.
4. Design can never be boring or uninteresting because we study different aspects of design.
5. By doing design one can become more aware about the world around and other people's needs.

So when I leave school I've left myself three options; one is to enter the medical field: the positions I've considered include doctor, physiotherapist, cardiac physician or a gynaecologist. Again my dad, who's gone through two major heart operations, has prompted these ideas because at the time I did read about the heart and its disorders and found the subject interesting. The other reasons for this choice were: I am interested in science and how its knowledge is used to help the sick and I think healing and helping the sick is a positive contribution to happiness. Another option has been influenced by design while doing a project on plastics. I received a sheet on careers in the polymer industry, and because it is a forward-looking industry on which all of us depend, I'd like to be a technologist or laboratory technician. I'd like to be responsible for running a lab or a research project and I'd like to decide on how to approach problems, and how to solve them.

If all else failed or if I were courageous enough, I'd like to go into the record/music business, because I have a very deep interest in modern music whatever variation. I'd love to produce records or run a music paper or manage a group but it's only an 'if' and it may not work. If I do become a technician or technologist I'll be able to say to myself that design did play a part in my actual getting there. If I don't, well I'll be able to look back on my projects with some satisfaction and with the knowledge that design was worth doing.

LISA QUATTROMINI

I chose design and technology because it was the most decent subject to choose from in that group. Also I had done design in the third year and I found it quite enjoyable so I decided to continue for O-level. Design and technology also trains the creative, artistic side of your mind and I feel that that is important for any career and to make domestic life more enjoyable and useful.

LISA WILKINSON

I chose design and technology because it was the best of the four options. The others were ceramics, cookery (which I can't stand) and needlework (well, I didn't actually really like needlework).

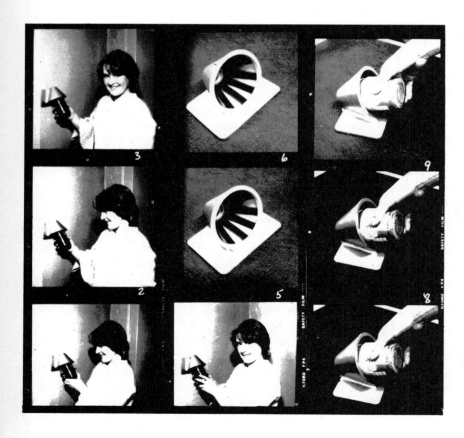

Figure 21.1   *Lisa Wilkinson and her work*

I continued with design and technology in the fourth year because I found it interesting and it kept my mind working. I found the thinking side of design most interesting. Now I also enjoy the practical side, though I still prefer the designing aspect.

When I have done my A-levels I want to go to university. Then I want to take up engineering.

The work of these girls was sensitive, detailed and dedicated, being easily comparable with the best efforts of the boys. Their interest never flagged and their cheerfulness and enthusiasm never waned. The boys in fact knew before much time had elapsed in the course that they would need to 'look to their laurels' to retain their 'resident expert' image!

It transpired that the work of one of the girls impressed the judges most at Olympia: Lisa Wilkinson, with her design based on a hollow cone, became runner-up.

To achieve this she had produced three different ideas, and developed one to a stage where it could well become a commercial product. (She has in fact been approached by a number of interested manufacturers.) She had produced a formal working drawing, a pattern drawing, made a split pattern, produced the mould and casting, machined and generally finished a prototype product – not forgetting of course, her very explicit report.

Needless to say, I was very impressed, though not surprised, by the work of all the girls in this large working group, and it is clear that *all* girls should be given the opportunity to participate in this important area of the curriculum. By far the majority do not at present, and, even if given the opportunity, tend not to opt for it for lack of understanding of the subject content – 'Better the devil we know?' They are missing out, at the very least in their preparation to cope with their future lives in a complex technological society. That same society will also miss out if it fails to recognize and subsequently rectify this totally unsatisfactory state of affairs – and further if it fails to develop what is potentially a great asset to its future existence and progress.

22 *CDT for children having 'special educational needs'*

● D. Lund

INTRODUCTION

I have taught CDT at a Comprehensive School to children of all abilities. My recent experience has involved teaching CDT to children categorized as being maladjusted and also to children who have 'mild' and 'moderate' learning difficulties. From my experience I am convinced that CDT should have a significant role in the curriculum for those children described as having 'special educational needs' by the Warnock Report (DES 1978) and the 1981 Education Act. In particular I have been interested in identifying the specific aspects of the subject which might be most useful.

The concept of 'special educational needs' stems from the Warnock Report (1978) which was the first-ever report to enquire comprehensively into the education of the handicapped.

In 1977 the extent of those children requiring and being given 'special education' was about 1.8 per cent of the school population in England and Wales; this represented approximately 176,000 children. Warnock recommended that the concept of 'special provision' should be expanded. This decision was based on the findings of the Isle of Wight Study (1964–65), a study which investigated the incidence of intellectual and educational retardation, psychiatric disorder and physical handicap. Warnock (DES 1978) stated therefore: 'That about one in six children at any time and up to one in five children at some time during their school career will require some form of special educational provision' (3–17 p.41).

This wider concept clearly expanded the previous idea of special educational provision and was meant to absorb other aspects of school provision, such as remedial departments which were not previously thought of as being 'special education'. The report highlighted those children who need some kind of additional help, most of whom are already in the mainstream of education.

My interest in the idea that CDT can be of special importance for children with SEN has shown that the subject is not being exploited as much as it should be for the benefit of such children. This seems perhaps to be because of other pressures, such as the constant striving to make the subject more acceptable for the brighter pupil.

WHAT CAN CDT OFFER TO CHILDREN WITH SPECIAL EDUCATIONAL NEEDS?

The underlying hypothesis on which I have based my ideas is the belief that most children enjoy 'doing things' in a practical rather than academic way. This is by no means a new idea when it comes to educating the 'less able'. I do, however, believe that teachers of CDT and many others are not aware of the vital role the subject can play in the education of children with 'special educational needs', needs which will vary but also which may have some common characteristics.

CDT is taught to smaller groups of children than most other subjects, and the equipment used is extensive and interesting. The materials used are varied and by the nature of the subject it is 'child-centred'. Essentially, there is tremendous scope for a child to learn and express himself in a safe and controlled environment.

The Schools Council (1980), after surveying the opinions of teachers, found that with regard to 'non-academic' outcomes of educational activities, art and craft, including CDT, came top in the following areas for disturbed children:

(a) relief of tension;
(b) personal enjoyment;
(c) sense of achievement;
(d) giving insight into personal and emotional problems.

The enjoyment and sense of achievement to which they refer is certainly something that I have witnessed when teaching CDT to children with mild/moderate learning difficulties and children categorized as being maladjusted.

Such achievement and enjoyment makes children want to return to the subject and progress onto more difficult projects. This could be the situation in many other subject areas; however, being a 'doing' or 'making' subject the results are much more obvious. This point would seem to have been recognized by the Schools Council (1975): 'It is a well established principle that the learning of slower children needs to be based on the concrete rather than abstraction' (p.18).

When a child meets the subject of CDT for the first time he could have behind him several years of failing in other areas of school life and possibly out of school life. He might have difficulty reading, doing arithmetic, getting along with other children and teachers. He might, because of these situations, lack confidence and be at the start of rejecting what school has to offer in order to avoid further failure, rejection being his 'defence mechanism'.

In the first or second year of secondary school, or the equivalent if he is in a middle or special school, a child will hopefully have the opportunity of working in a way not previously done in school. He will enter a workshop which contains a variety of new and interesting things, he will have the opportunity to produce 'something' using many skills which he has not already failed at using. If he succeeds the end result is visible and real for all to see and probably for him to keep. Perhaps at this time, we can help the child with 'special needs' the most by capitalizing on this interest.

> It is precisely at this time, the beginning of the secondary period, that an exceptional opportunity occurs for assisting the educational development of the backward child. (Eggleston 1953: 61)

Eggleston referred to children who are now described as having moderate learning difficulties. He went on to describe the great influence the CDT teacher may have, he continued:

> An interesting stranger with a new subject which is at once acceptable to the boys as an adult activity, is in possession of an outstanding opportunity to assist the whole development of the backward child. (p.61)

This is of course providing the teacher is aware of the needs of the child. Eggleston continued to suggest that not only is CDT (then handicraft) useful, but that it could lead to be:

> the key subject for the whole education of the backward child, which harnessing the practical interest of the boy, accelerates the whole of his educational development. (p.61)

This would seem to be quite a strong claim but one which I certainly subscribe to. Quite simply, what other school subject could be a better starting point for so many ways of using 'practical', 'concrete' learning? If we take, for example, a project of designing and making a toy lorry, apart from learning about the materials and tools to be used, why not include work about the history of transport, some simple science, e.g. fitting electric lights, road safety, etc? The possibilities are endless.

Others who have found the opportunity of working in concrete situations with less able children included Duncan (1942):

Attempts to educate them with an approach through the medium of words met with little success. We have seen, however, that in the ability to deal with relationships in concrete situations many of even the dullest children are at the same levels as children of middle ability, and that in this respect some are even above the line of middle ability. (p.66)

Duncan's experience was gained by teaching 'backward' boys woodwork. He also stated that it taught them self-criticism and gave them a sense of achievement. He did, however, add that children who had an IQ of below 66 did not seem to benefit from such a medium for learning. This, however, is contrary to the experience of Howard and Whally (1977), who experimented with some very basic woodwork with a group of mentally handicapped boys, brain-damaged and Down's Syndrome. They began with simple operations such as hammering nails, sorting nuts and bolts. They found that after the programme the behaviour of the boys improved.

Such simple operations cannot really be described as being true 'all-round' CDT activities. However, it is just an example of how one particular area of the subject may be of use to children with a particular 'special need'.

With regard to the use of CDT for children with emotional and behavioural difficulties, one of the pioneers of this work with maladjusted pupils was Wills (1941). He saw practical and craft activities as being a most useful medium for therapy. Laslett (1977) sees the most beneficial aspect of craft as being the so many different things available for children to use:

> The wide variety of materials and tools in the craft room meet the children's needs and moods. There are soft, malleable materials which offer little resistance to cutting and shaping, and hard materials which only strong blows and bold movements can affect. This at once indicates the therapeutic possibilities of craft. (p.132)

Many children with 'special educational needs' for one reason or another may have difficulty making friends and sustaining relationships. They may be introvert, lacking confidence, having experience of relationships failing in the past or just be unpopular due to their behaviour. I believe that in CDT lessons an ideal opportunity arises for children to work together as a group or in pairs on a project of common interest. If a child has a special need in this area it would not be too difficult for any teacher who is made aware of the need to manipulate the situation to help. Laslett (1977) refers to the strength of the subject for this purpose:

> Craft lessons give children opportunities to increase their skills, to co-operate with other people and to realise their own limitations and capabilities. The finished product reflects both their practical skills and their personal qualities. (p.133)

Problem-solving is an important feature of the 'new' subject CDT. The way of solving problems in the workshop is taught in a definite sequence and applied to progressively difficult projects and briefs. Children growing up have many problems, especially those who have learning and behavioural difficulties. If these children become interested in CDT, might they not learn an approach to solving real-life problems?

There are three specific areas in which I feel CDT can play an important role, under the headings of basic skills, self-image and motor skills.

BASIC SKILLS

By basic skills I refer to those basic ingredients which are needed to survive in other areas of the curriculum and post school, i.e. language (reading, writing and oral expression) and numeracy. My argument quite simply is: could not CDT be used as a medium for promoting such skills in a way which is interesting, relevant and enjoyable? I believe so.

A child who becomes interested in craftwork quickly learns the names of the tools and processes involved. If all of the equipment is clearly labelled and details of the processes he needs to know are written appropriately, this will surely help his reading? He would be reading for a purpose.

If a child wishes to make something special and communicate his own ideas to a teacher, he will be asked to draw a simple sketch and then perhaps a more complicated working drawing. These will be labelled to explain details, information may be needed from relevant books. The pupil would be writing because he can see a need to do so. It would take little imagination to extend this 'relevant' use of written skills into other areas, e.g. letter-writing for information on a specific topic, keeping a workshop diary, etc.

Turning to the oral use of language, it is widely accepted that a child's language develops best when the child is in conversation with an adult and for this reason the Bullock Report (DES 1975) recommended that: 'There should be more opportunities for children to be in a one to one relationship with adults' (p.70).

Surely the CDT teacher is in an ideal position here? Remembering that a child who is following an individual project will need to approach the teacher for specific help and advice (even the child who usually gets away with sitting quietly at the back of most other lessons!). With regard to home economics, which could be viewed as a branch of CDT, Devereux (1979) refers to the fact that many teachers may not exploit this opportunity.

Specialist teachers realise the opportunity Home Economics offers for developing practical use of communication and language skills – but how scientifically is this exploited? (p.16)

The use of language in school CDT workshops would seem to be relatively uncharted ground, but the new concept of CDT would seem to give tremendous scope for improving children's use of language. However, much more research is needed.

We may even move one step further from not only encouraging children who use verbal skills to explain what it is they are going or wish to do, but also by using lessons as informal counselling sessions. Not for every child, of course, but perhaps those one or two children in each class who may have 'special needs'. 'When the hands are occupied conversation on personal matters often arises more easily and with less embarrassment than formal counselling sessions' (Wilson and Evans 1980 : 180).

NUMERACY

Much criticism has been levelled recently towards the standard of maths in schools. The Cockcroft Report (DES 1982) recommends as part of the solution that maths should be given more relevance and used in different areas of the curriculum. He especially mentions art and craft subjects. I would suggest that CDT is a particularly important subject area for promoting concrete use of maths, if only we were to explore the opportunities.

Teachers of other subjects as well as mathematics teachers, need to be aware of the part which maths can play in presenting information with clarity and economy, and to encourage pupils to make use of maths for this purpose. (DES 1982 : 148)

I have been able to find few documented examples of where maths or English has been 'deliberately' taught through the medium of CDT type subjects. Burnett (1969), however, is one example. He decided to follow certain projects in wood to discover relevant 'maths in the environment', geometrical shapes, etc., which he followed up on. He did this with primary age children.

I am sure that with careful planning and choice of projects we would encourage most use of maths, perhaps even to help overcome a particular stumbling point a child may have in learning certain mathematical concepts. CDT teachers at the very least ought to be aware, as Cockcroft points out, of the importance of how to present and use maths.

SELF-IMAGE

The importance of a child's self-image and his subsequent success or failure at school has become more and more acknowledged as being closely correlated. Research has shown that a positive self-concept and high self-esteem is likely to result in higher achievement (Bledsoe NIR 1967; Bowden NIR 1957). One of the characteristics of many children with 'special educational needs' who may be failing at school is that they have a poor view of themselves and low self-esteem. Such a situation may contribute toward the formation of a type of 'secondary handicap' as described by Shakespeare (1975). Teachers are in an ideal position to help improve (or make worse) a child's self-concept, by the situations he manipulates and what 'message' he relates to his pupils, consciously or unconsciously.

I believe that by using the many attributes of CDT, teachers can help pupils improve their self-esteem. This can be done by careful selection and planning of activities and projects which will result in the child achieving success. Such success, will be visible and concrete, something for the child to show to 'mum'. Many children with 'special needs' badly need such reinforcement from parents, peers and other teachers. They may have few opportunities of achieving it in any other situation. Wilson and Evans's (1980) survey of special schools found that: 'Staff felt that after competence in the basic skills, craftwork offered the best opportunity for improving self-esteem' (p.138).

From my own experience of teaching children having 'special needs', care is needed to prevent too much failure. Just as pleasing results in practical subjects are easy to see and be proud of, a total disaster can also be very obvious and make a child reluctant to participate.

Clearly the CDT teacher responsible for teaching children with 'special needs' ought to be careful that appropriate projects are selected, projects which would seem to be commensurate with pupils' ability and interest level; realizing, of course, that making things too easy will do little to help. As Weiner *et al.* (1972) explain, unless the child is responsible for his success he will not accept it as being a positive contribution to his self-concept.

It is useful at this stage to consider some brief suggestions from Coopersmith and Feldman (1972) regarding the way in which a child best improves his self-esteem. They explain that it is very important for a child to have the opportunity for choice and refer to the most extensive programme for affording choice as being a 'responsive environment'. This they based on the Montessori tradition that 'schools should respond to the learner' rather than the other way around. In order to create a responsive environment five essential features are necessary (all of which quite easily relate to CDT).

(a) Child allowed opportunity to choose from several activities.
(b) Activities are self-pacing.
(c) Activities provide immediate feedback.
(d) Teachers respond to child by giving help when requested.
(e) Teachers establish limits of environment, activities, materials and organization.

In CDT pupils will have a choice of several materials and projects. They will have the opportunity to work at their own pace, they can see their project taking form. The craft teacher is on hand to give advice when needed, but will structure the environment, setting necessary limits which are usually obvious to children for safety reasons.

MOTOR SKILLS

I have left what might be one of the most obvious possibilities of CDT for children with 'special needs' as the last. Some children for one reason or another may have difficulty with co-ordination, both fine and gross. Where else in a school can one find more of a selection of equipment which can be handled by pupils?

Simple and more complex operations can give children the opportunity of developing motor skills, from using a pencil and cutting string to soldering tin sheet or shaping hot metal. I believe that the possibilities are endless, especially with an imaginative teacher. Each 'need' of course has to be considered and the appropriate type of work selected.

PROBLEMS AND PITFALLS

Providing CDT on the curriculum for children with 'special educational needs', even if it is viewed as an important ingredient in their education, may not be easy. There is still a shortage of qualified teachers of CDT – in special schools difficulty might be found attracting suitable teachers because of limited equipment as Butterworth (1983) points out. Economic constraints may prevent such investment. On a wider base, however, most CDT teachers will encounter children with 'special needs' in the ordinary situation. How these teachers approach such children and any others who may be integrated from special schools will vary with each individual teacher.

I wish to consider four points which I feel are important for the specialist teacher to do if he or she is committed to help meet the needs of 'special' children. I have formulated these points by drawing together some of the issues raised, but mainly from my own experience, having met CDT face to face with children having 'special needs'. The points are all concerned with what the individual teacher ought to do; after all, the ultimate responsibility on how we teach rests upon individual teachers – teachers who can choose to make an effort or not.

Firstly the CDT teacher must come to terms with the concept of 'special need' and be prepared to examine their own attitude towards such children.

Secondly, he or she must be prepared to be more flexible in their approach to such children.

Thirdly, they must be prepared to find out more about the type of needs children may have and match them to ways in which CDT can help to meet these needs.

Fourthly, the CDT teacher should be prepared to take positive steps to meet these in a deliberate and planned way. [Ed: This point is not included below.]

ATTITUDES

In my experience teachers prefer to teach the most able pupils. Why not? It is easier. How many teachers enjoy teaching the remedial class, or the class which contains several disruptive pupils? If the reader doubts my theory, I suggest a visit to a school staff-room when the new timetable is announced!

The majority of children with 'special needs' require more time and effort from their teachers. For this reason such children may not be popular and may be labelled. The consequence of such labelling has often been discussed, e.g. Becker (1963). Such labelling and the related attitudes towards such children could be the cause of other problems. An example is perhaps truancy, as Hamblin (1977) states:

> Truancy can be a response to both the perceived irrelevancy of the curriculum and a sense that the school is not only uninteresting, but uninterested in certain groups of pupils. (p. 75)

A great effort and determination is required for a teacher to overcome the pressures we may encounter from our colleagues, especially with regard to labelling. Staff-room language is very descriptive when concerned with children who have learning difficulties and behavioural problems. It is very easy to make excuses and opt out of making an effort with such children, blaming failure on *their* inadequacies not *ours*.

I believe that we must firstly examine our own attitude to children who have 'special educational needs' before attempting to meet their needs. This is perhaps one of the hardest things to do, especially at a time when CDT teachers may wish to jump on the bandwagon of their subject being more and more 'academically' acceptable for more able pupils.

In future the CDT teacher may be expected to teach more and more children with 'specific needs' in addition to those children with 'special needs' he will teach already. This may, for example, mean teaching a physically handicapped or visually impaired child. At this point the teacher may have the choice between making a real effort to help or looking for problems, not solutions. Hegarty and Pocklington (1981) found that generally teachers of craft subjects erred too much on the side of caution with children having 'special needs', sometimes restricting activities. However, they did state:

> Teachers who gave pupils scope while exercising normal standards of care found no problems. One metalwork teacher found that pupils with learning difficulties not only treated the machines with respect, but took pride in being able to use them confidently. Nobody had accidents to report and it would seem as if undue over-safety is unwarranted. (p.253)

It would seem clear, therefore, that the attitude and experience of teachers can open and close doors for such children. In addition to opening closing doors teachers can also, as previously suggested, give signals to children, both positive and negative depending on their attitude towards such children. Evans (1959) considered this point particularly important when teaching craft to lower streams: 'Relationships are important – let the children know that you enjoy teaching them' (p.3).

Adapting styles and methods of teaching

CDT teachers in my experience often tend to be quite disciplined into particular ways of controlling groups and methods of teaching. In many respects this would seem to be necessary due to safety considerations. I also believe, however, that this can sometimes cause such teachers to be cold and inflexible. When teaching children with 'special needs' we have to expect to help with problems which may not be experienced by other pupils in the group. It may be possible that such children may have characteristics which may be contrary to the attitude and expectations of the teacher. Evans (1959) listed eight characteristics of the 'backward' child, points which may be useful to consider when developing one's own philosophy and methods of teaching such children.

1) inability to concentrate.
2) slovenly appearance.
3) untidiness and carelessness.
4) attitude of 'anything goes'.

5) clumsiness.
6) poor retention.
7) resentment to correction.
8) behavioural difficulties.
   Due to the characteristics of the backward lad, it is plain that traditional methods of teaching woodwork will have to give way to unorthodox methods. (p.3)

Our acceptance of the pupils in our classes and our willingness to be flexible and innovative must have a great deal to play in the initiation of SEN children into the CDT workshop. I believe that we should be prepared to cater and meet individual needs and not expect pupils with difficulties to slot exactly into the framework of traditional approaches. We might, however, choose to use this as our overall aim for that child.

A personal and, I believe, telling example of an inflexible approach is from a 'maladjusted' school which I visited. The woodwork teacher would not permit the boys in his class to do craftwork because they were wearing training shoes. The well equipped room was unused, the boys did written exercises instead. The school served a run-down inner-city area, so the boys may well have not had the appropriate footwear which was thought necessary for safety. I believe that in the circumstances the teacher could have approached the problem in a more imaginative way, perhaps by starting on more basic craftwork, leading up to operations which really did require stringent safety rules hopefully snowballing their interest on the way to a point where more of an effort was made to provide the necessary footwear.

In order to make the teaching of children with 'special needs' successful, equipment may have to be adapted, decisions regarding content will have to be made. A CDT teacher should perhaps consider using aids which he may have totally rejected when considering projects for 'ordinary children'. He will have to decide whether it is more important that a child succeeds in making what the others have made with the help of a template and jig, or whether the child should chance failing.

Being aware of needs

Once a CDT teacher has accepted the responsibility of working in a positive way to help meet the needs of children with difficulties, i.e. has examined his own attitudes and is prepared to adapt his approach to teaching, I believe he should then be prepared to look at the type of needs we are concerned with. Especially how they relate to his subject content. Unfortunately, however, it would be difficult to draw up a problem and answer taxonomy for a child's 'special needs' as each need will vary. A teacher of CDT therefore ought to be prepared to consider particular needs and match these with his own knowledge and experience of how his subject can help to meet these needs. Hopefully I have begun to suggest some possibilities.

Teachers of CDT should be prepared to be critical of their own methods of teaching and also to extend their own immediate concerns into areas which they have previously given little or no thought. For example, the way in which they use language to communicate their ideas. Many children (unknown to the CDT teacher) may have difficulty understanding subject-specific language – words which they hear in the context of the workshop which might be totally out of touch with their own experience. Barnes (1971) has clearly explained that often specialist subjects use language which presents a barrier to their pupil's learning and should be introduced in a careful planned way.

Often CDT teachers will direct children to written material for reference, homework or punishment. How aware might that teacher be of the complexity of the material and the ability of his pupils? By being prepared to extend his or her area of professional knowledge, possible problems may be prevented, especially for children who have learning difficulties.

Moving away from the 'learning difficulty' aspect to more general social problems which may surface in the teaching of CDT, I wish to briefly highlight children who could be described as being disadvantaged. Many children with 'special needs' will come from homes which are disadvantaged. I use the word 'disadvantaged' as used by the National Child Development Study and later Wedge and Prosser (1973). They see these children as being part of large families, living in poor housing, and their families having low incomes. The study explains that: 'Disadvantaged children are thus over-represented in Special Schools in general and in schools for the ESN in particular' (p.43).

I believe that the implications this might have for such children who follow the subject CDT are considerable. For example, today more and more schools are expecting children to contribute towards materials because of the present economic climate – do we check to see why children do not provide what they are asked to? Or do we assume that they are just not interested? Children who continually forget their apron – have they got one? Or do they just borrow one when they can? These may seem minor points, but possibly the start of more serious problems. My view here is best summarized in the fictitious but nevertheless true-to-life novel *A Kestrel for a Knave* by Hines (1968), when 'Billy' has not got his PE kit and this then starts further problems. How many more children with 'special needs' will continue to gain little from the subject of CDT because some teacher fails to look beyond superficial behaviour and investigate the cause? If we fail to iron out these problems we cannot start to help the child with 'special needs' [...].

REFERENCES

Barnes, D. (1971), *Language, the Learner and the School*, Penguin.

Becker, H. (1963), *Outsiders*, New York, Free Press.

Burnett, A.R. (1969), 'Mathematics through Art and Craft', in *Primary School Maths*, no. 7, pp. 14–25 (December).

Butterworth, I. (1983), *Staffing for Curriculum Needs*, NFER-Nelson.

DES (1975), *A Language for Life* (Bullock Report), HMSO, London.

DES (1978), *Special Educational Needs* (Warnock Report), HMSO, London.

DES (1982), *Report of the Committee of Inquiry into the Teaching of Mathematics in School* (Cockcroft Report), HMSO, London.

Devereaux, H. (1979), 'How Valuable is Home Equipment?', *Special Education*, vol. 6. no. 2, pp. 16–19.

Duncan, J. (1942), *The Education of the Ordinary Child*, London, T. Nelson.

Eggleston, J. (1953), 'Handicraft for Special Classes and Special Schools', in *Practical Education and School Crafts*, vol. 2, 528 (December).

Evans, H.T. (1959), *Woodwork for the Lower Streams*, Technical Press, London.

Hamblin, D.H. (1977), 'Caring and Control: the treatment of absenteeism', in *Absenteeism in South Wales* (ed.) Caroll, H.C.M., University of Swansea.

Hegarty, S. and Pocklington, K. (1981), *Integration of Children with Special Needs*, London, Nelson/NFER.

Hines, B. (1968), *A Kestrel for a Knave*, Penguin Books.

Laslett, R. (1977), *Educating Maladjusted Children*, London, Crosby, Lockwood, Staples.

Schools Council (1975), *Teaching Materials for Disadvantaged Pupils* (Gulliford and Widlake), Evans/Methuen.

Schools Council (1980), *Special Provision for Disabled Pupils – A Study* (Dawson, R.L.), Macmillan.

Shakespeare, R. (1975), *The Psychology of Handicap*, London, Methuen.

Wedge and Prosser (1973), *Born to Fail*, Arrow.

Weiner, J. B. *et al.* (1972), *Child Development*, New York, Wiley.

Wills, W.D. (1941), *The Hawkspur Experiment*, Allen and Unwin.

Wilson, M. and Evans, M. (1980), *Education of Disturbed Pupils* – Schools Council, Working Paper 65, Methuen.

23 *Schools and industry – an overview*

● I. Jamieson

EDITORS' INTRODUCTION

This is taken from the first chapter of the book and it sets the scene for this issue. Details of the various aspects of the schools–industry movement are spelt out in the rest of the book from which we took this extract; as the title suggests here, an overview is given.

INTRODUCTION

It is now common to refer to 'the schools-industry movement' in this country, indeed some observers like to claim that it itself is 'an industry'. The 'industry' they refer to is of relatively recent origin, although it was built on the foundations of a series of older schools–industry infrastructures that date back to the beginning of the nineteenth century (Reeder 1979). The recent attempts to encourage education and industry to draw closer together can be conveniently dated by Prime Minister Callaghan's Ruskin Speech of 1976, although the modern movement pre-dates this event (Jamieson and Lightfoot 1982).

THE SCHOOLS–INDUSTRY MOVEMENT

What is the schools–industry movement? The movement is a diverse collection of employer and trade union groupings; specially constructed educational or quasi-educational 'projects'; government statements and exhortations – all designed to put pressure on the education system to change both the *content* of what is taught, *how* it is taught, and how it is *assessed* and *examined*. Its focus is largely on secondary education and within that primarily on the 14–19 age group, although there are some exceptions to this.

The schools–industry movement is *not* a homogeneous collection of groups united by a common purpose except in the most general of senses. All the groups wish to see schools draw closer to the industrial world – the 'real world' as it is often polemically described. They differ, however, in their conception of the real world: from narrow interpretations which stress the importance of manufacturing industry; those that stress the importance of the 'wealth-creating' sector of the community (usually a euphemism for private business); and finally those that take the broadest view and render industry as the 'local economic community' stressing the interdependence of the public and the private sectors and the manufacturing and service economies.

Not only does the schools–industry movement have a varied conception of 'industry' but, partly as a result of this variation, it also contains a wide variety of different motives for wanting to change schools. A fundamental concern of government and employers is that schools are not providing young people with the right blend of skills, attitudes and knowledge to maximize their productivity when they enter employment. That this concern is central can perhaps be demonstrated by noting that the interest in links between schools and industry seems to follow closely the vicissitudes of the economy (see Reeder 1979). Crudely, when the economy is in boom there is a tendency to allow education to fulfil the needs of individuals rather than the needs of the economy. In times of economic depression, there are pressures to force all parts of the social structure to conform to the needs of the economy. Education finds itself particularly vulnerable because it is a direct producer of a major and expensive commodity for industry–labour.

This analysis lies at the cornerstone of the schools–industry movement, but it is a contested analysis and certainly not one to which every member would subscribe. In the first place there are problems in deciding what an education which served the needs of the economy would look like. The simple assertion that a 'vocationally orientated curriculum', a phrase not without its own difficulties, would serve best, does not gain much support from the overseas evidence. In America, Norton Grubb and Lazerson (1981) have shown that their own education-industry movement has paralleled our own, and that vocationalism has largely failed to meet the economic requirements of employers. In Japan we are presented with a conundrum; a high-performing economy with a school curriculum which is 'narrowly academic, and is not much influenced by considerations of vocational application' (Watts 1984: 21)

In Europe, a fascinating study by Burkart Lutz compares the

contrasting educational systems of West Germany and France (Lutz 1981). He shows that because of the capacity of employers to adapt to the different structure and output of the two educational systems, the end result in economic terms is little different. Of course one must be careful in drawing simplistic conclusions from the study of other countries' educational systems, but such studies should at least make us cautious in accepting the view that there is any simple connection between the school curriculum and economic performance.

Whilst very many employers say that they want schools to adopt a more industrially relevant curriculum in order that industry might ultimately be more productive, there are understandably considerable divisions within their ranks. Some of the larger national organizations like BP, ICI, and the Bank Information Service have supported a radical revision of the school curriculum to embrace more experiential learning, a greater emphasis on economic literacy, and a more imaginative and relevant assessment system (Marsden 1983). Yet such rhetoric is not, by and large, reflected by the great majority of companies who operate solely in local labour markets. There is plenty of evidence to suggest that the majority of employers do not, in general, distinguish between job entry requirements and job performance requirements. Indeed, as the London into Work Study (Townsend *et al.* 1982) showed, many employers do not in fact *know* what is required to perform jobs in their own work organizations. Again, whilst leading employers claim to prefer more applied, industrially relevant qualifications, when it comes to expressing preferences for named A-level subjects, they opt for traditional subjects like physics and chemistry, rather than those subjects which have been specifically designed for industrial relevance (Central Policy Review Staff 1980). Overall, the evidence is suggestive of the conclusion that employers, like most others working in the schools–industry field, do not have any well-founded notions of what sort of school educations fits the demands for economic efficiency.

Not every employer or employers' organization involved in schools–industry work is specifically concerned with making the school curriculum congruent with the needs of industry. Another major concern is with *understanding* the world of industry and commerce and how these institutions fit into the wider society. The term 'understanding' varies in its meaning in schools–industry work. Sometimes it is used in its traditional education mode, meaning to comprehend, to see industry from a range of different perspectives. In this sense it is an objective widely embraced by the educational fraternity – who could deny that the world of trade and industry is a significant one for every adult? There is a widespread belief in both industry and the trade unions not only that they are misunderstood by school students, but that if those students came into greater contact with 'real' industrialists and trade unionists, then they would form a more favourable view. Such a position is perfectly legitimate if somewhat optimistic (see Jamieson and Lightfoot 1982; Jamieson 1983). It becomes less legitimate when the objective moves from 'understanding' through 'appreciating' to 'forming favourable views about'. It must be conceded that some aspects of schools–industry work amount to no more than propaganda.

I have argued that in times of economic depression the schools–industry movement takes on a new lease of life and that the demands to make the content of education more congruent with the needs of business grow stronger. In such times it often seems to those in power the socioeconomic system is itself in peril. Massive unemployment, violence in the streets, indiscipline in the schools give the illusion of system collapse. A moral panic often ensues (Mungham 1982). It is for this reason that certain elements in the schools–industry movement take on the task of defending and explaining the existing political and economic system to the schools. Many of these diverse points are caught by a written parliamentary answer from the Secretary of State for Education, Sir Keith Joseph, which was subsequently circulated to all chief education officers in England and Wales.

> Schools and business need to understand each other better. Business should be helped to appreciate the aims of the schools and the context in which these seek to achieve them. Conversely, schools and pupils need to be helped to understand how the nation earns its living in the world. This involves helping pupils to understand how industry and commerce are organised; the relationship of producers and consumers; the process of wealth creation; the role played by choice, competition and profit; and the traditional liberal view of the interdependence of political and economic freedom, as well as rival theories of how production and distribution should be organised and the moral basis commonly adduced by those theories. (Joseph 1982)

An important element in the schools–industry movement is the transition problem. The transition from school to work is essentially a problem of an economy with relatively full employment. It is concerned with the personal adjustments that young people need to make when they move from educational institutions which tend to treat them as dependents, to workplaces where some of them at least are treated as autonomous adults. Another concern is with the fit, in economic and technical terms, between the skills, attitudes and knowledge gained at school and those required in the world of work. It would have been a reasonable supposition that with the growth of the overall level of unemployment, and the even more severe rise in the youth unemployment rate, that the transition problem would have disappeared and with it much of the schools–industry movement. This has not happened. The transition problem has been redefined, transition in times of burgeoning youth unemployment has been converted to 'transition to adult life'. Adult life can contain periods of both employment and unemployment, and so the task of education has become to equip young people with a range of transferable and relevant work and social and life skills, that will allow them to cope with either scenario. If it is indeed true that the skills required to become an effective worker are, more or less, the same as those required to become a fully participating citizen, then this is a convenient discovery.

THE EFFECT OF THE ECONOMIC RECESSION

Why hasn't the schools–industry movement withered away with the rise of youth unemployment and the collapse of large sections of Britain's manufacturing industry? There are several answers to this question. In the first place the schools–industry movement as we have described it is a diverse movement; not every group or organization working within its framework has been concerned with preparing young people for work. Furthermore, the organizations have, in general, adapted to the changing educational and economic scenarios. For example, the rise to prominence of the small business sector has led many projects and organizations to embrace the concept of 'education for enterprise'. In the second place it is important to grasp both the *scale* of industrial collapse and the local *perceptions* of the economic and occupational scenario. Although it is true that large numbers of companies have gone out of business, particularly in manufacturing, there is enormous local variation in impact. In many communities the prediction of an economic wasteland looks decidedly premature. Furthermore, because the schools–industry movement is continually growing and becoming more efficient at penetrating the economic community, a large number of firms - and different types of firms - are being drawn into the educational net.

The impact of youth unemployment is also marked by substantial local variations and the position is masked by the variety and scope of the schemes designed to train or retrain prospective young workers. The effect of this, plus the widely reported reaction of teachers and students that 'unemployment is something that happens to somebody else', is to dilute the potential effect of unemployment on the schools. Many schools, even in areas of substantial youth unemployment, still cling to the traditional school to work scenario, and are happy to use the schools–industry organizations and projects to help their students become more competitive in job-seeking.

The effect of high levels of youth unemployment on the school curriculum is a conundrum. In one or two areas it is possible to see the signs of unemployment having cut, or at least severely damaged, the umbilical cord between the traditional curriculum and the job market for school-leavers. Paradoxically, in these areas the schools–industry lobby has had its greatest success. There are clear signs that the curriculum is becoming more industrially orientated. This means that the curriculum contains more material about the world of industry, commerce and the trade unions; more industrialists and trade unionists are working with teachers on both the design and the delivery of the curriculum; more young people are going out to industrial places of work in order to become familiar with aspects of the industrial world. It means a greater emphasis on experiential and experience-based learning. Finally, it means a gradual move towards new modes of assessment that involve students and industrial representatives as well as teachers.

Such changes are by no means mirrored in all or even most areas with high youth unemployment. In these latter LEAs the effect of unemployment is that the schools concentrate even harder on the traditional curriculum in order to make pupils more competitive in a tighter job market. Here the schools–industry movement's contribution to the curriculum is less radical. It consists of a range of essentially *ad hoc* additions to various elements of the curriculum – a little more work experience; the formation of a school-based company; a few more industrial examples in certain subjects.

There is little direct teaching for unemployment. Most of the teaching profession would agree with the sentiments expressed by John Tomlinson, then chairman of the Schools Council: 'We utterly refute the notion that we should, in the schools, train children for unemployment. This is not what we are for, any more than we specifically train them for particular employment' (quoted in Watts 1983a [...].)

Why, where levels of youth unemployment are similar, does the school curriculum vary so much in different LEAs? I think the explanation is as follows. Historically, high levels of youth unemployment are a necessary, but not a sufficient, condition for an 'unemployment induced' radical curriculum change. In the first place youth unemployment has to be *perceived* to be high. In the second place it has to be sufficiently high so that the vast majority of youngsters are seen to have no realistic chance of getting a job on leaving school. Finally, there needs to be the political will and leadership, both at the level of the LEA and the majority of schools, to bring about the radical curriculum change. Such a combination of factors has not been common in England and Wales.

RELEVANT EDUCATION

One of the strongest claims made on behalf of the schools–industry movement is its claim to bring a more *relevant* education to young people. On inspection the claim to relevance is a complex one. The first question is, more relevant to whom? We have already seen that part of this answer is constructed in terms of relevance to the supposed needs of employers, and this can be extended to the needs of young people as prospective trade unionists and citizens. To many people this claim to relevance is so obvious, compared with the claims of the more traditional curriculum, that it barely needs stating. And yet we have already noted the questionable connection between 'vocational education' and employee performance. Opposition to the claim for relevance of a different kind comes from another quarter. The Black Papers of the 1970s [1] contained an attack on trendy new subjects and on non-traditional teaching methods and assessment procedures. Although society might change there must remain certain fixed and immutable standards for judging curricula and educational standards, they argued. Recently Max Beloff has lambasted the curricular claims of the schools–industry movement. In a speech reported in the *Times Educational Supplement* of 7 October 1983, Lord Beloff attacked the 'progressive' view that just because 'the outlook for the economy was gloomy', there was a need to teach about economics. In the face of the 'necessary uncertainties' about the future he recommended 'that neglected subject history, in particular social and economic history', as offering 'the best hope of giving young people an awareness of the society they would enter'.

LEARNING FROM EXPERIENCE

At least part of the schools–industry case is based on the social and educational consequences of teaching all youngsters subjects like economic history in the traditional didactic mode, and examining it by a written examination. The evidence of a great legion of researchers like Willis (1977), Corrigan (1979), and Hargreaves (1982), appears to testify to the fact that young people vote with their feet on this sort of curriculum. Much of the schools–industry rhetoric is based on the assertion that young people do indeed see the relevance of studying subjects like English, mathematics and science, when they are applied to problems in the adult world of work; that furthermore they respond

---

[1] The 'Black Papers' were five papers published between 1969 and 1977 that attacked aspects of what they called 'progressive' and 'socially motivated' developments in the educational system (see Cox and Dyson 1969).

positively to new modes of learning that stress the active role of the learner, and the importance of learning by experience (the traditional adult mode of learning) [...] It is undoubtedly true that the majority of young people respond to what the Scottish report on schools-industry work (EISP 1983) likes to call the 'vocational impulse'. There is clear evidence that the majority of young people enjoy work experience. What is less clear is what young people learn in such activities (Jamieson 1983: Steinberg 1982). Some people have argued that work experience is enjoyable for students primarily because it represents a break from the routine of school. Whilst I do not think that the statements made by young people who have been on work experience square with such a view (see Watts 1983a or 1983b?), it is true that we do not know how they would react to extended periods of work experience as an educational activity. What has emerged from the extensive work of the Industry Project (SCIP), is that it is not invariably true that students respond warmly to those more active learning techniques, particularly if they are encountered for the first time in the fourth or fifth years of school. There is a tendency to regard such activities as role-plays and simulations as 'not really work'. Such views are often reinforced by the fact that there are no textbooks to guide them, no notes to copy down from the board – indeed, very often no writing to be done at all. Their suspicions about this sort of work are often confirmed when they find that these activites are not to be examined, at least in the traditional way. The conclusion to be drawn from this is not that there is something inherently wrong with the experiential mode of learning, but that it cannot be easily grafted on to traditional schooling.

If some pupils find it difficult to adjust to experiential learning after a solid diet of didactic teaching in most parts of the curriculum, then it must be reported that so do teachers. Most teachers have been trained to teach in the didactic mode, i.e. to make interesting presentations which students can understand, to set realistic exercises based on this presentation, and to assess subsequent written work. Experiential learning dramatically changes the task of the teacher. The teacher either constructs or selects experiences from which she hopes the students will learn. To assist this process she needs to train students to learn from these experiences. Not only are the majority of teachers untrained in such a pedagogic mode, but there are a wide range of impediments to its successful implementation. Experiential learning cuts across the traditional way in which time is organized in schools. One of the reasons why we have the traditional timetable slot of 35–40 minutes is that it, more or less, fits the attention-span of pupils in didactic teaching situations. It is however, extremely difficult to organize experience-based learning in such brief time slots. Learning about the world of industry and commerce in an experiential way tends to cut across the traditional academic organization of the school via 'subjects'. Unfortunately the issues and problems faced by the industrial world do not fit into neat subject packages. Finally, not only does experiential learning cut across the traditional organization of time and subjects in schools, but exercises which depend heavily on group-work and problem-solving tend to be noisier than the more traditional lessons. [...]

SCHOOLS AND INDUSTRY: A PERMANENT ALLIANCE?

We have noted that dialogue between schools and industry is not new. It has waxed and waned for over a century and a half. Ironically its buoyant phases have occurred when the economic activity of British industry has been on the downturn, although occasionally certain changes in the education system, like the raising of the school-leaving age in 1972, have provided an educational impetus. In its buoyant phases schools–industry work has been marked by a series of 'campaigns'. For limited periods of time a range of organizations from within education and industry have committed resources to pull education and industry closer together. The lessons from past campaigns – usually long forgotten and with few reminders left in the system – are rarely heeded. The literature on the implementation and dissemination of innovation lies undiscovered (campaigns are waged by men of action, practical people who are wary of 'theories' of change and dissemination).

The key question is, are there any reasons to believe that the current phase of schools–industry work will be different? The short answer is, yes. There are clear signs that this modern phase will mark the institutionalization of much closer relations between schools and the industrial world, and that the secondary school curriculum will include a clear industrial dimension. Although many features of schools–industry work remain the same, for example, the large number of 'projects' all trying to sell their different wares to the schools (start up a Young Enterprise company; run a 'Challenge to Industry Conference'; organize a work experience programme for your pupils), certain structural changes in LEAs who run the schools in England and Wales mean that success is both more likely, and more likely to become permanent.

The important structural change is the appointment by LEAs of Schools–Industry Liaison Officers (SILOS) whose brief is to bring local schools and industry closer together. By 1984 over three-quarters of the LEAs in England and Wales had such an officer.
[...]

Schools-Industry Liaison Officers act as a focal point for schools–industry work in a local education authority. They are the major brokers and disseminators of innovation in the schools–industry movement. They are a point of reference for industrialists and trade unionists who often find it initially quite difficult to deal with large numbers of local schools. The SILO also deals with the large number of educational projects and organizations in this field which have something to 'sell' to schools. As the SILOs gain in knowledge and experience one can see them starting to take over the functions of these national projects by devising their own local projects [...]

The existence of the SILO network marks the triumph of a model of curriculum change that is soundly based (Open University 1983). It stresses the importance of the local economic community in the change process; it reinforces the importance of *people* as change agents, not publications which tend to be inflexible and rapidly date; it gives the responsible authority – the LEA – the key role in the process. The revolution is not yet complete in that not all the SILO posts are currently permanent. The unique nature of the post in LEA terms also gives some of the SILOs problems of identity. This problem is ameliorated by the existence of the training and development network of SCIP, to which fifty LEAs belong, and by the attempts of UBI (Understanding British Industry) to network some of the remainder. Sooner or later, a SILO organization will arise, akin to the Advisers' Association (NAIEA) or the subject associations, to resolve this problem, and to give schools–industry work a clear-cut identity.

[...]

Despite these 'successes', which are high by the standards of the system in general, any outsider could legitimately ask: have schools in general made a concerted shift in their curriculum to give it an industrial dimension? The short answer is, almost certainly, no.

THE ROLE OF GOVERNMENT: THE TVEI INITIATIVE

It was against this background of frustratingly slow progress towards a more industrially orientated curriculum, which contained significant amounts of technical and vocational education, that the Conservative government of Mrs Thatcher introduced its Technical and Vocational Education Initiative (TVEI). The TVEI programme was operating in sixty local education authorities by September 1984, covering 320 schools. The cost for the five-year programme would be £150 million. It offered four-year courses of technical and vocational education for students between the ages of 14–18, and aimed to include children of all abilities and both sexes. The scale and cost of the 'pilot' project is itself remarkable, dwarfing that of any schools–industry initiative.

The government's determination to provide a large and radical initiative to change the balance of the curriculum can be seen by the way in which the change was instituted. The programme was announced in a written answer to a (planted) parliamentary question. There was no consultation with the usual professional interest groups. It has been argued that 'the devisers of the TVEI were seemingly determined to act quickly and wanted to avoid having their radical ideas smothered in a consultative morass, or at least amended out of all recognition' (Moon and Richardson 1984: 25).

The initiative was not given to the Department of Education and Science, but to that *dirigiste* arm of government, the MSC. The LEAs were not 'directed' to change curricular practices, rather they were 'invited' to submit schemes that would deliver pre-vocational education with a strong industrial element to a pilot group of pupils. A fundamental administrative feature of the scheme is the fact that the LEAs have to sign a contract to provide a mutually agreed curriculum to a specified group of students. The performance of the LEAs is being closely monitored by the MSC.

One of the requirements of each TVEI project is that a project director is appointed. In many LEAs these individuals have the role of schools–industry liaison officers with a clear-cut brief of curriculum development. There are now less than a score of LEAs with no post exclusively committed to the development of schools–industry work broadly conceived.

One of the traditional blocks to curriculum change in secondary schools is the examination system. Although this impediment is generally overweighted in education, it is true both that there has been a relative shortage of examinations which have a technical, vocational or industrial orientation, and there has been a reluctance on the part of many teachers, employers and parents to accept that these 'new' examinations are fully equivalent to the more traditional 'subjects'. The government has given considerable encouragement to the examination boards, particularly the non-traditional boards like RSA, CGIL and B/Tech to develop new relevant examinations. They have done this extremely successfully. The latest government-sponsored initiative, the Certificate of Pre-Vocational Education (17+), an initiative which involves all the above examination boards, is offered for the first time in 1985.

LOCAL INNOVATIONS

[...]
Not many of the school innovations reported here were part of nationally examined courses and subjects, and this reflects a common

tendency of schools–industry work. The stance of many teachers in secondary schools has been to concentrate on the subject curriculum, to get their students through the public examinations, and *then* do something interesting and relevant. Much of the industrially orientated curriculum is delivered in the period after the end of the public examinations.

Not only do teachers feel pressure from parents, students and industrialists to deliver the requisite number of public examination passes in 'traditional' subjects, but until recently there were few examinations on the market which had an industrial dimension. There are now signs of change. Another problem faced by interested teachers is the fact that the world of school 'subjects' does not fit the way in which the industrial and commercial world is organized. This fact has been recognized in some of the new examination syllabi, for example the various syllabi on industrial studies, and the examinations run by CGIL, B/Tech and RSA. Ingenious subject teachers have always got over these hurdles [...] Other recent developments include a gradual movement down the age range so that schools-industry work embraces the first three years of the secondary curriculum instead of being the near exclusive property of the 14–19 age group.
[...]

SPECIAL EDUCATION

If primary schools represent a new departure for the schools–industry movement, then it might be argued that special schools represent its oldest terrain. Historically there has always been a very strong strain in the final years of special schooling for a vocationally orientated industrial education. It has been argued that the overall aim of the curriculum in special schools has been 'work preparation: the teaching of certain basic manual skills has taken precedence over literacy and numeracy or the transmission of knowledge' (Rees 1984; see also Allason 1984). The aims of such a curriculum appear to be tacitly supported by the Warnock Report which recommended:

> A small amount of extra help for school leavers with moderate learning difficulties or emotional or behavioural disorders may enable them to hold down a job, and reduce the chances of them entering a cycle of frequent changes of job, leading to long-term unemployment and dependence on social or psychiatric services. (Warnock Report 1978: 163)

Neither of the the case studies on special schools reported in Chapter 3 and 4 of *Industry and Education* (Jamieson 1985) have curricula which exactly mirror the description put forward by Rees (1984), although it might be argued that both schools wanted to use the Industry Project to give their youngsters a better chance of future employment. Both schools made use of curriculum ideas that had originated in comprehensive schools, and in many ways much of their schools–industry programme was indistinguishable from what might have gone on in a comprehensive school. We might note, in particular, the desire to make the school more outward-looking; to get the young people to be more aware of the wider community and to make greater use of it; and finally, a concern to make the students less dependent on their teachers.

Industrialists played a more important role in the development of work in these two special schools than would be the norm, even in a project like SCIP. This is symptomatic of the community's caring attitude to many children with special educational needs. As long as it does not help perpetuate the cycle of dependence it is to be welcomed. Certainly the schools found it helpful to have a heavy involvement of industrialists, not least because of the belief that it would improve their students' chances of eventual employment. Teachers' worries about the destinations of students with special educational needs have grown in the last few years. The study of the labour market fortunes of the handicapped (broadly defined) based on the National Children's Bureau Cohort[1] shows a widening gulf between the handicapped and the non-handicapped (Walker 1982). As Rees points out, if YTS really does have the effect of sharpening the competitive edge of some school-leavers, and introducing some of them to networks which may improve their chances of getting a job, then handicapped youngsters will be at an even greater disadvantage (Rees 1984).

SECONDARY SCHOOLS

The largest section of this work on curriculum development in the schools-industry field is appropriately devoted to secondary schools [...] Chapter 5 in Jamieson (1985) takes a one-year snapshot of the efforts of one school to give its curriculum an industrial dimension. It represents a particularly good example of a 'curriculum enrichment' strategy, i.e. a wide range of teachers and subjects had contact with the industrial world. There are several particular points of interest. First, the school found it necessary to appoint one person in the school to act as a focal point for schools–industry work (there was no SILO in the LEA). In the second place the scheme gained an initial impetus by high-level backing

---

[1]A longitudinal study which is following through the lives of all children born in one week in 1958.

from the senior management of the school and senior local industrialists. Thirdly, that schools–industry liaison was manifest both in teachers and pupils going out to industry and by industry coming into the school. Finally, although the scheme started without any trade union involvement, managers from local employers suggested their inclusion.

The case study of T.P. Riley School reported in Chapter 6 of Jamieson (1985) is a good example of a school which chose to discharge its main responsibility in the industry area by the provision of a common core course on modern industrial society [...] Specific points of interest in the case study include the use of a curriculum review which showed that the school was 'not preparing students adequately for everyday survival in adult life, nor were we giving them any real understanding of the structure and working of the modern industrial society in which they live'. Such a diagnosis also prompted the provision of an 'education for leisure' module. The modern industrial society course reflects many of the dilemmas that are common in such initiatives – the temptation to overload the course with content, and the recognition that process goals are at least as important as content goals.

Kingsdown Cars in Chapter 7 of Jamieson (1985) reports another extremely common way of introducing 'industry' into the curriculum of the secondary school. Kingsdown School has a compulsory, non-examinable course in the fourth and fifth years called 'Living in Society', and this course discharges the school's curricular responsibilities in a number of fields, industry included. The case study describes a large-scale industrial stimulation (factory production lines using Lego bricks) that took place in the course for a whole-day programme for fourth-year pupils [...] Such events require a large amount of planning, but the impact and richness of the subsequent experience for teachers, pupils and industrialists is usually so great that the investment pays off. Within SCIP such strategies are referred to as the 'big bang' model of curriculum change – the event has such an impact on the school that it sends fissures throughout the rest of the curriculum.

Granville Barrand's case study in Jamieson (1985), 'What's in a Song?: Teaching about Industry through Music', represents a common approach to handling industry, through an individual subject, but the particular subject vehicle – music – is very unusual. Many teachers working in the aesthetic domain feel threatened by the schools–industry movement which they see as part of a more general attack on the 'arts' in the school curriculum. One of the merits of Barrand's case study is that it shows that schools–industry work need not imply a narrow vocationalism, and that with ingenuity and imagination subjects like music can themselves gain from industrial study, and can make an important contribution to the students' understanding of the industrial dimension.

Chapter 9 of Jamieson (1985) focuses on a one-week programme at Hetton School in Sunderland which was developed in response to some difficulties that were encountered in the LEA-run work experience programme. The difficulties are themselves instructive: in a period of economic recession, and growing competition from the MSC, there is increasing concern about the number of work experience places available to schools; in the second place, there is a difficulty in developing a curriculum framework in centralized LEA-administered work experience schemes (Jamieson 1982).

Kevyn Smith, the author of the Hetton study in Jamieson (1985), provides us with a particularly good analysis of large-scale industrial simulations in the school setting. The difficulties of using simulations amongst students unused to this mode of learning are discussed; the important issue of the 'realism' of the simulation, and the way in which industrialists and trade unionists should and should not be used both receive careful treatment. The case study also makes mention of the use of 'work shadowing' – a device commonly used in the USA but rare in this country (see Watts 1983b).

The final two case studies of secondary schools in Jamieson (1985) usher in a new and important theme in schools-industry work the theme of 'enterprise education' [...] At Hemsworth School in Wakefield worries about the numbers of work experience placements was one of the spurs to the development of Hemsworth Enterprises, a collection of school-based businesses that trade in the 'real world'. Dane Court School in Kent tackled the enterprise idea in quite a different way. Here small groups of sixth-formers planned and set up businesses in a two-day simulation. Although they exhibit differences in organization, the two case study schools show some similarities. In both schools a key aim was to try to get young people to make their own decisions and to be responsible for the consequences. This aim meant that the role of teachers and adults other than teachers required very careful thought and negotiation.

[...]

TEACHERS

Teachers have always been an important focus in schools–industry work. There has been an enduring theme in the movement that part of the 'problem' has been a lack of industrial experience in the teaching profession, and a consequent lack of knowledge and sympathy with the industrial world. Such a view certainly underlies the genesis of many teachers into industry schemes. [... This raises] important questions about the effectiveness of this form of in-service training. For example, is an industrial secondment an effective way of learning about *industry* as distinct from one firm? Are these schemes organized in ways which are likely to make them effective? Is there much evidence to suggest that classroom practice, and therefore pupils, benefit from these schemes?

The 'remedy' for the 'teacher problem' in schools–industry work has nearly always seen in in-service terms, i.e. training the existing stock of teachers. This policy is understandable when one examines the relatively modest flow of students into the profession compared with the size of the existing stock of teachers. Notwithstanding this point, in recent times more attention has been focused on initial training and a growing number of institutions are including some input on 'the world of work' or schools–industry matters. Such initiatives were given official blessing by the publication of the HMI paper, *Teacher Training and Preparation for Working Life*. This paper firmly recommended that:

> Initial training institutions should (also) make positive efforts to ensure that future teachers understand the part their subject plays in the economic and cultural life of their society, and that they have sufficient understanding of the economic foundations of that society, and the role of industry and commerce in wealth creation, to be able to pass on to their pupils both information about and respect for industrial and commercial activity. (HMI 1982:[1])

[...]

'Schools and enterprise' represents the latest theme in the burgeoning schools–industry movement. The decline of large-scale manufacturing industry and the rise in the esteem and importance of the small business sector has now been recognized by a growing number of schools. Jamieson (1985) calculates that some 850 of the 5000 plus secondary schools in England and Wales have embarked on mini-enterprise activities. He analyses this latest development and places it in the context of the curriculum development goals of schools and industry.

REFERENCES

Allason, C.H. (1984), *Schools to Working Life – Pupils with Special Needs*, York, CSCS.

Bray, E. (1983), 'Mini-Co's in Schools', in Watts, A.G. (ed.,) *Work Experience and Schools*, London, Heinemann.

Central Policy Review Staff (1980), *Education, Training and Industrial Performance*, London, HMSO.

Committee of Enquiry into the Education of Handicapped Children and Young People (1978), *Special Education Needs* (Warnock Report), London, HMSO.

Corrigan, P. (1979), *Schooling the Smash Street Kids*, London, Macmillan.

Cox, C.B. and Dyson, A.E. (eds) (1969), *A Black Paper*, London, Critical Quarterly Society.

Department of Education and Science (1983), *Schools/Industry Liaison,* letter to Chief Education Officers, SS 5/19/0127D, London, DES.

Education for the Industrial Society Project (EISP), Final Report (1983), *An Education for Life and Work,* Glasgow, Consultative Committee on the Curriculum.

Gray, L. and Waitt, I. (1983), 'If You Want to Get a Head ....', *Times Educational Supplement,* 24.6.83.

Hargreaves, D.H. (1982), *The Challenge for the Comprehensive School,* London, Routledge and Kegan Paul.

HMI (1982), *Teacher Training and Preparation for Working Life,* London, DES.

Holmes, S. (1981), 'Is Schools–Industry Liaison – a liaison dangereuse?' *Education,* 157, 17.

Holmes, S. and Jamieson, I.M. (1983), 'Further Uses of "Adults Other than Teachers"', in Watts, A.G. (ed.) (1983), *Work Experience and Schools,* London, Heinemann.

Jamieson, I.M. (1981), 'Schools and Industry: Some Organizational Considerations' (Part I), *School Organization,* vol. 1, no. 4.

Jamieson, I.M. (1982), 'Learning from Work Experience at 14–16', in Watts, A.G. (ed.), (1982), *Schools, YOP and the New Training Initiative,* Cambridge, CRAC.

Jamieson, I.M. (1983), 'Miracles or Mirages? Some Elements of Pupil Work Experience', *British Journal of Guidance and Counselling,* no. 11, 2 July.

Jamieson, I.M. (ed.) (1984), *We Make Kettles: Studying Industry in the Primary School,* York, Longman.

Jamieson, I.M. (ed.) (1985), *Industry in Education,* York, Longman.

Jamieson, I.M. and Lightfoot, M. (1982), *Schools and Industry,* London, Methuen.

Joseph, Sir Keith, Written Parliamentary Answer 29 July 1982 contained in DES Circular letter SS 5/19/0127D 15 March 1983.

Kolb, D.A. (1984), *Experiential Learning,* New Jersey, Prentice-Hall Inc.

Lutz, B. (1981), 'Education and Employment: Contrasting Evidence from France and the Federal Republic of Germany', *European Journal of Education,* no. 16.

Marsden, C.L. (1983), *What Industry Really Wants: Implications for Education and the Community,* London, BP (mimeo).

Moon, J. and Richardson, J.J. (1984), 'Policy-Making with a Difference? The Technical and Vocational Education Initiative', *Public Administrations,* no. 26, Spring.

Mungham, G. (1982), 'Workless Youth as a "Moral Panic" ', in Rees, T.L. and Atkinson, P. (eds) (1982), *Youth Unemployment and State Intervention,* London, Routledge and Kegan Paul.

Norton Grubb, W. and Lazerson, W. (1981), 'Vocational Solutions to Youth Problems: the Persistent Frustrations of the American Experience', *Educational Analysis,* vol. 3, no. 2.

Open University (1983), *Curriculum Innovation: Unit 19, From School to Adult Life: Innovation in the Secondary School,* Milton Keynes, Open University Press.

Reed, B. and Bazalgette, J. (1983), 'TWL Network and Schools', in Watts, A.G. (ed.) (1983), *Work Experience and Schools*, London, Heinemann.

Reeder, D. (1979), 'A Recurring Debate: Education and Industry', in Bernbaum, G. (ed.) (1979), *Schooling in Decline*, London, Macmillan.

Rees, T.L. (1984), 'Slow Learners: From Special Education to Special Programmes?' in Varlaam, C. (ed.) (1984), *Rethinking Transition: Educational Innovation & the Transition to Adult Life*, Lewes, Sussex, Falmer Press.

Steinberg, C.D. (1982), 'Jumping off the Work Experience Bandwagon', *Journal of Youth and Adolescence*, vol. 11, no. 3.

Stronach, I. (1984), 'Work Experience: The Sacred Anvil', in Varlaam, C. (ed.) (1984), *Rethinking Transition: Educational Innovation and the Transition to Adult Life*, Lewes, Falmer Press.

Tomlinson, J. (1981) *House of Commons Education, Science and Arts Committee*, para. 7.42. Quoted in Watts (1983a).

Townsend, C. *et al.* (1982), *London Into Work Development Project*, University of Sussex, Institute of Manpower Studies.

Walker, A. (1982), *Unqualified and Underemployed: Handicapped Young People and the Labour Market*, London, Macmillan.

Watts, A.G. (1978), 'The Implications of School-Leaver Unemployment for Careers Education in Schools', *Journal of Curriculum Studies*, vol. 10, no. 3.

Watts, A.G. (1983a) *Education, Unemployment and the Future of Work*, Milton Keynes, Open University Press.

Watts, A.G. (1983b), 'Work Experience: Principles and Practice', in Watts, A.G. (ed.), (1983), *Work Experience and Schools*, London, Heinemann.

Watts, A.G. (1984), *The Japanese Lifetime Employment System and its Implications for Career Guidance*, NICEC, Hatfield.

Willis, P. (1977) *Learning to Labour*, London, Saxon House.

Wood, B. (1983), *Schools Industry Liaison: The Development of Policy and the Role of the Schools Industry Officer*, unpublished MEd thesis, Worcester College of Higher Education.

VI TEACHING AND LEARNING TECHNOLOGY

From what is inevitably an enormous range of possibilities, we have selected just a few topics about how to provide a technological education. Problem-solving is one of the most talked-about aspects and also one which is poorly understood. Lewin (Chapter 2) and Cross *et al.* (Chapter 3) have already pointed out one common confusion: technological problem-solving and scientific method. If the merging of those two is one result of a wave of enthusiasm for problem-solving, an unquestioning acceptance of problem-solving *per se* is another. Much is claimed for it, and Bernard Down examines the claims, within the context of CDT, in Chapter 24. Whatever caution may be necessary about problem-solving, it is undoubtably important. One neglected aspect is its importance in enhancing group-work, one of the issues brought out by Paul Burton in Chapter 25.

Anita Cross (Chapter 11) has shown the importance of a psychological perspective, and in Chapter 26 Nigel Procter continues this. By arguing for a curriculum model based on a notion of multiple intelligences, he stresses some fundamental aspects of learning.

Project work has been central to technological education since the days of Project Technology. The three extracts we have included (Chapters 27–9) consider how to organize, assess and help pupils do projects. But, while we have included projects in this section on teaching and learning, it is important to remember that they are an end in themselves.

For any teacher wanting to embark upon teaching technology examples and case studies are the most helpful. HMI surveys and reports provide an ideal way of presenting details of what is happening in schools, informed by a national picture. Our selection from their examples (Chapter 30) shows a wide range of practical issues relating to teaching and learning. One such issue is accommodation, and in Chapter 31 we draw upon the results of a series of visits to schools carried out by the DES in 1984. The check-list produced, is a useful summary of the considerations to take into account when deciding upon accommodation needs.

Evaluation, so the rhetoric goes, is an integral part of teaching and learning. As with special needs there is much to be done in all areas of the work of schools, and the teaching of technology is no exception. There are few accounts of such evaluation and here we have had to confine ourselves to the evaluation of a CDT department.

24 *Problem-solving, CDT and child-centredness*

● B. K. Down

THE PROBLEM

While practical problem-solving seems to be central to the notion of CDT objections can be heard concerning its value as a teaching method, particularly for the child of average and less than average ability. Those who favour it argue that it helps to develop the ability to think effectively as well as providing opportunities for initiative and creativity. Practical problem-solving, they say, leads to an understanding of various materials and resources that can be used to achieve human purposes, as well as providing insights into areas of related learning. In what follows I intend to examine some of the logical conditions necessary for problem solving and apply some of these conclusions to the area of CDT. I offer these considerations as a continuation of conversations begun with teachers of this subject who feel uncertain about many of the changes that they perceive happening or about to occur.

TWO SOURCES OF PROBLEM—SOLVING

There might be said to be two main sources of the concern with problem-solving in CDT, namely (1) the work of the designer and the technological researcher and (2) such movements within education itself as child-centredness.

1. Traditionally some writers have distinguished between the craftsman whose concern is the realization of the end-product and the designer who draws up the ends to which the craftsman worked.[1] This view draws too sharp a distinction between ends and means and tends to support the view that it is the designer who does the thinking, thus underestimating the mental effort involved in the activity of craft. Those who have pointed out the ill-defined nature of design problems[2] were indicating among other things that in design there needs to be a

progressive clarification of the ends. The term 'design' covers environmental, communication, fashion, system and product forms of design, while 'technology' covers a wide variety of primitive and modern means and activities by which man controls or transforms his physical environment. In some senses design and technological activity may overlap; hence the description of the school subject 'design-technology'. In both designing and technological research there is some form of problem-solving. That being the case it might be straightforward to argue that problem-solving is logically necessary for the study of these subjects. However one needs to ask what one's aims are in the teaching of the subject. Children may study history at quite a high level without encountering the primary sources and problems of evaluation faced by the professional historian, and even when collections of primary source material are looked at there is very little attempt at what might loosely be described as original work. Similarly one could develop or attempt to develop an awareness of the impact of design and technology on our lives by numerous means, such as what has been described as the 'transmission model of teaching', which need not involve problem-solving methods. Indeed even if one's aim is to enable one's pupils to solve design or technological problems there is no guarantee, as we will see, that this is best done through learning by problem-solving. Learning in school need not reproduce the research methods of the professionals.

2. An interest in problem-solving, however, antedates the present interest in design and technology. Even if we concentrate our attention on the twentieth century we find that it is strongly advocated as a method of learning for child-centred and open education from the beginning of the century. (Incidentally within previous centuries we find a sympathy being expressed by supporters of this view towards craft activities).[3] In John Dewey this sympathy is maintained together with a conviction that education should be concerned with making children aware of the dynamic nature of knowledge which involves answers gathered for past and present problems.[4] Only in education – never in the life of the practical man – does knowledge mean a store of information aloof from doing. In his laboratory school Dewey used such occupations as carpentry and cookery as ways of providing active insights 'into natural materials and processes, points of departure when children shall be led into a realization of the historic development of man'. In *Democracy and Education* he explains by reference to gardening that children can be helped to understand the place that farming and horticulture have had in the history of man and the place which they occupy in present social organization. 'Carried on in an environment educationally controlled, they are a means for making a study of the facts of growth, the chemistry of soil, the role of light, air and moisture,

injurious and helpful animal life etc.[15] Applied to CDT we can see how certain materials, arts or techniques can be studied as a centre of interest with the raising of related historical, moral, scientific, aesthetic and social questions. It is to be noted that this approach involves some degree of curriculum integration, team-teaching and project work and is far from the efficient achieving of specified ends by problem-solving. It involves an introduction through practical activities to a liberal education. Dewey's much-cited account of the stages of problem-solving has its direct influence in many versions of the stages of designing in education, and his influence through Kilpatrick on the project method can be seen in the integrated movement of project technology. For these reasons I might be justified in relating Dewey's theories directly to problem-solving in CDT. However in what follows I will concentrate on some more general logical points about the conditions of problem-solving and the implications for CDT. I will even offer a modification of Dewey's five stages.[6] I do this because I want to make my concern more specifically problem-solving than an academic interpretation of Dewey. Nevertheless many of the points that I make will have their origin in the debate that is centred on Dewey's advocacy of this method.

THE NATURE OF PROBLEM-SOLVING

As Dewey was keen to point out, problem-solving occurs in many aspects of everyday life; when tradition or stereotyped habits of thinking and acting, or the replication of previous experience can provide no answer to a difficulty one encounters and one has to use one's intelligence and imagination to overcome the problem and adapt to the environment. In saying this I have tried to show that problem-solving is related to biological and evolutionary processes and that as a concept it overlaps with other concepts. Writers on the sociology of scientific ideas have suggested that there are two levels at least of problem-solving, that in which a revolution of thought occurs and a new model or paradigm of science is offered (exemplified by Einstein), and that in which an everyday scientist who presupposes such a paradigm of science fits his own research into the model like pieces of a jig-saw.[7] The genius of the model-maker lies in finding problems where others do not. The everyday scientist is seen to be operating in a more determinate situation. With a determinate problem the issue can be clearly defined, the mode of tackling it can be known and what would count as a perfect solution can be judged beforehand. In the case of creative work, such as aesthetic expression and production or the problem-finding of the model-maker, as with many everyday problems, the goal-states and the methods of achieving them are not so clearly defined, so that what is originally regarded as a possible solution may be changed. In short, problems vary in their degree of openness and complexity, as well as in their type of objective. One question that arises from this is the extent to which the use of problem-solving methods in the learning situation will enable one to develop a general capacity to solve problems. The answer to this should become more evident from an analysis of the logically necessary stages of problem-solving.

Writers have suggested something like four stages: (1) perplexity, (2) problem identification, (3) plan construction, and (4) evaluation.

Perplexity

Logically a problem must be a difficulty, an obstacle or a state of confusion or uncertainty for someone. It is the individual or group who defines what is to count as a problem. What is a problem for you is not necessarily a problem for me. This means that for the person who regards something as a problem some degree of tension is experienced, some impetus is felt to reach the goal. It is for this reason that problem-solving can be seen as an ideal form of active learning, though it differs from learning itself in its goals and in the predetermined nature of its material.

Problem Identification

A problem is not a problem until one can specify and identify the actual perplexity. One requires the appropriate knowledge, experience of conceptual framework to categorize the problem and to realize what might count as a solution. Problems are not just problems; they are particular kinds of problems, and one needs to be initiated into the relevant way of thinking in order to correctly analyse the situation. Even the problem-finder standing at the frontiers of knowledge does not stand in a position of discontinuity with tradition. Consequent upon identification is the consideration of alternative hypotheses and the planning of a possible solution.

Plan Construction

The problem may be tackled in two ways: symbollically and abstractly at first and then by a more demonstrable working out of a solution. For the first stage a number of different strategies can be employed. A frequently made distinction is between the algorithic strategy (which involves the extensive and systematic working out of every combination and alternative) and the heuristic strategy (which involves working by hunch, intuition or insight). Using the algorithic method may involve too long and complex a search and may not apply to all kinds of problem-solving (especially those which are ill-defined or involve creative work), while using the heuristic method does not in itself provide a mechanism for selecting suitable solutions so that after the first few attempts one may be forced to adopt an unsystematic trial-and-error approach. While previous knowledge may be of direct or analogous help in situations sufficiently similar to previous experiences, it can also act as an inhibiting factor in situations where a totally new answer is required. One needs somehow to see the problem from a different perspective. In order to translate the hypothesis into action one requires the necessary skills and know how. Indeed one of the conditions for a suitable solution is that is must take into account the practical problems involved in its realization.

Evaluation

Just as a problem is a problem for someone so what counts as a possible and satisfactory solution must be acceptable to the originator of the problem. We often have occasion to question what someone else has accepted as a solution to their problem. We fail to grasp what their intentions are or how their original goals have become re-defined.

CLAIMS FOR PROBLEM-SOLVING EXAMINED

Among the claims that have been made on behalf of problem-solving are the following four: (1) a supposed motivational superiority, (2) a supposed superiority of learning from experience, (3) its openness and democratic view of authority, and (4) its contribution to a general capacity to solve problems. [8]

Motivation

Dewey himself made it clear that the motivational impetus with problem-solving could be seen when the pupil has a problem and with it a tension and psychological need to solve the problem. In other words when the problem is our own rather than one imposed upon us we have a basic desire to solve it. But in so far as the problems offered within school are artificial then, as Ausubel noted, 'problem-solving can be just as deadening, just as formalistic, just as mechanical, just as rote as the worst form of verbal exposition'.[9] The teacher is more important than the method and a stimulating teacher can make what might seem to be a weak method come alive so that the children become excited and acquire new interests. The question we need to ask with respect to this in CDT is whether we need to introduce this method for *motivational* reasons. As many reports have indicated, for the majority of pupils the craft subjects seemed enjoyable because they were practical and relevant.[10] It may not always be this way if less and less time is spent in making things and more and more time is spent on design work or technological theory. Of course for some of the brighter pupils, who have opportunities not previously available to them to explore some personal interest into whatever material or medium they require, into fascinating areas of electronics for example, the workshop has come to offer something significant. Obviously the more tailor-made a subject can be to everyone's individual requirements the more pleased everyone can be. But there is a need to ask upon what aspect of the subject and for what purpose teachers should spend their major effort.

Learning from experience

One main reason why child-centredness stressed problem-solving as opposed to transmission models of teaching is because they believe that learning from experience is a more active and valid way of learning. But it was Rousseau who offered the objection to this view:

> To acquire knowledge it is not enough to travel hastily through a country. There are plenty of people who learn no more from their travels than from their books, because they do not know how to think because their mind is at least under the guidance of the author, and in their travels they do not know how to see for themselves.[11]

It is part of the art of teaching to know what kind of structuring and preparation to offer for any form of learning, when pupils are learning from their own mistakes, and when there ought to be intervention. We learn both from experience and guidance from teachers. In many ways the traditional teaching of craft skills can be seen as employing a form of transmission model. The teacher demonstrates, instructs, corrects, warns or encourages; the pupil models himself on the teacher, learns something of the theory of skills and tools, and practises and applies the skills that have been demonstrated. As Warnock put it in respect of the music teacher: 'He will show me, help me to practise, give me tips (along with some theory, no doubt) and the hoped-for result will be that I shall discover how to play'.[12] The point is that discovery learning,

learning by experience in the sense of learning by trying out or by attempting to act[13] is an essential feature of acquiring and practising skills. So the traditional teaching of skills by demonstration and pupil practice involves both transmission and discovery methods. Where problem-solving in CDT differs from the acquisition of craft skills is not that one involves learning from experience and the other does not, but that what is learned through the two methods is different. CDT is concerned with the rationale of designing, the understanding of aspects of technology and the development of an awareness of different kinds of material. The concern of traditional craft education is towards competence in certain limited skills on a restricted range of materials.

The democratization of authority

One reason that radical educators prefer the problem-solving model to the transmission model of teaching is that they regard it as less dogmatic and authoritarian, paying more respect to the student's individual viewpoint. There are two claims that are being made: (1) about knowledge, and (2) about the position of the teacher.

1. With regard to knowledge, it is maintained that while doubts can be cast on absolute claims to truth, since all that we know is socially constructed or based within a form of life that is immune to outside criticism, then ultimately instruction must be based on unjustifiable assertion. In such a situation indoctrination can be avoided only by open discussion, problem-solving and a co-operative teacher–pupil construction of reality.[14] Against this argument I want to make two points, one a general logical point, and the other a specific point about practical or craft activities. There is something logically odd about the argument, for if there can be, in principle, no agreement about what counts as truth or evidence, problem-solving and the child's construction of reality cannot produce a greater insight into truth: they can only create a greater psychological satisfaction. More specifically, since craft and technology assume the pragmatic principle that knowledge is what works, practical instruction in their skills could not be regarded as exemplifying epistemological dogmatism. As the Newsom Report pointed out, practical subjects lead to something which can be seen or handled and to a success which is easily recognized.[15]

2. By teacher's 'authority' we mean something like his competence and right to make statements and to demonstrate know-how which reflect the methods and conclusions of the discipline and the academic community to which he belongs and which he mediates for his pupils. As such, authoritative statements can be checked against the findings of current research. In life we accept many statments on someone's

authority and it is, in principle, not irrational to do so, for we cannot critically examine for ourselves the truth of everything we hear or read; nor are we capable of doing so. However we can compare the statements of different authorities and we distinguish 'authority' from 'authoritarian' in that the latter implies a dogmatic manner of assertion or a refusal to submit one's opinion to the impersonal tests of the appropriate discipline. Therefore we can recognize that while there may be teachers of the transmission model who are authoritarian there is no necessary connection between transmission or instruction and authoritarianism. It is also perfectly possible to exercise authority and yet to respect pupils as persons and to encourage them to think for themselves. Indeed it may be argued that the more open the situation the more important the model for imitation and the more powerful a socializing agent the teacher becomes because of the premium placed on social trust.[16] Nevertheless there is one major difference between the position of the teacher in the transmission and the problem-solving models. In the latter case, when the problem is allowed to go beyond the teacher's present knowledge and skills, he has to use resource material and to find out information or to practise new skills. There is a sense, therefore, in which he is placed in a more vulnerable position, his knowledge no longer being superior to his students. In this situation he needs a more general knowledge than the average subject teacher and he has to be willing to expose his ignorance and to learn occasionally from his students. It is this aspect of the change in authority that may be most worrying to the teacher of traditional craft, whose expertise was made obvious through the demonstration and by a control of the products to be made. In the new circumstances the behavioural outcomes are not always predictable. Yet it can be said that the view of authority that this assumes is one of the rational authoritative teacher, whose aim is always to point beyond himself to an evolving tradition of knowledge.

Problem-solving as a general thinking capacity

It is sometimes argued that problem-solving is a general capacity to think reflectively, consisting of a set of general skills which can be regarded as independent of particular knowledge or context. On this view anyone who has ever solved a problem has employed these skills. Mere information is insufficient in itself to develop them, though one can be trained or taught to become more efficient in their operation. In particular, practice in problem-solving methods is one of the best ways of developing this general capacity, and it ought to be the aim of education to develop it. Dewey and others since have stressed as the aim of education the development of such related capacities as reflective thinking, effective thinking, intelligence and creativity, often used synonymously for problem-solving. Part of what is being said through such statements is that in such a society as that in which we live, education cannot concern itself mainly with the storing of facts and the separation of theory from practice, or on an undue reliance on authorities. We need to educate pupils to think for themselves, to possess the skills necessary to find things out and to cope with the changing nature of society and the many problems that emerge. As a corrective to existing practice such aims may be useful, but as Dewey himself discovered they can be so mis-used as to underplay the value of authority and tradition. They also overstress the importance of the intellect and individual. Schools rightly regard, as Dewey himself recognized, other factors as important – the social and community life, as well as physical, practical and aesthetic activities. Education must involve the whole person so that not only the intellect is expanded, but also a person's wants, attitudes, dispositions and emotions – indeed his whole awareness – must be extended, regulated and sensitized.[17]

But this is only part of the difficulty with a problem-solving aim. It assumes that problem-solving and the acquisition of knowledge can be regarded as logically equivalent, and as I have already indicated, it regards problem-solving as a general set of skills acquired independent of context. The first assumption leads to an instrumental view of knowledge so that what is studied is not so much for intrinsic value or enjoyment but for the sake of the solutions found to present problems. Consider the way that history, music or literature can be distorted when pursued with these motives solely. Against the other assumption I have already argued that problem-solving is a specific set of achievements that needs to be informed, both in the identification of the problems and in the method of working on the problem, by previous experience as well as relevant skills and knowledge: it is therefore context-bound. People cannot be taught to think without some particular content to think about and without some awareness of the logic and methodology of the appropriate discipline. What counts as effective thinking in one discipline will not necessarily be transferable to another discipline. Ausubel makes the point that empirical researchers have failed to establish 'any impressive degree of transfer to problem-solving situations in other contexts, disciplines or sub-disciplines. Their efforts foundered on the improbable thesis that there is a general heuristics of discovery.'[18]

Most everyday problems are solved by the replication of skills or the application of knowledge. Insights can also occur, as Koestler was keen to show, through the use of analogy, the relationship of cabbages and kings.[19] Even in this latter case where the transfer is extraordinary, the researcher is prepared and even searching for ways of formulating the problem or solution upon which he is working. If problems are, as I have argued, context-dependent then transfer must be generally within contexts rather than between them. As Toulmin puts it, 'If we ask about the validity, necessity, rigour or impossibility of arguments or conclusions, we must ask these questions within the limits of a given field, and avoid, as it were, condemning an ape for not being a man'. However Kilpatrick long ago pointed out that schools can improve thinking by engendering certain attitudes and habits, such as the habit of stopping to think before rushing into a possible solution and the concern about appropriate evidence, relevant data and consistency as well as care about the planning of details for any complex matter.[20]

While each discipline tends to have its own logic, skills or conceptual framework which constrain the uninitiated from solving problems in it, some freshness of approach or lack of habituation and general attitudes of concern or confidence can be of help. When Glenister claimed that in craft practical ability develops character and logical thinking he could only have such a limited claim in mind.[21] Since one cannot learn the logic of the different forms of knowledge without being taught them and since this is unlikely to occur in the kind of craft lesson that Glenister was concerned with, it would be impossible for craft students engaged in practical activities to master the logic of other disciplines, though they might acquire from the teacher an awareness of the importance of analysing any problem by whatever means are relevant. In a CDT situation where there might be interdisciplinary work being carried out there could be a development of understanding in other disciplines. In any case it is possible to argue that where students are put in the position of having to generate much of their own learning they may ultimately become more self-reliant. But this is an empirical point that would require further investigation.

CONCLUSION

The last decade has brought about a number of major changes in the CDT area. It is against such a background as well as considerations about the future of society that the nature of this subject must be debated. We have seen the movement of equal opportunities for girls, an increased social pressure for technological competence and curriculum concern with interdisciplinary studies. There has been some desire to upgrade this practical area and to encourage pupils to choose the more technological areas. There has also been increased unemployment and a reduction of educational resources. Problem-solving has been one way of encouraging the development of individual interest, though perhaps at the expense of the coherence of the subject and the teaching of the older craft skills. It offers an awkward compromise between those who see technology as applied science with a strong theoretical element and those who want to retain the old craft skills in modern terms that take account of advances in material technology or perhaps even those who want to equip us all for the practical DIY tasks we encounter in the home. I am uneasy about some of the claims made for problem-solving as I have indicated in this paper, but I am also most uneasy about attempts to increase the subject's status by turning competent teachers of practical skills into teachers of scientific and technological theory – as illustrated by some moves, for example in teacher education. Is problem-solving a way of teaching mixed abilities a variety of things? In designing through problem-solving are we aiming at producing competent designers or a more general design awareness? It seems to me that in the end my problem and the problem I find in this area is a lack of clarity about aims. Can others help?

REFERENCES

1. R.G. Collingwood, *The Principles of Art*, Oxford University Press, 1938, chapter 2.

2. Bruce Archer and Phil Roberts, 'Design and Technological Awareness in Education', *Studies in Design Education, Craft and Technology*, Vol. 12, No. 1, Winter 1979.

3. Rousseau, Froebel, etc.

4. J. Dewey, *Democracy and Education*, Macmillan, 1916.

5. *Ibid.*, p.200.

6. J. Dewey, *How We Think*, D.C. Heath, 1933.

7. T.S. Kuhn, *The Structure of the Scientific Revolutions*, 2nd edn, University of Chicago, 1970. [See Chapter 3 of Reader.]

8. D. Ausubel *et al. Educational Psychology: A Cognitive View* 2nd edn, Holt Rinehart and Winston 1978, chapter 15.

9. *Ibid.*, p.524.

10. Ministry of Education, *Half Our Future* (The Newsom Report), HMSO, 1963, chapter 17.

11. J.J. Rousseau, *Emile* (translated by B. Foxley), Everyman's, 1911, p.415.

12. M. Warnock, *Schools of Thought*, Faber, 1977, p.65.

13. J. Passmore, *The Philosophy of Teaching*, Duckworth, 1980, p.66.

14. G.M. Esland, 'Teaching and Learning as the Organisation of Knowledge', in Michael F.D. Young (ed.), *Knowledge and Control*, Collier-Macmillan, 1971,

15. *Ibid.*

16. K. Morgan, 'Socialization, Social Models and the Open Education Movement: Some Philosophical Consideration', In D. Nyberg (ed.) *The Philosophy of Open Education,* Routledge and Kegan Paul, 1975, p.123

17. Writings of R.S. Peters.

18. Ausubel *op. cit.*, p.583.

19. A. Koestler, *The Act of Creation*, Hutchinson, 1964.

20. W.H. Kilpatrick, *Foundations of Method*, Macmillan, 1925, quoted in I.A. Snook, Teaching Pupils to Think', *Studies in Philosophy and Education,* vol.8., no.3 (Winter 1974), pp 146–61.

21. S. Glenister, *The Technique of Handicraft Teaching*, 3rd edn, Harrap, 1968.

25   *Analyse, evaluate and realize*

● P. Burton

A tentative knock at my office door shattered the silence of my concentration. The forlorn and distressed little figure of a first-year girl stood gazing up apprehensively, eyes brimming near full with tears.

'I've got a problem,' she blurted out, and then proceeded to explain her predicament concerning the broken zip on her school bag containing her dinner money and that she had cut her finger trying hard to mend it. Well, being a good CDT teacher, I analysed the situation, applied the appropriate technology (in this case a large pair of pliers), arrived at a successful conclusion, and so away went another happy and satisfied customer.

A few days later I was giving a talk on problem-solving activities to a group of post-graduate science students at the Roehampton Institute, and during a plenary session a young lady about to start her probationary year in a school looked at me very apprehensively, just like the little first-year girl, and said: 'I've got a problem.'

She explained that she was very keen and enthusiastic about this approach to teaching, but unfortunately those lessons involving problem-solving activities had not been successful and that when she had asked for help from experienced teachers the reply from colleagues was 'Leave it alone – not worth the trouble – always fails – ends up in chaos.'

This set me to thinking about my own experiences with problem-solving approaches with which I have been involved for nearly a decade, both within my own teaching and that of the CDT department, and made me decide to set down some of my observations concerning their application as a learning strategy for pupils. I thought this might help those practitioners who may be a little reluctant to employ these approaches in their own teaching.

My first observation, and what I would consider to be the underlying basis for all problem-solving activities, is that the more relevant the problem to an individual, the more motivated he or she is in finding an appropriate solution, as is clearly illustrated in the previous two examples. Keeping that in mind, let me first try briefly to explain problem-solving.

Most contemporary approaches to CDT within the secondary school curriculum have placed their main emphasis on the activity of problem-solving in design. Within this activity a number of design strategies have been proposed and adopted by practitioners of CDT; chief among these are the linear and the cyclic processes. These two processes involve analysing a problem, offering various possible solutions, evaluating these and finally realizing one of them with the use of appropriate materials.

I employ both these approaches, but predominantly the linear approach, which is logical and systematic in character. It takes the form of a procedural path which begins with the awareness and identification of a need or problem and ends ideally with a successful solution. This procedural path can be broken down into a developmental sequence consisting of a number of related areas of activity (see below)

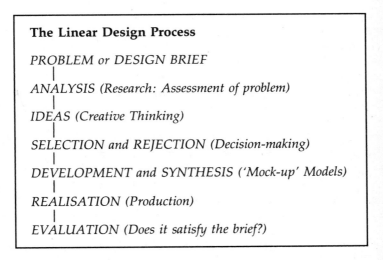

The Linear Design Process

PROBLEM or DESIGN BRIEF
|
ANALYSIS (Research: Assessment of problem)
|
IDEAS (Creative Thinking)
|
SELECTION and REJECTION (Decision-making)
|
DEVELOPMENT and SYNTHESIS ('Mock-up' Models)
|
REALISATION (Production)
|
EVALUATION (Does it satisfy the brief?)

Alternatively, instead of the 'linear path' we could implement a 'cyclic path' (more commonly referred to in CDT departments as the 'design loop'). Unfortunately, with both these 'paths' two major, and difficult questions arise:

1. Who makes the child aware of the need or problem and how to identify it? Is it the teacher's responsibility?
2. What determines the number of sequences needed to bring about a successful solution?

Bearing those questions in mind it becomes very apparent, when I visit schools and departments, that they employ what I would call an 'antiseptic' view of problem-solving.

Basically I refer to it as the 'TCP method' which stands for 'Teacher-directed problems', 'Closed-end problems' and 'Pupil-orientated problems'. I would suggest that possibly all three are employed to a greater or lesser extent in departments.

For example, with first-year pupils I initiate them into the problem-solving approach, using a simplified version of the linear process, incorporating simplified terminology. This approach is very much teacher-directed. The problem is given; material constraints, tools and techniques are carefully orchestrated.

However, I must emphasize very strongly that the responses are very individual and unique to the pupil and that no two solutions are the same. Alternatively, one can incorporate the 'Closed-end problems' which tend to be used more by departments in the design technological end of the CDT spectrum, where specific components are given in such areas as mechanisms, electronics, structures, pneumatics, and the solutions are nearly always predictable, especially when using 'constructional kits' which have become very popular with departments.

But I will be at pains to point out that once the basics have been understood using this approach it then lends itself to the third area of TCP methods – Pupil-orientated problems, that is problems deriving from a need or situation peculiar to that individual, in simple terms 'personal ideas'.

For example, one young boy had been to a drag-racing competition with his family and he had seen a car fitted up with a jet engine. The boy then produced several sheets of drawings, sketches and a cardboard version of a proposed scale working model he wanted to construct using a small 'glow plug' aeroplane motor.

Unfortunately, at that time his technical knowledge was limited and his ideas a little impractical. However, fantastic or impractical as such ideas may appear, there is no doubt that they have a significance for the individual. However, I can hear the readers say the problem with 'Pupil-orientated problems' is that they cause many more problems, such as organizing workshop facilities, materials, teaching techniques, contact time, staff involvement, and so on.

How can this all be managed when teaching twenty-one individuals each with his or her own needs, interests, situations and problems? There is no easy solution, but one possible means of direction is to develop or create situations in which the individuals in a group can direct their own energies and yet make a collective response. We all have our own interests, likes, dislikes, but sometimes we can be collective in our responses as in buying a particular brand product, record, car, television, book, home computer – three million people buying a 'Boy George' LP must have something in common.

Group-work thus provides the basis of the possible solution to the problem of catering for individual needs. What I am suggesting is finding, selecting, creating 'common' situations or needs from which pupils can develop an individual response or the 'SDP' approach.

No, it does not stand for the Social Democratic Party – what it stands for is Stimulus, Discussion, Problem.

By producing the right stimulus and involving the pupils in discussion, a problem common to them all can evolve, from which an individual response can emerge, but with the teacher orchestrating the learning situation and in control of the use of materials, techniques, skills, and knowledge to be learned.

Such a situation occurred recently when a young boy in my third-year design and technology group was very upset because his granny had fallen down and hurt herself, and had lain on the floor for nearly one and a half days before help came. This provided a 'situation' on which I expanded by providing 'stimulus', posters of old people, rooms, statistics on accidents in a home, newspaper cuttings. From this I directed discussions on the topic of emergencies and accidents. The pupils found it easy to relate to this because common to both boys and girls in the group were elderly relatives.

The scene was set, and a 'brainstorming' session held, with ideas flying fast and furious – emergency alarms, something to attract neighbours, a noise, flag, signals, sirens. Collectively, the 'problem' emerged – design and make an emergency alarm system for a senior citizen.

The specification developed, size no larger than a video cassette, mounted on the outside of a wall, operated mechanically or electrically, that should have a signalling device, such as lights, alarm, speakers, bells. What I then allowed was pupils to work in teams or groups, to have a project director, secretary, project co-ordinator, and to establish a company with an identifiable logo. A time limit was given on the final presentation of their solution, which included a twenty-five-page design brief, packaging format and advertising campaign.

My teaching strategy involved lessons on designing electronic circuitry, using 'Locktronic' equipment, material considerations, communication processes (technical graphics), modelling and researching techniques – all very much interrelated and illustrating to the pupils the need for team work and that each of the separate skills and experiences they developed, collectively, produced the final product.

Opportunities sometimes come unexpectedly, and taking advantage of situations which present themselves and having a fairly flexible approach towards a syllabus can reap rewards, beneficial to both staff and pupils. At the beginning of this school year there were installed on the school 'Redgra' pitch some large spotlights which required an even larger crane to place them in position.

The operation fascinated the younger pupils and it became a talking point in CDT lessons – so much so that I showed slides on different types of cranes and lifting mechanisms, not just to one group but to several. Subsequently the staff set a 'problem' based on lifting a 400 g weight from a TD desk to the floor and back again. The response was tremendous – mechanisms, electronics, materials – all combined in one project theme.

Using the SDP approach in a traditional technical graphics lesson can transform the subject area. Recently the Queen officially opened the Thames Barrier. Here was an opportunity to create a 'situation'. I showed the class a video of highlights of the ceremony which included a synopsis of the function of the barrier, illustrated diagramatically. 'What would happen to London if saboteurs blew it up when river water levels are critical?' The question provoked an immediate response. Carefully directing, I channelled the group into discussing the design of a survival module for 10–20 people for use in emergencies, and the production of a 'model' of their chosen solution.

The project 'took off' into data research on methods of power, energy conversion, heating, food storage, calorific intake, living conditions, unit shapes, materials, and so on. Technical graphic techniques involved organizational diagrams, pie charts, free-hand sketching, orthographic presentation, modelling processes.

Again I used the 'team' approach for this particular project although the value of groups working in problem-solving situations is rather undervalued in CDT. Group-work should not be undervalued in this way. Most people, I consider, want to 'belong'.

Being part of a group gives feelings of security and more opportunities for recognition, and I believe most pupils find a group situation acceptable; as G. Morris remarks: 'All organizations can meet this potent need. Not all do. Many still underestimate the enormous motivational power of "team" work, especially a team with an effective leader.'

But I wonder whether many CDT teachers encourage group projects or activities. Perhaps they do not think such situations can produce 'motivation' in pupils. I consider that group work offers something more than positive recognition. It should be the opposite of being a mere 'cog in a wheel'. Each pupil needs to feel that he is contributing something of importance to the group activity and that he is necessary.

Whether one incorporates TCP or SDP approaches in instigating problem-solving, there are what I consider fundamental points to bear in mind and I have listed five, not in any specific rank order:

1. Let the problem evolve naturally and preferably through the individual's need or situation. The more related the problem is to the pupil the more motivated he will be in producing or finding a solution.
2. Research and catalogue ideas for problem-solving and be flexible enough to allow for taking advantage of unusual situations, circumstances or events reported in the media, both locally and nationally. Sometimes the novelty approach pays dividends.
3. If trying to create artificial situations through stimulus techniques, make sure they can be related to needs or situations common to the group. Find out what their interests, dislikes and fads are and try to tap this ready-made resource.
4. If applying the linear approach to problem solving, remember what Eric Hoyle wrote in his book, *The Role of the Teacher*, in which he suggests that part of a teacher's function is 'to move to the periphery and merely create the right conditions for pupil-oriented activities and self-direction'. In creating these situations a teacher can still orchestrate or manage the workshop activities by providing the necessary tools, processes, equipment and materials and steering the pupils without too much over-direction.
5. Team or group-work – try to employ this approach in your teaching. It is more advantageous to direct groups of pupils engaged upon the same task, but make sure each individual is doing his own bit to help!

Finally, for those teachers who have not yet endeavoured to come to grips with this method of teaching CDT, and who still rely on the traditional approach, I leave you with a quote from Isaac Asimov who said in a recent interview:

> But people resist change, and it is difficult to blame them for that. Change is uncomfortable – even frightening. We like what we are accustomed to; we feel warm in our pleasant cocoons of habit. To alter this, we have to accept the very notion of change – its desirability, its inevitability.

Perhaps in some schools it may be too late?

REFERENCES

Eric Hoyle, *The Role of the Teacher*.

G. Morris, *Motivation – the Other Need*. Emas Ltd, lecture notes.

26 Educational psychology and curriculum design: a child-centred approach.

● N. Proctor

EDITORS' INTRODUCTION

Nigel Proctor is concerned about the lack of relevance of educational psychology to curriculum design. In this extract he takes up the question of what forms the basis of the curriculum and goes on to suggest a framework based upon five communication skills.

[...] Instead of proposing wholesale changes to the curriculum, it might be better to focus attention on these 'fundamental skills' and investigate what opportunities they provide for curriculum development and renewal. After all, H.M. Inspectorate (1977) makes the point that. 'No one disputes the irrefutable case for basic skills and techniques,' while *The Practical Curriculum* argues that 'knowledge without skill has a long, sad history. We believe schools need to make a conscious effort to ensure that their pupils acquire skills, many of which may prove to have a life-long value. A handful of fundamental skills form the highway to education' (Schools Council 1981: 15.) If this is true, then 'fundamental skills' could represent the basis of a common curriculum. The most 'fundamental' of all skills are those we use to communicate.

COMMUNICATION SKILLS IN A COMMON CURRICULUM

[...] There are five forms of communication all of which are 'languages' – literacy (written language), oracy (spoken language), numeracy (number language), graphicacy (graphic language using maps and pictures) and physiognomacy (body language). All five 'languages' have productive and receptive elements, since communication is always between two or more people, one the source, the other the receiver (Table 26.1).

Table 26.1 The forms of communication

Mode of communication	Form of language	Productive element	Receptive element
Literacy	Written language	Writing	Reading
Oracy	Spoken language	Speaking	Listening
Numeracy	Number language	Number manipulation and calculation	Number appreciation
Graphicacy	Graphic language	Sketching and map-making	Map and picture reading
Physiognomacy	Body and sign language	Movement, dance and expression	Watching and interpreting

In terms of the school curriculum the five communication skills or 'languages' underpin all education in that they allow the transmission of thoughts, concepts, feelings, judgements and instructions. Without these skills a person is disadvantaged practically, emotionally and academically. Psychologists such as Inhelder and Piaget (1964) have shown that communication is basic to a child's development; they are 'basics' since they represent some of the prerequisites for learning (Proctor 1985a) and are therefore an essential part of teacher education (Proctor 1984a).

To consider the five 'languages' purely as 'basics' is, however, short-sighted. Not even the most gifted children can master all the skills of communication, for these can be continually refined and developed. Indeed the great achievement of the so-called masters is that they developed these skills, to an extraordinary level; they could 'express' themselves supremely in a 'language' – whether this was through writing, oratory, painting or movement and dance. Genius is not only about knowledge, ideas and imagination in one area. It is also about the ability or skill to communicate these to others. Many geniuses – such as Einstein – master only one language. Others, such as Leonardo da Vinci, have transcended normal boundaries, but the all-round genius has perhaps never emerged. Communication skills are clearly not just 'basics'.

Similarly, it is misleading to consider communication skills as having only a utilitarian function, focusing on preparation for working life, since they also provide a framework for the 'Expressive' arts, comprising literature, drama and music, visual arts and dance. Indeed any dictionary definition of 'expression' will emphasize communicative qualities; wording or phrase in literature; intonation of voice; symbols together expressing algebraical quality; mode of expressing character in painting; aspects of face or performance expressing feeling. Arguably expressive arts represent ultimate aesthetic achievements growing out of each of the 'basic' communication skills (see Proctor 1985b).

A common curriculum based on the five communication skills could, it is argued, be used in any school – infant, junior, secondary or special – since acquisition of such skills represents a realistic goal for the vast majority of the school population. Continuity and progression in children's learning – epitomized in the 'spiral curriculum' of Bruner (1961) would be emphasized. Pupil profiles or Records of Personal Achievement (RPA) could also be based on children's abilities in the five 'language' skills, leaving evidence of their factual and conceptional knowledge to their performance in formal (subject) examinations.

Planning a curriculum around a 'language' framework need not diminish the importance of the learning of facts and concepts, or the development of values, attitudes and social skills, within the subjects, as indicated by Stones (1971: 128):

> Language enables us to create categories of things which have no existence in the real world. Language facilitates the formation of concepts. Concepts abstract the essence of things in the real world and enable us to classify and index reality. Through language we create concepts which would not otherwise exist. [Also] language not only conveys information: it carries affective overtones. The affective content of words develops while the words are being learned.

Again, McGuire and Priestley (1981: 68) state that 'Most forms of social interaction are dependent on some kind of direct communication. Communication is the basis of all social skill.'

A 'language' framework could also help to develop a 'whole-school' curriculum strategy to which *all* staff could contribute. After all it is generally recognized that interdisciplinary programmes, such as humanities or creative arts, do not solve the problems of school fragmentation or departmental isolation, since they merely represent groupings of 'like' subjects. In contrast, an 'across the curriculum' policy for the five languages, extending the Bullock (DES 1975) and Cockcroft (DES 1981b) recommendations for literacy, oracy and numeracy by including the two other languages, would mean involving departments – such as art (Proctor 1984b) and physical education (Proctor 1984c) – which have traditionally been peripheral to whole-curriculum debate and planning. The potential for school-based curriculum development would be considerable; the focus of this development would be more on the 'needs' of the child, than on the subjects, so more attention would have to be taken of work done by educational psychologists.

EDUCATIONAL PSYCHOLOGY AND COMMUNICATION SKILLS

In a new book, *Frames of Mind: The Theory of Multiple Intelligences*, which has received support from Jerome Bruner, Howard Gardner argues that there are at least five 'intelligences', apart from the verbal and logical/mathematical; he proposes a musical intelligence, a spatial intelligence (with which, for instance, Eskimos and artists are richly endowed) and a bodily-kinesthetic intelligence, which is well developed in dancers and gymnasts. He goes on to suggest that there may also be two 'personal intelligences' with which individuals understand their own, and other people's feelings and intentions, but the original five undoubtedly have the greatest bearing on the school curriculum. Indeed Isaac Asimov, reviewing the American edition, suggested that the framework opened a door onto a new way of looking at individuals; it could enable children to acquire and develop a wider range of skills and abilities.

The 'intelligences' match almost exactly the forms of communication identified earlier, apart from the 'musical intelligence'; as a means of communication, a musical score is part of literacy while the making of, and listening to, sound is part of oracy, which should be part of the 'common curriculum' for all children (Proctor 1985b). Gardner contends that far too much emphasis is placed on verbal and numerical intelligences by teachers and education psychologists alike.

Research on the 'three Rs' has certainly dominated the curricular work of educational psychologists throughout this century. Stones (1971: 118) in a chapter on 'learning and language' illustrated the importance of literacy and oracy to psychologists by commenting that 'emphasis has been placed on the role of language in human learning because it is the key to meaning'. Inhelder and Piaget (1964, from 1959 French), after stating that 'language accelerated the processes of classification and seriation and helps to complete them' added that, 'we do not propose to study how it does so in detail. In the first place the importance of language is a commonplace.' Again, Piaget (1970, from 1946 French) had previously considered some aspects of numeracy: 'the concepts of movement and speed touch upon the fields of mathematics and general science teaching, in which it would be of great value to know precisely the way in which these concepts develop; in other words their psychological as well as their logical build-up'. Piaget's work in these three 'languages' has been augmented by many psychologists, including Lovell (1962, 1966) Murray (1975, 1978) and Smith (1971) while testing of children's ability in literacy, oracy and numeracy is commonplace.

Spatial ability – the first of Thurstone's (1938) primary mental abilities – is clearly related to the development of graphical skills. Even animals possess spatial ability, and must inevitably form their own mental maps of territory, but they are unable to communicate this spatial information to other animals: only mankind can do this through the drawing of maps and sketches. Some research suggests, of course, that there is a clear relationship also between poor spatial ability and reading problems, but the most recent studies show that dyslexics, for instance, do not have a disturbed spatial ability and may well have a predisposition to spatial and graphicate skills (see Tansley and Panckhurst 1981: 112; Ernest 1983).

Piaget and Inhelder (1956 from 1948 French) produced the pioneering work, *The Child's Conception of Space* including chapters on spatial relationships in drawing (pictorial space) and on the co-ordination of perspectives. Nearly twenty years later (1969, from 1966 French) they drew attention to Luquet's celebrated studies on children's drawings (1927) and showed that, 'Drawing is a form of the semiotic function which should be considered as being half-way between symbolic play and the mental image. It is like symbolic play in its functional pleasure and autotelism, and like the mental image in its effort at imitating the real.'

There are, of course, many tests of spatial and graphical ability. The Goodenough-Harris Drawing Test (formerly called Goodenough Draw-a-Man) is a long established test of intelligence, but its use as a single indictor of ability is not recommended. There are a number of other tests of graphicate ability. The NFER *Catalogue of Tests for Educational and Clinical Psychologists* lists two, one being a non-verbal drawing test, the other – Make a Picture Story (MAPS) – using a projective method in which the subject chooses a pictorial background and populates it with figures before accounting for his arrangement. The NFER *Catalogue of Educational Guidance and Assessment* lists three spatial tests: Stuart's picture test for 7 to 8-year-olds, MacFarlane-Smith's Spatial Test, requiring subjects to translate two-dimensional material into a three-dimensional form, and Watt's Spatial Test, which, using three-dimensional material, tests the hypothesis that differences may exist in children's ability to deal mentally with two-and three-dimension problems. The *British Ability Scales* (Elliot 1978) include twenty-three scales which tap five major behavioural processes, one of which is spatial imagery.

Physiognomacy is closely allied to Bloom's psycho-motor skills domain as well as Gardner's five intelligences but has been inadequately researched from the point of view of curriculum content. Rudolf Laban (1956) initiated research into relationships between movement, human personality behaviour and experience and invented a system of movement notation which has been adopted internationally. North (1972: 41) used this scheme and concluded that, 'the assessment of the pattern of a child's present capacities (in movement) can be helpful for teachers and psychologists'. She included case studies of children's personality tests which were compared with performances in standard tests.

The Assessment of Performance Unit of the Department of Education and Science (DES) also included a study of physical performance in its research programme. Its first director, Brian Kay (1975), identified various 'kinds of development' to monitor pupil performance across the curriculum. In addition to verbal (reading and writing, listening and speaking) and mathematical (communication through number) abilities which have since all been closely monitored, he included physical performance, including the pupil's developing muscular control and his ability to use his body efficiently and expressively; this progressed from dexterity in using a pencil to 'movement and dance in communication'.

The recent report on *Physical Development* (APU 1983) concludes that any programme of assessment aimed at determining the attainment of children in schools must pay due regard to their motor development, which should be seen as the responsibility of *all* teachers in all schools. Furthermore children's motor performance should be monitored as a normal part of teachers' school activity, and should be compared with their performance in basic skills 'to provide necessary data for those responsible for administering educational provision'.

It is clear then, that children's acquisition and development of 'basic' skills are seen as among the most important aims of the curriculum and as a major responsibility in school and local authority administration and planning. The role of educational psychologists in identifying the rationale and structure, and in the later evaluation and monitoring, of this curriculum, should not be undervalued.

It is not suggested that the five 'languages' should become a focus for educational psychology, since

> 'Psychology is a science and as such is governed by a code of rules which calls for the empirical verification of its propositions. Its purpose is to elaborate an increasingly comprehensive theory of human behaviour. The curriculum is something other than this... Educationists [need to be] very clear about the role of psychology and aware that its goals and those of the curriculum are different' (Taylor 1968: 93)

Nor is it suggested that the framework based on five language skills represents a panacea for all the problems of the school curriculum.

Schwab (1969) recognized the difficulties involved: 'What is fatally theoretic...is the dispatch, the sweeping appearance of success, the vast simplicity which grounds the purported solution to the problems of the curriculum.'

It is argued, however, that used in conjunction with other curriculum schemes, the model could provide a more practical framework on which local authorities and schools could plan their own curriculum programme. Additionally it could provide a platform on which educational psychologists could build a more clearly defined relationship with curriculum planners and decision-makers.

REFERENCES

Assessment of Performance Unit (1983) *Physical Development*, London, Department of Education and Science.

Bruner, J. (1961) *The Process of Education*, London, Oxford University Press.

Department of Education and Science (1975) *A Language for Life* (Bullock Report), London, HMSO.

(1981) *Mathematics Counts* (Cockcroft Report), London, HMSO.

Elliot, C.D. *et al.* (1978) *British Ability Scales*, Slough, NFER.

Ernest, C.H. (1983) 'Imagery and Verbal Ability and Recognition Memory for Pictures and Words, *Educational Psychology*, vol. 3, pp. 227, 244.

Gardner, II. (1984) *Frames of Mind: The Theory of Multiple Intelligences*, London, Heineman.

H.M. Inspectorate (1977) *Curriculum 11–16* (The Red Book), London, HMSO.

Inhelder, B and Piaget, J. (1964) *The Early Growth of Logic in the Child*, Henley, Routledge and Kegan Paul (original French edition, 1959).

Kay, B. (1975) 'Monitoring Pupils' Performance,' *Trends in Education*, vol. 2, pp. 11–18.

Laban, R. (1956) *Principles of Movement and Dance Notation* (London, Macdonald-Evans) (new edition, 1975).

Lovell, K., (1962) *The Teaching of Arithmetic in Primary Schools*, London, University of London Press.

(1966) *The Growth of Basic Mathematical and Scientific Concepts in Children*, London, University of London Press.

Luquet, G.H. (1927) *Le Dessin Enfantin*, Paris, Alcan.

McGuire, J. and Priestley, P. (1981) *Life After School: A Social Curriculum*, Oxford, Pergamon Press.

Mouly, G.J. (1968) *Psychology for Effective Teaching*, New York, Holt, Rinehart and Winston.

Murray, F.B. and Pikulski, J.J. (eds) (1975) 'The Acquisition of Reading', in *Delaware Symposium on the Curriculum*, Newark, Delaware.

Murray, F.B. with Ehri, L.C. (eds) (1978) *The Recognition of Words* (IRA series on the development of the reading process), Newark, Delaware.

North, M. (1972) *Personality Assessment Through Movement*, London, Macdonald-Evans.

Piaget, J. (1970) *The Child's Conception of Movement and Space*, New York, Basic Books (original French edition, 1946).

Piaget, J. and Inhelder, B. (1956) *The Child's Conception of Space*, Henley, Routledge and Kegan Paul (original French edition, 1948).

Piaget, J. and Inhelder, B. (1969) *The Psychology of the Child*, New York, Basic Books (original French edition, 1966).

Proctor, N. (1984a) 'Professional Studies and the QTS Review,' *Journal of Education for Teaching*, vol. 10, pp. 61–72.

(1984b) 'Art as Graphicacy in the Common Curriculum,' *Journal of Art and Design Education*, vol. 3, pp. 203–14.

(1984c) 'Problems Facing Physical Education After the Great Education Debate,' *P.E. Review*, vol. 7, pp. 4–11, 'Physical Education in the Revised School Curriculum.' *P.E. Review*, vol. 7. pp. 106–12.

(1985a) 'Redefining the Basics of Primary Education,' *Education 3–13*, vol. 13, pp. 5–8.

(1985b) 'From Basics to Aesthetics in the Curriculum,' *British Journal of Aesthetics*, vol. 25, pp. 57–65.

Schools Council (1981) *The Practical Curriculum*, London, Schools Council.

Schwab, J.J. (1969) 'The Practical: A Language for Curriculum,' *School Review*, November.

Smith, F. (1971) *Understanding Reading: A Psycho-linguistic Analysis of Reading and Learning to Read*, London, Holt, Rinehart and Winston.

Stones, E. (1971) *An Introduction to Educational Psychology*, London, Methuen.

Tansley, P. and Panckhurst, J. (1981) *Children with Specific Learning Difficulties*, Slough, NFER-Nelson.

Taylor, P. (1968) 'The Contribution of Psychology', in J.F. Kerr (ed.) *Changing the Curriculum* London, University of London Press, pp. 79–98.

Thurstone, L.L. (1938) 'Primary Mental Abilities,' *Psychometric Monographs*, 1.

27 *Project work*

● Schools Council

EDITORS' INTRODUCTION

In the two extracts from the Schools Council 'Modular Courses in Technology', the importance and organization of project work are spelt out. Although the points made are in the context of these specific courses, they are of a general significance to other courses.

THE EDUCATIONAL IMPORTANCE OF PROJECT WORK

There are many good educational reasons for the inclusion of projects in all school disciplines, not least of which is their real-life multi-disciplinary nature. A few of the educational reasons for the inclusion of projects in technology courses are highlighted below. Project work in technology develops:

(a) skills in the application and use of knowledge and expertise in solving particular problems;

(b) the ability to work with others;

(c) divergent and convergent thinking by giving due consideration to intuitive inspiration, guesses, and accidental developments as well as those achieved by means of a logical step-by-step progression;

(d) self-discipline and responsibility, as the success or failure of the project is pupil-centred;

(e) creative abilities and encourages enterprise and dedication;

(f) speculative thought and exercises ingenuity.

In the past these important aspects of educational development have been largely ignored because of the difficulty in assessing them quantitatively. However, their importance to personal development is now being given due consideration.

The main justification for project work is that it enables pupils to develop their capabilities fully at their own pace. This provides them with a greater breadth of education than could be achieved by following the traditional narrow academic path, and so better equips them to solve the real problems which will have to be faced in their future professional lives.

So for educational reasons it is of fundamental importance that project work should form a part of every pupil's educational programme at some time. Teachers should therefore discuss the importance of project work with parents, industrialists, and colleagues from further and higher education, so that the inclusion of project work in technology syllabuses is both understood and encouraged.

[...]

ORGANIZATION OF PROJECT WORK

From the teacher's and pupils' point of view, technological project work can be exhilarating, instructive, fulfilling and enjoyable. Equally, it can be boring, frustrating and de-motivating. The point of view which develops will largely be dependent on four factors.

1. The suitability of pupils for the work undertaken.
2. The teacher's approach to project work and the teacher/pupil relationship.
3. The teacher's advice on project selection.
4. The teacher's overall preparation, planning and organization of project work.

Without thorough consideration of the above factors, project work can get out of hand and culminate in failure. It is hoped that the following information in this section will act as a useful guide in helping teachers think and plan carefully their approach to project work and so minimize the chances of failure.

The suitability of pupils for technological project work

In the context of the Schools Council's 'Modular Courses in Technology' Project, the materials that have been developed and the projects that have been suggested are designed for CSE grade III pupils and above. The school trials have confirmed that pupils attempting the course below this level are unable to cope with the course content. This applies particularly to the major projects as, unlike in many other subjects, a project will not be acceptable for technology if it is merely a collection of

Figure 27.1 *School technology projects*

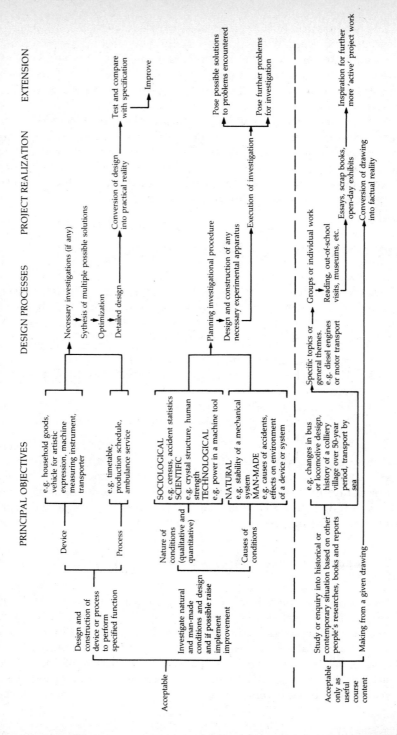

factual information, or if it is just making an end product from a set of drawings, although either of these activities could form a useful study element of a technology course. For a project to be acceptable it must involve investigation by pupils, followed by their own solution to the problem. Figure 27.1 indicates acceptable types of mini and major projects above the dotted line, and unacceptable types of project below, although the latter could be used for a useful component of a technology course. It is the active element of analysis and synthesis in the projects above the dotted line which pupils below grade III CSE find beyond their ability. There are, of course, exceptions such as the pupil who is very interested in engineering activities, and therefore highly motivated by the course, who rises above his or her general ability level in this subject. But even with this type of pupil, success has not been observed with pupils having a general ability level below grade IV CSE.

When advising pupils whether or not to take technology as a CSE or GCE subject based on the Project's modules, it is advisable that the following questions can be answered in the affirmative.

1. Is the pupil considered to be in the top half of the ability range?
2. Is the pupil interested in any aspects of engineering, be they mechanical, chemical, biological, civil, etc.?
3. Is the pupil practically inclined?
4. Is the pupil interested in science?
5. Is the pupil competent in mathematics?
6. Is the pupil interested in drawing?
7. Is the pupil interested in experimenting and innovating?

Point 1 is of fundamental importance to success on a technology course and, when linked with a positive response to any of the other questions, would indicate that a pupil is suited to take a technology course based on the Project's modules. If a pupil has no positive responses to points 2–7 then their inclusion on such a technology course should be considered very carefully.

The last generalization that needs to be made regarding the suitability of pupils for project work is that the more able the pupil the quicker you can progress to open-ended project work. Conversely, the less able the pupil, the more detail and care that are needed in setting project briefs with achievable parameters.

The teacher's approach to project work, and the teacher/pupil relationship

As in any other teaching situation, the teacher must organize the pupils' work from the simple task to the difficult one. In project work this progression from simple projects, having very few parameters for investigation, to those of greater complexity is essential, if semi open-ended projects are to be tackled successfully in the fifth year. In secondary schools we have five years in which to achieve this development. This means setting progressively more difficult project briefs which relate to the pupil's knowledge and skills. These briefs must be clearly defined, achievable and aimed at arousing pupil excitement and curiosity. (Failure of project work is usually the result of presenting ill-considered briefs during this stage of development.) During this development the teacher, while indicating a logical approach to solving problems, must also encourage a sympathy for short-cut creative approaches. Such approaches may be instinctive and emanate from intuitions, guesses, inspirations or accidents. Too much emphasis on logical development may stunt creativity. If this stage is successful, fifth-year pupils will be capable of initiating and conducting their own projects with minimal guidance. This means that pupils must have had some experience of project work *before* undertaking a two-year O-level or CSE technology course, especially if it involves a major project of more than one term.

For major project work to be successful the right relationship between the teacher and pupil must exist. To achieve this the following points should be borne in mind.

1. The teacher should talk with pupils and not at them.
2. The teacher should aim to develop a joint learning situation where both teacher and pupil gain new knowledge and experience, with the teacher acting in a consultancy capacity and only giving advice when the pupil is faced with what seems an insurmountable problem.
3. The teacher and pupil should develop a mutual trust and respect for each other. This trust can be helped from the beginning by giving the pupil a detailed knowledge of the means by which the projects will be assessed.

The teacher should set high professional standards, and expect his or her pupils to follow suit. To help accomplish this, the teacher should develop a stimulating environment by having high quality work from previous pupils on view. The participation in local or national competitions can also stimulate a raising of standards.

Varying degrees of teacher involvement will be needed for different projects, but this must never reach the stage of giving the answer or directing the project, as this would defeat the object. However, a watchful eye must be kept to see that pupil motivation is maintained. This may result at times in the teacher taking the initiative to re-motivate the pupil.

The teacher must at all times be careful not to stifle the pupils' natural sense of wonder and curiosity (this may mean letting the pupils follow lines of enquiry which are felt to be fruitless) or he/she will be guilty of destroying their natural creativity.

Teacher's advice on project selection

When the pupils choose their major project, the teacher must help to ensure that it matches the pupils' abilities and interests. For this reason a discussion of all the predictable factors that will have to be faced when carrying out the project must take place with the pupil before work is started. In this discussion particular attention should be paid to the following points.

1. The pupil's personal need to find a solution to a problem will give increased motivation and involvement.
2. Projects should be encouraged which build on knowledge and skills gained during the course.
3. The pupils should be encouraged to be optimistic regarding their own knowledge and skills, as this will enable them to develop projects which will extend their ability to the full.
4. Consideration and viewing of previously successful projects can give pupils an insight of what can be achieved.
5. The limited time in which the project is to be achieved must be discussed in detail.
6. Problems relating to organization of the project, e.g. if readings need to be taken every two hours for two days, can the necessary arrangements be made?
7. Will the necessary resources be available in the school or from outside sources?
8. Can the pupil meet the costs of the project? Where this is a problem, suggestions for community or industry-based projects may overcome this difficulty, e.g. a local handicapped people's home may need help with designing and making a particular item and be prepared to pay for it.
9. Will the project conform to safety regulations?

The teacher's overall planning and organization

When planning the introduction of project work, careful consideration must be given to the types of projects that will be undertaken and the differences between mini and major projects. To help with these considerations the following information may be useful on different types of project with respect to the number of pupils involved and the nature of the project.

The individual project

This has the advantage of relative ease of pupil assessment, when compared with group projects. Its disadvantage is that if you have a group of twenty pupils each doing different projects, the time spent by the teacher with each is minimal, especially if problems arise requiring considerable teaching consultation. This sometimes results in the waning of individual interest and enthusiasm. It also does not equate to real life project work which always involves a team.

Small group projects *(1–4 pupils)*

It has been found in practice that pupils working in pairs, or groups of four where each pair has specific responsibilities within the project, work well. It has also been observed that where three pupils work together, one of them will often become a bystander.

This type of project has the advantage of reducing the number of projects within a class, and therefore allowing the teacher to spend at least twice as long with each project. This reduces the possibility of pupils wasting time. Another advantage is that of reducing the quantity of materials and resources needed, which in turn leads to less capacity being needed in terms of equipment, machinery and storage. It can also help to develop meaningful pupil interaction.

The main difficulty with this type of project is that of assessment. This can be alleviated by organizing the project in such a way that pupils of like ability work together, and individuals have particular responsibilities with the project. The SUJB O-level requires that pupils work in pairs for the major project. Thus this type of project is suitable for major projects in some cases and very suitable for mini projects.

Large group projects *(5 pupils or more)*

It is suggested that it is preferable to use large group projects for mini projects because they create real life situations in which the pupils learn to understand what team-work really involves. This type of project fulfils many educational aims which could not be achieved through small group projects, e.g. giving pupils the opportunity to identify abilities in organization and leadership.

Mini and major projects

The basic different between mini and major projects, for O-level and CSE technology courses based on the Project's material, is that of time.

A mini project will last from one to two weeks whilst a major project will last from one to two terms. For a project to be acceptable in either form the following aspects must be present:

(a) A problem to be solved.
(b) The problem broken down into component parts (analysed) and these parts investigated.
(c) Several solutions considered and the best selected.
(d) An end product produced which may take the form of a report, a piece of equipment, a model, or a combination of these.

A project will not be acceptable as a technological project if it is merely a collection of factual information compiled from literature, or if it is just making an end product from a set of drawings. To be acceptable it must involve investigation by the pupils, followed by their own solution to the problem.

MINI PROJECTS

Mini projects test the pupil's ability to use knowledge (gained from a module) when investigating and solving a problem. For this reason the mini project briefs are usually given by the teacher, and involve a small number of parameters for specific investigation.

A typical two-week mini project brief to test the students' understanding of the *Mechanisms* module is given below.

> With the equipment and power source provided (e.g. variable dc voltage source and Fischertechnik Kits UT 1 and 2) design the most efficient energy system which will lift a 2 kg mass from the floor to a height of one metre.

This project will involve the investigation of several methods of gearing, power transmission and machine efficiency. A decision will also have to be made with regard to the best solution devised.

The pupil's transition from mini to major projects is achieved by a series of mini projects which increase in difficulty and complexity as the course progresses.

The time allowed for mini projects makes it unrealistic to expect the depth and breadth of research or written work which is associated with the major project. However, evidence of analysis of the problem, planning of time and resources, statement of why the particular solution was selected, together with a presentation of any supporting information is essential if the project is to be acceptable.

MAJOR PROJECTS

The major project is included in courses developed from the [Modular Courses in Technology] Project's materials to enable the pupil to obtain a meaningful understanding of the technological process. [...] It also enables the teacher to assess the pupil's ability to handle this process. Because of the significant amount of time allocated to the major project, it can vary from an expanded mini project with a very limited number of parameters for investigation (suitable for the less able pupil) to a complex almost totally open-ended project (suitable for the most able pupil). Whether the major project is simple or complex the following elements must be present for it to be acceptable. The pupil should have:

(a) defined a real need for the project;
(b) analysed and researched the various problems posed;
(c) planned the project work with regard to skills, time and resources;
(d) considered several solutions and selected and developed the best, giving evidence of good reasoning and communication; and
(e) produced an end product, and given a detailed report of the project.

Ideally the major project should originate from a pupil's own interests since this automatically guarantees a self-motivating factor. In practice, however, the teacher will need to provide many project ideas from which the pupils, in consultation with the teacher, can choose.

The major project should also be produced bearing in mind social, energy, materials and economic implications, followed by the solution and real-life implementation. However, in practice, the real-life implementation of the solution cannot always be achieved in the time-scale involved. For example, pupils might have made a detailed study, by the use of analogues and models, of an integrated traffic system which could provide greater efficiency for a region, but it is unlikely that they would be able to convince the local authorities to implement their ideas, particularly in the allocated time scale.

Constructional and investigational projects

The traffic system previously mentioned is a good example of a technological investigational project which fulfils the basic requirement for a major project. This type of project is not totally theoretical as it involves the making of models, but even so there are many teachers and pupils who would prefer to see a greater quantity of constructional involvement. To satisfy such people, projects are undertaken which could be classified as constructional projects, an example of which is given below.

Design and make a device for bowling cricket balls at various pre-determined speeds, and at various pre-determined lengths.

Although this type of project has a large element of practical activity, there is still a meaningful amount of theoretical work required, particularly at the planning stage, and as such it fulfils the requirements for major projects in technology.

Organizing major projects

No project will be completed successfully within a given time-scale without a clear plan of action which allows for unforeseen problems. It is therefore advisable to get a detailed work plan from the pupils, for discussion at the beginning of the project. This plan should consider the criteria laid out clearly in the assessment procedure. Having agreed the plan, the pupil should be encouraged to keep a diary of the project's development, which should include all costs involved. This diary will be found helpful when a pupil comes to write up his or her project report. It will also allow the teacher to observe whether the project is progressing satisfactorily.

By compiling all the pupils' plans for projects, the teacher can decide whether or not there are sufficient resources available, and plan the use of machinery and equipment to avoid bottlenecks and wasted time. The teacher should also encourage the use of photographic records for experimental work and constructional progress. These may be needed later for moderation purposes where kit constructions have been the answer to mini problems, or the final equipment is too large to take to moderation. The pupils will also find them useful to illustrate their written reports.

Resources for major projects

No project will be successful unless the necessary resources are available. In real life when faced with a problem, we make maximum use of available help and resources. No one would make a standard bolt which was readily available. Major projects should be viewed in the same way. Teachers should therefore encourage their pupils to obtain whatever help is possible for any stage in their project. It is surprising what can be achieved by use of good communication.

At the beginning of the project it will be necessary to discuss with the pupils where and how they can obtain help and advice. It should be possible to give them some specific leads as to local experts, and specialist books which can be obtained from libraries, together with any assistance that is obtainable from the local education authority, e.g. suggest teachers' centres, science and technology centres, etc.

When the project gets under way, the emphasis will be on the accommodation that is to be provided. Workshops or laboratories can both prove satisfactory bases, and the first consideration by teaching staff should be that of maximizing the use of facilities and equipment which are already available in the school or authority. It should, however, be borne in mind that while most laboratory activities can be conducted in workshops, workshop activities are more difficult to accomplish in laboratories. If a choice has to be made, project work should be undertaken in workshops to avoid undue restraints. Storage of projects also needs careful consideration since it is normal in schools for such space to be at a premium.

[...]

28 **The assessment of the design project**

● JMB Exams Council

EDITORS' INTRODUCTION

Again, although this is taken from the assessment of the scheme of a particular course, the framework presented has general application, with regard being made for the age of pupils.

In order to make possible reliable assessments in quantitative terms it is necessary to establish criteria for the award of marks for each of the assessment categories. It is considered to be unrealistic to attempt to provide precise and detailed criteria to enable the teacher to make fine distinctions within the mark ranges and it is recognized that criteria cannot be applied entirely objectively since at any stage in a candidate's work any combination of abilities and factors may be present. The assessment criteria provided on the *Individual Assessment Form* are intended to indicate the essential characteristics which should be identifiable at the various levels of performance to be expected from advanced level candidates and the accompanying mark scales indicate the appropriate award of marks for the various levels of performance.

Zero marks should be awarded where a candidate has failed to consider any one of the assessment categories, unless it can be shown that such an omission is not an oversight but a conscious act of design strategy. Zero marks may also be awarded to a candidate who has produced work of such quality that it fails to meet the criteria for an award of a mark of one in the category concerned.

The scale at the head of the *Individual Assessment Form* is to provide teachers with an approximate indication of the grades appropriate to the various levels of performance in the design project.

THE BRIEF

Although the brief is not included in the list of assessment categories, candidates are required to produce a brief prior to undertaking any research.

The candidate is required to identify, within the context of the syllabus, a design problem he or she wishes to explore. A clear statement of the problem to be tackled should be provided which shows an appreciation of the design factors involved and of the potential the topic offers for a successful outcome in the time available.

In advising the candidate on the choice of design project the teacher is involved in making some estimate of what the project will involve. In so doing the teacher is opening up the candidate's mind to the nature and possible consequences of a particular project. The object of these discussions should be to eliminate the impossible or over-ambitious elements of a project and to avoid the frivolous. The candidates should, therefore, be advised to select projects which show promise of success, given the time and facilities available. While candidates should be encouraged to select their own topic for a project, the teacher must exercise control over the final choice. It may even be necessary, in certain circumstances, for the teacher to make the choice for the candidate. It is important that the carrying out of the project to completion should be seen as an integral part of the whole design process and that modifications should be allowed right up to completion.

The main elements of this part of the design process are as follows;

(a)   The identification of a suitable design problem.
(b)   A description of the setting/situation/environment into which the product is to be placed.
(c)   The specification and outline of the envisaged parameters of the problem.

The candidate should not propose possible solutions in the brief. The brief is an essential part of the design process and teachers should ensure that candidates produce a satisfactory brief before embarking upon subsequent stages of the design project.

AMPLIFICATION OF THE ASSESSMENT CATEGORIES

In the following paragraphs each of the categories under which the design project is to be assessed is amplified and guidance given on the method of assessment and the factors to be considered in each assessment category.

The categories by which the design project are to be assessed and the sequence in which they are presented is intended to reflect the way in which designing is most usually carried out and it is expected that the work of most candidates can be readily assessed on the basis of these categories and in the order in which they are presented. However the assessment categories are not prescriptive and they are not necessarily hierarchical. It is recognized that some candidates might follow a design procedure which is quite acceptable but does not conform to the assessment categories given below or to the mark allocations given for the various categories.

Research (5 marks)

Some preliminary research is necessary to determine the feasibility of the design project before it is submitted to the board for approval on the *Project Outline Form*. Once approval has been given candidates may commence in-depth research. This research can take the form of:

(a) a survey of similar contemporary products;
(b) a survey of similar historical products;
(c) considerations of analogous products, materials or technologies designed for other purposes, which can have relevance to the design project;
(d) special investigations;
(e) questionnaires.

This section should be well illustrated.

Analysis of brief (5 marks)

When the researching has reached a sufficiently advanced design stage then the candidate will be in a position to commence a detailed analysis of his/her and other designers' ideas. The following aspects of design need to be considered;

(a) Environment
(b) Function
(c) Aesthetics
(d) Materials
(e) Technologies
(f) Processes
(g) Economics
(h) Social considerations

It is possible that there will be a considerable written content to this section.

Alternative ideas (10 marks)

When the basic analysis is complete the candidate must produce as wide a selection as possible of alternative ideas that could be considered suitable design solutions to the project. This section should consider the following:

(a)   variety of viable solutions,
(b)   sketches/drawings of the overall concepts of each idea,
(c)   critical observations about each idea.

Development of final design (15 marks)

When all alternative ideas have been stated, the most appropriate solution should be selected and may be developed as follows:

(a)   critical analysis to show why the chosen solution is more suitable than the others
(b)   development and analysis of each component to determine final forms
(c)   use of mock-ups, models, experiments or test rigs
(d)   production of working drawings and lists of components.

(Projects may range from the complex using sophisticated manufacturing techniques to the development of relatively simple projects which have evolved through a number of prototype stages and may include systems for their production in quantity.)

Planning (5 marks)

Any designer must plan work to be completed by a certain deadline and within appropriate economic constraints. This planning can be usefully accomplished in the following manner.

(a)   The research and data collection phase to be completed by a certain date. The candidate must allow time to consider all written and graphic sources of information, visits and letters to firms and institutions of education.
(b)   The time taken to analyse and synthesize must be determined and broadly outlined.
(c)   When the working drawings are complete then times must be estimated and checked against experience for the realization of each component. Specialist materials must also be ordered.

(d) If candidates are falling behind schedule then they must do more work, re-design certain aspects, or incorporate more manufactured components. The construction work should total about fifty hours. This planning should be in diary or calendar form.

Manufacture (40 marks)

This is an assessment of workmanship/craftsmanship. Marks can only be awarded for those parts/components of the realized design that the candidate has made and assembled. These skills can be assessed under the following headings.

(a) Accuracy
(b) Shaping
(c) Forming
(d) Assembly
(e) Quality of finish
(f) Imaginative use of materials/technologies in both orthodox and unorthodox situations.

It is expected that the teacher will carry out assessments of this work throughout the period in which it is undertaken. The examiner will not have the advantage of seeing the process of production. The external appraisal of the quality of the work will therefore be based on the evidence of the material available when the examiner visits the centre, including the notes in the candidate's design folio and on the examiner's discussions with the teacher and the candidate.

Evaluation (10 marks)

In order for the product to be 'field tested' it is essential that it is complete. Photography is a useful way of showing the project in action. It could be critically analysed in the following manner;

(a) Determine to what extent the brief has been fulfilled.
(b) Field test results.
(c) Obtain independent appraisals.
(d) The good and poor features should be discussed, the latter developed to show how improvements could be made.
(e) If the original brief has been modified in any way then it must be fully explained at this time.

Communication (10 marks)

This is to show the processes and skills involved in communicating ideas as an important tool of the designer. All preliminary sketches and notes should be included in the design folio to illustrate the enquiring mind of the designer as well as more refined drawings giving clear and precise information. The following techniques could be used:

(a) Any form of graphical representation considered appropriate.
(b) Annotation.
(c) Variety of media and techniques.
(d) Illustrative material such as photographs, collected illustrations, graphs, data, etc.

[...]

29 *Project guidelines for O-level technology*

- K. A. Shooter

EDITORS' INTRODUCTION

Whatever course uses project work, Ken Shooter's hints for starting and guiding pupils through project work are useful for teachers.

A considerable number of schools nationally are now following the O-level University of Cambridge Syndicate examination in technology. Not only does the organization and teaching of the selected modules of study pose problems but the methodology and approach to the 'design and make' project often presents major headaches for many teachers. In this article I have drawn upon my own teaching experience of the above course and my own role as team-leader for projects assessment for the Cambridge Syndicate in order to assist teachers organize an effective framework around which pupils can work successfully.

In the first section I have formulated some helpful hints concerned with the initial stages of project choice and development. In the second, I have drawn up some guidelines which pupils can use in order to see some structure in the design process. These closely follow the Syndicate's procedure for assessment.

HELPFUL HINTS FOR THE INITIAL STAGES OF THE MAJOR 'DESIGN AND MAKE' PROJECT

Encourage your pupils to start considering tangible ideas for the 'project' area by May of the first year of the two-year course. Set aside some time for general discussion with the whole group on the purpose of the design project, the educational objectives, the assessment procedure and the format of the folio.

Highlight the following: the severe time limitations which are placed on the project, in spite of the apparent and deceptive time-span of two full terms in the second year; the need to allow adequate time for realization and evaluation; and the cost and availability of resources and components, some of which will inevitably have to be purchased outside the school by the pupil.

Encourage pupils to examine problem areas for their project where the solution will be of a 'technological' nature and will utilize some of the knowledge and skills gained from the modular study. Try to harness individual interests and hobbies as a means of initiating ideas for projects. This will probably stimulate greater and more effective progress over what, to a pupil, is a very long-term project. One of the major problems is to maintain interest and enthusiasm over a long period of research and development when there is a natural tendency by pupils to wish to see immediate results.

Spend some time with each pupil at the outset of the project trying to identify any major problem areas before the design process commences. Be realistic and honest with pupils, do not allow them to get into blind-alley situations where, after a substantial period of fruitless research, either the problem is found to be too difficult or resources are just not available. Make sure that a pupil who has previously encountered major difficulties in sophisticated technical skill acquisition does not choose a project with a substantial and complicated constructional element. It may be convenient to have a list of acceptable problem areas for possible projects and suggested avenues of research, ready for the uninspired pupil. Such projects might include security devices, timing devices, animal feeding mechanisms, sorting devices, etc.

Develop your own format for presenting the design folio, perhaps using specially printed sheets for each section, asking appropriate questions at each stage. The second section gives you an example of a system of guidance. These help the pupil to visualize a progression and utilize his or her time more effectively, particularly in a homework situation. Emphasize the high standards of presentation necessary, both in the project folder and in the realization/production of the prototype.

Draw up deadlines for your completion of particular sections and check the work at each stage. There will be some obvious blurring at the edges as the design process is not always linear. It is however important to ensure that pupils start some element of construction early in the second year of the course. Investigation, research and development in another area can continue simultaneously. Emphasize the importance of a completed project by early March to allow for adequate and carefully structured evaluation.

Finally, encourage pupils to use their spare time to develop and implement their design ideas. I found that an after-school club solved many of the problems of access to specialized equipment by pupils and helped to foster a successful working relationship between pupils and staff.

PUPILS' GUIDELINES FOR THE DESIGN OF THE MAJOR PROJECT

Description, specification and analysis of the problem

Statement of need.

Identify a real-life problem and then establish a specific need, e.g.:

> My uncle has a large garage/workshop which is situated at the bottom of a long garden and out of sight of the house. He stores a considerable amount of expensive equipment in it. There is a need for some kind of security device which would:
>
> (a) alert members of the house to intruders;
> (b) frighten possible intruders and deter them from continuing their robbery.

Formulate a design brief and specification

This should consist of a detailed listing of information, constraints and limitations which all bear on the problem. At the conclusion of the project the final evaluation should bear a close relationship to the original specification.

Questions and information may include such items as:

(a) Where will the device be used? – drawings, notes, dimensions.
(b) When will it be used, how often?
(c) Who will use the device?
(d) Are there any special requirements?
(e) Does it have to be adjustable?
(f) Does it have to be portable?
(g) Under what sort of conditions will it be used?
(h) Will it have to withstand loads, forces, etc.?
(i) Does it have to conform to a standard size?
(j) How can safety in operation be ensured?
(k) Does any part of the device need regular maintenance?
(l) Does it handle materials, if so, how are these stored ready for use?
(m) Is the device going to be a reasonable cost effective answer to the problem?

General analysis

A block diagram or flow chart is a very effective way of displaying the analysis. At this stage the analysis is very broad. There are no specific details of how the problem might be solved. We are concerned only with a detailed specification listing all the important design aspects of the problem. Drawings and dimensioned sketches of the situation of the problem are often of assistance.

It is advisable to produce a broad time schedule for the various stages including a timetable for construction of the eventual project. This time available will feature in the specification.

Finally set out the main points you consider necessary to test and evaluate the effectiveness of the device. What are the essential points that you are going to test?

Investigation and research

In the initial stages of analysis and research a block diagram is recommended so that as many elements as possible are considered. In order to carry out research into each of these areas, you may find it necessary to:

(a)   read books and magazines;
(b)   consult people with experience of these systems;
(c)   write to manufacturers;
(d)   conduct some experiments, e.g. circuits on prototype boards;
(e)   examine catalogues of materials, components, etc.

When using manufacturers' information, i.e. catalogues, only extract the data which is of use. This can be achieved by either copying drawings or explanations and acknowledging the source or cutting out sections of a catalogue and mounting them on card. Full catalogues are not required, neither are all the copies of letters. A list of companies contacted and reference to particular information gained, is all that is required.

Conclusions should be drawn from this research and analysis. All diagrams drawn and notes written should be of a high standard and clearly laid out. Try to remember that the examiner should be able to read the folio easily and follow the reasoning.

Three or more solutions to each area should be considered in depth, i.e. detailed sketches, notes and conclusions drawn – advantages and disadvantages.

Possible solutions should be realistic and not merely to satisfy the examiner's requirements. They should be quite distinct and different ideas, not merely variations or adaptations on the same theme.

It cannot be emphasized too much that ideas should be developed by means of *good clear sketches*, circuit diagrams, flow charts, etc., rather than by masses of unrelated prose.

Good reasons must be given for developing an idea to conclusion and for rejecting the alternatives that you have considered in your investigation. An analysis of the different materials which could be used is also important at this stage.

Close examination of the several ideas that you have put forward may reveal good points in each. You may wish to combine these to form a new solution. If this is the case, explain the development of the final solution. Comment on its possible shortcomings, and identify any parts which may prove difficult to manufacture.

Give a brief account of how the device will work, in staged notes. At this stage, it may be appropriate to *develop your ideas through models and experiments*. Keep a record by using photographs. Mount these with notes, graphs, results, etc. on A4 card and include them in your folder. Always consider the most effective way of presenting the information. Use coloured card for mounting graphs, photographs, magazine illustrations. Spread the work out neatly. Sectionalize your folio according to the Examination Board's marking scheme. Use pencil crayon, highlighters, felt tips and line weighting on diagrams.

For maximum marks in this section you must provide 'much evidence of good investigation and research into the problem. Good collection of data and/or organization of experiments, very well written up and presented. Three or more solutions considered in great depth. Good reasons for rejecting alternatives clearly stated'.

Quality of the finished work (production of the prototype)

This is the realization of the project in terms of actually producing a completed piece of hardware.

Before the project can be made, the chosen solution should be presented as a set of working drawings. These drawings are assessed as part of this section. The drawings may be presented in a variety of ways, not necessarily in formal orthographic projection. Good clear freehand sketches, exploded views, isometric views on grid paper are all acceptable. In deciding which methods are appropriate, use as a guideline the fact that drawings should be in such detail that someone else could construct the device. Dimensioned drawings and cutting lists, lists of components, etc. are therefore essential.

The practical element will be assessed on the basis of:

(a) Evidence of thorough work, appropriate to two terms of two–three periods per week. (There is no doubt that successful projects over the past few years have involved a greater amount of time and effort).

(b) Evidence of a high level of technical skill, attention to detail, a completed construction and realistic use of materials and techniques.

As the realization progresses better ideas may come to light and modifications made. This is an acceptable part of the design process. However, all such changes should be recorded by means of annotated sketches and reasons given for the changes. These can form an essential part of the evaluation.

It is important that the teacher's help is sought continuously in this manufacturing stage. Very often new techniques have to be learned and a considerable amount of time can be saved by listening to careful instructions or watching a demonstration.

The folio should not contain detailed notes on the actual construction of the device or the techniques used in its manufacture, e.g. how to braze or solder joints. The practical work should be completed by mid-March ready for evaluation and testing.

Testing and self-evaluation of the project by the candidate

This is a very important and often neglected part of the project and you should allow adequate time for its study. There are several approaches to evaluation.

Setting up for operation

You should give details of fine-tuning in order to put the device into operation. Any problems which are encountered should be fully recorded, together with necessary modification.

Testing

A test programme should be drawn up based on the original specifications. The results of each test and the performance of the device should be recorded, using graphs, diagrams and statements. You may need to return to the brief in order to revise the essential points that you wished to consider.

Modifications

Most prototypes need modifications or alternatives in order to increase the performance or success rate of a device. These should be developed in detail, in sketch and note form.

Conclusions

You should analyse the test programme results and draw conclusions about the effectiveness of your chosen solution in terms of: (a) how it meets the original specification; (b) how it exceeds, or fails to meet the original specification. Comment on whether other ideas may have been more effective or more appropriate.

Self-congratulation does not gain marks.

CDT in schools: some successful examples

● DES (HMI)

EDITORS' INTRODUCTION

Here we have selected three of the twelve schools reported by H.M.I. They illustrate among them a number of issues in teaching technology.

SCHOOL 6

Context: 11–18 comprehensive school with 1100 boys and girls, serving rural and city communities and nearby RAF bases.

Balance

This is a balanced department. No one aspect of craft, design and technology predominates. There is quality to be seen wherever the visitor cares to look. The pupils work with absorption, confidence and independence. They talk readily and fluently about their work. They produce design notebooks which reveal a capacity to draw and to write. The workshop environment is planned with care. The work areas are alive with examples of pupils' work. There are photographs, design sheets and posters. Resource areas house colour-coded packs of reference material. It is an orderly and safe workplace. There are carefully positioned, purpose-built tool racks. Machine tools are well maintained. There are working instructions and warnings of potential safety hazards in many work areas. These are the immediate impressions: balance and quality happily combined.

Team-work

The reason for this balance lies in a unifying philosophy of designing and making. The craftwork is one element in a design department which encompasses art, craft, fabric work and housecraft. This 'design faculty', as it is called in some schools, has compiled a guide booklet on the nature and method of design education. It is the product of staff meetings held at frequent intervals.

In addition to statements of course content, the booklet contains sections on assessment of pupil progress, teaching method and the forms of communication, for example, 'Discussion as a way of learning'. The guide is studded with precepts which are translated into practice.

> Since the workshop environment forms the base for activity there should be a real effort to create an environment which is stimulating . . . Visual material should be relevant, and should not stagnate . . . We run as a team . . . the technician will prove a most valuable asset if he is treated as a member of the team.

Some important factors

Between the policy statements and practice lie a number of factors which help quality to emerge. First, three hours each week are allocated to the design department throughout five years. This time-block is subdivided at the discretion of the faculty. In effect there is a foundation course in many media followed by increasing specialization in two or three. Secondly, there is a progressive build-up of competence and confidence in designing. Sketching is taught, for there is no assumption that a pupil has this skill or is unafraid to commit ideas to paper. 'All pupils fear sketching . . . they envisage all forms of line as straight and decisive.' Thirdly, pupils learn that in order to undertake designing they must combine their skill of making with power of expression. For example, a pupil may be given the following brief: Design a kitchen utensil in laminated wood. Such a brief means that he must learn the techniques of laminating and shaping, but teachers also expect him to consider a wide range of possible forms and to produce a number of sheets of sketches, explanations and procedural notes.

Design briefs can be demanding for all and daunting to less able pupils. Whatever their ability, pupils are expected to produce work of quality. It was 'effort' that was recorded on school reports and on departmental records. The attainment of each was relative to his own ability and not to the achievement of others. In one fourth-year mixed ability class the teachers had set the design brief at three levels of difficulty and had also prepared supporting material for various investigations at three levels of difficulty. In short, the teachers gave their time and effort across the spectrum of ability.

There was balance in the acquisition of all communication skills. Mention has been made of the progressive development of sketching and this also applied to other forms of graphic communication such as formal projections. Language and number skills received similar consideration. Competence in the use of language was being built up through listening, talking, reading and discussion. Dialogue between pupils and between staff and pupils was conducted in a quiet informal manner with uncontrived use of language.

The fourth factor contributing to quality was the care which went into the planning and use of the workshops. Everybody helped to create a stimulating environment. The work of the pupils predominated. As a contribution to safety education each upper school pupil designed and prepared a safety poster. Although space was at a premium the staff had created small areas for particular purposes – for resources, for specialist craft activities and for displays. The workshop technician was a key figure in the organization, creation and maintenance of the workshop environment. His duties, role and status were recorded in the department guide. He had designed and made many of the tool racks and carefully maintained equipment and machines. He was a full member of the team. [...]

SCHOOL 10

Context: rural township. 11–18 mixed comprehensive school, 1000 pupils. New workshop accommodation.

Technology: but is it craft?

One expects to find pupils working with wood and metal in a school workshop. That can indeed be seen here. But in one room, pupils are not sawing, filing or hammering; instead they are assembling constructional kits. Some of the kits are familiar to any visitor. There are the perforated metal wheels and strips of Meccano kits. There seem to be more gears and shafts than are usually seen in family sets and the pupils are clearly not building models from the trade catalogue. There are other less familiar construction kits being used on the tables and benches. One group is working with short lengths of extruded plastics, like those used in office buildings for carrying electric cable. Each length forms a box which has terminals and a label such as 'diode', 'resistor' or 'capacitor' to identify the encased components. Wire leads enable the units to be coupled into systems made up from these 'black boxes'.

This is part of a technology course which is offered by the CDT department. The aim of the course is to give pupils the chance to learn how things are controlled. The use of kits places emphasis on understanding such matters as the relationships of components in a system. For example, 'How do gears work? What is the effect upon speed of movement or power transmitted when gears are intermeshed in various combinations of size and type? Suppose this shaft has to be driven at three times the speed and at right angles to that shaft – can it be done with the gears in this set?' Such understanding is part of the repertoire of knowledge and skill which pupils use in order to design and build structures, machines and devices to control things which are remote from them (such as a light-triggered switch across a room), which require an energy input other than their own (such as a fire alarm system) or which are too small, too large or too fast or sensitive for humans to handle (such as an electronic gauge which records minute strains in the framework of the school staircase).

No, this is not craft-work – which is the handworking of so-called 'primary materials' such as wood and metal. Most teachers and other educators would be reluctant to replace craft-work experiences by the use of constructional kits. In fact there is no replacement at this school: the core of craft-work is offered to all pupils for the first three years and continues as an option beyond that. The technology course is taken by middle band and upper band pupils from the third year. It leads to a Mode 3 CSE or an O-level GCE in control technology. For sixth formers taking A-level GCE, the department offers a technology course entitled 'Elements of Engineering Design' which is compatible with the control technology course. All students design and make a personal project of their own choice which contributes to their final assessment.

Design is central

Critics of technology courses are quick to jump to the conclusion that the use of constructional kits and work-sheets, with the associated build-up of systematic knowledge, gives a pupil no chance to design. It is true that the early part of the course in this school is structured to enable pupils to discover facts and principles. But after each of these explorations pupils apply their knowledge in the course of mini-projects. For example, there is much to learn about the behaviour of pin-jointed structures. This is taught through a sequence of constructional exercises in which pupils begin to discover how structures can be made stable, rigid and light.

The whole course is broken down into modules on 'structures', 'motion', 'electrical/electronic control', 'pneumatics' and 'logic circuitry and programming'. Each module has its mini-project assignment, and as the pupil builds up a foundation of knowledge and skill, so intermodular projects can be undertaken. For example, understanding gained from work involved in an electronic module and a gears module enables pupils to build vehicles which stop, start, reverse, turn and oscillate automatically. Minor projects are set by teachers in the first year. Later, major projects are devised by pupils.

In-service commitment

Where did the teachers acquire the knowledge to teach this course? Not in initial training, for this kind of technology course did not exist ten years ago. One teacher, like most pioneers of what has become known as 'school technology', saw a little, read a little, was helped by LEA advisory staff and backed by his headmaster. Fortunately, published curricular material for technology had become available. But the major effort to launch a course of this type came from one traditionally trained craft teacher who set about learning the 'T' dimension of CDT. He took courses, including the Open University Technology for Teachers post-experience course and, on partial secondment, an in-service BEd at the National Centre for School Technology. He had gradually translated his own knowledge into classroom practice, introducing one module at a time. He had taken pains to think out the most effective way to rack and to store the multitude of components which the course employs. He also helped other teachers to learn how to conduct the course.

Figure 30.1

This, then, is one example of commitment in technology teaching within the framework of CDT. The course runs parallel to craft experience in order to achieve other objectives, and combines the craft-work when the need arises. Although highly structured in the early stages, it offers pupils experience of thinking and making through the solving of design problems characteristic of the technological changes of modern life.

SCHOOL 12

Context: rural community college, 11–16 mixed comprehensive school with education services for the local community of twenty villages. 600 pupils.

Resource-based learning

Over a hundred second year boys and girls were hurrying to the crafts centre – a large, open-plan single storey building which houses art, needlework, pottery, home economics, woodwork and metalwork. Some went straight to work at tables and benches with hardly a greeting for the teacher. Others studied a notice board headed 'Demonstrations' which listed a number of craft activities that were apparently 'on offer' at various times of the day. A number began hunting for video tapes and slide sets in a large resource area. Many pupils glanced briefly into pocket-sized booklets before hurrying away to work. These booklets were the clue to the bustle of diverse activities that now began.

Figure 30.2

Each booklet contains check-lists of practical activities. One girl was asked to indicate what she had done during the term. Her check-list showed 'T002 BG C – Planning a kitchen layout' and 'T029 G O – Make a lamp'. She explained that the first number was a resource reference. Each activity had an associated work card, a set of instructions, a demonstration or an audio-visual aid which helped pupils to carry out some practical activity. The letters B or G indicted that some activities *might* have more appeal to a boy or to a girl. For example, there was a 'make a tie' activity for boys and 'make and dress a rag doll' for girls but there was no restriction on the choice of these activities. There were school service jobs too, for example, 'tidy the pattern library' and 'clean a workshop sink'. The final letter indicated that the activity was core material (C) and must be finished before choice was made from optional (O) activities.

There was a booklet ('work schedule') for the workshop crafts (planning and communication, woodwork and metalwork) and one for art, home crafts and home economics. The activities could be carried out in any order, provided that work space was available. Lists on the notice board indicated demonstrations for the day. Sometimes it became necessary to limit numbers of pupils taking an activity. This was done by asking pupils to sign on a numbered list or by making a limited number of aprons available. For example, for a forging demonstration each pupil had taken a coloured apron from a peg, and when all the aprons had gone this indicated that no more pupils could watch on that day.

In this department, the basic belief is that each pupil should bear some responsibility for organizing an individual practical timetable in which learning takes place with the aid of as many resources as the school can muster. The principal resource remains the teacher, but many of the learning activities use other resources. For example, tape-slide sequences are available in the resource bank. Unaided, the pupils are able to load the tape recorder and projector and follow a set of instructions on setting up a lathe for wood turning. Many of the photographs gave an operator's eye view, which pupils do not have when watching a demonstration while grouped around a lathe. Live lectures and demonstrations have their place, of course, but much of the imparting of straightforward information is by illustrated work-sheet or audio-visual aid, which leaves more time for consultation and dialogue.

Why should it work?

Many teachers might feel apprehensive about such a system: there seemed to be so many things that might go wrong. For example, might there be bottlenecks – groups of pupils queueing to get at some specialized item of equipment – with, at best, inactivity and at worst destructive uproar? Then what about the loafer, who might use the system to escape work, or to avoid tidying up? Indeed, how could teachers keep track of pupils at all?

In fact, there were fewer bottlenecks than are sometimes seen in conventionally taught lessons. Pupils who found that they were unable to carry on with one activity turned their attention to other work or assignments in the work schedule. The pupils themselves liked the system: 'You're expected to be responsible and grown-up.' A third-year pupil who had transferred to the school that year much preferred to be self-paced rather than teacher-paced and enjoyed discovery instead of didactics.

Most of the checks on the system were inbuilt. The work schedules had a simple, non-numerical method of recording progress and quality of achievement and it was easy to glance through the booklet to see if quality was being sacrificed for speed or if less work was being done than it was reasonable to expect. A teacher had to mark the completion of each activity before a new one began. Some of the work-sheets had tests included in the assignment and there were some activities that were designed to test knowledge of tools and materials and which involved no making. Finally, there were conventional tests.

Prerequisites and pay-offs

If such a system is to start, let alone grow, all the staff involved have to agree. In this case, an entire faculty of teachers (three each from art, craft and home economics) had to agree to experiment as a team. There had then to be an enormous investment of non-teaching time in the

Figure 30.3

preparation of lectures, demonstrations, models, work-sheets, slides, tapes, collection of posters, drawings, photographs and, above all, the establishment of a storage and retrieval system pupils could use unaided. Tool racks had to allow for easy identification, and simple, safe withdrawal and return of tools. Damaged or blunt tools needed to be identified. There had to be accessible storage systems, and methods of issuing prepared material, charging for the cost of consumables, and noting depletion of stocks.

The result of such care is that children become self-confident, self-reliant and highly responsible. The workshops become a natural setting for individuals to organize time to fit the demands upon facilities made by others.

A group of older pupils were asked, 'How would you cope with making a project that was *not* on the work schedule, and for which there were no work-sheets or visual aids?' 'We do that all the time,' they replied, and pointed out that the work schedule gave many opportunities for 'free choice' work. They were confident that somewhere, someone, some book, or some film could provide the help and guidance needed when tackling unfamiliar practical work. They knew where and how to begin looking, how to plan a sequence of activity, and how to approach each new task with confidence tempered with caution. That is no mean achievement.

31 *CDT: accommodation in secondary schools*

● DES

EDITORS' INTRODUCTION

In the extract from this DES publication we reproduce the 'Conclusions' and a checklist of useful questions.

CHANGES IN THE SUBJECT

Though the nature of the CDT curriculum is still changing, links with other areas of the curriculum are being established and are growing. Some of these links can be enhanced by physical proximity. In the past, heavy craft departments have often been grouped with home economics and art departments but the degree to which these links have been exploited varies. Other schools have established links between these subject areas and CDT regardless of location. Nevertheless, with the increased emphasis on design work, there is a case for sharing equipment and expertise with art departments and this is obviously easier when accommodation is nearby. The greater emphasis in many schools on scientific and technological principles and on testing and evaluation has led to a need to use facilities traditionally found in a science department. Indeed it is possible that some work in this area could be taught in spaces provided for science and some science work taught in areas provided for CDT. In the past, heavy craft departments were frequently built as free-standing blocks on the perimeter of schools. It is clear that this relationship with the rest of the school is no longer ideal and, whilst it is not possible to put all areas next to each other, CDT needs to be 'brought in from the cold'. This may not be easy to achieve in existing schools but should be given a high priority when building new ones, or when considering improvements or extensions. The 'design and make' approach involved in CDT has meant a move away from the dominance of the skills training of traditional woodwork and metalwork. The widening range of activities and the greater emphasis on the decision-making aspects of the work requires a different environment from the traditional workshop.

IMPLICATIONS OF CHANGE FOR ACCOMMODATION

The main working areas need to be more flexible than those provided in the past, permitting work in more than one material and capable of supporting design work. For the latter, pupils and teachers need to form groups for discussion and demonstration, but pupils are also required to work on individual or small group-work involving reading, writing, talking, drawing and model-making. The main working areas must be planned to allow easy access from one to another and to supporting areas so that pupils can use all the department's facilities. With the increased emphasis on pupils preparing and developing design briefs, a wide range of resources needs to be readily available and easily used locally. An awareness of the importance of displaying inspirational material and students' work (both design work and completed projects) has grown. Displays in each of the working areas, in the centre of the department and elsewhere in the school are desirable. The overall environment of a main working area has been described as that of a studio; the design of the whole department should reflect a concern with materials, colour, texture, scale and ease of use. This attention will ensure that the department is designed and furnished in a way appropriate to what is being taught in it.

Although in some parts of the country the 'design and make' approach central to CDT has been present for twenty years or more, it has only recently become widely adopted and physical provision has yet to catch up. Much accommodation still comprises specific material workshops, heavily equipped with large pieces of machinery that are often under-used and which sterilize large areas of floor space. A desirable range of equipment is often lacking and the variety and type of furniture is not appropriate to current teaching. The environment in which design activities take place should not be underestimated as an influence on the quality of work itself. Whilst recognizing that the subject area is in transition, enough is understood about it and the way it will develop to be able to make sensible decisions about accommodation which will hold good for many years. There are real difficulties in teaching in accommodation which is badly planned and does not readily support the broad range of activities taking place. Small-scale extensions or alterations can often go a long way towards improving the balance of accommodation and may stimulate a review of the whole of the accommodation used for teaching the subject.

Remodelling also provides an opportunity to improve the balance of accommodation, but even when modest in scale, it needs to be done within a clear set of concepts and reference points. Where new schools or new departments are being built it should be possible to achieve optimal solutions.

CHECK-LIST FOR BRIEFING AND DESIGNING CDT ACCOMMODATION

Curricular considerations

1. **CDT within the whole school curriculum**

   (a) What is the intended allocation of curriculum time?
   (b) What are the curriculum links with art, science, information technology and other subject areas?
   (c) Does the location of the departments within the school promote these links?
   (d) Has advantage been taken of the principal linkage areas (i.e. graphics and technology) to facilitate these?
   (e) Have the needs of the pupils with learning difficulties been considered?

2. **Organization of the CDT curriculum**

   (a) Is the number of main working areas appropriate for present and projected use?
   (b) Are the sizes of main working areas appropriate for present and projected use?
   (c) Is the nature of the main working areas appropriate for present and projected use?

3. **Planning of a CDT department**

   (a) If additional facilities need to be provided in the future can this be done conveniently?
   (b) Does the department link up to the rest of the school in such a way as to advertise its presence and nature?
   (c) Is the entrance to the department attractive and welcoming, and is there provision for displaying the pupils' design and project work and other two- and three-dimensional material?
   (d) Does the support accommodation provide a focus to the department and is it readily accessible from the main working area?

(e)   Is there easy physical access to and good visual links between the main working areas?

(f)   Are the circulation routes for people, materials and portable equipment between spaces direct, adequate in size, and free of danger spots?

(g)   Is there access from outside to allow bulk materials to be delivered to the material store?

(h)   Have the requirements of *Fire and the Design of Schools*[1] and the local fire officer been met?

(i)   Have the requirements of *Access for the Physically Disabled to Educational Buildings*[2] been met?

Main working areas

1.   Briefing, planning and evaluating projects

(a)   Is there provision for the teacher to gather together a group of pupils for a presentation or group discussion?

(b)   Is there an area where a small group of pupils can work together?

(c)   Is there an area where individual pupils can read, write and draw?

(d)   Is there provision for display of inspirational material and pupils' work in the areas?

2.   Working with materials

(a)   Is the range of equipment appropriate for the processes provided for and the age range of users?

(b)   Is the equipment safely sited and is equipment which is used solely by the staff and technician sited outside main working areas?

(c)   When equipment is to be used in an unsupervised space is aural and visual supervision possible from adjacent spaces?

(d)   Are the work benches and vice systems appropriate for the materials being used and for the age range using the space?

(e)   Are there safe working and circulation areas around benches and equipment?

(f)   Is the material store accessible? Does it have appropriate racking systems?

(g)   Is there separate storage for work in progress?

(h)   Is there storage for flammable and other dangerous material?

(i)   Is there storage for hand tools and tools associated with machines?

---

[1] *Fire and the Design of Schools*, Building Bulletin 7, HMSO, 1975.
[2] *Access for the Physically Disabled to Educational Buildings* (second edition) Design Note 18, DES, 1984

3. **Other considerations**

   (a) Has provision been made in the main working areas or elsewhere for the storage of pupils' coats and bags?
   (b) Has provision been made for the storage of stacked stools?
   (c) Have rubbish bins been provided?
   (d) Has provision been made for the storage of loose drawing boards and T-squares?

Supporting accommodation

1. **Resources**

   (a) Is the storage and display of reference materials suitable? Is it located in an appropriate place, with an associated study area?
   (b) Can resource materials be moved easily to adjacent rooms?
   (c) Is there provision for work with computers?

2. **Storage**

   (a) Is provision made for the storage of bulk materials separately from the main working areas but with ready access to them?
   (b) Is there access to the outside and are the doors big enough to allow supplies to be delivered with ease?
   (c) Is there provision for storing flammable, noxious and other dangerous materials?
   (d) Have the storage needs of adult education and any other community use been considered?
   (e) Is there secure storage for valuable equipment centrally in the department?
   (f) Are students' portfolios to be stored in the department and if so has provision been made?
   (g) Has consideration been given to the use of mobile as well as fixed storage?

3. **Display**

   (a) Has the role of display in presenting the various aspects of the work of the department to the school been considered?
   (b) Is display positioned centrally within the department but in a way that allows passers-by to see at least some of it?
   (c) Is it well lit both in the daytime and evening?
   (d) Does it allow for the display of related two- and three-dimensional items of varying sizes?
   (e) Has the need for security been considered?
   (f) Is there an opportunity for the CDT department to display work in other parts of the school, such as the main entrance foyer?

4. **Staff accommodation**

   (a) Is there provision in the department, or associated with it, for staff to prepare lessons and mark pupils' work; have a conversation or hold interviews in private; use a telephone; leave personal belongings; and to keep secure pupils' records, examination papers, etc?

   (b) Is staff accommodation required on a departmental or wider faculty basis?

   (c) Is it easy to find?

   (d) Can it provide the opportunity for indirect supervision (e.g. overlooking study/resources area)?

5. **Base for technicians**

   (a) Is there a suitable working base for a technician?

   (b) Does its location in the department facilitate the flow of tools and equipment to the technician for maintenance?

   (c) Is there easy access to the area which contains equipment and tools used solely by staff and technicians?

   (d) Is there a secure store for small tools, expensive materials and flammable and other dangerous substances?

   (e) Are the links with adjacent working areas such that the technician can be aware of activities in the department?

6. **WCs and hand-washing provision**

   (a) Are there toilets accessible from the CDT accommodation for pupils and staff of both sexes?

   (b) Is there sufficient hand-washing provision in the main working areas?

7. **Cleaners' cupboards and provision for services**

   (a) Is there provision for storing cleaners' equipment and materials in the area?

   (b) Has the floor area that will be occupied by boilers, electrical switch gear, etc. been taken into account?

Environmental considerations

1. **The character of spaces**

   (a) Has consideration been given to the overall character of rooms, in terms of scale, proportion and use of colour, texture and lighting, to create an environment appropriate to teaching visual awareness?

(b) Do the visual links between spaces give a feeling of unity to the department?

2. Lighting

(a) Does this meet the requirements of *Health and Safety in Workshops of Schools and Similar Establishments*[1] and *Guidelines for Environmental Design and Fuel Conservation in Educational Buildings*[2]?

(b) Has the need for dim-out or blackout to enable the use of visual aids been considered?

(c) Is there appropriate lighting for machines and equipment and for areas used regularly for drawing work?

(d) Are display areas illuminated?

(e) If lighting and displays are enclosed, has consideration been given to the problem of the build-up of heat?

3. Heating, ventilation and extraction

(a) Does the heating and ventilation meet the requirements of *Health and Safety in Workshops of Schools and Similar Establishments*[3] and *Guidelines for Environmental Design and Fuel Conservation in Educational Buildings*[4]?

(b) Is the heating system chosen and designed so that the heat sources in individual spaces do not circulate dust nor reduce wall space and floor area that could with advantage be used for machinery, benching, storage or display?

(c) Has extraction been considered for machines producing chips, dust or toxic fumes?

(d) Where mechanical ventilation has been provided generally, have steps been taken to ensure that negative pressure has been maintained (to contain dust)?

(e) Should the whole department be considered as a separate zone, for heating and ventilating purposes, if it is required to operate independently of the rest of the school?

---

[1] *Health and Safety in Workshops of Schools and Similar Establishments*, BS 4163, British Standards Institution, 1984.
[2] *Guidelines for Environmental Design and Fuel Conservation in Educational Buildings* (revised edition), Design Note 17, DES, 1981.
[3] Op. cit.
[4] Op. cit.

4. **Services for teaching**

   (a) These consist of electricity, gas, water and compressed air supplies and coaxial cabling. Do they comply with the requirements of *Health and Safety in Workshops of Schools and Similar Establishments*[5]?
   (b) Are the services appropriate for the processes undertaken in each room?
   (c) Are they adequate in number for the group sizes and activities?
   (d) Are they designed and positioned in a way that will allow easy alteration and expansion?
   (e) Does the coaxial cabling need screening or other protection?
   (f) Have safety knock-out buttons been provided to stop all machines in an emergency?
   (g) Has consideration been given to co-ordinating service runs and outlets with display surfaces, furniture and fittings in a way that maximizes valuable floor and wall space?

5. **Acoustics**

   (a) Do acoustics comply with *Guidelines for Environmental Design and Fuel Conservation in Educational Buildings*[6] and has the approach in *Acoustics in Educational Buildings*[7] been adopted?
   (b) Has the need for sound attenuation between separate teaching groups been considered?
   (c) Has the positioning of noisy machinery and equipment within particular rooms been considered relative to the quieter activities likely to take place in the same space?
   (d) Have steps been taken to reduce noise generation at source?

6. **Signing**

   (a) Are the graphics used in the department good examples?
   (b) Is the entrance to the department itself and are the teaching and supporting areas correctly and clearly named?
   (c) Are any directional signs required in the department?
   (d) Is it possible for any graphical information produced by the departments to be co-ordinated with this in style, size and colour?
   (e) Are information on safety and instructions for using equipment clearly displayed?

---

[5] Op. cit.
[6] Op. cit.
[7] *Acoustics in Educational Buildings*, Building Bulletin 51, HMSO, 1975.

Finishes, furniture and fittings

1. Selection

(a) *School Furniture Dimensions: Standing and Reaching*[1] and *Furniture and Equipment: Working Heights and Zones for Practical Activities*[2] give guidance on furniture heights for different age ranges.

(b) Is the furniture and equipment of the appropriate type, number and size for the age range?

(c) Has a storage area been provided for stacked stools?

(d) Are the character and colour of furniture, fittings and equipment co-ordinated with those of the rest of the room?

(e) Do the main working areas have adequately sized rubbish bins?

(f) Is there provision for storing temporary or interchangeable working surfaces when not in use?

2. Finishes

This is an area in which a degree of compromise is required. There will be a different emphasis in each type of space, but considerations include the following.

3. Floor finishes

(a) Do they meet the requirements of *Health and Safety in Workshops of Schools and Similar Establishments*[3]?

(b) Are they easy to maintain?

(c) Are they slip resistant when wet, dry or dusty?

(d) Are they easy to clean at frequent intervals during the day?

(e) Are they warm and do they have some resilience so as to be comfortable to users when standing for long periods?

(f) Is there a risk that floor surfaces will damage tools, if dropped, or produce flying chips of steel or other hard material when damaged?

(g) How do they affect the acoustic environment of the space?

(h) How do they affect the overall lighting level?

4. Wall finishes

(a) Are they easy to clean?

(b) Are there splash-backs for sinks, acid baths and any other wet process areas?

---

[1] *School Furniture Dimensions: Standing and Reaching* (second edition), Building Bulletin 38, HMSO, 1974.

[2] *Furniture and Equipment: Working weights and Zones for Practical Activities*, Building Bulletin 50, HMSO, 1973.

[3] Op. cit.

(c) Do the wall finishes ensure large continuous areas of wall space for display (i.e. uninterrupted by services)?

(d) Do they contribute to good overall lighting conditions by having a good light reflection?

(e) Have the corners of doors and door frames been protected against damage by trolleys and other large items?

5. Ceiling finishes

(a) Are they easy to clean especially in hot and dusty areas?

(b) Do they reflect light well?

(c) Do they contribute to the acoustic environment of the room by offering some sound absorption, particularly if ceilings are high and there are long sound reflection paths?

Health and safety

(a) Have the publications *Health and Safety in Workshops of Schools and Similar Establishments*[4] and *Safety in Practical Studies*[5] been consulted? This publication does not attempt to cover details of health and safety requirements that may be applicable to any particular project.

(b) Is there a local authority liaison officer, and, if so, has he been consulted?

---

[4] Op. cit.
[5] Op. cit.

32   *Evaluating the CDT department*

● P. Toft

INSIDE CDT DEPARTMENTS

Structures

[...] Before comprehensive reorganization, many secondary modern schools ran courses in 'Arts and Crafts', 'Housecraft' and 'Handicrafts'. Grammar schools offered rather less and those few technical schools operating, mounted enhanced programmes in technical and pre-vocational areas. Most of these schools had an important feature in common: they organized their courses through a number of small and separate departments. These departments differed from each other within the school but between schools there were many similarities between art departments or housecraft or handicraft departments. In the smaller schools, the 'departments' frequently consisted of one teacher in a single room.

The reorganization of secondary schools into larger comprehensive units changed all this. A few schools retained the fragmented pattern with a large number of individual departments, comprising one or two teachers (Figure 32.1).

At the opposite end of the organizational spectrum, huge conglomerations were formed, which bound together the above small units and, in some schools, others as well. Figure 32.2 shows such a 'Faculty'.

Within these extremes lies a plethora of different patterns. Some reflect the policy of the school and some the policy of the Local Education Authority (LEA). Compared with other major groups like English and science, there is a confusing complexity of activities

Art	Pottery	Metalwork	Woodwork	Technical Drawing	Cookery	Needlework

Figure 32.1

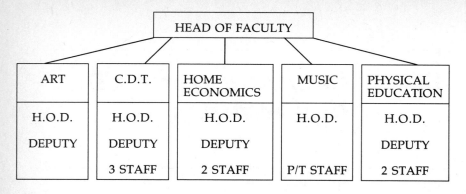

Figure 32.2   *Faculty of expressive and creative studies*

pursued. In broad terms though, there is a tendency to link together art, craft, design and technology, and home economics in a great majority of creative departments or faculties. Because this paper is intended to be of sound practical use, it focuses on day-to-day practice. To sharpen its focus, I have restricted its coverage to craft, design and technology. Other areas, need a specialized angle.

Craft, design and technology is a mixture of different activities: despite its apparently polymorphous nature, it is a highly coherent 'subject'. Its coherence rests on strong threads which powerfully bind together these activities. Because the threads are barely visible and frequently not recognized, I wish now to examine them. In doing so I hope to isolate those features which are distinctive to craft, design and technology departments and which conceptually hold them together.

Distinctive features
[...]

Lying at the roots is the generic concept of CAPABILITY. This concept is not only of vital importance to personal development and to society, as it complements understanding; it also enshrines the root activities of the CDT department and this forms its central distinctive feature. In doing so, it gives us an important clue about evaluating this department. It should be the source of departmental aims and its very essence – *doing* – points to the kinds of activity-based learning strategies which will be adopted. I will return to these ideas in the section on what to evaluate.

CULTIVATING THE RIGHT CONDITIONS FOR DEPARTMENTAL EVALUATION
[...]

If you want to run a departmental evaluation programme in your department your first task will be to consider just how threatening it might seem to your staff. The first reaction may well be to see evaluation as an implied criticism of current performance. Those of you who have attempted to develop ideas in school which run counter to the values of the teachers who will be expected to implement them will be sharply aware of just how easy it is for colleagues to undermine the effort. In extreme cases there would be a counter-reaction to evaluation strong enough to ensure that the idea is never resurrected.

Having analysed this problem at some length, we must now consider ways of solving it. If evaluation, as a new and potentially threatening force, is to succeed in your department then it will have to be introduced very carefully and be carried out with great sensitivity and tact; it will only work effectively if relationships within your department are good.

A creative and co-operative interpersonal climate may emerge in a department as a happy accident. I would not bank on this however. One of the primary roles of a head of department is to create such a climate within his team, and until it reasonably exists, it would be counterproductive to attempt to initiate a comprehensive evaluation programme. The first step in developing the right climate is to accept fully that you need to do it. After this you must work to create an atmosphere of discussion and the sharing of ideas; this means listening as well as talking; reacting to the ideas of others; and encouraging colleagues to talk to each other. The exchange of greetings, coffee break discussions, departmental social events, are important, just as are regular departmental meetings. At all times the head of department needs to signal the idea that he is interested, will listen and be available for consultation, and respond with actions where appropriate. In complex CDT departments where the head of department is likely to have emerged from one of a number of distinct subject areas, it will also be important to ensure that everyone understands that he has no favourites and always takes an overall view.
[...]

WHAT TO EVALUATE IN THE CDT DEPARTMENT

Rome was not built in a day; nor will you develop a comprehensive evaluation programme for your department overnight. Your approach needs to be gradual, but not piecemeal. Work within an overall plan but try to keep it flexible: tackle the less contentious or less difficult areas first. In this way your team will gain confidence, accumulate experience and make continued progress.

I have already attempted to identify the distinctive features of the CDT department. When developing your programme, however, you will need to include activities which are common to the whole school, as well as those which are unique to your department. Compared with 'academic' areas, creative education has not been subjected to a great deal of research, and its literature is very sparse. In identifying those important areas of your department which are to be evaluated, you will have very little guidance to rely on from this field of literature. You will therefore have to take the plunge yourself, and to do this with the knowledge that, so far, not many other people have really begun to tackle the task you are now undertaking. It will help considerably to do this with the collaboration of other members of your team.

An early phase in evaluation will be to gather information. A recent trend has been to make use of check-lists and a number of LEAs have drawn these up for the use of their teachers for self-assessment. They vary in length and approach, and have brought upon themselves some philosophical and methodological criticisms. Despite these they can focus your attentions sharply, and in doing so provide an excellent starting point for gathering information.

Given the wide variety of approach in CDT departments and their many different types of structure, it would be foolish of me to prescribe a detailed check-list. Not only would this fail to meet fully the requirements of different departments: it would also remove the highly educational (for your colleagues) activity of producing your own check-list. It would also remove an excellent focus for collaboration and purposeful discussion. I am therefore arguing that each department should produce its own check-list, that all members should participate in some way and that the head of department should lead the exercise. To help you draw up such a check-list I list below a number of important categories for reference. The list is long: an effective check-list would be much shorter particularly at the outset. It may be wise to take only a section at a time.

Underlying philosophy

(a) Is there a clear philosophy underlying the work of your department, e.g. to be concerned essentially with the development of capability?

(b) If not, are there threads that could be woven into a coherent philosophy? What steps are you taking to bring this to fruition?

(c) Is your philosophy expressed in aims and objectives?

(d) Do these reflect and support the aims of the school?

(e) Do they promote cumulative experience, building on the work of your feeder primary schools and looking forward to post-school education, training, work and life generally?

(f) How far do they match your school's cross-curricular policies, e.g. multi-cultural education, language and numeracy across the curriculum, equal opportunities for boys and girls, catering for pupils with special needs?

(g) How clear are colleagues in the department about these aims and objectives and to what extent is there consensus?

(h) How effectively are they understood and accepted by the rest of the school?

Translation of philosophy into curriculum

(a) Does the CDT curriculum contribute in quality to the curriculum followed by *all* children?

(b) Does it reflect the characteristics of those areas from which it draws? Have you avoided dilution or distortion of capability to gain 'academic respectability'?

(c) Are all staff aware of up-to-date thinking in their specialisms? Are there routine systems for tracking new developments and absorbing their acceptable features into your curriculum?

(d) Are you sufficiently responsive to social change? Does the curriculum meet the changing needs of pupils and community?

(e) What leads you to believe that it will have the intended effects on your pupils? Can you justify its structure?

(f) Is it arranged to make full use of the interest and special abilities of staff, and your facilities?

Courses and schemes of work

(a) Is there an acceptable scheme of work for each course?

(b) Do they reflect the structures of the areas of knowledge and activity from which they draw?

(c) Are they sequenced to optimize learning and to match the ability and interests of pupils?

(d) Are they broken down into units of appropriate length, each with a clear purpose which is explained to pupils?

(e) Is there an appropriate balance of activity and expository teaching, between negotiated and imposed work?

(f) Does expensive equipment lie idle whilst pupils pursue learning activities which might be more profitably done for homework?

(g) Does each unit of work have a basis in skills, concepts and attitudes?

(h)   Where necessary, have you adapted your teaching methods to accelerate skill development so that pupils are given sufficient time to explore concepts, to engage in problem solving and to apply skills?

Quality of learning and teaching

(a)   Are teaching strategies varied enough to match the wide range of activities, e.g. structured for skill development, open-ended for certain types of problem-solving, flexible for investigative project work?

(b)   Is there a distinctive creative and productive atmosphere in the department at all times? What contributes to and detracts from the maintenance/creation of such an atmosphere?

(c)   Is there a quality of motivation and discipline appropriate to practical activity rooms?

(d)   Are staff enthusiastically engaged? Do they expose pupils to their own creative work?

(e)   Are pupils exposed to outside representatives of the 'culture' of capability from the adult world of the home, the arts, design and industry?

(f)   Do you attempt to overcome sex-stereotyping and to cater for multi-ethnic and mixed-ability groups?

(g)   How are staff made aware of their own successes and failures in teaching, and pointed towards improvement?

(h)   Is there an effective use of educational technology?

Pupil assessment

(a)   Are you clear about assessing products and artefacts as evidence of pupil achievement/development, rather than as simple ends in themselves?

(b)   Do you assess all major areas of creative endeavour or do you focus only on the most easily assessable areas?

(c)   How aware are you of recent developments in the assessment of creative work?

(d)   Do you use a full range of assessment methods, including objective tests, multiple choice items, conventional written examinations, practical tests, course-work assessment, project assessment, interviewing pupils, etc.? How far do your assessment methods reflect the distinctive nature of capability? How far do they distort what you aim to teach?

(e)   Are your systems practical, reliable and valid?

(f)   How far do you use pupil self-assessment?

(g)   Do you attempt to produce positive profiles of achievement for all pupils?

(h) To what use do you put the information when gathered? Do you use information to modify your teaching methods?

Use of resources

(a) To what extent are furniture, equipment and machinery arranged to promote efficient use?
(b) How efficient is pupil access to equipment?
(c) How watertight is your security for equipment and tools?
(d) How far are rooms safe to use? Have you recently consulted outside experts, e.g. LEA safety officers, advisers/inspectors, the local factory inspector?
(e) What systematic routines do you have to ensure maintenance of safe conditions and to rectify problems as they occur?
(f) What training have staff had in 'health and safety'? How do you ensure that staff and pupils are always aware of 'health and safety' in their work?
(g) Is the system(s) of stock control thorough and practical?
(h) How accurate and up-to-date are departmental accounts? Who keeps them? To which of the senior staff are you responsible for accounts?
(i) Is the department always reasonably prepared for a visit from the LEA auditor? Are all records of stock, equipment and accounts up-to-date?
(j) Is stock control structured into the learning experiences of pupils?
(k) How effective are in-school systems of equipment maintenance? Are technicians properly deployed across all areas of the department?
(l) How effective is your method of obtaining specialist LEA or outside contractor maintenance service?
(m) What steps do you take to ensure that your department receives an adequate share of school capitation? How successful are you in obtaining materials and money from other sources, e.g. parents' association, your LEA adviser/inspector, local industry?
(n) Does your department work co-operatively within the school's annual timetabling cycle? Are all your courses mounted in appropriate specialist rooms? Do pupils have sufficient time in your department? Are group sizes small enough for safe practical work?
(o) Does the visual environment reflect the educational aims of the department? How much responsibility for this devolves onto pupils?

(p)   Is there a regular system for the display of pupils' projects, staff work and exhibits from out of school? To what extent are these linked into the formal curriculum?

(q)   How far do you make use of the community and the outside world through visits and work in galleries, libraries, museums, factories, studios, etc? Do you integrate such experiences into schemes of work?

(r)   Do you invite representatives of the adult 'culture' of capability to share experiences with pupils? Is this built into your routines or merely incidental?

(s)   Do you use further education and art colleges for link courses? How effective is liaison?

(t)   How far do you tap industry and commerce for help with technical problems, materials, work experience?

Management

(a)   Do roles of responsibility within the department adequately match the work to be done?

(b)   How effectively are roles carried out? What methods are in operation to monitor role performance?

(c)   Is there a policy to regularly review roles with a view to change and enrich experience? Would 'role rotation' be feasible?

(d)   Is there adequate senior staff support for all staff? Do you regularly canvas the views of junior staff on this issue?

(e)   Do you systemically attempt to analyse INSET needs, linked to the needs of the department and to the needs of your staff for personal development? Do you participate in departmental, school, LEA, and regional/national courses?

(f)   Are there adequate and systematic methods of looking after probationary teachers, student teachers, technical and ancillary staff?

(g)   Do you contribute effectively to the general middle management of your school, making both general and specialist contributions, and advocating the cause of CDT education?

Organization

(a)   Is departmental decision-making compatible with the annual decision-making calendar of the school, e.g. timetable construction, examinations, reports, stock purchase, etc.?

(b)   Do you delegate decision-making to the lowest level at which it can be done effectively – to the 'point of expected delivery'.

(c)   Is communication clear and effective? Are meetings conducted in a business-like and purposeful manner?

(d) Do you monitor the implementation of decisions and ensure that those with power use it responsibly?

(e) Is there a clear system of pupils' referral and counselling, and does this match the whole school system?

(f) Do responsible staff keep their 'fingers on the pulse' by regular checking of the work of pupils?

(g) Is routine administration and control of information on registers, mark books, pupil profiles, reports, storage of examination results, etc. effective?

[...]

HOW TO EVALUATE THE CDT DEPARTMENT

In essence, evaluation is an exercise in collecting specified information and then assessing it using certain criteria. It should follow a sequence as in Figure 32.3.

As a general principle any new method to be introduced into a busy school needs a clear aim in mind, a workable process and great care to ensure that it slots into existing school routines, wherever possible. If your school has a formal evaluation policy then you will key your department's process into this, making any necessary adjustments to sensitize the process to the specific characteristics of your department. If not, you must create your own, after obtaining the support of the head, and ensure that it works. To help you do this, the rest of this section is devoted to: general design principles for such a process; ways of conducting important tasks; a brief look at one process which I have used successfully. This is meant to be illustrative, not prescriptive and undoubtedly you will need a great deal of care to adapt my suggestions to the conditions you experience in your own school.

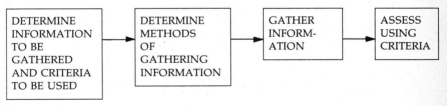

DETERMINE INFORMATION TO BE GATHERED AND CRITERIA TO BE USED → DETERMINE METHODS OF GATHERING INFORMATION → GATHER INFORM-ATION → ASSESS USING CRITERIA

Figure 32.3

Design principles

(a) There must be a reasonable climate of co-operation within your department; if this does not exist it is your job as head of department to build with the help of senior staff if appropriate.

(b)   The purpose of evaluation must be made quite clear, i.e. that it is a supportive tool to ensure that you formulate aims and methods, determine your successes and failures, and make changes where necessary. Any sinister 'Big Brother' fears must be dispelled at the outset.

(c)   Attempt as much as you can collaboratively. One sure way of gaining co-operation, and of devising a system acceptable to all, is to make use of everyone's ideas. However, to do this requires some skill in group management and the extent to which you 'open up' proceedings will depend upon your current level of skill.

(d)   If you prepare a check-list of what to evaluate, or a list of evaluation methods to use, have them appraised by your head teacher and specialist adviser(s). Between them, they will have accumulated a lot of wisdom and you can save time and effort by tapping this.

(e)   Devise a process which is:
   – systematic and matches school routines;
   – workable and realistic;
   – sensitive and non-threatening;
   – capable of inspiring confidence;
   – broad enough in scope and technique.

No one technique will give a totally accurate picture; the more techniques you focus onto a particular area, the more accurate a picture you can gain as you cross-check evidence. Researchers call this 'triangulation'.

Techniques to use

Running profitable means

[...]

PREPARATION

Before calling a meeting, make sure that you have clearly worked out its purpose and be sure to explain this purpose to participants. Meetings can be used for a number of purposes, e.g. to exchange information; to explain or confirm ideas, or to determine how clearly your team understands them; to identify and discuss issues, developments and problems; to offer support. In a more Machiavellian manner, they can be used to apply peer group pressure to encourage members into certain kinds of action.

Agendas, minutes and any supporting papers should be circulated in advance to give people time to prepare, digest, and marshall thoughts.

Members should also be given the opportunity to place items on the agenda. Items should be listed in order of importance. Staff will then be dealing with the most important questions at any given time. Whenever possible attach a time limit to each item. This provides a disciplined framework for discussion and will promote a business-like atmosphere.

Immediately prior to the meeting create the right atmosphere within the room. Lay out the furniture to facilitate discussions and if appropriate, to focus attention on the chairman, and arrange for any necessary aids such as an overhead projector to be available and working. If the meeting is to be held at lunchtime or after a hard day's teaching, try to arrange for refreshments to be available.

PROGRESS

The main task of the chairman will be to ensure that the meeting keeps to its purpose and progresses efficiently. Control should be firm yet patient and tactful. The chairman needs to be well organized, efficient and supportive. His authority will be enhanced if he has a good grasp of the issues and a competent way of speaking and listening. These are skills which can be developed. At all times discussions should be through the chair and should stick to a point. Discussion of more than one item at a time is confusing, counter-productive and should never be allowed. Points of disagreement should be thrashed out logically; where possible a consensus should be arrived at, and decisions agreed upon and noted. The chairman should allow for personal views, and humorous comments but should not let the meeting become anecdotal. Discussion can be instrumental in changing attitudes and stimulating co-operation, but if badly handled can be a time waster. All members will have something to contribute and one very important task is to help them to make this contribution.

[...]

CONCLUDING

At the end of a meeting, briefly summarize decisions reached, the jobs that have to be done, the staff responsible for doing them and their deadlines. This will clarify things and help to ensure an equitable work-load. It also helps reassure staff that they are making progress and that time is not being wasted. Depending on your own situation you may have to check that jobs are being carried out and cajole people if necessary.

[...]

Observing lessons

To be observed by another teacher can threaten both experienced and inexperienced teachers alike; it can also be just as embarrassing for the observer as for the observed. Without question though, it can reveal deep insights into the quality of teaching, and recognizing these is a first pre-condition for improvement. It is well worth the effort therefore to create the climate within your department in which mutual lesson observation is welcomed. Those of you who work in open-plan areas and are therefore used to performing in front of other colleagues may find that the climate already exists; others may have to work hard to achieve it.

The best classroom observation is reciprocal. Teachers can learn from watching their head of department, just as the head of department will find it invaluable to view his staff. Teachers may increase their own confidence in their head of department by watching his expert performance; they also should welcome the change to show him their own skills. By observation he should become aware of the pulse of his department; to see how well aims are being transacted in the studios, workshops and classrooms; to assess the suitability of teaching approaches, learning materials and equipment; to learn something of the relationships between his teachers and their pupils; and to become aware of and acknowledge hard work and good performance. It should also help the teacher to demonstrate any difficulties under which he works, as a prelude to seeking improvements.
[...]

Although the head of department should be able to visit any lesson in his department simply by virtue of his job, he would be most unwise to begin without discussion and mutual agreement. The vital task is to *negotiate access to the classroom, workshop or studio*. Barging in may be one way of entry, but it is quite likely to land you on the floor. Ask any teacher to suggest the lessons you attend and to include a 'successful' and a 'problem' class.

Of course, many teachers will not have 'problem' classes but they will always have some misgivings about the performance of some classes. You should attend both 'successful' and 'problematic' classes. Once you have committed yourself to attending a lesson, do all in your power to turn up; and be on time! Familiarize yourself with the scheme of work and lesson content in advance – be as informed as possible before you arrive.

PROGRESS

Stay for the whole lesson to see how effective each phase is, and how they are linked. Be as unobtrusive as possible: you do not want to put the teacher off his stride; nor do you want to influence the behaviour of the group. Talk to a selection of pupils about their work to see if they clearly understand what they are doing and making, and if they are learning. Look in particular for a sense of purpose, creativity and problem solving; one way of gauging this is to try to assess just how much pupils are committed to achieving the results they have been pointed towards. Check the pupils' work for evidence of long-term development, achievement and the setting of homework. Pay particular attention to the organization of resources, equipment, tools and machines, and the extent to which pupils are using them safely and confidently.

Also try to gauge the quality of the whole lesson. Are control and management satisfactory? Does the teacher have a good rapport with the group and do you detect a sense of pupil involvement, creativity and accountability? Was the lesson adequately prepared and did it fit into the scheme of work? How far was the teacher (and pupils) aware of the concepts, skills and attitudes underlying the lesson content? Were all levels of ability catered for? Was sex-stereotyping minimized? Were administrative procedures (registers, marks, issuing and collecting of stock, tools, and equipment) satisfactory?

CONCLUSION

Making notes may be necessary: if so keep them brief, make them unobtrusively, and show the teacher afterwards. If you feel that writing them during the lesson is inappropriate, write them immediately afterwards. Follow up observations by holding an 'appraisal interview', guidelines for which are given below.

Appraisal Interviews

Appraisal interviews can be used in a variety of situations, for example when following up lesson observations. Arrange to see the teacher involved as soon as possible after the lesson, so that events are still fresh in both your minds. Your comments will seem more relevant and have greater impact as a result. The meeting may only take fifteen or twenty minutes, but if there are problems or implications for organization, INSET or curriculum, it may take longer. Further meetings ought to follow each lesson visit.

PREPARATION

Before the interview clarify its purpose, do all you can to allay any fears, ensure a comfortable and private venue, so that you will find it relatively easy to progress in a relaxed and reassuring manner. Make it quite clear that the meeting is confidential, and that others, for example the head-teacher or deputy in charge of INSET will be involved only with the awareness of the teacher.

PROGRESS

Begin discussion with things that are going well: explain your views and invite your colleague to express his own. Try to manage the discussion so that the teacher himself identifies any problem areas, having done this he is more likely to want to discuss them frankly. Reassure him that you are aware of any difficult circumstances under which he works and try to ensure that problems new to you are aired. Try to be sensitive to underlying feelings which your colleague may find difficult to express in words.

CONCLUSION

End the discussion on a positive note. Having identified difficulties suggest possible solutions and make it clear that you will seek solutions elsewhere. As head of department you are much more than observer, you must advise and support. Follow the session up to monitor progress on those areas of development which were identified in the meeting. This will help sustain the interest of the teacher. It is also vital to attempt to satisfy any needs that have been identified, for example, for new equipment or a change in the timetable; if this is not done, the purpose of appraisal interviews may well become lost to some teachers.

Running such an interview is a delicate and skilful task and many heads of department may be tempted to shy away. This would be very sad as sensitively run appraisal interviews can be of immense value in identifying good and bad practice, creating solidarity and support, stimulating curriculum development and suggestions for INSET, and generally helping you to raise overall performance. It goes without saying that the ultimate beneficiary will be the pupil.

Following up lesson observation is only one use of the appraisal interview technique. CDT teachers today have much more to do than perform within their specialist lessons – they are managers, developers and administrators, and also members of your team. You should hold a fairly lengthy interview with each of your teachers at least once a year to discuss performance in all of these areas. A check-list can be useful to give structure to such meetings but should not stifle discussion of topical issues. In such an interview you should encourage the teacher to comment at length on your own performance – when good relationships have been built frank and honest exchanges of this nature can be most illuminating. There are no certain guidelines on the timing of such meetings although I have usually held mine towards the end of the academic year to review progress over the whole year.

Setting Targets

[...]

When setting targets, you will find it helpful to bear the following in mind. You need to be aware of present conditions before listing targets for their improvement – target-setting is thus one stage in the whole sequence of review and should not be conducted in isolation. It is often productive to set them collaboratively – two brains are usually better than one and teachers are more likely to be committed to achieving targets if they have played a significant part in setting them. Set targets which reflect your aims, which are realistic in the light of conditions prevailing in your department or school, and which are not going to meet rejection because they need more resources than are available. Setting targets which are nearly unattainable might keep some of your teachers striving for perfection, but repeated failure is more likely to sap morale and dissolve interest.

Set deadlines for achievement, identify those people who will do the work, ensure that they have the information and resources to do so, and keep tabs on progress. Too often targets can be set in a state of mild euphoria, but when the day dawns for the results to be delivered, all kinds of reasons for inaction may surface. Analyse the barriers that lie in the way of your target achievement. If you do not do this carefully and specify ways of raising the barriers, any development which does occur will be merely accidental. Frequently banging heads against barriers will do little for high morale in your team. In this day and age, of course, there is no guarantee that requests to lift barriers will be granted if they include extra resources. If you fail to make such requests in a clear and well-justified manner you can be fairly certain they they will not be granted, however.

Analysing data

Not all areas of your work will succumb to useful data analysis and the first task here will be to identify those areas which can be appropriately examined this way. You may find some of the following areas of use in your departmental evaluation:

(a) The results of public and internal examinations and project assessments in comparison with results of the same pupils in other departments.
(b) Capitation allocated to your department in relation to costs per pupil and to capitation awarded to other departments.
(c) The distribution of general ability (as diagnosed through your school's overall assessment processes) within CDT groups to determine whether pupils of all abilities are given access to CDT education.

(d)   The numbers of pupils opting for fourth-, fifth- and sixth-form CDT courses in comparison with numbers opting to study in other comparable departments.

(e)   Safety record, particularly accidents.

(f)   Loss of tools and equipment through wear, theft and vandalism.

The use of outside consultants

The education service has experts at many levels whose job is not just to direct but also to support and facilitate. Your senior staff will have a vast pool of experience and you would be wise to tap this whenever possible. It will always be essential for your head-teacher's approval if you are to initiate major change. Tactically, therefore, you should involve him whenever appropriate if he is to be persuaded of the logic of your ideas.

Most LEAs have specialist advisers or inspectors who will be talented people of wide expertise. Although they tend to be extremely busy people, they are the main source of specialist advice open to you and you should tap their expertise whenever you can. They may, like H.M. Inspectors, make formal inspections of your department from time to time; the results of these can be most illuminating as they reflect your practice within the context of other schools, and they should always be carefully considered by your team.

If you are close to an institution of teacher training which employs specialist lecturers in your field, you can sometimes make informal links which can be mutually profitable. The teacher trainers can be given access to events on the 'chalk face' and you can glean from them their perception of your performance.

In some LEAs, the specialist adviser/inspector may have grouped the CDT departments into geographical consortia for the purpose of regular local meetings. If you are fortunate enough to be involved in one of these, and inter-school relationships are good, you should be able to use them as a broad forum for the discussion and evaluation of cross-school departmental issues.

Pupil consultation

Any good department will have cultivated relationships between staff and pupils which are based on mutual respect and consideration. In such circumstances feedback from pupils is freely offered and readily accepted. However, a more systematic attempt to gather the views of a broad spectrum of pupils can pay much greater dividends if conducted wisely. A former senior colleague of mine, when he was a head of department, used to plan his lower school CDT courses annually on the bases of the interests and hobbies of incoming pupils. He used questionnaires to gather such information, analysed the results to identify topics of interest and overlaid these onto the skills, attitudes and concepts which were the cornerstones of his curriculum. The effort was well rewarded in course popularity, effective learning and high take-up of CDT courses at option time.

It can be worthwhile to use questionnaires at other times of the year, for example at the end of courses or projects to determine pupil reaction.

Confidentiality can be arranged by omitting names from papers.

Group discussions can also be usefully focused on review topics but this needs to be skilfully steered to minimize the distortion that peer group pressure can force onto pupil views.

VII PLANNING THE TECHNOLOGY CURRICULUM

The section on 'Technology in Education' has already dealt with curriculum planning issues at a very general level (Chapters 14–17). Here we go into more details; thus Ray Page picks up from Tom Dodd (Chapter 14) in considering a variety of curriculum strategies. Again we draw upon a survey by HMI to illustrate several kinds of courses which include technology. Increasingly, concern is being expressed about continuity of technological education throughout the whole period of secondary schooling. Austin Underwood faced this issue more than ten years ago when many focused upon the two years before 'O'-level or CSE courses. In Chapter 35, we give his ideas for a design and technology curriculum covering the seven years of secondary school.

Picking up the gender issue highlighted earlier (Chapters 19–21) Martin Grant provides the rationale for planning a course which will make technology more attractive to girls.

33 *Strategies for introducing technology into the curriculum*

● R. L. Page

EDITORS' INTRODUCTION

Although this was written prior to the introduction of GCSE, the general principles are still relevant.

The three aims the STF (School Technology Forum) has set for school technology are as follows:

(a) To develop in all pupils an understanding and appreciation of technological and industrial development, so that the ordinary citizen of the future will exercise some control over these developments, as well as recognize that his or her standard of living depends on them, while others with particular skills will seriously consider careers in these fields. (AWARENESS)

(b) To enable all pupils to experience all or part of the technological process so that they understand how decisions are made and conflicting factors are resolved in technological and industrial situations, as well as develop a confidence to solve problems themselves that they may face in the future in their own lives. (SELF-SUFFICIENCY)

(c) To increase technological skills and knowledge in all pupils so that a better discrimination may exist about the usefulness of technological products, and a better appraisal of personal aptitude with respect to technological and industrial careers may be made. (SKILLS)

No single mode of teaching can hope to give a comprehensive view of technology and industry. Usually one or a combination of five modes have been used.

1. As a structured course in its own right, based on either the science, technical, or craft, design and technology departments or a combination of these, and frequently offered as a choice subject and taught on a team basis. This mode has much to recommend it, because it fits into the existing school framework and can be examined at sixteen-plus and eighteen-plus, but suffers the disadvantage that the accent may still appear to be on the acquisition rather than the application of knowledge, and pupils do not experience the technological process for themselves unless a project is specifically included.

The main advantages of a structured course can be summarized as follows: (a) it offers an examinable subject which gives it status in the sight of head-teachers, parents, and local industrialists, as well as pupils themselves; (b) it makes less demands on a school's resources than more open-ended project work; (c) teachers do not need to be highly expert in anticipating and dealing with unpredictable problems at short notice; (d) it works within a framework in which disorderly behaviour is more easy to control; (e) it is more easy to timetable; (f) it is important for pupils to learn about technology and industry as well as behaving as technologists and experiencing how industry operates; (g) for many pupils the demands of extensive project work for rather more diffuse general studies, with no pre-skill and cognitive development, are beyond them in terms of self-confidence, the necessary craft and self-study skills, and basic scientific knowledge; (h) placed in the 'science' and 'craft' option bands, a structured course can enrich the science of more able pupils and keep a craft element in their curriculum, while for the less academic, it can offer an element of science. If a project is included as well then that can offset the criticism that a structured course tends to foster the acquisition rather than the application of knowledge.

Frequently a structured course is used to replace existing courses such as physics, or offer an acceptable alternative (e.g. engineering science for physics at 'A'-level). Alternatively, it can act in a complementary capacity (e.g. the Schools Council Modular Courses in Technology Some structured courses try to give an overall view of technology and industry, while others look only at one facet (e.g. control technology). Finally, some structured courses are not long enough to stand fully in their own right but form part of a larger course (e.g. Project Technology's 'A'-level fibre chemistry unit).

2. As enrichment of existing curriculum subjects, in particular science, craft, and sometimes the humanities (e.g. geography). Although this may be the only way a school can introduce technological activity, the disadvantages of this type of approach have already been alluded to. However, the gains of such an approach can be listed as follows: (a) in the early years (e.g. nine to thirteen) it can provide the necessary base for later structured courses or extensive project work; (b) it can show the dependence of society on technology and industry and raise their

esteem; (c) it makes the least demand on existing timetables, and thus meets the least resistance from teachers. On the other hand, the dangers of the enrichment approach must not be overlooked, namely; (a) in science and craft studies, technology can become confused with applied science and design; (b) it puts technology in second place; (c) it does not easily change attitudes and develop skills unless the enrichment spreads right across the curriculum.

However, more consideration of this approach ought to be given in the first instance to the nine-to-thirteen period of education (e.g. the School Technology Forum's middle years development) and it must be admitted that at present it is likely to be as an acceptable way of introducing technology into schools as the structured course approach. The science inspectorate have already indicated that they believe science teaching in secondary schools should include an element of 'technology for all'. The renaming of craft departments as craft, design and technology reflects this.

The recent development of modular resources (e.g. the School Technology Forum's modules and the Schools Council Modular Courses in Technology) also suggests that there is likely to be equal take-up of both approaches in the future. Modular resources offer schools the possibility of enriching existing courses by introducing individual modules or the development of structured courses using a fixed number of modules. At 'O'-level and CSE level, for which the School Technology Forum's modules and those of the Schools Council project are designed, two structured schemes in practice seem to be successful. The Hertfordshire scheme uses three modules spread over three terms in the fourth year followed by a major project of two terms in the fifth year, and the choice of modules to make up the full course will decide whether it gives a balanced view of technology or focuses on only one aspect, and whether it is an alternative or a complement to existing courses. The Avon scheme, by insisting on a common core of three ten-week modules followed by two optional modules and a project, tries to give a broad view of technology. The common core consists of energy resources, materials technology and technology problem-solving and these modules attempt to give an insight into the resources, constraints and process of technology.

3. As part of a general studies programme, whereby it is easier to achieve a balance between the various components. However, unless care is taken they may not experience much decision-making or working to a particular brief. Students may also form the impression that technology has nothing to do with the other subjects of the curriculum, while nearly all such subjects do in practice have a contribution to make. At a practical level however it can keep a technological component in the programme of sixth-formers and further education and higher education students who would otherwise drop work in this area. The BP 'decisions' kits have proved to be very successful in giving students a

taste of real decision-making from an industrial viewpoint and the book *Hidden Factors* by Edward Semper and Philip Coggin gives a general view of an advanced technological society. The School Technology Forum's Minority Time Working Party is also developing resources for this general studies area.

4. As a unifying factor throughout the curriculum where several departments link forces to develop a particular technological theme or topic from time to time. Until more schools become less subject-bound in their organization, this approach, while having much to commend it, will suffer from lack of sustained and continuous activity. It raises the conflict between a subject-based and a problem-solving-based curriculum.

5. As extensive project work, frequently based on a technical activity centre, and therefore often run as an extra-mural activity. As a consequence it is beyond the capacity of many maintained schools, and it is the independent schools which tend to adopt this mode, where as an afternoon/evening/weekend activity it does not interrupt their 'classroom' teaching. It poses the problems that it: (a) is not easy to timetable; (b) demands a large resource bank, ties up equipment needed for other courses, and needs its own accommodation and storage; (c) requires pre-project skills and knowledge and an extensive back-up library; (d) is difficult, but not impossible, to assess in objective terms for examination purposes; (e) requires experienced staff and takes several years to build up effectively. On the other hand, when run successfully it allows: (a) pupils and teachers to work alongside one another as co-workers; (b) pupils to experience the technological process (providing they have developed the necessary skills in the work that precedes the project); (c) decision-making skills to be developed and knowledge to be applied rather than acquired ; (d) cognitive, effective and psychomotor development to be integrated in the problem-solving aspect of the work; (e) pupils to work at their own pace, within their own abilities, so that they are thus more intrinsically motivated. Thus, although project work by itself may leave pupils knowing about how technologists work, but ignorant of the range and scope of technology and its relationship to manufacturing industries, in terms of motivation this mode has much to recommend it as it is central to technological activity, modelling itself on the core process of technology.

The need for these different strategies for introducing technological activity and industrial awareness into schools is inherent in the nature of the two activities, which it must be stressed are not defined areas of knowledge but rather processes drawing on man's knowledge and resources to improve the quality of human life. Put another way, they are the processes by which man copes and learns to live with his environment in an increasingly complex world. Many of the resources useful in this context have been produced nationally rather than locally and as a consequence teachers expected to use the resources have not been fully trained in their use. There is a need for much better dissemination and training programmes.

A technological or industrial career cannot be fostered by the career service alone. The School Technology Forum, and in particular the Teacher Education and Dissemination Committee, would like to stress that it is their view that unless an impact is made on the curriculum, it is unlikely that the careers' service, even if it is more effectively trained to do so, can alone undertake such a task.

TECHNOLOGY THROUGH SCIENCE

Although applied science by itself gives less than a rounded view of technology, if coupled with an enrichment of craft and technical studies much can be achieved. Recently, pressures have begun to build up on science teachers to include a technological component in their teaching. In a recent article in *TREND*, Norman Booth, recently retired staff inspector for science, wrote that science education should have three elements in it; 'science for science sake' (pure science), 'science for action' (technology applied science), and 'science for citizenship'. H.M.I. Winnerah, the present staff inspector for science, has made similar comments at recent meetings. The Association for Science Education is proposing three models for 11–16 science programmes for the 1980s in its pamphlet *Alternatives for Science Education*. For example model 3 is organized as follows:

Years 1 & 2	Environmental Science	(8 periods per week)
Year 3	Experimental Science	(8 periods per week)
Year 4	Applied Science	(8 periods per week)
Year 5	Science and Society	(8 periods per week)
Years 6 & 7	Independent Studies	(16 periods per week)

Time does not permit a full discussion of these ideas or where the resources to enrich science teaching in this way may be found. However, STF *Working Paper No. 3* gives several case studies on the technological enrichment of science, and together with such curriculum development as the Schools Council Integrated Science project offers a starting point.[1]

---

[1] Editors' note: Recently the Secondary Science Curriculum Review has issued a discussion document on technology in science teaching: *Science and Technology Education*, SSCR, 1985. Also HMI have conducted a survey of science departments: *Technology and School Science: An HMI Enquiry*, HMSO, 1985.

34 *Technology in schools: developments in CDT departments*

● DES (HMI)

EDITORS' INTRODUCTION

In this extract from the HMI survey of ninety schools, we have included the description of six of the eight types of courses they identified (they saw some 170 courses or forms of technology).

The technological activities seen included courses leading to public examinations, non-examinable courses, and elements of work within courses. In this document the activities have been divided into groups, each with a particular characteristic.

GROUP 1: MODULAR COURSES IN TECHNOLOGY

As the name implies, the principal characteristic of modular courses in technology is that they consist of self-contained units of work which are compiled into courses of study.

Over thirty courses were seen which were modular in nature. All led to a Certificate of Secondary Education (CSE) or to a General Certificate of Education (GCE). A typical course was prefaced by a common area of study about the place of technology in society, its history and possibly some reference to the implications of technological development for the environment. But the principal feature was that the pupil then undertook 'modules' of practical work involving designing and making, each of about one term in duration. These modules were usually a selection of 'options', chosen by the school to reflect the expertise and training of the teachers or the facilities available in the school. Typical titles for such modules were 'structures', 'mechanisms', 'electronics', 'pneumatics', 'aeronautics' and similar areas of specific technology.

However, some courses included compulsory modules of a more general nature such as 'problem-solving', 'energy' or 'control'.

In each module pupils learned a body of knowledge which they had to apply during or at the end of a module by undertaking a 'mini-project'. For example, in a module entitled 'mechanisms', pupils studied gears, linkages and loci, using work-sheets and constructional kits. They were then asked to:

(a) Design and make a door mechanism for a rabbit hutch. It should allow the rabbit to get in, but close securely after it.

or

(b) Design and make a mechanism that will open a garage door when a motor car approaches it.

In each case the teacher exercised some control over the size and complexity of the project. For example, in this school, the second problem could only be modelled using hardboard, wood scrap, springs and string. Any gears used in the solution had to be manufactured from these materials.

Similarly, a 'structures' module had a mini-project which required pupils to solve the problem of bridging a specified gap with a structure which carried a specified load, or, alternatively, to design and build a jib crane to carry a given load. In each case, the pupils were required to use the knowledge that they had acquired when experimenting with beams and frameworks during the module.

Modular courses culminate in the building of one or more complex 'major projects' which use the knowledge acquired in several of the modules. Usually the pupil chooses his or her own problem. For example, a pupil described his work on an automatic door-opening system:

> The aim of my project was to aid people in wheel-chairs or on crutches who have difficulty in getting through doors. This was to be done by having an automatic door-opening system that incorporated an electromagnetic bolt. The system was to be designed so it could easily be fitted on to any hinged door, and remain as cheap as possible.

Some preliminary suggestions for solutions had been made, based on the knowledge acquired during work on the modules. In addition, the pupil had learnt which types of motor were suitable, had considered possible ways in which a car ignition switch might be used to modify a door lock, and mastered the practicalities of fitting the device to a full-sized door.

The quality of pupils' work was often extremely impressive. At its best, it indicated a sound grasp of technological principles coupled with an ability to apply those principles. The solutions showed ingenuity, good exploration of alternative possibilities and good craft skills, together with excellent supporting design folios which included pupils' evaluation.

Where less satisfactory work was seen, this was usually associated with the major project. A pupil would sometimes attempt to build a project which was too far outside the range of his experience. For example, having taken modules in mechanisms, structures and electronics, a pupil devised a chair-lifting device on pneumatic rather than electromechanical principles. Neither he nor the teacher knew enough to anticipate the problems involved. Such a departure is permissible in many modular course examination syllabuses and may even be encouraged by some teachers who feel that able pupils should not be constrained by lack of previous knowledge, but it rather negates the principle of building up knowledge and skills in a modular fashion and then seeking to integrate the content. Further, in order to undertake a major project in the limited time of one or two terms, it is difficult for the pupil to carry out the research, acquire the additional knowledge and necessary skills and buy or borrow the specialist equipment.

Despite this weakness which was seen in a minority of courses, the modular approach, initiated in East Anglia and the south-west, has valuable characteristics. First, the modular format is a deliberate tactic on the part of the course designers to help schools to introduce technological studies without a considerable investment of time, equipment or in-service training. For example, most teachers of craft, design and technology have some experience of mechanisms, materials and structures during initial training. Fewer have experience of, say, electronics or pneumatics, but those that do are able to prepare material and run courses for those that do not.

Secondly, teachers from several disciplines are able to contribute one or more modules according to their training or expertise. For example, a physics teacher can teach an energy or electronics module and a CDT teacher can offer modules in mechanisms or structures. This type of co-operation enables a school to select modules according to available expertise, specialist accommodation, or even local interest. To illustrate, a school near an aircraft firm had chosen to include a module in aeronautics run by a mathematics teacher, a module in electronics taught in the physics department, with the remaining modules taught by a CDT teacher.

Thirdly, the content of the courses was often developed, particularly in the south-west, after consultation with representatives from industry, further education or higher education, thus helping to make the syllabuses relevant to working life, and the examination qualifications acceptable for employment or related further study.

These examinations now include, in addition to a variety of Mode 1 and Mode 3 CSEs, GCE O-levels offered by the Southern Universities Joint Board and the Oxford, Cambridge and Welsh Joint Boards. There is also an A-level course of modular format entitled 'Technology' which the Cambridge Board has introduced as a logical extension to the O-levels. The advanced course includes a module in automation and requires all candidates to show an understanding of programming in BASIC and of the use of microcomputers in control systems.

The Schools Council has funded a curriculum development project to support 'modular courses in technology', and at the time of writing, materials which support the various CSE and O-level courses are being published, and a dissemination programme is in train. Although primarily intended for modular courses, the material is also designed for use in other technology courses.

GROUP 2: CONTROL TECHNOLOGY

This is the title of a particular modular course developed under the auspices of Schools Council Project Technology.

The growth and influence of this course make it sufficiently strong and distinctive to merit separate description, although it could be considered to be a form of modular course and indeed was in existence several years before the courses described in the previous section were introduced. Indeed, much of the curricular material produced for the courses in Group 1 has its origins in the control technology course.

Twenty control technology courses were seen, all similar in format and all leading to an examination at CSE or O-level. The principal difference between these and the courses in Group 1 is that the modules are compulsory, and that control concepts and control devices form the heart of the work.

The early stages of the course usually consist of basic modules taught in the following sequence:

(a)   structures;
(b)   gears;
(c)   electricity;
(d)   electrical switching;
(e)   electronics.

This enables gears to be built into vehicles, cranes or similar machines which the pupil assembles. Gears can be driven by electric motors. Motors can be controlled by electrical or electronic switches. Thus at the completion of the basic modules a pupil had the competence to build, for example, a vehicle which would travel at a specified speed, stop, start, reverse or turn as a result of striking an obstacle, entering a magnetic field or cutting a beam of light. Teachers can vary the order, pace and emphasis of the modules, provided that all the compulsory parts of the syllabus are covered. As in Group 1, 'mini-projects' may be associated with each module.

In the later stages of the course, pupils have greater freedom to choose, design, model or build major projects. These projects draw upon the knowledge developed in the compulsory modules and result, typically, in the making of automated devices and machines such as those employed in commerce and industry. For example, in one school an automatic drinks dispenser had been made similar to that seen at a railway terminus or motorway restaurant. In another, a telephone exchange was being developed for the school. In short, it was possible to see examples of devices which would sense, warn, dispense, sort, repeat, display, react, select or in other ways control a machine or system. The ideas for projects arose from the identification of needs in diverse fields: local industry, handicapped people in the community, leisure interest, or control in the home.

The quality of the best work seen lay not so much in the extent to which knowledge had been acquired for its theoretical interest, or even to illustrate principles applied in industry, but rather in the extent to which pupils used it to design and make devices and machines to perform specified tasks. In each case, the production of hardware was not the only aspect of the course to be assessed. Pupils were also marked on their ability to plan, modify and record the progression of the work, to indicate the variety of solutions considered, to make an assessment of their validity, to note any modifications or necessary departures from the plan of work and to arrive at a critical evaluation of the success of the project.

It was in these aspects, as much as in the production of a machine or model, that the pupils' work showed quality.

These courses, and also those in Group 1, can be improved in two respects. First, there is plenty of opportunity to use and understand electrical and mechanical control devices, but few teachers took the opportunity to relate a concept taught in one field (say 'feedback' in electronics) to related concepts in other modules of the same course.

Secondly, there is a preoccupation with the use of constructional kits, such as Meccano, Fischertechnik, Proto, Lego and one which is produced especially for this course, called Danum Trent Kit. These are excellent aids which enable pupils to assemble parts rapidly and accurately. But over-preoccupation with kits means, in some schools, that while pupils often develop great facility with these kits and use them with speed, flair and imagination, they cannot necessarily model and construct with real components. For example, some pupils could build electronic circuits using components encased in the plastic boxes of the Danum Trent Kit, but when shown the uncased component they did not recognize it; others recognized the component, but without its 'box' were unable to incorporate it in a circuit which they had correctly designed. Or, to take another example, pupils showed that they could build a model bridge in Meccano or Fischertechnik, but were confused when designing in wood, metal or plastics, where the different methods of joining, the need to consider sectional shape and, above all, to consider the properties of the material became far more important than an understanding of statics in modelling kits.

However, the reliance upon kits is not a weakness in itself. It is a result of the way in which the course has developed. Although conceived as a three-year course for average and above-average pupils, the enquiry showed that it had, in most cases, been compressed into a two-year course and offered to pupils of a wide range of ability. Thus time was short for work beyond the stage of modelling with kits.

To take a more positive view, the control technology course is one of those which appeals to most pupils and industrialists alike. Providing, as it does, a good grounding in the understanding of how artefacts and systems can be controlled, it is also a natural preface to a study of microelectronic control and in that sense it is particularly topical.

GROUP 3: ELECTRONICS

Many examples of electronics or microelectronics were seen as modules in the courses described in Groups 1 and 2. The self-contained courses in electronics described below appeared to be somewhat different in nature, as well as in duration.

From fourteen courses seen, only one school offered a spectrum of courses in CSE, O-, AO and A-level examinations in electronics. The majority of schools offered CSE courses only and from enquiry there is no reason to suppose that CDT departments offer O-level courses in electronics. This suggests that, as a general rule, electronics courses in CDT tend to be fairly low-level and unrelated to other courses in CDT departments. However, almost without exception, electronics courses were taught with considerable drive, enthusiasm and pace. Pupils were usually strongly motivated and the standards of project work were high.

The teaching approach to electronics invariably placed the practice before the theory. Early exercises often followed a 'recipe' pattern, where pupils learned to couple 'black boxes' of components together to achieve desired effects. For example, a pupil might be shown a basic circuit, such as an electronic switch which turns on and off as the result of being exposed to a particular level of light, and utilize it in a project such as an automatic parking light which could be activated as darkness fell. The explanation of *why* a device should respond to light would be deferred. Teachers thought that pupils could and should discover what the switch could do and how it could be made to do it. Understanding of the related physics was not regarded as a prerequisite for solving simple problems. In the view of teachers, to commence with theoretical principles could 'blunt motivation', and underlying principles should be studied against a backdrop of practical experience and self-confidence. The high level of application which pupils displayed supported this view.

The dearth of GCE O- and A-level courses can be attributed partly to the fact that these syllabuses usually contain large theoretical elements which do not suit the pragmatic approach of CDT teachers. It may also be the case that a CDT department is already offering a set of CDT O-levels, and the inclusion of electronics could be difficult to staff and to resource.

In the few schools offering A-level courses, the Associated Examining Board's A-level in electronic systems was chosen.

The following titles illustrate the range and complexity of work which was seen:

(a) measurement of speed and sound;
(b) monitoring the effect of noise on human reaction time;
(c) design of an electronic lock, with alarm system;
(d) design and manufacture of an electrocardiograph.

The fact that the work was of good quality can be almost entirely attributed to the dynamism of the teachers. Possibly the fact that the technology itself is changing at an exponential rate may have some relationship to the forward-looking attitudes of teachers.

At the time of writing, the more extensive introduction of electronics into CDT departments faces difficulties. The first is the shortage of CDT teachers who have either the initial or in-service training to teach the subject beyond an elementary level.

Secondly, CDT departments which wish to include full electronics courses, leading to public examinations, usually face a shortage of physical resources. Purpose-built electronics rooms are rare and the purchase of even modest equipment will often force a department to distort its budget at the expense of other aspects of CDT.

A third and more fundamental difficulty is that some CDT teachers are wary of the introduction of complete courses on electronics on the grounds that these can only be included at the expense of time spent upon other aspects of designing and making. For example, it is argued that electronics teaches a limited range of physical skills and is an activity devoid of aesthetic content.

On the other hand, if it is accepted that technology courses should be (in whole or in part) the province of CDT, then electronics as an *element* of those courses has considerable worth. In the first place, it considers the design of systems, as much as the design of artefacts – the traditional province of CDT. It deals in an uncontrived way with a wide range of technological concepts. And it is an aspect of technology which exemplifies control of the remote and the inaccessible.

It is therefore difficult to envisage a practical technology course in which electronics would not be an *element*. But, with the exception of the fortunate school which can benefit from the drive and expertise of a teacher who is likely to remain in the school for some years, a CDT department would be wise to be cautious about offering a complete and free-standing course in electronics.

GROUP 4: APPLIED SCIENCE, ENGINEERING SCIENCE AND ENGINEERING DESIGN

Many of these courses include the word 'science' which suggests a scientific content, although taught in a CDT department.

The titles 'applied science' and 'engineering science' are familiar in higher and further education but in this enquiry the labels proved a poor guide to their content in the schools. They were umbrella terms which sheltered an extraordinary variety of courses with little in common beyond a title. Forty-two courses were seen and of these the largest and most diverse groups were those at CSE level. For example, in one part of the country a CSE Mode 2 called engineering science had core content which carried 30 per cent of the marks but the remaining 70 per cent was allocated to one of the following 'branches', which could be chosen by the school:

(a)   automotive engineering;
(b)   mechanical engineering;
(c)   materials technology (metals, polymers, concretes);
(d)   applied science;
(e)   experimental technology;
(f)   control technology;
(g)   agricultural engineering.

One school was taking the control technology branch; so that, although the course was entitled 'engineering science', it was virtually the same as courses described in the section on 'control technology'. In another part of the country, a CSE Engineering Science course proved to be entirely concerned with electronic projects. The quality of work seen in CSE courses was as varied as the content and approach, so it is impossible to make useful generalizations.

At GCE O-level, courses in engineering science were not common in CDT departments. The syllabuses in this subject which are offered by the London and the Cambridge Boards were not taught in the schools visited, but it was interesting to ask teachers why this should be. First, neither examination had a major practical project and therefore it was not easy for a CDT department to fit the course to the CDT philosophy of planning, designing, graphic communication and making. Secondly, at the time of the visits, neither Board had a complementary A-level examination. The Cambridge Board had no A-level equivalent and London had a syllabus which, paradoxically, calls for evidence of designing and making abilities in a major project. Therefore a department which offered A-level engineering science (London) preferred to preface this with an O-level examination in which pupils could develop general skills in designing and making.

On the other hand, a course entitled 'elements of engineering design', offered by Cambridge Board at both O- and A-levels, was popular, and a selection of these courses was seen.

The stated intention of the courses is to provide a sound understanding of mechanics as an aid to good (mechanical) design. Consequently, the project work which forms a major part of course assessment consists of designing and making small machines or mechanical devices. For example, projects included special jigs to hold oddly shaped components, presses for producing blanks from sheet metal and a tool for wrapping wire on to an armature. The work seen was characterized by good quality metalworking; often including complex casting and machining. The quality of designing varied and sometimes, as was found in some modular technology courses, a mechanical solution was chosen when a different technology, such as electromechanics or pneumatics would have been more appropriate.

The major theoretical element in the course consisted of a close study of the structure of materials and their behaviour under working conditions. In order to do this work in materials science, specialized tools such as tensometers, hardness and impact testers were essential. If the school did not possess such things, either they were borrowed or pupils had to visit nearby colleges or industry in order to use the equipment. The materials science element was well taught and pupils understood the main concepts. However, this aspect tended to be divorced from application in the main practical project. Furthermore, it was often limited to a deep knowledge of metals rather than general understanding of the properties of *all* materials and how they behave under various conditions.

Despite the reservations expressed by HMI concerning the narrow, if thorough, emphasis upon mechanical aspects, teachers indicated that the examination was acceptable not only to faculties of mechanical engineering but also to related areas of engineering.

With the exception of the Cambridge 'elements of engineering design', GCE A-level courses in applied science or engineering science are rarely taught in CDT departments. Although both the Associated Examining Board and the Oxford Board have an engineering science A-level, no course was being offered in the schools visited. Two schools offered the

Northern Universities Joint Matriculation Board A-level engineering science. This exceptionally well devised examination includes a major practical project. In one case it was taught entirely by CDT teachers and in the second by physics and CDT teachers working as a team. The complex and detailed syllabus, which covered thermodynamics, tribology, heat transfer and fluid flow, was very well taught in each case. The examination included the assessment of related practical projects such as a wind tunnel, heat exchanger and friction test bed.

Several points emerge from the consideration of this group of courses. First, they are diverse in nature; so diverse that it is extremely difficult for parents and employers to know the content and emphasis upon assessment in a particular course. Secondly, it requires a major effort on the part of a head of a CDT department to select a compatible set of CSE, O- and A-level examinations. It was clear that the title 'engineering science' in many CSE courses was pretentious, and the work had little relationship to courses at a higher level. Thirdly, the A-level examination course, though well taught, required a level of staffing provision and resources not often to be found in CDT departments. The fact that the courses required a high degree of specialization on the part of teachers, access to good machine shop facilities and expensive or sophisticated laboratory equipment, suggests that the advanced work might best take place in further education, where this level of resources can be justified.

GROUP 5: DESIGN-BASED COURSES

As the name suggests, design-based courses are those which seek primarily to develop a pupil's ability to design. When first devised, the inclusion of technological content was fortuitous – now it may be deliberate.

The word 'design' is usually incorporated into the title of these courses. They normally lead to examinations at CSE, O- and A-levels. The word emphasizes the importance given to the development of a pupil's ability to design. Craft skills in woodworking, metalworking, or work in other media are regarded as important concomitants, but greater weighting is usually given to the reasoning skills associated with designing and making. Pupils learn how to identify problems, consider possible solutions, gather relevant information, plan the production of an artefact and evaluate the outcome. In some examinations it is as acceptable for a candidate to design and execute a mural for the school hall as it is to design and make an electronic organ. Other syllabuses specify the type of problem to be solved or the medium to be employed. Both types emphasize the process of designing and the acquisition of applicable practical skills and relevant knowledge, as the task demands.

Examples were seen of the following A-level work: the Oxford Board's design, London Board's design and technology, and Welsh Joint Education Committee's (WJEC) design, craft and technology. Although it was possible in some examinations for candidates to avoid a 'technological' project and choose purely 'expressive' designs, in practice a large proportion appeared to undertake projects which were entered subsequently in the 'Schools Design Prize', sponsored by industry and organized by the Design Council, the 'Buildacar' competition organized by British Petroleum, or the 'Young Engineer for Britain' organized by the Department of Industry. Projects were seen which were entered in regional or national Science Fairs, or the BBC's 'Young Scientists of the Year' series – even though the projects were not necessarily connected with school science departments and were built in CDT curricular time. In fact, teachers sometimes remarked wryly that their pupils were 'Young *Technologists* of the Year'.

The supporting theoretical work seen in a design-based course was often specifically technological. For example, in a course leading to the WJEC examinations, the teaching included the topics of mass production, conservation and the history of technology. In the Oxford A-level examinations teachers pointed out that candidates had to be prepared to answer questions on such topics as automation, mechanization and ergonomics. Since the visits, several more A-level design-based syllabuses have emerged. The Associated Examining Board's (AEB) design communication and implementation has specific sections on technology (ergonomics, structures and control systems) and the Northern Universities Joint Metriculation Board's design has very detailed sections on structures, electronics, control systems and motive power. Cambridge Board now has a design-based A-level CDT examination, with technology in the syllabus.

In short, many A-level courses seen contained far more teaching of specific aspects of technology than their broad-based emphasis upon ability to design suggests and the trend is to make the inclusion explicit. AT CSE or O-level, the teaching of technological concepts was less evident, since the emphasis was upon the development of design skills. Nevertheless, an assignment often required the acquisition of specific technological knowledge. For example, some projects from the following list in a CSE design course were seen in an 11–18 comprehensive school:

(a) Investigate the theory of weaving and design and make a loom.
(b) Design and make a model of a slimming machine.
(c) Design and make a model of a car or motor bicycle exhaust system to reduce noise and exhaust fumes.
(d) Design and make a safety device to eliminate the danger of pots and pans being pulled from cookers by small children.

(e) Design and make a transmitter that could be used by police patrol cars on motorways to warn drivers of any dangers into which they may be driving.

The quality of the work seen at all levels was high in most respects. Problems were carefully specified, well researched, correctly planned, recorded and evaluated. The only real cause for concern was that occasionally a pupil was allowed to undertake a project which betrayed a lack of understanding of technological principles on the part of the teacher. For example, since gearing systems are inherently inefficient, a pupil should have been made aware of this before being allowed to make a series of coupled gear boxes in order to change the speed, direction and force transmitted by a driving shaft. Several examples of ineffectual solar heaters were also seen which showed scant understanding of simple heat exchange. It could be argued that it is up to the pupil to 'research' the problem in order to discover the underlying technological principles and teachers pointed out that to place this responsibility on the pupil has 'educational validity'. Against that view, the pupil has limited time, materials and resources to spend in the exploration of 'blind alleys'. Greater control of the chosen project by knowledgeable teachers is necessary in design-based courses, since the syllabuses sometimes lack the structured build-up of knowledge which characterizes the modular technology or control technology courses. [...]

GROUP 8: TECHNOLOGICAL AWARENESS

These courses seek to make pupils aware of technological change and the implications for society which result from that change. The courses are usually intended to be taught by teachers from several school departments, thus creating a cross-disciplinary view of technology.

Some examples were sought of courses, not necessarily leading to an examination, which attempted to develop 'technological awareness' across the curriculum. Such an approach to technology, taught by a number of different subject teachers, is sometimes advocated in contrast to courses which are based primarily on one department. After widespread enquiry, fifteen examples were found and they had little in common. In the majority of cases the technological awareness courses did not extend across all school subjects. Eight courses consisted of a study of topics such as 'pollution', 'technological futures' or 'energy crisis'. Pupils read books or articles, saw films or held discussions. The courses took place in the early years of secondary schooling and did not link with related examinations in the upper school. Since 'designing and making' was not a necessary characteristic, these courses were not central to the survey.

In another two schools, technology was an element in GCE O- and A-level general studies. CDT teachers contributed to the courses by lecturing on 'industrialization' and helping to advise pupils on written projects. Although the work was competently taught, the breadth and diversity of the syllabus made it difficult for teachers to convey any coherent view of technology, and the general impression was that topics were taught in a random and unrelated fashion.

In the total sample, there were seven schools in which some form of practical activity took place. Of these, two schools ran CSE technology courses 'for those not taking three sciences'. In both cases the CDT department was clearly expected to give pupils of low ability a mixture of simple constructional project work and general information, which drew upon knowledge and skills in other subjects but which did not involve other subject teachers.

For example, in a topic entitled 'bridges' pupils were looking at local bridges, collecting historical information and building simple models. However, none of this work attempted to teach elementary principles of structures, or to analyse why bridges were of a particular configuration, to consider the nature of the materials chosen, or to design bridges which might be modelled and tested.

In an independent school, a CDT teacher ran courses in technological awareness as part of a sixth-form general studies programme. For a variety of reasons it was not possible to see these non-examinable courses being taught. However, the teacher gave an extremely clear and well ordered account of two aspects, and showed examples of work:

(a) Alternative technology: a practical course which was based upon the problems of developing nations. For example, pupils had investigated the problems of fuel shortage and had built models and prototypes of wind-pumps and water irrigation systems.

(b) Possible futures: an attempt to look at the wider implications of technology. A non-practical course based upon a number of technological issues: resource depletion, food supply, predictive studies of technological developments and moral issues in modern medicine.

In the remaining two schools in the 'sample' a sustained attempt had been made by groups of teachers to evolve a course in the first three years of 11–18 secondary schools to which most subjects could contribute. In each case the topics were chosen and interpreted by individual subject teachers, according to their own perception of technology. For example, in one school the historian proposed to study medieval architecture and also the evolution and use of tools. The biologist saw, in a study of skeletal and plant structure, prime examples of 'design related to function'. The European studies teacher had developed a series of lessons on the Channel Tunnel. The social consequences of a 'Chunnel' were considered as well as the technical difficulties.

Both schools had managed to attract some outside finance in order to help with curriculum development and the production of materials. The importance of designing and making was recognized. The work was still evolving and discussions were continuing between teachers who were attempting to move from a miscellany of perceptions of technology held by individual teachers, to a coherent course with agreed aims and objectives.

Beyond these embryonic examples, no model for courses in technological awareness emerged. In common with other attempts to establish courses which cross curricular boundaries, successful practice is a function of the extent to which teachers can meet and thrash out a course framework to suit their particular school context.

35 *An integrated design and technology curriculum*

● A Underwood

EDITORS' INTRODUCTION

For many teachers who want to base technological education on project work, the problem is planning such work to give pupils a coherent experience throughout their schooling. Despite being over a decade old this article offers one such plan.

RECOGNITION IN CURRICULUM DEVELOPMENT

In technological education, we have now had nearly a decade of massive pioneering work to establish recognition in the curriculum of school technology, school project work, technology projects, design and technology, call it what you will. The necessity to establish this recognition within schools is perhaps the most necessary part of our work. Yet in many ways, this recognition so often goes little beyond lip-service.

It was for this reason that I asked at the last meeting of the School Technology Forum for the inclusion of a fifth requirement in the Forum's appeal letter on teacher education – the encouragement in schools, through headmasters, of the climate in which design and technology shall be accepted as part of an integrated curriculum.

TECHNOLOGY AND THE TIMETABLE

An encouraging number of schools are succeeding in producing individual and group project work of first-rate quality, and carrying out technical project working as a normal part of the timetabled curriculum.

This contribution is intended to show how the project method is being used at Bishop Wordsworth's School not just for the occasional group-working method, but for normal teaching in the design and technology department. In this, we have had great encouragement from the immediate past headmaster, Mr R.C.R. Blackledge.

Timetabling for the department runs as follows:

Year 1.   2 periods of art and design ($\frac{1}{2}$ year in each of workshop and studio).

Year 2.   2 periods of design and technology ($\frac{1}{2}$ year in each of two workshops).

Year 3.   2 periods – pupils' choice of workshop with ability to interchange as materials or specialized requirements demand. (One of the periods is primarily concerned with electronics, plastics, metals, applied science, lapidary, etc. The other period is concerned mainly with wood and GRP, with an annexe for large projects.)

Year 4.   4 periods or 2 periods:
4 periods blocked with history/biology/music/geography (intended as Mode 3 CSE or GCE periods if required);
2 periods – in a technical projects block across the whole year with art/biology/music/TD. (Intended as an opportunity for project working in all subjects in a technical projects group.)

Year 5.   4 periods or 2 periods as for year 4.

Years 6 and 7.   8 periods in each year to Oxford design A83 syllabus 'A' level.
3 periods in one afternon a week of technical projects in workshops, science laboratories, electronics laboratory, or at the Salisbury College of Technology.

In form 1, pupils investigate the design of forms, their shape, texture, structure and function, and explore the working of materials with simple tools, and have some sketching experience.

In form 2 we begin with 'all together' work in mensuration, marking out, cutting, shaping, drilling, and finishing, from simple working drawings of a small object whose production involves all of these processes – e.g. a name tag in brass. We regard spending half a term on this as being very worthwhile for every child.

FIRST DESIGN PROJECTS

In the rest of the time (1 term +), the pupils design and make something in wood in the wood/GRP workshop, and in the alternating half-year in the other workshop, they choose their first design from a number of briefs. These are on a duplicated sheet which is given to them about a fortnight before they finish their work described above. One of the sheets, which we have now used for two years, explains:

Where to obtain INFORMATION
How to COMMUNICATE their ideas
MATERIALS and PROCESSES available
TESTING facilities available

The typical choices on one sheet are to design and construct:

1. A simple device to:
    (a) Measure up to 0.5 kgm force.
or (b) Convert wind power to rotary motion.
or (c) Convert water power to rotary motion.
or (d) Convert steam power to rotary motion.
2. A device which will run over very rough ground and powered by a spring or elastic band.
4. A simple toy for a young child involving converting rotary motion to reciprocating motion.
5. After finding out about intermediate technology: either
    (a) A machine to raise water for irrigation from a river using only the water flow to work the machine.
    (b) A machine for making use of the sun's heat for producing a hot-water supply.

RESOURCES – INFORMATION AND MATERIALS

We have endeavoured to produce our own resources centre on the inevitable shoe-string of the whole scheme. Some eighty envelope files contain relevant information on topics that we restrict to general titles. An example at the beginning of the alphabetical classification is:

Adhesives
Air – air power – flight – ventilation
Aluminium
Anodizing
Astronomy
Batteries – battery vehicles etc.

These reference files are supplemented by an encouraged use of the school and public libraries, and a six-page handout on how to set about information searching. In the Upper School we have a lecture by the librarian at the Salisbury College of Technology, and are encouraged to use their library, their British Technological Index, Satis, etc.

Each pupil works with a design sheet on which he defines his aim or problem, and refines his design brief. By sketches and notes, which include design restrictions, he works out his suggested solutions. The design sheet poses questions on proposed materials and the reason for their use.

Group-working at this first stage is not permitted and partnerships are discouraged. It is the individual child we are attempting to encourage to think, make decisions, and carry them out in what is, to some extent, a diagnostic exercise. It is difficult to break up a sleeping partnership once it has begun. Intense and animated discussion often takes place between the children during the course of their work, and is an indication of the ebullient thought processes taking place.

Materials for this work must be as diverse as the information sources in the variety and form of materials offered. Good relationships with friendly firms and parents stand us in good stead, as they do with certain government establishments, and we pay regular visits to the Southern Science and Technology's Forum Stores. Recycling is part of the work of the department and mention is made of this later.

Among the principal raw materials used at this stage are expanded polystyrene, tinplate, assorted sizes of steel and bronze welding rod, aluminium and steel in a variety of sections mostly from surplus equipment, rubber (from old inner tubes), elastic bands, glass tubing in a variety of sizes, a great assortment of bolts, nuts and washers, mostly stripped from equipment, and the traditional stock of wood and metal. A wide selection of adhesives and fixing methods is also provided.

We try to get to the testing and evaluation stage by the end of the year. This puts a time restriction on the design, and we find this a useful training asset in avoiding unfinished work in the future.

During that part of the year in which they undertake their first design project, children will use, and others learn of their use, by watching demonstrations of a number of basic processes. These will include: use of the hot wire cutter, soft soldering, blow moulding of plastics (the blow-moulder, as the hot wire cutter, vacuum moulder and other equipment, have been made as a technical project in the school), and simple turning, for example. The more involved successful designs are only finished by extra time put in outside of the normal design and technology periods.

THIRD YEAR CHOICES

In Form 3 we begin a period of working in the project method which continues throughout the whole school. Children have a free choice of workshop, and to this extent there is still an underlying bias of their interest in particular materials. This is dictated only by buildings; and we rightfully envy those schools where a really free interchange of rooms and workshops can be effected and this bias removed.

We have two workshop areas – one a single breeze-block walled 1943 ex-wartime Air Training Corps building, the other a wooden army-type hut of late 1920s vintage. A third similar hut is used for larger project work and GRP.

Throughout the three years that begin with this choice, we try to keep knowledge and skills abreast of the ability to think out solutions to problems by investigation, reasoning and understanding. We believe that there is no proven success of the design process without realization and evaluation.

Whether, for example, among his work the pupil is engaged in a project with copper enamelling, where, without knowledge of the chemistry of oxides and fluxes and a 'feel' for kiln temperature and fusion, a first-rate sign can be ruined; bridge construction where basic principles need first to be investigated; or a transistor circuit where principles and precautions must be known before the design can begin – there is an underlying need for knowledge and skill on the part of the designer.

When pupils first come in to form 3, they are given a resumé of the areas in which they may undertake their design project, and they can' suggest others. Design briefs arise from further exploration of working techniques in the materials of their choice, or an investigational project. This may be in plastics, GRP, wood, metal, jewellery, glass, technology, lapidary, enamelling, a wide range of applied science topics, electronics, or any other topic chosen for an investigational project providing it can be dealt with within our physical ability to cope with the class demands. In this may be included a project in industrial archaeology or intermediate technology.

RECYCLING MATERIALS AND EQUIPMENT

At this stage, too, mention should be made of our recycling policy. Recycled materials and components play a key part in our work. Without them the wide range of interests and activities catered for by the department could not possibly be pursued.

Making the maximum use of recycling and of materials and components recovery also forms a valuable training in the social economics involved in sixth-form studies in the wider design course at A-level. By recycling, we are able to conserve our valuable allocation of money for those supplies not obtainable by other means, such as resins, solvents, finishing media, balsa, sheet and stock metals, batteries, and electronic components not readily recovered by recycling.

A brief list of the materials we salvage, collect and store is: From parents and friends of the school – a constant supply of TV sets (for components, connecting wire and fittings), washing machines (for aluminium sheet, motors, pumps, tanks and fittings), electric cookers (for components), vacuum cleaners (for various blowing and suction needs), and a vast array of containers that are used in themselves as a source of plastics and tinplate. From local firms we are given Dexion, electronic components, enamelled wire for winding, offcuts of copper tube and wire, steel tube and sheet, Perspex, Formica and expanded polystyrene.

FOURTH AND FIFTH YEARS

In forms 4 and 5 the project nature of the work is developed, and while we run O-level courses for those who wish it, we also have our own Mode 3 technological studies, with a syllabus ranging approximately over the areas described in form 3 work, and we are working towards a CSE Mode 3 design and technology. Factory visits are also included at this level.

Typical project working in year 3, for example, in a class of sixteen children, gave rise to the following variety of work at one time: an electronic metronome, electronic organ (simple 8-octave circuit), radio reception with semi-conductors, pressure forming perspex, indication signs in perspex, strip heating and fabrication in perspex (bookends, tape recorder table), lapidary using indigenous stones for decoration, forgework, transformers (to give 12v DC supply for model railway), design and construction of bridges, hammered metalwork.

The term's work involved four major introductory talks and demonstrations. Once everyone has begun, the rest of the class are gathered round to see important stages in the work where guidance has to be given. It is at these stages when most of the cross-fertilization and spin-off takes place between projects.

In forms 4 and 5, some of the projects undertaken may demand a high degree of either specialized theoretical knowledge or particular skill. This often tests our resources to the limit, as does the need for programmed learning where specific processes need to be mastered before the next step is taken. Flexibility in standards allows for the degree of investigation or testing demanded at each stage to be varied according to the ability of the pupil.

In the case of underwater swimming equipment being developed by a sixth-former for example, quite a degree of research was carried out into the tubular riveting method he had devised for joining nylon sheet to stainless steel in a cylinder harness. This included the testing of one rivet which, tested to destruction, would not yield under a load of 250 kgm. This gave a calculated breaking strain on the whole harness of several tonnes. Investigations were carried out in the laboratory into flotation, density and co-efficients of friction measured between nylon belts and plastic dip-coated lead weights.

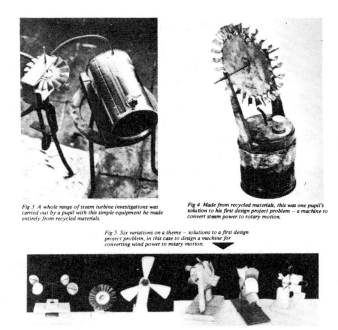

Fig 3 A whole range of steam turbine investigations was carried out by a pupil with this simple equipment he made entirely from recycled materials.

Fig 4 Made from recycled materials, this was one pupil's solution to his first design project problem – a machine to convert steam power to rotary motion.

Fig 5 Six variations on a theme – solutions to a first design project problem, in this case to design a machine for converting wind power to rotary motion. ▼

SIXTH-FORM WORK

The impact of technology on society is developed at sixth-form level, where in the Oxford A83 A-level design syllabus course, studies in such topics as roads, and traffic and town planning, include attendance at major public planning enquiries, participation in traffic counts, and discussions on local town planning proposals.

Here, in the environmental problems of planning, highways, pollution, recycling, energy sources, and transportation systems, there is an unlimited field for project activity.

The objectives of some of our projects at sixth-form level give an indication of this concern in the nature of topics chosen by the students themselves. These include, in the last two years: design of self-contained flat for the disabled in a wheel-chair, safety on motorcycles, design and layout of a compound for farm milking, highway lighting, alternative methods of propulsion of vehicles, fire prevention and fighting in warehousing, new designs in underwater swimming equipment, a town car, impact of traffic on the city of Salisbury, and an ergonomically designed car seat.

In addition to these projects were the more specialised: linear air track, computer memory unit, digital frequency meter (which won the designers a fortnight in America), biological amplifier, earth resistivity meter, and so on.

BEGINNING TECHNOLOGY PROJECTS

What is the most helpful advice one could give to those about to start? What have we learnt from our five years of development?

Firstly, cheap, available equipment is at hand. Listed are some of our most useful pieces of equipment (besides those traditionally supplied, such as lathe, forge, and hand tools). Most have been built in the school at very low cost or for nothing: blowers and vacuum machines for blow-moulding and vacuum-forming; gas furnace blast supply and testing wind-powered models; ten-inch diamond saw; dip fluidizer; hot-wire machine for expanded polystyrene and foam cutting; hydraulic test bed made from washing machines; kiln; lapidary machines; materials test rig; multimeter; electric cooker oven for plastics processing; combined blow-moulding and vacuum-forming machine; strip heater for thermoplastics, and variac control for mains supply and wind tunnel.

Add to this, oxyacetylene welding and cutting equipment, and especially the small lead-welding blowpipe – excellent for silver soldering, and there is very little that cannot be made – as a technical project of course! Those schools which are, as our own, fortunate enough to have College of Technology workshops and laboratories, and the odd factory nearby, should be able to find ready co-operation in dealing with the occasional difficulty. With the College of Technology there is too, of course, an admirable opportunity for timetabled course work which forms part of our curriculum. This is done in computers, electronics, surveying, material science and testing.

A last word on information resources – we find it necessary constantly to prune the content of our resources centre because of its growing physical size and to make for ease of reference. A youngster at third-year level, for example, trying to find out about resin casting, machine acrylics or moulding PVC sheets, finds a large file marked 'Plastics' a formidable collection to tackle.

Needs for the most common activities have been met by duplicated information and instruction sheets, but our next objective is the construction of a back screen projection system with film loop and programmed teaching on tape for what are found to be the constantly recurring needs of specific techniques or basic information.

I hope that there has been at least something sufficiently helpful in this account of the work of our department to assist others in stimulating the curriculum development of their school.

36 *Starting points*

- M. Grant

EDITORS' INTRODUCTION

Martin Grant shows how courses, based on project work, can be planned to attract girls to design and technology.

[...]

In recent years some clues have emerged from educational research and from practice in schools which indicate the kind of technological activities that might be welcomed by most girls. Omerod (1979) found that girls who choose a physical science subject are likely to have a more positive attitude towards the social implications of science activity than those who don't. This factor did not seem to influence the choice of physical sciences by boys. Head (1982), from his work on the psychological aspects of subject choice, concluded that:

> To obtain a major qualitative improvement to recruitment in science with more girls and with students possessing imaginative, flexible minds it would be necessary to make science more appealing to boys and girls . . . The probable implication is that science would need to be presented in the context of the needs of society and individuals.

The implications for design and technology are probably the same. Physics and chemistry share obvious curriculum interests with CDT and they also experience a similar, though less acute, deficit of girls in option courses. The GATE project (GATE 1982), in a limited study of pupil entries in a national design competition, found a difference between girls' and boys' design projects that would tend to support the view that a greater emphasis on the social aspects of technology in school 'design and make' activities would be generally welcomed by girls. However, of the three components of design and technological understanding – skills, knowledge, and values (see Figure 36.1) it is the third that receives least attention in existing teaching approaches.

In traditional handicraft courses, the concern is principally with the acquisition of knowledge – knowledge about materials, construction and techniques. Although this approach is still widely practised in schools, it is seen by educationists as being largely irrelevant to the needs of boys

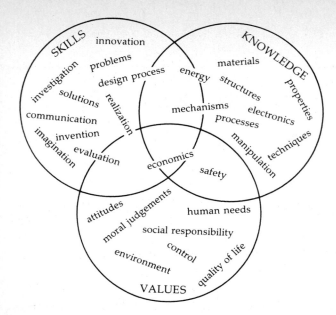

Figure 36.1   *A model showing the three components which combine to constitute an understanding in design and technology*

or girls, and is being gradually replaced by either a broad-based design approach or a structured technology approach. Both approaches emphasize the intellectual skills involved in designing and making in a technological context but neither have successfully managed to involve the values component in Figure 36.1. It is assumed that by being involved in the practical solution of technical problems, pupils will somehow become aware of the impact of technology on society and society's influence on the direction of technological change. Figures 36.2 and 36.3 illustrate these two approaches.

In the 'design and technology from problems' approach, the emphasis is placed on problem-solving and decision-making skills. The starting point for any individual pupil or group activity is the presentation of a 'problem'. Typically it is stated thus:

'A device/artefact/system is required to solve the problem of . . .'
or
'Design and make a device/artefact/system that will perform functions XX and comply with specifications YY'.

Pupils are then expected to research the problem and offer alternative solutions. Through a process of investigation and discussion an optimum solution will be arrived at and this will be further developed with the help of models and tests. Following modifications, a device or system is constructed using the necessary materials and techniques and on completion is evaluated against the original specification. A feature

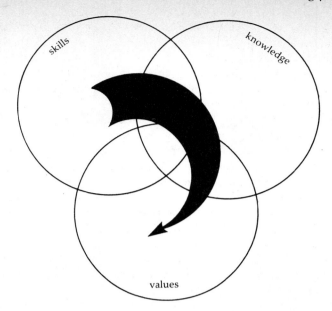

Figure 36.2 *Design and technology from problems*

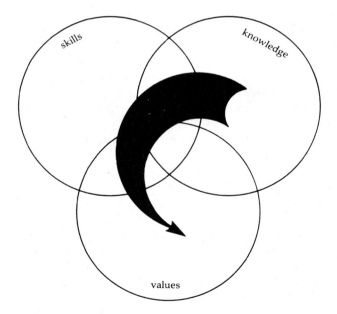

Figure 36.3 *Design and technology from knowledge*

of this approach is that knowledge of materials, scientific principles and motor skills is ill-defined and is less important than the development of intellectual skills. The particular medium (be it wood, metal, plastic, electronics, etc. or a combination of these) in which the design process is executed is relevant only in so far as the most appropriate choice is made for the solution to the problem under study.

'Design and technology from knowledge' is a more structured approach and requires pupils to be given a grounding in a series of 'knowledge areas' related to modern technology. Three or four modules from a wide range (materials, energy, electronics, hydraulics, pneumatics, mechanisms, etc.) are selected by the teacher, and pupils follow a series of guided exercises in each in order to build up a knowledge base. After three or four terms pupils undertake a major design project in which they can bring the knowledge gained by working through the modules to bear on the selected problem. A feature of this approach is that while intellectual skills are still of paramount importance, the knowledge content is well defined and provides the foundation for subsequent design activities.

In both approaches the 'values' component receives scant attention. Its existence is usually acknowledged in department and course syllabuses but its relationship to the other two components is unclear. When this component is actively pursued it usually receives separate treatment and is unrelated to ongoing practical activities.

In either approach the implications for girls' education in design and technology are the same. The subject is, and is seen as, largely concerned with technical solutions to technical problems. Technology's association with objects, things, techniques, scientific concepts, inventions and 'technical fixes' becomes its overriding image; and technology's relevance to people, quality of life, social problems and values become submerged and invisible. As long as the subject so continues to be associated with the impersonal and objective it may remain as anathema to girls.

A third approach – 'design and technology from issues and situations' – would change the emphasis from objects to people and from the impersonal to the personal (Figure 36.4).

In this approach the 'values' component is highlighted and is used to guide the designing and making activities. Instead of employing a 'problem' or a 'knowledge area' as the starting point to a teaching activity, an 'issue' is selected for study on the basis that it has some relevance to technology. Problems connected with the issue are identified by pupils (with the use of resource material such as newspaper cuttings, reports and film) and the appropriateness of technological solutions are examined. This will, of necessity, involve pupils in the making of value-judgements about the nature of technology and in some cases could result in the rejection of the 'technical fix' and the proposal of social solutions. However, it is likely that some aspect of the issue or situation under study will be amenable to a technology input (in some cases this might come about through the redefinition of the problems exposed). Pupils can then proceed to designing and making activities with the knowledge that *their* work has a social relevance outside the school/workshop and that *their* moral decisions are controlling the direction of *their* technological activity. This approach – design and technology from issues and situations – would ensure that pupils had the opportunity of becoming fully involved in the design process, that they acquired knowledge related to materials and scientific principles, and above all, that they developed an awareness of the interactions between technology and society.

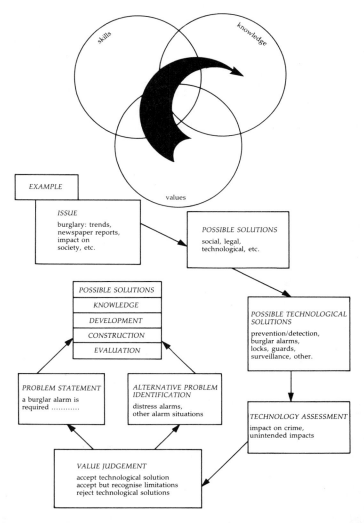

Figure 36.4 *Design and technology from issues*

By giving full recognition to all three components – skills, knowledge, and values – craft, design and technology can provide a better technological education for boys and girls and, at the same time, create a subject ethos that is, in practice as well as in image, more attractive to girls than most existing approaches and less likely to be regarded as a 'masculine' subject.

AUTHOR'S NOTE

The example shown in Figure 36.4 – designing and making a burglar alarm – was chosen simply because it has become a popular project in schools and has been submitted in many variations to national design competitions. Other examples would have served equally well. In schools having a particular expertise in, for example, electronics, the outcomes of pupil projects will be influenced in that direction. Other schools may be particularly strong in engineering science and projects will be influenced in this direction. Either case would not alter the basic teaching experience outlined here.

REFERENCES

Head, J. (1982) 'Personality and Attitudes to Science', in Head, J. (ed.), *Science Education and the Citizen*, Chelsea College/Bristol Council.

Omerod, M. B. (1979), 'The Social Implications Factor in Attitudes to Science', in *British Journal of Educational Psychology*, 41.

GATE (1982), 'The Involvement of Girls in National Design Competitions', GATE Project Report 1982:1.

Index